The Arts Management Handbook

Revised

SECOND EDITION

By

ALVIN H. REISS

Preface by Nancy Hanks

Law-Arts Publishers, Inc.

New York

1974

Library of Congress Cataloging in Publication Data

Reiss, Alvin H.
    The arts management handbook.

    Articles which appeared in Arts management, 1962-1972.
    Bibliography: p.
    1. Arts—Management. I. Arts management.
II. Title.
NX760.R45   1973   658'.91'7   73-13517
ISBN 0-88238-050-8

Library of Congress Catalog Card No. (First edition) 70-132371
Library of Congress Catalog Card #73-13517

Printed in the United States of America by Meilen Press Inc.

TO ELLEN AND FOR THE ARTS

TABLE OF CONTENTS

PREFACE

In recent years art as a way of life has become an important new business force in society. As Harold Schonberg put it in the *New York Times* (April 29, 1973), it is a "sector of American industry" and, he adds, "the word 'industry' is used advisedly."

This understanding of the relationship of art and economics is growing rapidly, but must become even more positive. If we are to have thousands of people in America building life-time careers in the arts, if thousands more participate as an avocation, and if millions make up the audience for orchestra, theatre, and dance performances and wear out the museum floors 300 million strong annually, then it is even more important for us in this country to attend to the housekeeping details, the money management, and the long-range planning for our great cultural institutions.

Only by wise management will the galleries and museums exhibit and conserve properly our great heritage in painting, sculpture, graphics and the crafts; only with creative administration will our institutions be able to continue to operate and provide careers and a productive living for musicians, dancers, actors, and filmmakers; only with the most imaginative and humane thinking can the long-range possibilities of the arts and their enormous social potential for improving the quality of everyday life be realized.

Communication between people is a deep concern of our time. So is the environment, education, constructive change, and basic human values. The arts are central to all of these issues, and increasingly the nation and its citizens are becoming aware of the arts as growing participation in them indicates.

Thus, careful management and planning are daily more important to the growth of the arts. The proliferating university courses in arts administration and the expanding institutes and workshops devoted to operational concerns all indicate the wide need to examine management methods and evaluate traditional approaches especially in view of the technological developments which are reprogramming so many aspects of our society.

The first edition of the "Arts Management Handbook" served a useful purpose as an information manual, not only for professionals but for all those interested in the arts.

I wish the editors equal success with this second edition.

Nancy Hanks
Chairman
National Endowment for the Arts

ABOUT THE AUTHOR

ALVIN H. REISS

Alvin H. Reiss has personally played a major role in American cultural development and in the growing business-in-society movement. Co-founder and editor of the first journal for cultural administrators, *Arts Management,* he has written extensively on the arts and business for leading magazines, and has developed pioneer programs in both areas. His recent book, *Culture & Company,* has been hailed by critics as "the needed pathfinder work" and "the definitive account" of the changing roles of the arts and business in modern society. His earlier book, *The Arts Management Handbook,* is a standard reference work in its field.

The host of his own WNYC radio series, Alvin H. Reiss also directs the Performing Arts Management Institute, an annual training program for cultural administrators, and is communications consultant to the American Council for the Arts in Education. He is a consultant to many cultural institutions and a trustee of national arts organizations. He has worked directly with the business world as a consultant, symposium and program organizer, writer for company publications, director of a corporation foundation, and as head of his own corporate public relations firm, Related Arts Counsellors.

In his distinguished career, Mr. Reiss has pioneered in the educational field as well. The creator of the nation's first college course in arts management, he has developed first-time courses at the New School for Social Research, lectured at scores of universities and has organized and led seminars for such diverse groups as the American Management Association, the Association of Junior Leagues of America, and the New York State Council on the Arts. He recently was named Visiting Consultant on the Arts to the State University of New York.

Introduction

The sixties were a decade of tremendous change. In virtually every avenue of American life, the familiar and accepted ways were questioned, challenged and at times, uprooted. This was especially true in the arts, where in a few momentous years, profound developments altered not only the form and content of artistic presentation, but also the social and economic foundations on which arts organizations had been structured for decades.

Change, however, even positive change, did not trigger any so-called cultural explosion. Nor did change solve the chronic financial woes of the arts. For as significant as each new development was, it was not a solution but a beginning and a beginning often accompanied by complex problems.

The National Endowment on the Arts, for example, the visible symbol of Federal subsidy to culture, received such minuscule doles from Congress that it was unable to match either the rising tide of fund expectations by arts groups or the emergency needs it recognized. States which enacted legislation creating official arts councils often were guilty of abandoning their offspring immediately following their birth. Title Three education programs which poured millions of dollars into cultural coffers sometimes were developed haphazardly and diverted cultural groups from achieving their major goals. Business support of the arts, a much-heralded concept, meant business exploitation at times. The cultural building boom resulted in much more money for bricks and mortar than it did for the economically moribund users of the new facilities. But there were some very positive notes in this cacophony and one of them was the emergence of an important force onto the scene. For in the vanguard of this incredibly compressed swirl of

1

change, a new professional was carving out a new profession. Arts management, as a career, was coming of age.

Although cultural activity today is not yet at the center of daily life, the arts manager has helped to move it from the periphery to a point well within the circle. The non-profit arts institution he administers — the symphony orchestra, dance company, resident theater, opera troupe, and museum—may still be the stepchild of philanthropy tottering on the brink of financial crisis, but it is a lively stepchild, in tune with the times and clamoring for and winning a larger piece of the action. It has cut through the velvet walls which once surrounded it, spread its influence into every corner of the community, and embraced new and different kinds of audiences.

The accomplishments of the arts manager have seldom been noticed beyond the board room of his own institution, but, by any measure, they have been considerable. In many instances good administration has spelled the difference between organizational life and death. Working in a field where, until recently, the transferrable body of knowledge was limited, and opportunities for formal training were virtually non-existent, the arts manager shaped and developed his craft while on the job. Eager to do, eager to relate, eager to adapt the techniques which worked or gave promise of working elsewhere, he sought out his counterparts in his own and other artistic disciplines, and learned from them.

And while he was learning and doing, a four-page newsletter called *Arts Management* was playing Boswell to his Samuel Johnson: reporting his approach to problems through case histories; relating his successful experiences in "how-to" stories and brief tips; interpreting the changing climate in which he worked in background articles; exploring his expanding horizons in "think" pieces; and summarizing the key developments in his field in news and round-up stories. *Arts Management* spoke directly to him, and opened up a new channel of communications between him and other cultural administrators throughout the country. In short, it is this same kind of dialogue for arts managers, by arts managers and about arts managers and their institutions, which comprises the handbook which follows.

The new, updated handbook, with selective material drawn from the 79 issues of *Arts Management* published between February, 1962 and February 1973 is a carefully organized compendium of practical information. A new section included in this revised edition focuses on publications of direct interest to the arts administrator. Following chapter ten, for example, there is a series of articles about books and reports published between 1969 and 1973 which may be useful as an annotated bibliography. Also included is the popular Newsletter feature, "Checklist," which carries year by year listings of relevant newspaper and magazine articles published between 1969 and 1973.

The handbook is shaped to meet the needs of today's and tomorrow's cultural administrators, who will find within it, precedents and ideas to help them resolve the chronic problems inherent in managing an arts organization—how to raise funds, how to promote programs, how to attract audiences, or how to organize a board of directors. To facilitate its use, material has been grouped into five basic sections, each containing one or more related chapters. For maximum readability and pragmatic value, illustrative case histories often immediately follow theoretical or "how to" articles on the same subject. Thus, an article explaining how to arrange guest interviews on radio is followed by a study of an opera company's highly successful broadcast publicity program featuring guest interviews. The

3

number in parenthesis at the end of each story enables the reader to determine in which issue of *Arts Management* that story originally was published. A key to these issue numbers follows the last chapter in the book.

Of course, the reader must recognize that changes may have occurred since some of the articles were originally published. Individuals quoted or written about may have moved to other institutions, costs for some of the services described may have increased, and certain statistics may not be as meaningful now as they were at publication. But hopefully, the reader will find most of the material to be timeless in its relevency and application.

This briefly, is the handbook, but because it is planned as a working guide rather than a mere compendium, it is somewhat different from the newsletter from which its material is taken. Some background information on *Arts Management,* its editorial concept and its journalistic mission, may prove useful in helping the reader to understand the context and framework in which the following articles originally appeared.

Since its first issue in 1962, *Arts Management* addressed itself not only to the practical aspects of arts administration, but to the broader social aspects of the arts as well. While laying down guidelines for meeting the challenges of the day to day operations of a cultural institution, the publication dedicated itself also to uncovering trends not immediately discernable and preparing managers for the changes which lay ahead. Often, it was the initial publication to draw attention to new developments. In its fourth issue, for example, the first of its two part survey of chambers of commerce, *Arts Management* pinpointed rising business interest in the arts. The very next month, June 1962, *Arts Management* clearly indicated that a cultural building boom of significant proportions was underway. These articles attracted national attention and were cited in such pub-

lications as the *New York Times,* the *Reader's Digest* and
scores of newspapers throughout the country. Similarly,
in the following years, *Arts Management* traced, step by
step, such developments as the creation of state arts councils, labor involvement in the arts, and growing government activity in the arts. For practical reasons, many of
these news stories and in-stage progress reports have not
been included in this handbook.

Equally important has been the focus, and at times initiative, provided by *Arts Management* in broad areas of
concern. It has consistently promoted the concept of cooperative endeavor; cited the need for increased management training programs, (*Arts Management* editors created the nation's first college level course in arts management and the newsletter has reported on every new
course or program); called for increased economic and
sociological research into the arts (*Arts Management* undertook its own surveys when data was unavailable); reported regularly on virtually every new book, magazine,
and newsletter of interest; and spurred journalists to
greater coverage of cultural activities and events. But,
perhaps most importantly, *Arts Management* editors,
sought and found ways to make the newsletter and its information resources available to arts managers and arts
institutions without charge. As a result, hundreds of thousands of free copies of *Arts Management* were distributed
over the years.

The *Arts Management Handbook* was conceived primarily as a tool, as a useful and timeless reference work for
professional administrators, for students, for artists, for
trustees, for businessmen, and for all the people who in
some way, relate to the activities of cultural institutions.
But although pragmatism is a key objective of this volume,
it is not the only one. It is hoped that the reader dipping
into these pages will sense also, the boundless energy, the

5

unfailing spirit and the sheer joy of doing, which has characterized the work of the arts manager and the profession of arts management over the years. For it is these qualities found so abundantly within the field, which have made my reporting task over the years, a true labor of love.

ALVIN H. REISS

ACKNOWLEDGMENTS

Whatever value *Arts Management* has had, first as a newsletter, and now as handbook material, is related directly to the validity of the concept on which it was founded. In this respect, Alvin Toffler deserves a good deal of credit. Back in the summer of 1961, Al, then an associate editor at *Fortune,* conceived the idea of developing a journal specifically for the administrators of cultural institutions, an idea which, at the time, seemed utterly impractical. But Al's persuasiveness, clear logic and deep sense of commitment won me and won Alden Todd and Sidney Green, the two other members of the original team, to the cause. It was Al, a truly fine journalist and the author some years later of several important books, *The Culture Consumers* and *Future Shock* who developed the format and articulated an editorial concept which I have since tried to maintain.

Throughout *Arts Management's* earliest days, the faith and support of a number of arts leaders like Phil Hanes of Winston-Salem, North Carolina, helped the publication to find its audience. In 1963, the concept of free newsletter distribution to cultural organizations was initiated by John H. MacFadyen, then director of the New York State Council on the Arts, who made *Arts Management* a Council-sponsored publication. This policy continued under Mr. MacFadyen's successor, John B. Hightower, with the result that thousands of individuals and groups, in and out of New York State, received *Arts Management,* and the State Council's newly created newsletter, without charge for more than three years. To both of these pioneers in the state arts council movement, I owe a special debt of gratitude. Thanks are due also to Roger Stevens who, as chairman of the John F. Kennedy Center for the Performing Arts in Washington, D. C., made *Arts Management*

7

part of the Center's own publication, *Footlight*, in 1964. During the period that *Footlight* was published, more than 10,000 people received free copies of each issue with the *Arts Management* insert. My lasting thanks go to Neil H. Anderson and Sybil Simon of the New York Board of Trade, who inspired many corporations to support the arts. They recognized the validity of a free distribution program, and arranged for the Board's Business and the Arts Advisory Council to sponsor and distribute *Arts Management,* a policy which enabled thousands of individuals and groups to receive *Arts Management* without charge from 1967 through 1970 when the newsletter was forced to adopt a new subscription policy.

Over the years many people have assisted me in proof-reading, researching, and writing for the newsletter and my gratitude goes to all of them—to Sylvia Auerbach, Louise Esteven, Isabelle Fisher and Jerry Miller, to name a few. To my wife Ellen, a special thank you for her continued patience, assistance and warm encouragement when I most needed it.

Along with handing out some well-deserved plaudits, I must acknowledge shortcomings as well. Whatever errors are to be found in this book are mostly mine. As editor, and as researcher and writer of most of these articles, I must assume responsibility for any inaccuracies.

In closing, I extend my deep appreciation and thanks to the thousands of people who contribute much but receive little recognition in return. Without them, there would be no handbook. To arts managers throughout the country, who have helped to make so many good things happen for so many people, this book is dedicated.

A. H. R.

PART ONE: ECONOMICS AND SOCIOLOGY

Chapter I – Money Matters

Chapter II – Audiences and Programs

Chapter I – Money Matters

THE ECONOMIC PICTURE

Performing Arts Face Dim Economic Future

By

W. J. Baumol and W. G. Bowen

One can read the prospects of the arts tomorrow in the economic structure which characterizes them today. The evidence will suggest that the prospects offer no grounds for complacency — that there are fundamental reasons to expect the financial strains which beset the performing arts organizations to increase, chronically, with the passage of time.

It is apparent that the live performing arts belong to the stable productivity sector of our economy, offering little opportunity for major technological change.

Even if the arts could somehow manage to effect technological economies, they would not solve their long-term problem if such savings were once-and-for-all in nature. In order to join the ranks of the rising productivity industries, the arts would somehow have to learn not only to increase output per man-hour, but to continue to do so into the indefinite future.

True, some inefficiencies of operation are to be found in the field and their elimination can help matters somewhat. Moreover, performing arts organizations can reduce the rate of increase in their unit costs by permitting some deterioration in the quality of their product, by fewer rehearsals, the use of more poorly trained performers, shod-

11

dy costumes and scenery. But such a course is never popular with organizations dedicated to quality, and, furthermore, it may lead to loss of audience and community support. Nevertheless, it is not an uncommon "temporary" expedient, imposed by the realization that the cutting of corners may be the only alternative to abandonment of the enterprise.

There is one other important avenue for cost saving open to the performing arts. We refer to wages paid performers. The live performing arts constitute a rather special labor market, a market in which the need for great native ability and extensive training limits the supply, but in which the psychic returns to those who meet these tests often offer a very substantial inducement to remain in the field.

Performing arts organizations in financial difficulty have often managed to shift part of their financial burden back to the performers — and to the managements, who also are generally very poorly paid by commercial standards. The level of the incomes in this general field must be considered remarkably low by any standards, and particularly so in light of the heavy investment that has often been made by the artists in their education, training and equipment.

However, there are limits to the financial sacrifices society can extract from the performers, in exchange for psychic returns. One may reasonably expect that rising incomes in other sectors will ultimately produce untoward effects on the supply of talent. At what point this will occur depends partly on the income elasticity of the demand for psychic income.

In sum, the cost structure of the performing arts organizations promises them no easier future. One might anticipate therefore that this structural problem would produce discernible effects on pricing policy. There is a wide-spread impression that the arts have indeed behaved in accord with this anticipation — that ticket prices have been soaring. Yet our preliminary data indicates that the rate of increase of ticket prices has barely managed to keep up with the price level and has lagged substantially behind increases in costs. We suspect that a valid explanation is the role of a doctrine of just price in the objectives of arts organizations.

The tendency for increases in prices to lag behind increases in costs means simply that arts organizations have had to raise larger sums from their contributors — and our analysis leads us to expect this trend to continue. If, as may be suspected, there are limits to the amounts that can be obtained from private contributors, the question is obviously raised whether society can find other sources of support for the performing arts if they are to continue their present role, and especially if it is intended that they will expand their role and flourish.   (35)

—◆—

HOW NONPROFIT GROUPS CAN BOOST THEIR INCOME

The August 1972 issue of Institutional Investor, *a journal for professional money managers, was devoted to the theme, "The culture crisis: Can our nonprofit institutions be saved?" Although the focus was broader than the arts,* AM *is reprinting the following article in a slightly abridged version (copyright 1972 Institutional Investor Systems, reprinted with permission) because it discusses key trends worthy of consideration by arts managers.*

Sorting Out Priorities

Despite widespread belief that government, directly or indirectly, is going to play a bigger role in financing nonprofits, the trend, needless to say, does not meet with universal acclaim. Thus nonprofits are faced with some tough choices in sorting out their priorities. The key concern here is about the types and quality of services which would be available. And no less an authority than the Carnegie Corporation has called for establishment of a national committee to "think through and articulate" the requirements of a massive campaign to deal with the future of nonprofits. Certainly, many city museums and cultural institutions would collapse without even the amount of state support they get now, and legislation has been proposed to allow them to use larger amounts of their tax-exempt receipts for lobbying in behalf of their case. But the trick is in trying to develop a consensus on how the government could best meet the needs through direct support, grants and loans, public subsidy of user services, or through tax incentives — or some combination of the three. Muddying the water still further, notes John Jay Iselin, managing director of New York's educational TV station, which raises more than $2 million annually from "subscribers," is that "we can no longer be beholden to any one group, public or private. We must deal with the fact that we must *qualify* for support; we must prove our value to the consumer."

Going Into "Business"

While nonprofits are not by definition designed to make money, there is nothing to prevent them from owning profit-making enterprises. Numerous colleges own coal mines or oil wells and one (Knox College of Galesburg, Illinois) even owns a race track. Frank Jennings, secretary of Columbia's Teachers College, a proponent of a mixed-economy approach, points to the fact that Columbia was bequeathed the land upon which Rockefeller Center stands. Private schools, for instance, could aim for better land use, and many non-profits — including museums, which make money from restaurants and book stores on their premises — are eyeing this approach to additional income with special interest. MIT, among others, looks longingly at the profits which result from research done in its laboratories, and other schools are also interested in the kinds of fees professors can make when they take their ideas off campus. The Stanford Research Center is cited as an example of what can be done, with its approach of conducting research and development for both private and public customers.

Better Utilization of Assets

The emergency task force at NYU has proposed weekend sessions to use its plant more efficiently, and the prospects for leverage elsewhere are almost limitless. Museums can get more mileage out of "the billions they have in their basements," according to Wilder Green, director of the American Federation of Arts, and universities have a plethora of rooms that aren't being fully utilized.

Sharing of Facilities

Every hospital in the land seems to want a cobalt treatment center and every university an urban studies program. But some sharing is already beginning to take place, particularly among hospitals, and there is a notable increase in the number of interchanges between other nonprofits which have expensive new technologies that they can share and jointly underwrite. "Why should the library hold art

15

shows and why should we have a library?" is the way a director of a leading New York museum puts it. Needless to say, there is considerable vested opposition to this, but foundations increasingly feel they will be called upon to become merger makers among nonprofit institutions which so far have seemed unwilling to share their identities.

Moving Toward Decentralization and Specialization

"Institutions that are not individual or different will either be absorbed or go out of business," warns an Eastern university president. An oft-cited example of what could be done is the old University of Paris, where traditionally the only common facilities places were meeting halls and the library. There, students took care of their own food and lodging requirements.

Tapping the Potential of the "Third Sector"

A phrase coined by Amitai Etzioni, director of the Center for Policy Research, the third sector describes using an approach that would avoid both the too-profit-oriented business world and the too-bureaucratic government world in seeking solutions. Sample patterns are the new postal service and Comsat. A great many non-profit organizations already fit the pattern, says Etzioni, adding, "imagine what an effective attack could be made on heroin addiction, for instance, if government funds, hospital staffs, community groups, law enforcement officials and local business got together to tackle the problems under a well-coordinated and well-financed system."

Seeking New Financial Remedies

Clearly, economizing will not solve a problem of the magnitude of the one facing nonprofits, so many of them are seeking new ways to balance the books. Some are considering how traditional capital-raising drives can be put on a continuing basis, such as getting a commitment from university alumni to repay, over their lifetimes, the difference between what they paid for their education and what it actually cost. Various tithing schemes have been proposed, including one whereby the Internal Revenue Service would collect 1 per cent of a person's income each year after he graduates and return it to alma mater. Residents of suburban St. Louis, to cite one example of what can happen, recently imposed a tax upon themselves to help support a series of urban institutions, including the St. Louis Museum and Zoo. "Somehow," concludes one foundation administrator, "we are going to have to provide a continuous stream of support."　　　　　　　　　　　　　　　　(77)

WHAT CULTURE NEEDS NOW
IS A GOOD LOBBYIST

BY KYRAN M. McGRATH

Culture in the United States has been the stepchild of national priorities since America declared her independence from England in 1776. Through the years that followed, groups concerned with education, labor, management, construction, and defense have identified their needs, convinced the American public of their importance, and successfully lobbied their way on to the list of national priorities for funding. Cultural institutions, however, our museums and performing arts groups, have failed to keep pace with these other forces and, as a result, we see them faced with financial obliteration.

During the past 30 years, museum attendance has skyrocketed — over 560 million visits during 1967 — and public attention to the performing arts has blossomed in every community in the country. Still the impression persists that the arts serve only the rich, and not the middle class or the poor. Before any case can be made for national attention to the financial crisis facing our cultural institutions, local and national organizations involved with the arts must examine their purposes closely and decide whether or not they can allow this false impression to continue. If not, they must mount a public relations campaign to educate the public to the contributions which have been and which can continue to be made by the arts and humanities to the life of all Americans. Relaxing in self-satisfaction with ever increasing attendance records is not enough to satisfy the obligation to our enlightened self-interests. The will to survive must be honed to the point where cultural associations and individual members will cry for unity and positive action on a local and national basis to bring relief to their distress.

Relief must be based on the broad value of art and culture and indeed education to the public, not on the specific needs of individual institutions. Once the case has been made on a grassroots level, the public should be encouraged to have their governmental representatives see to it that these needs are properly met.

All of these wonderful things do not happen by accident. Miss Nancy Hanks, chairman of the National Endowment for the Arts, wrote in the January 1969 issue of *Museum News* that after passage of the legislation creating the National Foundation on the Arts and Humanities in 1965, those people concerned for the future of the arts in America indulged in self-congratulations and relaxed in the belief that Washington would give a big hand to solving the financial problems of the arts. She concluded, "Those of us concerned for the future of the arts and humanities —

professionals, trustees, or interested citizens — have failed
to make a valid case for our cause with the nation's leadership." Because Miss Hanks is now chairman of the Federal
agency directly involved with promoting government programs in the arts, let us not again indulge in self-
congratulations over her appointment and rest easy that
she can solve our problems singlehandedly. She is answer-
able to the President, and her programs will be dependent
upon Congress for funding. If concerned citizens do not
provide the backup support, we will see the arts languish
still further, as institutions expire one by one and the
public suffers.

Section 501(c)(3) permits qualifying institutions and associations to receive charitable contributions and allows
certain deductions to the donors. Such 501(c)(3) organizations are prohibited from engaging in substantial lobbying
activities under present tax laws, and under the proposed
tax legislation they would be prohibited from any legislative
activities. Who then will speak to Congress on behalf of
our needs and the needs of our members if all of the
organizations directly concerned with the arts, culture, and
education persist in qualifying under Section 501(c)(3) and
not, let us say, 501(c)(6) as do many other national associations? There are no lobbying restrictions on 501(c)(6)
organizations.

We saw what happened when popular support was not
organized behind the National Endowment for the Arts'
programs and appropriations, when Roger Stevens was
chairman. Let us not repeat ourselves now that Nancy
Hanks has assumed this vital role. The philosophy of shared
responsibility too often leads to a rationalization of no
responsibility. Changing the nature of an organization from
a charitable organization (501(c)(3)) to a mere non-profit
organization (501(c)(6)) requires a worthy amount of soul-

searching. Establishing a new organization to enable arts and culture to compete with the other areas of our society might be easier. The need remains the same: some group, or groups, willing and able to go to bat for performing arts, for visual arts, for museums of art, history, and science, with the full resources of competition available. Think about it! (66)

Community Theaters Pay Way Through Box Office

The preliminary findings of a new theater survey offer some interesting insights into the operations of non-profit semi-professional and professional theater companies throughout the country. Undertaken by the Theater Resources Development Council and the Eugene O'Neill Memorial Theater Foundation, the survey was based on questionnaires sent to 68 professional theaters, those operating with partial or total union personnel, and 57 semi-professional groups, which, although they sell tickets and often pay management and creative staff, use volunteers on stage and in the front office. When the cutoff date for responses was reached, completed questionnaires had been received from about half the groups in each category.

As a general rule, semi-professional companies pay their way through box office receipts and operate within their budgets, while the professional groups rarely cover costs through ticket sales and operate beyond their budgets. Of 27 professional theaters responding, 19 covered less than 75 per cent of their expenses through box office and subscription income, as contrasted to the 20 of 26 responding community theaters which covered from 75 to 100 per cent. Only five professional groups operated within their budgets during the past three years—15 community theaters did—and 20 went into deficit operations during all or most of this period. Obviously, with large paids staffs, the operating budgets of the professional groups were considerably higher than those of the community groups. The average cost of mounting a production for two of the professional groups was over $50,000, five groups averaged $20,000 to $50,000, and nine averaged under $20,000. In contrast, ten of the community groups listed costs under $2,000 and 13 were over $2,000.

The professional companies, faced with deficits, also have a greater need for outside support. Thus, although none of the community theaters reported receiving important support from government sources or national foundations, and only four indicated that local foundations helped them, the picture was quite different for the professional groups. Here, 15 companies received support from government, 10 from national foundations and 19 from local foundations. Groups in both categories, however, 15 professional and 16 semi-professional, reported undertaking regular annual fund-raising campaigns.

Data on "bricks and mortar" provided by the companies is revealing. Of the 26 semi-professional groups responding, 12 own the theaters in which they perform, 17 have accumulated capital funds, 11 have capital funds invested in real estate, and 13 have obtained mortgage money.

In contrast, although 11 of the professional companies own their homes, only six have accumulated capital funds, only three have capital funds invested in real estate and only two have obtained mortgage money. In response to the question, "Have you any access to loans for basic capital needs?" 12 of the professional groups and 18 of the semi-professional groups answered yes.

The number of people involved in theater activity both

as paid staff and as volunteers is staggering. Cumulatively, the 26 professional theaters employ 522 actors and actresses, 207 directors, designers and coaches, 209 stage personnel, and 246 in front office capacities. Although only two of the community groups use paid actors or actresses (the others use amateurs), 18 non-professional companies use a total of 76 paid creative staff members, 9 use 22 paid stage personnel, and 15 use 53 paid front office workers. In addition, thousands of volunteers serve in creative or technical capacities, and over 400 serve as board members. Among the professional groups, there are more than 800 board and advisory board members.

The professional theaters rely heavily on paid personnel for most administrative functions. Of the 27 theaters reporting, 25 use professional general managers and house managers; 23 use professional publicity managers and accountants; 20 use professional treasurers; and 19 use professionals for audience development. In fund-raising however, only 8 groups use professionals.

According to survey data, professional regional theaters average 25 weeks of continuous performances plus a significant number of extra programs including theater readings, and children's school and street performances. The 27 respondents spend $7,000,000 annually in playhouses with an estimated capacity of more than 17,000 seats. The community groups do an annual business of $2,000,000—mostly on weekends—in playhouses seating about 10,000.

(62)

Study Reveals How Theatre Costs Climb

By

Thomas Gale Moore

Where has the audience for professional theatre gone? Why are its costs skyrocketing? Is professional theatre dying? These are some of the questions that the Carnegie Institute of Technology, under a grant from the Rockefeller Foundation, has set out to answer in a three-year study of the economics of the theatre.

Research has focused on non-musical productions in the professional theatre, with emphasis on the factors affecting supply of plays and demand for tickets. While most of the work has been devoted to Broadway, many of the conclusions are applicable, with modifications, to the stage outside New York. Our studies cover economic changes in the theatre between the 1927-28 season and the 1960-61 season. This article, giving some preliminary results based on the first year's work, analyzes the rising costs of drama production.

While theatre costs in general have increased, the pre-opening outlays, known as production costs, have risen far more rapidly than regular weekly operating expenses after opening night. With costs of the two-season period 1927-29 pegged at an index of 100, production costs, expressed in constant purchasing power dollars, for the average straight play had risen to index 211 by the mid-1950s. But in the past six years these pre-opening costs have shot up even more rapidly, to index 305 by the end of the 1960-61 season.

Why have production costs tripled? What elements have expanded the most? Building and painting scenery (the largest single item, amounting to nearly a quarter of all

23

pre-opening costs) has a little more than doubled in the past thirty years. Costuming bills and cast salaries during rehearsal have each about quadrupled. Together these two account for about 15 per cent of the total. Costumes cost about 50 per cent more than the salaries paid during rehearsal and tryout weeks to the people who wear them.

There has been an upsurge of about 650 per cent in relatively small items, such as cancellation of contracts, telephone, insurance, secretarial services, acquisition of stage rights, mail order expenses, health and hospitalization premiums, music and orchestration fees, and transportation of stars and directors. Expenditures for advertising and publicity, both in the pre-opening production stage and in weekly operating costs, have risen dramatically. Producers now spend eight dollars to advertise a straight play before opening night for every dollar spent in the 1927-29 period. Ten years ago advance advertising outlays were only half the present figure.

These expenditures have been made necessary, at least in part, by a changing pattern of theatre-going. Before sound motion pictures, the stage furnished a major form of recreation; people went to the legitimate theatre then as people go to movies today. In recent years television has provided another substitute.

Because of such competition people are unwilling to attend mediocre plays. A show accordingly tends to be either a hit with a substantial run or a flop that closes promptly. A poor reception by the critics can lead to a quick shuttering of the production. If, however, enough tickets can be sold before opening night, much of the investment can be recouped, even in the face of pallid reviews. Producers have therefore pushed up advertising expenditures so as to market as many tickets as possible before the opening. The average straight show in the 1960-1961 season cost more than $12,000 to advertise in advance, and another $1,455 was spent for a press agent to publicize it. Together these make up about 13 per cent of total pre-opening production costs.

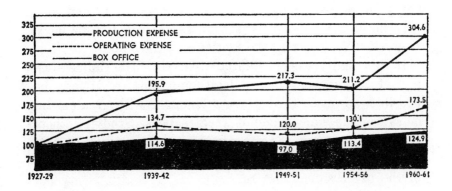

WHY THE THEATRE IS HURTING. *The graph shows how pre-opening costs, after dipping slightly between the late forties and mid-fifties, have shot spectacularly upward, making investment in a straight play riskier than ever. Box office has climbed, too, but not nearly so fast. Plays must run longer to break even.*

After opening night, publicity expenses (which include advertising) take a slightly greater proportion of the total weekly operating costs—$3,029 of a total $18,055 spent to maintain the average straight show. The only item that costs more is that covering actors' salaries—$6,691 a week.

25

Other major categories of operating cost are authors' royalties, crew and stagehands' salaries, and those of stage and company managers. Together these represent $4,200, or 23 per cent of the weekly costs.

The smaller expenses for productions on Broadway are multiplying in number, and the forces at work there are likely to be affecting the legitimate stage elsewhere. Taxes are up everywhere, insurance has become more important, social security must be paid, and paperwork of all kinds has proliferated. Even increased advertising is undoubtedly necessary all over the country to lure the audience from its TV sets and local motion picture Bijous.

If this analysis is substantially correct, little can be done to reduce expenses in the legitimate theatre. It may be possible, however, to increase attendance with greater and more certain knowledge of theatregoers. Studying them and their preferences in theatrical entertainment will perhaps point to ways to solve some of the economic problems of the professional theatre. (9)

—◄●►—

The Arts Future: A Cultural Common Market

By

George C. White

The "salad days" of fund raising in the arts may be over. Increasingly, those sources of support which helped seed many arts programs are turning their consideration to new and more pressing areas, such as inter-racial relations and ghetto re-development. Arts leaders acknowledge that new sources of subsidy must be found.

Many argue that business and industry must shoulder the burden, but corporate support is often tied to specific self-interest. Moreover, big business cannot be expected to experiment.

Within the business world, only one industry exists which can be expected to benefit from experimentation in the arts—the entertainment industry. The relationship between the so-called "experimental" and the commercial is becoming intermixed increasingly, and a growing number of productions which originated in regional theatres or off-off-Broadway, have been purchased by major film companies. Yet, the large entertainment corporations continue to look at non-profit performing arts groups as panhandlers rather than as product development centers. With several notable exceptions, the entertainment industry has failed to provide support to the non-profit arts field.

If the mass entertainment media and the highly commercial "cultural" enterprises are to survive, however, let alone raise their standards, they must contribute to their own long-range development. As surely as the technologically oriented corporations must invest in the future through grants-in-aid and through the sponsorship of countless courses, seminars and conferences, the performing arts in the nation—whether leisure-time activity or true cultural achievement—will have to be sponsored by those who will receive the greatest commercial benefits. The alternatives, stagnation or complete government control, are too grim to contemplate.

With the fear that the time is already late, I propose an "Entertainment Foundation," supported collectively by the great entertainment corporations and administered by a staff similar in character to that of a Ford or a Rockefeller Foundation.

If, for example, C.B.S., R.C.A., A.B.C., Paramount, Columbia, U-I, B.M.I., and their proliferating subsidiaries turned over just the income from a reasonable number of their shares of treasury stock—not the stock itself—to this proposed foundation, the result would be an entertainment "community chest." This growing fund would remove the support burden from private foundations which have so effectively primed the pump.

The establishment of this foundation would provide us with one central fund to which non-profit performing arts organizations could apply for grants. In addition to centralizing the grant-giving function, this would give the entertainment giants a central bank of developing talent and a real and useful knowledge of "what's going on."

In today's world of theater, where, for example, a 90-minute television program may cost close to $1,000,000 and an off-Broadway "experimental" may be capitalized for $25,000, no room exists for failure, for true experimentation or for growth. Regional theater companies are discovering daily that the gap between income and expenditures is growing wider and wider, and few can be expected to survive without outside help.

The cultural community chest I propose is highly practical and could be implemented from within the existing entertainment complex. Administration of such a program has precedent in existing foundations and talent is available to manage it. The contributing corporations could benefit just through elimination of the "if-we-do-it-for-this-one-then-we-must-do-it-for-that-one" kind of decision-making. And the projects or individuals they save today, may, in many instances, provide them with their artistic strength in the future.

Here's another point for the entertainment giants to keep in mind. When government investigators point their fingers at them and ask what television and motion pictures are doing to upgrade and improve their products, here is an answer which these corporations have not had in the past: support and development of the non-profit performing arts.

I realize that in many ways what I propose is full of problems—not unlike Churchill's wartime proposition of eventual amity between France and Germany—but the European Common Market is a reality today. Why not a Cultural Common Market in a country which, in the 1950's and '60's, has proved it need never again take a second place in the arts to any nation on earth? The ultimate beneficiary is American civilization and its cultural heritage.

(61)

———◄●►———

Philanthropy a Significant Institution
Says Noted Sociologist

By

Arthur Vidich

The expansion and growth of private philanthropy is consistent with the rise of the service state insofar as the philanthropic redistribution achieves the same economic ends as secondary and tertiary job expansion in industry and government. In effect, philanthropy is another mechanism by which the problem of overproduction finds a resolution counter to the Marxian prediction.

It is of the essence of modern philanthropy that it produces nothing but services, but that it produces *only* services is its major economic significance. Theoretically, the market for services, in contrast to other forms of economic goods, is limited only by man's capacity to imagine ways of marketing services. . . . Philanthropy facilitates the marketing of services by providing them for nothing or so far below cost as to allow calling it philanthropy. . . .

It is abundantly clear . . . that both the government and private sectors share in meeting the costs of philanthropy. Though the absolute volume of government investment in philanthropy is incomparably greater than private philanthropic investment, the structural terms which define how the burden is shared must be specified. For example, what is one to make of the fact that even though the government carries a disproportionately heavy share of the burden, the number of units distributing these vast amounts of money is small in comparison to private philanthropic units. Of private non-profit *foundations* alone, there are more than fifty thousand, while the number of welfare, religious, educational, etc., charitable and philanthropic organizations defy enumeration. It would appear that on a dollar-for-dollar basis, the government distributes its philanthropy much more efficiently than the private sector, and indeed it is the case that where one committee in Washington can decide one afternoon to give a physics department in a university one million dollars, it takes many more people and much more time for the physics department to spend the million, the more so as the proportion spent on services is greater than equipment costs. . . . To the extent that the government stands as the symbol for the large-scale production of philanthropic dollars, the difference between government and private philanthropy can be likened to the distinctions between industrial and pre-industrial economies.

Private philanthropy is essentially pre-industrial, being better understood on the model of the craft system where the item is produced for a specific client. . . . Generally speaking, private philanthropic welfare expenditures take the form of servicing the client, whereas the government as a general but not universal practice prefers bulk purchasing of units of service. . . .

It is in this sense that government philanthropy is technologically advanced in comparison to much of private philanthropy which remains in the labor intensive handicraft stage, *i.e.*, large staffs relative to size of budgets. . . .

In the short run, it is always difficult for the government to spend money on projects that do not have a socially useful appearance. Tax dollars are supposed to be reasonably rational, to provide services which the community needs, and to have some relationship to the community's resources. In fact, at any one point in time public philanthropy will always have some number of ideologists who can justify the rationality, the necessity, the usefulness and perhaps the indispensability of the purposes for which the money is being given away. As for the public, it is wont to accept what is as if it had always been so and will be forevermore.

The picture that emerges for the long run is quite different, since with time there are great changes in the definition of social needs, the rationality of social expenditures and the proper ratios between expenditures and resources. It is at this point that private philanthropy begins to play another role. Because private philanthropy has no public accountability, it can indulge itself in the continuous and never-ending activity of creating new service needs, of embellishing and elaborating old needs, and of expanding the availability of all needs to all groups. As a result of these efforts, new areas of needs are accepted as legitimate by the public mind. Once such legitimacy is achieved, the need eventually can no longer be met by private philanthropy alone and must be taken over by government or

31

subsidized out of tax funds. In this way we increase our range of public welfare, health, educational and cultural programs and in the long run the tax load as well. Once the government steps in and takes over any area of new needs, the private philanthropic dollar is free to engage in the exploration and creation of other areas of need, and the whole cycle starts all over again. . . . In this sense private philanthropy . . . provides a perpetual mechanism of expansion.

The heroic role of the fund-raisers must be seen in the light of the above discussion. These entrepreneurs who create new causes and then go out and collect the money to support them are capitalism's current equivalent to the risk-taking entrepreneur of an earlier stage. The philanthropic entrepreneur performs the functions of stimulating the flow of currency from the market economy into non-productive channels. The stimulation of the consumption of non-productive services supports the market economy.

(25)

ARTS GROUPS SPURN AVAILABLE FUNDING AND SURVIVE

Selling tickets and winning grants may be among a non-profit performing arts group's most essential activities, but there are at least two theaters that *deliberately* ignored this normal course of action and survived.

The University of Toledo Theatre, for example, sent out notices at the beginning of the current season to announce a new free-ticket policy which it termed, "legit and exciting madness." The notice read, "We're poor, so we've gone free ... We can't afford a subscription campaign so we'll be passing the hat instead."

Dr. Bernard Coyne, the head of the university's theater department, decided to initiate the new policy in an attempt to broaden the theater audience beyond students. A highly successful small-scale free admission experiment the previous season had drawn large attendance from every area of the community including residents of old age homes, participants in vocational rehabilitation programs, factory workers, blacks and youngsters. Under the new policy, overall attendance has increased by some 40 per cent.

"Theater in Toledo has been a big society splurge," Sheila Sabrey, the theater's public relations director told *AM.* "But as an urban university we have a responsibility to break down the barrier of elitism and bring theater to all the people. The people we're getting now are the people we want."

The theater, which receives operating funds from the student union board, discovered after starting the program that it couldn't accept donations because of university auditing procedures. However, with attendance vastly increased and with operating costs pared to the bone, it is confident of operating free theater again next season.

Thousands of miles away, in Lucaya/Freeport, Grand Bahama Island, the Freeport Players Guild is awaiting the opening of its newly-built theater early this summer. However, but for the Guild's desire to "make it" on its own, it could have been in a new building two or three years ago.

In 1967, when the community theater was six years old, and housed in a converted shipbuilding facility, it decided to raise funds to build its own theater. Almost immediately, the Grand Bahama Port Authority offered the group a site and a basic structure, an estimated $50,000 gift. According to one of the theater members, ''The vitality of the company was based on our ability to overcome difficulties. The gift would have made things too easy.'' The gift was rejected.

With the fund drive moving haltingly, one of the theater's founders offered to donate $150,000 to build the theater. Again, for the same reason, the offer was rejected. Finally after three years the fund drive raised $150,000 and construction started. Then, having proved it could fund its own theater, the Guild accepted a $50,000 donation from the Port Authority to complete the project. (70)

Economic Note

A study of museum staff salaries sponsored by the New York State Association of Museums shows that curators are very low on the salary scale. In New York State, after six or seven years' service, the average curator's salary is below starting wages in many other professions. (78)

LOWRY DISCUSSES NEW FORD FOUNDATION SURVEY

(In Spring 1971 the Ford Foundation announced a full-scale economic survey of 200 performing arts groups, covering the five year period ending with the 1969-70 season. The data bank resulting from this survey will be computerized and updated annually. Also an audience market study in the arts will be undertaken in several key cities. In this interview with AM editor A. H. Reiss, W. McNeil Lowry, Ford Foun-

dation vice president for the humanities and the arts, discusses the new program and its ramifications.)

Q: How and when did the idea for developing the economic survey originate?

A: When Ford Foundation trustees approved an arts program in 1957, one of the subjects the staff proposed for exploration was the economic and social position of the artist and of organized outlets for his career. Between 1957 and 1962 Ford Foundation staff collected a large quantity of data on the operations of non-profit arts groups although the data was not on a comparable basis, and it became apparent that only the deliberate construction of a uniform survey could provide the kind of information most needed. Other agencies about the same time announced plans for performing arts studies. The Rockefeller Brothers Fund Report was one illustration; the important volume done by Professors Baumol and Bowen was another. The need for a more comprehensive analysis of the non-profit arts sector continued to be stressed, however, not only by performing arts managers but by many private and public agencies, including the newly emerging national and state arts councils. In 1970 the Ford Foundation, in consultation with these other agencies, moved to undertake such a survey.

Q: What kind of advance study and pretesting preceded the actual formulation of the questionnaires?

A: Case histories of a small number of performing arts groups were prepared by the staff of the Ford Foundation and discussed in June 1970 with the Foundation's Trustees, who gave approval in principle to a national economic survey. From that date until January 1, 1971, with the help of performing arts managers, economists and systems analysts, the data collection form was revised and tested by more than a dozen groups in the field. The data collection form distributed in May to 200 arts groups was the result.

Q: Do you agree that most groups will have difficulty in answering the questionnaire? Not only will they be asked to provide accurate material on seasons which were completed four or five years ago, but they must also exercise judgment in many cases. How can you be sure that the material you receive from performing arts organizations will be accurate and valid?

A: There will undoubtedly be difficulties. The responses of the groups included in the pretests, however, were more encouraging than had been anticipated. The administration of the survey includes assistance from the project staff when this is called for by performing arts groups required to exercise judgment in accommodating their own records to the data form.

Q: On what basis were the 200 participating arts groups selected? How do you define a professional group?

A: The 200 participating groups are largely those who have associated themselves in particular categories of operations in the fields of theater, dance, opera and symphony orchestra, namely, American Symphony Orchestra League (major and metropolitan orchestras), League of Resident Theaters, Association of American Dance Companies, the Central Opera Service and O.P.E.R.A. America. In each field the groups included are non-profit, use union personnel, and operate at a minimum budget level comparable to other groups in the same field that are embraced by the survey.

Q: How will non-participating arts groups benefit from this material?

A: The report, which is expected to be published and distributed in 1972, should be of great benefit even to the performing arts groups who operate at a lower budgetary level or do not have sustained performance seasons. Pro-

36

jections and extrapolations from the data supplied by economists and experienced performing arts managers should reveal many important trends applicable to the smaller as well as to the larger groups.

Q: Is it an intention of this program to develop a uniform system of accounting for all performing arts groups? If so, will you be making guidelines available to the arts?

A: The Ford Foundation, of course, does not presume to offer a uniform system of accounting for all performing arts groups. Reactions of managers of some of the groups in the pretests suggest, however, that a by-product of the survey may be the development of more consistent and uniform definitions of expenditure and income categories.

Q: Considering the impact of change on the arts and the development of new kinds of programs and problems, how helpful will the material you've gathered be?

A: The first aim of the survey is to describe and analyze operations of a significant number of non-profit groups over a five-year period. The impact of change and the development of new programs and problems should be more visible as a result of the analysis and not less.

Q: Why didn't the studies start four months later and include the 1970-71 season?

A: The time lag in financial statements and fiscal year audits at the conclusion of one season ranges between 90 and 120 days. The survey will, however, include the 1970-71 season and all seasons subsequent, since the Foundation has announced its intention to keep the data up to date by an annual canvass of information from the same groups.

Q: Considering the many problems affecting the arts and the fact that the data bank will cost $500,000 a year to update, why did you view this program as a current need?

A: In the 14 years the Foundation has operated in the arts, the demands for a better economic analysis on a national scale and for more uniform data have increased every year. The results are important not only to artistic producers and managers but to private and public agencies at every level, local to national. A consistent theme of all writing and discussion about the arts in the United States is the tentative nature of the economic and fiscal projections. The $500,000 figure is a tentative budget estimate for all research and development activities of the Foundation in the arts. We do not know exactly what it will cost to update the data bank but it clearly will only be a small fraction of $500,000.

Q: The Ford Foundation has invested considerable money in the arts ($238-million) since 1957. Will the current program in any way adversely affect the future arts funding policies of the Foundation?

A: The survey will in no way adversely affect the policies of the Ford Foundation in its support of the arts. As stated by the Foundation, the objective sought by the survey is not related to grantmaking plans and policies. The large investments in the arts since 1957 testify to the sustained character of the Foundation's commitment in these fields.

71)

FUND-RAISING TECHNIQUES

Nine Key Steps to Successful Fund Raising

Fund raising and development campaigns require careful timing and conscious, step by step planning. According to John Price Jones Company, a leading fund raising firm, there are nine key phases in a development program.

The first is stating the case. A definitive statement of an organization's case must be prepared and then placed before the organization's leaders and its prospects. Every conceivable method of communicating this case to the public should be used.

Second is the identification of all prospects—the prospecting phase. Once the list is drawn, it must be carefully screened and evaluated. Next, prospects must be rated according to interest in the organization and potential to give.

Organizing the campaign structure is the third key phase. Leadership, especially on the top level, must be organized early in an institution's schedule of operations. Committee heads must be appointed and the campaign headquarters must be carefully planned so that volunteers will have sufficient support and service to function efficiently.

Next, comes the cultivation and motivation of prospects. A solicitor must personally meet the prospect and stimulate his interest in the organization, its case and its needs. This calls for private luncheons and other meetings in social settings as well as public functions to which prospects should be invited.

A fifth key phase is finding pace setting gifts to get the campaign moving. This phase is particularly crucial. It can

39

make or break a campaign because big gifts offer a "parade of enthusiasm which leads to others climbing on the band-wagon." Pace-setting gifts usually come from someone within the organization itself, such as trustees or other members of the organization's official family.

Timing is another essential. Ideally, each step in a campaign should follow the one before it in a natural and logical manner. Thus, prospects are best approached when a sense of urgency has been developed in them and the person who is best suited to contact them personally is found.

Momentum is equally important. Although campaigns start slowly, they will, as a rule, gradually accelerate until a point of intensity is reached. This point of intensity should be sustained as long as it is necessary to do so. In short campaigns, momentum cannot be sustained for very long unless organizations work at maintaining it. Special climax points such as organizational dinners, parties, and campaign announcements, are essential to developing momentum and sustaining it.

Soliciting, the eighth phase, is the most important. No matter how well planned the rest of the program is, the campaign will fail unless someone asks someone else for a gift. At times, one direct call may produce results. Frequently, however, much follow-up work is necessary. If everything else fails, then a "mop-up" mail campaign may have to be used. But whatever the methods used, every prospect *must* be asked for a gift.

Lastly, comes acknowledgment. By thanking prospects for their help, a doorway to continued future support remains open. (27)

Advice On Fund Raising

Free advice on the planning and execution of fund raising campaigns, may often be obtained from executives of health and welfare organizations who face financial problems similar to those encountered in the arts. Get to know these leaders and maintain cordial relationships with them, but avoid requesting information during their fund drives when they have little free time. (16)

———————◄•►———————

High Standards Vital to Fund Drives for Arts

Sound fund-raising practices are important to arts groups for the efficiency of their operation, and for the continued success of their fund raising drives. Basic standards have been established by the National Information Bureau, a non-profit, consultant group that evaluates national philanthropic and cultural organizations for its subscribers—foundations, community chests, and corporations—that want to be sure the money they donate is being properly used.

AM interviewed Erich Gottlieb, a member of NIB's research staff, to find out the basis for NIB's ratings. According to NIB, the following standards are basic.

The board of directors should be an active, responsible group, and its meetings—or those of its executive committee—should take place at least five times annually, preferably eight times.

Members of the board should not be letterhead figures only; they should be well informed about all the institution's activities, should discuss basic matters of policy and should participate in decisions.

NIB, in many cases, actually goes to the offices of a group it is evaluating and meets and talks with the staff. It suggests that new board members be invited to do the same, as part of an orientation program.

The arts group's purpose should be clearly defined and it should be able to show, if asked, that it does not duplicate or overlap the functions of other groups. It should also be able to demonstrate that its schedule of events have been planned so that they don't overlap or compete unnecessarily with other groups.

The fund raising practices of an arts group should be above reproach. This means there should be no payment of percentage commissions (i.e., as distinct from fees) for fund raising, no mailing of unordered tickets or merchandise with a request for money, and no telephone solicitation of the general public.

It also means that the money raised should be used for the purposes specified in the group's promotion. For instance, if a group solicits funds specifically for an orchestra tour, it should not use any part of the money raised for other purposes.

Ethical promotion is a very important part of fund raising. Promotional claims should be justified in terms of the actual services and programs offered. Specifically, if an arts group advertises that it is offering a series of first rate performances, the orchestras, theatre troupes or soloists must, indeed, be first rate. If the group cites attendance figures at events or exhibits, these figures should be based on some system of counting, rather than on loose estimates.

Who does an arts group's audit can be just as important as how well it is done, according to NIB. It should *not* be done by the treasurer of the group, by a committee of the board, or even the treasurer's company, if he is a member of an accounting firm. The audit should be signed by an independent outside firm.

The statement itself should conform to the best accounting practices. There should be no catch-all categories; all items should be as specific as possible, although lack of standardized classification has plagued the accounting practices of philanthropic groups. Instead of administrative expenses, for instance, there should be a breakdown of salaries, publicity, promotion, mail, etc. The expenses of administering a concert series, as an example, should be separated from the year-round administrative expenses. Cash donations should be separated from donations of "goods-in-kind," so that a painting, for instance, would be listed as a "painting, valued at" instead of setting a cash valuation on a painting and then listing it as cash received.

Finally, says the NIB, every group must submit an annual detailed budget, that projects a plan of expenditures and sets monetary limits on the various parts of its program. It is true, the NIB notes, that cultural groups often are not sure how much money they will get, and therefore find it difficult to set a budget. The answer is that the budget need not be immutable—there can be minimum budgets, maximum budgets and even "in-between" budgets. But there must be a plan of expenditures, and it must be seen, discussed and approved by the board.   (20)

The Special Gifts Campaign:

Eight Fundamental Preconditions for Success

No type of fund raising is more important than the "special gifts" campaign. It may be part of an overall effort that employs direct mail, house-to-house canvassing and other solicitation methods; or it may be used by itself.

What are special gifts? In the parlance of the professional fund raiser, they are relatively large donations solicited on a personal and highly individual basis. They contrast with the small contributions sought in a mass effort. While canvassers may seek five dollar contributions from householders, or a street-corner solicitor may collect quarters and dimes, the special gift is usually that of $100 or more.

Measured on a dollar-spent-per-dollar-raised basis, the special gifts drive is usually the most economical and efficient of all forms of fund raising. Moreover, its special characteristics make it particularly suitable for smaller institutions.

The small institution frequently cannot solicit over a broad geographical area, or may lack a large corps of volunteers, or it simply may not be able to afford the relatively high costs of other methods. For these reasons, the special gifts campaign has become the staple of the small organization. However it is the most important part of the effort of the larger groups as well. It is the chief weapon in the armamentarium of the effective fund raiser.

However, not every institution can conduct a successful special gifts drive. Certain pre-conditions must be met before an effective push can be made. To determine whether your institution can make use of this method now, asks yourself these eight questions:

1. How strong and clear is your "case"? Define your mission and the specific purpose of the contemplated fund drive. You must show your donor how, by giving, he will be helping a cause larger than the institution itself. A fuzzy case will not convince.

2. Are your board members well known and widely respected in the community? Your board is not only a major source of special gifts, itself, it is also your most important line of communication to other donors. Its strength and public reputation may compensate for other weaknesses in your situation. You may want to consider adding judiciously selected members before entering the campaign.

3. Is your board a paper body? It may include some of the most important and respected members of the community, but, if it is not a working body, your special gifts campaign may never get off the ground. The brunt of the effort in this form of fund raising necessarily falls on the board. It will cost its members time and money. They must set the pace, both in terms of gifts and of effort. Without its enthusiastic support, a special gifts drive is doomed in advance.

4. How well known in the community are your activities and accomplishments? Donors hesitate to give to an unfamiliar institution. A sustained public relations drive before the campaign begins can help let people know about you.

5. What is the economic health of your community? Check with your local united fund to see whether it has met its target in the most recent campaign. Check, too, with specialized health and welfare funds. Their fund raising results are usually a matter of public record, and you should have no difficulty getting them. A general

pattern of fulfillment suggests that the community is able and willing to give; a consistent pattern of failure suggests the opposite.

6. Is the time right? Even if there is clear evidence that patronage is available, it may be foolish to start a drive just when other drives are under way that may involve your potential supporters.

7. Is the community disposed to support your kind of activity? Is it generally culture-conscious? Here any information about the success or failure of recent drives by other cultural groups can give a clue to the prevailing atmosphere. If it appears negative, it may be improved by a carefully planned, energetic public relations effort calling attention to the role of your institution in raising the quality of community life.

8. Do you have the resources? Even though the special gifts campaign is the most efficient of fund raising methods, it can require months of close attention by one or more staff people and considerable clerical time. It will require brochures, press releases and other such material. You will need money for fund raising events like a banquet or a cocktail party; you may even want to engage outside professional assistance to do research, make surveys or to manage the drive. It takes money to raise money, and your institution must be prepared to foot the bills.

Realistic answers to these questions can give you a fair estimate of your chances for success in a special gifts campaign. (2)

The Special Gifts Campaign:

How to Rate and Reach Your Prospective Donor

The success of a special gifts campaign depends heavily on the committee that develops the list of prospective donors, rates them, and assigns them to solicitors. If this part of the campaign for large gifts is well planned, the drive can succeed; if not, it will probably fail.

The listing committee should first draw up the basic list of possible donors. Members of the soliciting organization are, of course, the first source of names. But other sources should carefully be screened for additional leads. Some of these sources are: programs or publications of similar, non-competing organizations; business and city directories; social registers; and club membership lists.

The name of each potential giver should be entered on a card, along with as much relevant data about him as possible, such as: his occupation or business affiliation; positions held; record of past giving; club connections; personal friends or interests. Omit nothing that might help determine the best approach to the individual or the appropriate size of the donation to be sought.

An evaluation committee should then study these cards. Such a committee should include people who, through their business or social position, are able to estimate each prospect's ability to give. Its members are ordinarily found in the board of trustees of the campaigning institution. It is their task, once having rated each donor's potential, to assign prospects to solicitors. In doing so, the committee should ask itself:

1. Does the proposed solicitor have the right relationship to the potential donor? A business relationship can be

of great value, especially when the prospect wants to maintain the good will of the committee member calling on him.

2. Is there a committee member or solicitor in the same giving class as the prospect, who has social connections with him? It is natural for the donor to contribute an amount close to that given by his solicitor, if that solicitor is also a friend.

3. Have members of the solicitation committee made "pace-setting" gifts? A solicitor is far more effective in asking for a generous contribution, if he, himself, has made one.

No solicitor should be assigned more prospects than he is willing or able to handle. He should always do so personally, though the setting may be business or social. Some donors are best approached at their office; others at lunch, cocktails, or an intimate dinner party where there is adequate time to explain the financial needs and program goals of the institution.

It is vital that the solicitor be thoroughly familiar with the purposes, program and financial status of the organization. He should always have printed material to leave with the donor as a reminder. Sometimes it is effective to bring with him a staff member of the institution to answer detailed questions.

Above all, a special gifts campaign must be based on personal, face-to-face contact. It has been proved through the years that other methods—mailings or telephone calls alone, for example—will not produce special gifts as large as the evaluation committee may have planned or hoped.

(4)

Acknowledgement Vital to Special Gift Repeats

When an organization has run a special gifts campaign for large contributions solicited on a personal basis, proper acknowledgment of the gift is often the key to repeat giving.

In fact, repetition of special gifts through the years on the part of those people who are permanently, not only temporarily, interested in the group's work, is essential if the institution is to build a sound base of support. Solidifying givers into permanent friends is the goal of an acknowledgment program.

Acknowledgment can take several forms. For example, large donors as a group can be thanked by invitation to special events organized for the purpose; such as a banquet, an opening night cocktail party, a preview of an exhibition, or an intimate dinner party at the home of a socially prominent person of the arts.

All contributions over $25 should be acknowledged by personal letter. One letter should be sent over the signature of the person who actually solicited the gift. In addition, a formal letter signed by the president of the organization can be included. But if there are so many acknowledgements to be made that duplicated letters must be used, they should be written in the same type employed to fill in the contributor's name, address and amount of gift.

From this point on, contributors of $25 or more should receive all informational mailings, as a step to bind them to the organization. (7)

How to Spot, Woo and Win a Foundation

In making an approach to any foundation, cultural organizations should take the same professional attitude as that exhibited by the educational, health and social welfare groups that win the lion's share of foundation money.

The primary step must be the careful choice and delineation of the project to be supported. It should be timely, important, and something that your institution could not finance in any other way.

The next step is painstaking research into those foundations that are possible sources of support for the project. Not all are.

Generally, larger national foundations like Ford and Rockefeller prefer to aid "risk ventures"—new departures in the grant recipient's field of endeavor. They view their grants as "seed money", and only rarely grant funds for maintenance needs or similar routine demands. Smaller foundations, mostly local, family or local-corporate, are more likely to help close the financial gap in a community organization's regular program.

The right foundation to approach is one whose stated purpose would be furthered by the project for which you seek assistance. Canvassing foundations whose expressed aims would not be advanced by your project is a waste of time for applicant and potential giver. To locate the appropriate foundation in a field of 13,000, consult the *Foundation Directory*. Also, a visit to one of the six regional depositories of the Foundation Library Center offers a chance to consult conveniently a wide range of relevant literature. Keep an eye peeled for new foundations in your field opening for business and looking for their first grantees.

50

The first contact with a foundation may be a sounding-out session in person or a very brief description of the proposed project in a one- or two-page letter. If this piques the interest of the foundation, you will be invited to follow up with a full presentation. Although requirements of individual foundations vary widely, here are a few cardinal points no application should fail to cover.

1. The project—its significance, timeliness and relationship to the foundation's own aims.

2. Your organization—its qualifications to carry out the proposed project successfully.

3. Carry-over value—the usefulness of your project results to others in your field.

4. Plan for inspection and review—the foundation's opportunity to oversee work in progress and evaluate results.

5. Need—proof that the foundation's aid is absolutely essential.

You should also include such essentials as a description of the precise nature of your organization, its history, legal form, and controlling body. List names and addresses of officers and professional staff. Explain its financial status and provide a detailed budget for the current year, along with the name and address of the auditor and a copy of your federal tax exemption certificate. Offer to supply any further information the foundation may request.

Your presentation should take into consideration the sensibilities of the foundation and of the community. One foundation executive, for example, may be known to court projects that pay off quickly with community approval, and to shun those whose results are long-range and less obvious. The more you know about your target foundation, the better.

To the old claim that "knowing the right people" can be as much help with foundations as elsewhere in our society, foundation people offer mixed comment. Jeanne Brewer, an expert on foundation relations, writes of one foundation official who remarked: "Acquaintanceship is no substitute for a soundly constructed proposal." Yet another, she says, put it this way: "Personal connections with us are important. We look for good proposal ideas first, but they're rare, so we give generally where we know the man or the institution asking us."   (1)

Foundation File

If your organization is interested in foundation support, it will be worthwhile for you to maintain a foundation card file. On each index card, list the pertinent information about each local foundation, such as name, address and phone number, and the names of key personnel within the foundation. Then every time you come across some new information concerning the foundation, such as the size or purpose of gifts given, or a statement of policy made by an executive, jot it down on the card. Also keep a record on the card of any foundation person who is a member of your organization or a ticket subscriber.   (21)

How to Start an Effective Bequest Program

(Bequest programs offer non-profit groups a major source of income that is far from being fully exploited. In the following article, John Price Jones, a leading fund raising firm, tells how to develop a successful bequest program.)

One can make a strong case for bequest programs in the next few years. As taxation eats into large fortunes, bequests offer a means of offsetting this drying up of large pools of private wealth. Moreover, bequests to non-profit arts groups are exempt from federal estate taxes.

The organizations which have set up bequest programs in recent years, and stayed with them, have built additional, stable sources of income in a period of increasing competition for the philanthropic dollar. Records show that bequest programs per time and dollar invested pay off better than many other fund-raising programs.

Moreover, there is less wear and tear on volunteers and their consultants in bequest programs than in campaigns. Many volunteers find such programs suit their temperament more than campaign solicitation.

Bequest programs frequently raise funds that would not, and could not, be otherwise secured. In a period of increasing taxes, bequests offer a means to the middle income person—and there are more and more of them—to make a substantial gift to the organization of his choice. Bequest giving is on the increase.

A question often raised is that bequest program results cannot be measured. This is not true. Measure them the same way you measure other fund-raising costs—by the money coming in and what it costs you to obtain it. Simply figure results over a longer period of time than 12 months. Figure them on a 5- or 10-year basis.

Here are some ways to increase your bequest income. First, have a sound case—valid reasons why people can and should leave you money in their wills. And your program should be broad enough to offer a range of gift opportunities. Second, get your explanatory literature into the hands of your prospects, lawyers, bankers, tax consultants as well as others in your area.

Third, capable volunteers are needed and they may require technical assistance at some point in their work. Tax, legal, accounting and other matters must be determined by qualified persons who may be employed by the person making the bequest, or who may be on your staff. Both are often involved.

Fourth, make specific suggestions or presentations to your prime prospects—geared to their known interests and desires. Persistence is particularly necessary in bequest campaigns.

The volunteer who has himself written an organization into his will makes its best ambassador. He is enthusiastic and he is not asking anyone to do what he has not done himself. However, a bequest program to be successful, must be supported by a broad publicity campaign.   (37)

Insuring Success

Cultural organizations named as beneficiaries in life insurance policies can realize significant future income. This kind of contribution may also have special appeal to some donors since annual premium payments, which are tax deductible, cost less than annual payments on a cash pledge of the same amount. However, it should be remembered that the organization must be named an irrevocable beneficiary and the donor cannot reserve the right to change beneficiaries. The total value of the gift is ensured the moment the policy is enforced and remains so as long as the premiums are paid each year.   (33)

Bequest Form

To ease the way for bequests to your organization, keep sample bequest forms on hand for distribution. The forms should bear the name of your organization as beneficiary. In addition, printed information on the tax benefits to the testator should be made available to contributors.   (42)

Motivating the Donor

An approach used by a college to increase donations through wills, trusts and insurance policies may be of interest to arts groups. Swarthmore College, in Pennsylvania, devoted the entire March issue of its bulletin to the topic *Creative Giving and Swarthmore College.* More than half of the handsome 16-page illustrated publication was devoted to a section which discussed in detail eight different forms of gifts. Through charts and hypothetical examples, it carefully explained tax benefits and advantages to the donor in each of the listed categories.   (50)

A Stock Answer

Contributions of stocks and bonds, which have special tax advantages to the donor, can be encouraged by cultural organizations. Securities, which may rise in value after they are donated, can still be deducted by donors at the market price for which they were bought. The higher value is not counted as income subject to capital gains tax.
(34)

A Trust Fund Program Can Help Arts Groups

A trust fund program is one method of fund raising sometimes overlooked by arts organizations.

Trusts typically are repositories of money, securities or property to be used as specified in an agreement establishing a trust corporation. Having perpetual life, permanent trusts continue to earn money even after the death of the donor.

Often, persons who might not directly contribute to an arts group will establish a permanent trust for it because of tax benefits and trust permanency. Contributors to a trust are entitled to a 30 per cent tax deduction on their gift. This rule applies when the recipient is a non-profit organization receiving at least a third of its support from the public, or from government agencies. On the other hand, no taxes need be paid by non-profit groups on income earned from a trust. (Note: The implications of new tax laws were still uncertain at press time. Check with attorneys first.)

One trust form, the temporary trust, has a special advantage because it may be set up for as short a period as two years to benefit a tax-exempt organization. At the end of that time, the principal of the trust reverts back to the contributor. But in the meantime, the non-profit group benefits from the income earned from the trust.

Because trusts take many forms, and each state has specific statutes governing them, arts groups wishing to promote trust programs should consult an attorney first. Information on local trust laws should then be made available to potential contributors. (40)

How to Plan and Conduct a Benefit Performance

The benefit performance generates funds through the sale of tickets at prices increased to include contributions.

The first step in developing a benefit campaign is to organize a strong committee. This is usually composed almost entirely of socially prominent women, and should be headed by a member of the board of the benefiting institution.

This committee should be led by a chairman, a vice-chairman for publicity, and one for planning and arrangements.

The event should be chosen with care. It may be an opening night, a preview, or a special program. Whatever event is selected should have broad popular appeal.

The group must next decide on how many tickets it thinks it can sell, and on an appropriate price structure. Guests pay the regular ticket price, plus a premium (the contribution). This premium seldom exceeds $20 per seat, although in rare cases it may go as high as $100. Ordinarily, at an event at which the top premium is $20, a section of seats are set aside at the $20 level; other blocks at $15, $10, and $5 above the regular price.

Experience indicates that the top and bottom price seats sell better than those in the middle range, and so, in planning for a sale of, say, 600 seats, the committee might set aside 200 at $20, 100 each at $15 and $10, and 200 at $5. Such a distribution would yield a gross income of $7,500, if all 600 seats are sold. Of course, the price levels and particular distribution chosen should reflect the potentials of the benefiting organization.

The next step is to work up a list of sponsors—prominent business and community leaders who agree to allow their names to be used in the accompanying publicity.

Once this is done, invitation kits must be printed. These include the invitation itself, which should contain not only the time, date, place, and a description of the event, but also the names of the committee, the sponsors, and the trustees of the institution. The invitation should also carry a statement explaining the work of the institution and spelling out its need for funds.

The kit must also include a reservation card listing seats available with prices, and a return envelope for checks.

Once these preliminaries are concluded, the publicity vice-chairman should arrange for a dinner or meeting at which the first public announcement of the benefit is made. It is vital that this meeting be reported in the press, preferably in the society pages. Photos of the principals should be given the press. Releases should contain the names of sponsors, committee members and others associated with the event.

This initial public relations effort should be followed by a continuing flow of releases, pictures and progress reports to local newspapers.

In the meantime, the vice-chairman for planning and arrangements should call upon members of the committee to submit the names of potential ticket buyers whom they will agree to solicit. These names are put on a master list and culled for duplication. A list of more general prospects is compiled from the Social Register, chamber of commerce members and similar sources. Members of the committee agree to solicit those with whom they are personally acquainted. Unassigned names are divided arbitrarily, or accepted by the committee leaders as their assignments.

Committee members then mail invitation kits—along with personal, preferably hand-written, notes to each of

ARTS MANAGEMENT HANDBOOK

their assigned prospects. The return envelope in each case is coded with the name of the committee member sending it out.

The committee holds periodic meetings to follow the progress of the campaign and inspire greater effort. Additional assignments are made as necessary.

As checks arrive, they should be ticked off against the master list of prospects. Return envelopes will indicate which committee member sent out the invitation, and this member should be notified, so that she knows which of her prospects have made purchases and which need additional prodding.

The benefit campaign described above usually takes between three and four months. As the date of the event approaches, final arrangements for seating and other details must be worked out. (8)

———— ◄●► ————

Taxes and Tickets

Are you selling tickets to a fund-raising event? According to guidelines published by the Internal Revenue Services, only that portion of payment which exceeds the fair market value of any consideration received by the purchaser can qualify as a tax deductible gift. Thus, if $25.00 is charged for an opera ticket which normally sells for $10.00 only the $15.00 above the normal ticket price is deductible. The I.R.S. urges sponsoring organizations to indicate in their promotional material what the amount actually is of the gift being solicited. (57)

How to Maintain Ties With Old Contributors

A new fund raising drive logically begins at the conclusion of the old one. During the period preceding the start of a new campaign every effort must be made to maintain a friendly and continuing relationship with contributors. Too often, in the understandable zeal to discover new prospects, institutions neglect the constituency that has already demonstrated an interest. However, past contributors already "sold" on the institution may become bigger givers if properly cultivated. Moreover, they are excellent possibilities for future volunteer work and can become effective fund raisers themselves.

The first step in developing a continuing relationship with a contributor is a suitable acknowledgment of his gift. This should be done as quickly as possible after the gift is received. Donors of large gifts should receive personal acknowledgments from top leaders in the campaign. In the case of exceptional gifts, the board of directors might consider a formal resolution of thanks.

Since it is impossible to acknowledge all gifts personally in a large campaign, form acknowledgments should be drafted with care. They should be attractive, and the wording should impart the feeling that the institution is sincere in its appreciation of the gift, whatever its size.

After acknowledgments have been sent, the institution should have a prepared program to assure continued report-back to contributors. Initially, contributors should receive an accounting of the funds raised and an explanation of how these funds are being used. Regular written reports, inexpensively prepared in newsletter or simple letter form should go out under the signature of a top officer of the institution to keep the donor aware of the continuing program of the institution. These should be supplemented by verbal reports at periodic organizational functions to which donors and/or volunteers are invited.

Although extra work and money is involved in maintaining relationships with past contributors, such a program will more than pay its way when the next drive rolls around. (26)

———————— ◄●► ————————

The Personal Touch

As a change from the coldness of the typical acknowledgement card sent to donors, the head of an arts organization might try sending out one with a personalized look. This can be done by reproducing a pen-and-ink message on a card that bears a printed heading—the reproduction of the hand-written message and signature being in a typical blue-black ink that gives the impression of a personal thank-you note. (59)

———————— ◄●► ————————

Progress Report

A record of organizational growth should be an important part of any fund raising case statement, but too many groups either forget to include it, or don't present it to its best advantage. A good example of how to emphasize progress is found in an eight-page brochure recently issued by the Indianapolis Symphony Orchestra titled "State of the Symphony." The report includes a description of all current orchestra activities, but also features a "then and now" comparison between its program and budget in its early days and today. The brochure's two-page centerspread dramatically demonstrates the orchestra's rising income and expense picture by featuring a color graph of the period between the 1965-66 season and the 1970-71 season, which uses actual figures for the completed seasons and estimated figures for the current and coming ones. (64)

Tax Deduction

Taxpayers often have difficulty recalling exactly how much they gave to charitable, non-profit groups months before. If the receipt given donors at the time of giving is plainly marked with a reminder that the gift is tax deductible, it will help the busy donor place it with records he will need at tax time. A standard phrase imprinted on receipts and a reminder in acknowledgement letters should be automatic. (7)

Who Gets the Check?

A campaign to raise funds for a health charity recently mailed elaborate printed material to potential contributors. But along with all the handsome literature came a mimeographed card clearly made necessary by the failure of someone to indicate how checks were to be made out. Often contributors and those ordering tickets by mail are left in doubt on this point. Organizations can save themselves and the public trouble by remembering to print clearly in bold type or capitals: "Please make checks payable to . . ." (27)

How Professionals Maintain Records in Fund Campaign

Keeping accurate and adequate records may be unglamorous, but it is an important part of any fund raising effort. Some large campaigns require that literally thousands of individual accounts be kept up-to-date and within easy access. In one $15,000,000 campaign, for example, fund raisers maintained 15,000 regular accounts, plus thousands of additional ones for direct mail respondents. The women's division of the campaign maintained records on still another 25,000 prospects solicited by its members. In a drive of this magnitude, punch card systems are almost a necessity. But even small campaigns require detailed attention to the record keeping function. Good record keeping one year can be of inestimable help in the following year's drive.

A typical master file of 4 x 6 index cards ought to contain the following information for each giver or prospect: name and address; name of person to be interviewed, if the account represents a business; up-to-date information on the type of business and number of employees.

Many professional fund raisers keep a ten-year giving record on the card, indicating the size of the gift each year, the date of each gift, and the name of the successful solicitor. Space should also be provided in which the solicitor can jot down the reasons given for a refusal to contribute.

Where there are a great number of very small contributions, it may be wise to establish a cut-off point for record keeping. Thus, while every contribution must be posted somewhere for bookkeeping purposes, it may be uneconomic to bother with additional data on those who give under $5.

While such painstaking record keeping takes time, it is essential to effective fund raising. (18)

————— ◄●► —————

Cautious Use of Surveys Can Help Gauge Fund Potential

Many cultural organizations reach a point in their development at which they need professional help in gauging their fund raising potential. To do this, they often call on a professional fund raising firm to undertake a study that will help them plan realistic fund drives.

Some studies, designed for organizations with very large constituencies, are based on questionnaires sent by mail. These are simple, and responses are given in yes-or-no form. A survey of this type may reveal which aspects of the institution's program are most "saleable" in the fund campaign. However, this type of survey cannot indicate the depth of individual commitment to the organization.

Another type of study focusses on a relatively few individuals, but attempts to probe their reactions to the institution in depth. For this type of survey, interviewers spend from one to three hours with each interviewee, attempting to provoke value judgements about the institution's program and effectiveness. Such interviews can indicate the degree of support the institution can expect during its drive. Sometimes, interviewers cannot only elicit information, but obtain a significant campaign pledge then and there.

Success of either type of survey depends heavily on careful drafting of questions and thoughtful evaluation of responses. In the interview type, much also depends on selection of interviewers. Organizations should not rush into a survey without careful consideration of its objectives and cost. Interview-studies are costly, and may range in price from $1,000 for a one-month study based on 25 interviews, to $10,000 or more for a three month study of a larger sample. (22)

―――――――――◄●►―――――――――

Variety of Printed Literature Needed in Fund Raising Drives

Booklets, fact sheets, handbooks, and other printed materials are vital tools of every fund-raising campaign. They are important for explaining the reason for the drive, for helping cultivate donors and for supplying factual information.

What is needed and how it is used depends on the purpose of the campaign, and the group appealed to. According to the John Price Jones Company, a New York-based professional fund-raising firm, these are the most used printed materials:

The case statement, the first piece, is basic. It explains what service the institution provides, why this service is needed, what opportunities exist for greater service, and what funds are needed. Subsequent publicity is often based on this statement, and it can be used to indoctrinate campaign leaders. Since it is not for general distribution it is usually mimeographed or duplicated rather than printed.

The second major piece is a pamphlet intended for the general public. It contains the same material as the case statement, but sets the institution's goals within a larger framework by explaining the community's problem and then noting the institution's role in helping solve it. Since it is meant for mass distribution it should be printed, and made attractive with pictures of present activities, and various kinds of art work.

Each campaign worker should receive a handbook that contains tips on effective canvassing, a chart of the institution's needs, and a list of campaign committee members. It may include a section presenting the most-often-asked questions and their answers.

A preliminary campaign announcement is usually the first notice sent to prospective donors. It lists the institution's needs and the details of campaign preparations.

There are several categories of specialized campaign pieces. Many groups prepare a tax leaflet that lists the various forms that gifts can take. Sometimes there are personal appeals to more important prospective donors. These often list separately the special purposes the funds will benefit and are usually hand-typed or otherwise personalized.

Many drives prepare leaflets for particular groups, such as business.

For building drives a gift and memorial opportunity leaflet presents the pro-rated cost of each unit, such as a meeting room or gallery, along with floor plans and a text pointing up the opportunity to name a unit after a donor.

Careful attention to the preparation of printed materials can make an important contribution to your fund-raising drive. (18)

Cultural Stocks and Bonds

The Winston-Salem Arts Council used parchment type paper for a fund drive promotional letter. A three part folder, the outside is printed in green and is made to resemble a share of stock. The text in the folder informs the recipient that: "The holder of this share is entitled to the benefits of a rich community life through the varied and ever-expanding facilities of the Winston-Salem Arts Council and its members. Very negotiable." The reverse side refers to "The Arts: Winston-Salem's Unique 'Growth Stock' ". (27)

Making a Date with the Donor

A New England school for the deaf has used an unusual and effective fund-raising reminder that places its appeal before potential givers 12 times annually. Every year it sends out a calendar, with each month printed on the back of a business reply envelope. When the user tears off a month, he finds himself holding the institution's message and a self-addressed contribution envelope. (1)

Sense of Humor

A humorous approach can help to promote a fund raising event successfully. When the Art Gallery of Toronto, in Canada, initiated a "Happening" to raise funds, attractive posters proclaimed, "Make your own junk sculpture right in the Art Gallery of Toronto. (Junk available cheap at the Gallery.) Learn the truth about Pop. It's a wise child who knows his Dada."   (37)

———— ◄•► ————

More Arts Groups Hire Fund Raising Pros

By

Richard Trenbeth

Although cultural organizations have lagged behind most non-profit institutions in hiring professional counsel to help with their financial development, many more are turning to skilled firms and consultants to guide their volunteers and executive staff in their promotional and fund raising efforts. Lincoln Center in New York, the Los Angeles County Museum, the Lyric Opera of Chicago, the Stratford Shakespearean Festival Foundation in Canada, and the New York Museum of Modern Art are among those which have successfully used professional help.

Far from being an admission of inadequacy on the part of the organization's board, the hiring of professional development counsel is a forward-looking, efficient approach to a problem as demanding of specialized help as a medical or legal problem. Effective money raising is a business. It makes use of the marketing, sales promotion and advertising techniques with which board members are familiar from their own business interests.

Almost any cultural group can make good use of counsel, but the following conditions virtually demand it:

1. When capital funds are needed for new construction, rehabilitation, endowment or other specific purposes;

2. When annual gift support is inadequate to meet budget needs;

3. When membership or subscription enrollment is lagging.

Capital fund drives generally require the complete services offered by large firms specializing in campaign management. Most of these are members of the American Association of Fund-Raising Counsel, a highly regarded professional association with offices at 500 Fifth Avenue, New York, N. Y. 10036. Smaller firms specializing in continuing annual support appeals are to be found in most large cities. Still other consulting firms tell their clients how to organize their own development programs, then guide them through the first three or four years.

Some cultural organizations have employed the part-time counseling services of professional development men working for similar organizations. An increasing number are creating their own development staffs, with or without outside counsel.

Whether hired for a capital campaign or a continuing annual appeal, most consultants start with an extensive study and survey of the organization, its needs and potentials. Sometimes they conclude that an intensive campaign is not feasible; in other cases they decide that the tentative goal is unreasonably low. Campaign management firms next project a timetable and preliminary strategy, working at the same time with staff and volunteers on list analysis and rating of prospects. This is followed by the organization of committees, the recruiting of volunteer leadership and the assignment of duties. Then specialists are called in to write campaign literature, form letters, to set procedures and handle publicity.

Continuing counsel, after the initial survey, builds for the long pull. It stresses definition of objectives and cultivation of prospects through published information, orientation meetings and special events. It sets up personal solicitation plans and works out regular direct mail solicitations to broaden the base of support. Extensive direct mail promotion always requires expert counsel from the first planning stages through each step, including gift acknowledgment.

Where membership or subscriber promotion is needed, counsel suggests sales techniques and list testing procedures to get the maximum benefit from the promotional budget. Volunteer trustees are reminded at this stage that the money they are spending now may not produce substantial profits until a renewal pattern has been established.

Where there is an acute or impending financial need, counsel can usually save both time and money through orderly, economical planning and skillful direction. Further, counsel brings to the organization an objective, practical point of view, playing the disturbing "role of the stranger" who candidly points out weaknesses that may have been swept under the rug for years. Seasoned counsel shares with the organization years of experience in all aspects of fund raising and promotion, providing sound rules for judging success or progress, offering reassurance, or prodding, when necessary.

Counsel's greatest value often lies in bringing skilled communicators to bear on publicity and promotion. They

71

know when to drop false modesty and how to obtain invaluable public service space and time from communications media. But experienced counsel is also the first to warn that even though good and continuing publicity is essential, it is not a substitute for one person's asking another for money.

Perhaps most important of all, hired counsel stimulates trustees and other volunteer leaders to act immediately to protect their investment in counseling fees and campaign expenses. Sometimes this changes a board's concept of who its own members should be in the future to assure continuing financial support. Finally, counsel provides continuity of direction, offering the services of skilled professionals of higher caliber than most organizations can afford for their own staff. (12)

Fund Raising Counsel:

The Cost is High, so Choose With Care Before Hiring

By

Richard Trenbeth

The main objection to hiring professional counsel for a fund raising drive is the cost. Often small organizations are in such a bad way financially that a large promotional effort is needed to prevent untimely death and speed the patient on the road to recovery. There are natural fears that there just isn't enough money on hand to pay the doctor's fee.

Costs are usually substantial, but well worth it in view of the alternative. It must be kept in mind, too, that the initial expense is compensating for years of neglect of orderly work at building a sound financial base.

Counseling fees and campaign expenses must be faced long before any practical returns can be expected. Most reputable firms, and that includes all member firms of the American Association of Fund-Raising Counsel, refuse to work on a commission basis. They evaluate the potential through their initial survey, estimate the time and manpower required to accomplish the goal, and charge a fixed fee plus reasonable expenses.

Almost all firms charge for the initial survey, whether they are eventually hired for a campaign or not. Fee for an adequate survey can range from $500 to $10,000. Few qualified consultants will agree to work for less than $250 per day per principal executive. The client also pays a premium for experienced short-term help to carry out details.

Many organizations not familiar with development planning and operations ask for a program with a price tag attached, without defining their goals and true needs or authorizing an adequate study by the prospective counsel. Such a procedure is unfair both to client and to the counseling firm. When a campaign is required, absolute candor is necessary on both sides if the costs are to be balanced by results.

An arts group considering counsel should be careful to evaluate what type of counsel will best accomplish its objectives at the most efficient cost (not necessarily the lowest) over the period when counsel is required. Does it need a major gifts campaign for capital funds? Or is the main problem to obtain regular annual support for a fairly stable budget plus minor improvements? Does it have on its staff a qualified but inexperienced person who can be given full-time development responsibilities? Or does it need a new person with experience?

Often it is wise to invite several counseling firms for short interviews, and eliminate those which would not be interested. Serious applicants should be asked to present their record in similar campaigns and submit references from groups they have served. Perhaps most important of all, they should bring for personal interview the account executive to be assigned if the firm is hired, because he is the one the client will be working with.

In checking references, try to ask for opinions from at least three people in the organization previously served; at least one should be the top staff executive. This is to reduce the chance that you may get a false picture from one person who may have had a personal difference with the account executive, or generally denigrated the value of counsel.

Good sources of names of fund raising counsel are the A.A.F.R.C. mentioned above, staff executives of community fund drives, and college and university development executives. As firms are interviewed, do not be discouraged by lack of definite promises or estimated costs at the first meeting. Most reputable firms will not make a commitment until they do some investigating of their own, or until they are hired to make a preliminary survey.

When costs, promises and services are compared and a choice of counsel is made, insist that the contract state clearly what services the fee covers and any limits to be placed on expenses. Reputable firms ask the client to pay actual costs in addition to their fee. It is up to the client to place a realistic limit on these expenses, subject to review. But the organization should make provision for swift authorization to spend more in an emergency.

It should be clearly understood at this point that all major policies recommended by counsel are to be cleared quickly with one or two officers, or a small executive committee. Nothing cripples counsel more than indecision. Precision timing is a fundamental of effective development.

(13)

———◄●►———

Counsel May Cost 10% of Total Fund Raised

By

Richard Trenbeth

If your fund raising counsel recommends an intensive campaign at first, to be followed by a long-range development program, don't be surprised. The really sound organization should expect years of strong support long after the campaign ends.

Some indication of the length of the campaign itself may be found in a recent survey by the American Association of Fund-Raising Counsel, covering thirty-seven recent campaigns for colleges, universities and professional schools. In campaigns for goals under one million dollars, counsel service averaged 13 weeks in preliminary work and 16.6 weeks of active campaign period. Campaigns for $1,000,000 to $7,000,000 averaged longer—34 weeks in preliminary work and 45 weeks in the active period.

The same survey of campaigns under a million showed costs ranging from a high of $68,080 for total contributions of $600,000 to a low of $13,832 for total contributions of $294,830. In the larger goal group, costs ranged from a high of $290,681 for total contributions of $7,070,161 to a low of $39,245 for total contributions of $1,748,461.

For arts groups, costs may be expected to run as high as ten per cent or more of the goal, especially if there has been little or no development activity in the past.

Firms or individual consultants handling continuing annual support programs usually work on an annual contract basis, although some may insist on a minimum initial contract of at least two or three years. They bill on a monthly basis in terms of agreed-upon services usually ranging from eight to 40 hours per month, plus fees for special writers or analysts as needed. Total fees might range from $250 to $1,500 a month or even more.

Annual support programs are based on careful planning, a detailed time table, and professionally prepared printed material and letters. Such consultants usually offer sound advice on the buying of printing, envelopes, lettershop services and other requirements, and these recommendations eventually add up to substantial savings.

Annual drives for an arts group always involve considerable effort on the part of the organization's own staff and trustees, but with able counsel the effort is put to more effective use and usually requires far less time, which must also be considered in computing true costs.

For the very small organization or one just getting started, the independent counsel or the part-time services of someone already working fulltime for another organization may be the best alternative. For as little as four hours a month such a consultant can often save the organization many times the amount of his fee, and though some may require contracts of at least two years, others may agree to work for six months or a year.

Don't expect miracles from a short-term agreement. It usually takes a competent staff department under the most capable supervision at least a year to show any kind of results from a standing start, and often longer to do more than get expenses back. Under a limited counsel arrangement, the organization's own staff must be prepared to do all the work except planning, major writing, and other creative work.

A growing trend in organizations fortunate enough to have a qualified staff development executive is to employ outside counsel on a limited basis. The outsider, with an objective point of view, can make the staff man far more effective by pleading his case and his recommendations before the board or other policy group.

The old saying that it takes money to make money certainly applies in development or fund raising work.   (14)

How to Select a Staff Director to Head a Development Program

To meet expanding financial needs, many arts institutions have reached the point in their growth at which they need a staff director of development. This is one of the most crucial positions in the organization.

In searching for a staff fund raiser, you may find it useful to explain your needs to a professional organization, such as the National Society of Fund Raisers or the American Association of Fund-Raising Counsel, Inc., both in New York City. Similarly, a large employment agency specializing in fund raising personnel may also be helpful.

Fund raisers, unlike lawyers, doctors, and scientists, are not required to have formal training. Therefore, it is much harder to determine their competence. In choosing the right man for an arts institution, one must rely on good judgment, intuition, and a thorough analysis of the candidate's qualifications and experience.

There is no standard questionnaire that can be used to measure the candidate's capabilities, although success in other campaigns, even those conducted for unrelated kinds of institutions, may be a valid indication of competence. Be sure to check on a candidate with both the executive directors and lay leaders of organizations he cites in his employment record.

Each institution, of course, will have its own criteria for selection. However, a staff director of development should have a knowledge of fund raising techniques, a knowledge of community life and organizational structure, an ability to interpret and sell the institution's program, the ability to communicate to top echelon leadership through a direct approach and through written materials, the capacity to establish effective working relationships with important community leaders, aptness in selecting the most pertinent aspects of the program for exploitation, and the ability to write brochures, speeches and presentations for corporation and foundation prospects. Although no individual fund raiser will possess all the above qualities, a good one will be a synthesis of many of them.

Check 10 Points When Choosing Fund Drive Head

Planning a fund raising campaign? A basic decision that must be made is the choice of your drive chairman. G. A. Brakeley & Co., Inc., of New York, a leading firm of professional fund raisers, has devised a 10-point test to help select an effective chairman. Score candidates from one to ten points for each item. A score of 85, says Brakeley, makes a good chairman. However, the firm warns, if a two-man team is involved, the score should total 95 or better. Here are the ten checkpoints:

Does the candidate have:

1. A thorough familiarity with and understanding of the basic philosophical and practical reasons why the cause or institution should be supported; a consequent conviction and desire to do the job. _____.

2. The calibre of a good trustee (if not a trustee at the time), a "leader" or "leader-designate." _____.

3. Ability to make an important gift personally—if not sacrificially at least the top level proportionate to his means. _____.

4. Ability to get a leadership gift from his corporate affiliation(s)—assuming this to be a cause to which corporations can logically give. _____.

5. Ability to obtain leadership gifts (or to assure this through others) from the trustee group and wealthy "friends" of the cause or institution. _____.

6. Enthusiasm in asking for big gifts—in most instances, by amount or at least "range"; often teaming up with an institution president, a top researcher or department chair-

79

man, and often with the idea of identification of the donor with a specific project. _____.

7. Willingness and ability to enlist and work with a top-level team ("executive" or "steering" committee) for policy decision, planning, organization, and delegation of authority where necessary. _____.

8. Availability for periodical meetings of the "executive" committee, probably weekly to begin with, but tapering off as the organization and delegation of responsibility proceeds; adequate time for key enlistments and solicitations, also tapering off. (How much time? Tremendous variations, but we generalize for the average capital campaign at between one and a half and two working days or their equivalent in time per week, including lunch, later afternoon, and occasional evening meetings.) _____.

9. Willingness to accept "professional" advice and adhere to a responsible and prepared plan schedule. _____.

10. Ability to preside with enthusiasm and inspiration over meetings of his associates. _____.   (23)

FUND RAISING CASE STUDIES

Telethons Can Play a Key Role in Boosting Financial Support

Cultural organizations seeking to bolster their fund raising programs might consider sponsoring telethons. Although telethons require long planning, careful coordination, and an advance outlay of funds, they can yield major financial returns. Recently, the Pasadena Playhouse in California, faced with an emergency fund raising situation, received $21,000 in pledges from a telethon.

Telethons have been successfully used by health and welfare organizations for a number of years, and the techniques employed by such organizations as the Muscular Dystrophy Associations of America, Inc., for example, can offer helpful guidelines to arts groups. On a 20-hour M.D.A. telethon held on WNEW-TV in New York City beginning on Labor Day, more than $1,000,000 was pledged. By November 1st, M.D.A. had received 85 per cent of this amount.

According to Lila Brigham, Manhattan district director of M.D.A., planning for the recent telethon began more than a year in advance. The first step was finding a television station which would commit free air time. Choices were limited to local independent stations with strong records of public service. WNEW-TV met these criteria, and a top M.D.A. volunteer helped win station approval late in 1965, for a Labor Day airing.

Next, a host had to be found. In January, the organization asked its national chairman, film star Jerry Lewis, to be master of ceremonies. His early acceptance motivated many others to participate.

Although talent and a variety of services were contributed, the organization decided to hire a top television producer to recruit celebrities and mount the show. M.D.A. recognized that a professionally presented production would help to attract and hold an audience, and thus spur donations. Next, the organization rented four floors of the Americana Hotel at a discount rate for the week preceding the show and for the telethon.

With confirmation of station, date, place, producer and star, the organization, under the overall supervision of its director, began the tremendous task of coordination. An organizational chart was prepared, headed by the director, who was responsible for budget, purchasing and contract negotiations. Three separate divisions were established under the director—operations, promotion, and show production.

About six weeks prior to the telethon, the operation moved into high gear. The paid producer began lining up his talent and assembling the production. The promotion division, manned by paid staff members, began an all-out campaign geared to motivating stay-at-homes to watch the Labor Day telethon. A printing firm donated posters which were distributed to stores and supermarkets throughout the city; and 750,000 fliers were posted in large housing developments, enclosed with rent statements, and distributed through other organizations. Also, spot announcements featuring Jerry Lewis were aired regularly on station WNEW, Lewis and other celebrities "plugged" the telethon in radio and television interviews, and scores of newspaper stories were released.

The operational division, headed by staff members, coordinated the efforts of more than 2,000 volunteers recruited from within the ranks of the organization, through publicity, and through specially established suburban offices.

Well in advance of the telethon, cards were sent to volunteers informing them of their four-hour work shift, their specific assignment, and where and when to report.

The telethon, which began at 10 p.m. on September 4th and ran till 6 p.m. on September 5th, proceeded according to advance planning. The producer kept the show moving, while batteries of volunteers, armed with written instructions, handled the pledges phoned and wired in. Calls were taken both at the Americana and at 12 regional centers. During the show, everyone who phoned in a donation of more than $100 was immediately called back for verification. Volunteer drivers picked up pledges from out-of-the-way areas. Figures were totaled and announced on television following verification.

Follow-up was essential. Within 24 hours after the telethon, staff and volunteers had mailed out cards to everyone who had made a pledge.

Although telethons can be highly lucrative, Mrs. Brigham offers these cautions to arts groups: never anticipate receiving everything that's pledged; be prepared to spend money to make money (M.D.A. budgeted $200,000 in advance for the program); and anticipate some difficulty in working with celebrities. (53)

Arts Groups Try a Fun Approach
To Win Dollars and New Friends

In an attempt to attract new audiences and win friends, arts groups throughout the country are developing fund raising events which emphasize informality, excitement and fun. In fact, in many communities, such traditional offerings as black tie dinners and formal balls may be a thing of the past.

In Wichita, Kansas, for example, the Symphony's Women's Association, aware of declining interest in the annual symphony ball, decided to do something different this year. The long-closed main waiting room of Wichita's Union Station, with its three storied ceiling and once-elegant Harvey House dining room, presented both a unique setting and a party theme. Following months of discussion with railroad officials beginning in the fall of 1970, permission was given to reopen the room the following spring for a benefit, the Symphony Station Stop.

On May 27th, after a 15-year accumulation of dirt and dust had been removed, a capacity crowd of more than 400 people assembled in the restored waiting room, illuminated by kerosene lanterns, for an evening of fun and entertainment. Dressed in everything from overalls to white tie, the guests, who paid $15 a couple, arrived in a driving rain and experienced two tornado alerts during the evening. "It was one of the worst nights in memory," Wichita Symphony manager Dewey Anderson told *AM*. "There was a tornado on the other side of town but it didn't bother anyone—they were having too good a time."

Although the weather prevented the use of railroad handcarts, which were to have transported guests from the parking lots to the station, the old-fashioned railroad theme was in evidence everywhere. Old station scales, shoe-shine stands and outdated baggage carts served as bars, and a large ice sculpture of a train dominated the buffet table. Entertainment included dancing to the Kansas City Philharmonic Rock Band, banjo playing in the lobby, tours of a restored caboose and nearby Historical Railway Museum and continuous showings of two silent films, "The Great Train Robbery" and "Freddy Takes the Throttle." Guests posed for pictures in front of a large train mural and purchased antique dining car silver from a benefit boutique. They feasted on the buffet in the old Harvey House and quaffed draft beer.

Publicity before and after the event was excellent and although it was planned "as a fun event involving many new people and good will for our organization," according to Anderson, about $1500 was raised. "I think that we learned from this event," he added, "that the old Symphony Ball is now past history in a city like Wichita." (73)

A Three Day Radio Marathon Is Effective Fund Raising Device

Radio marathons can be effective fund raising and pro-motional tools as several symphony orchestras, Boston and Cleveland among them, have discovered within recent months. In Dallas, Texas, a 72-hour marathon organized by the Dallas Symphony Association this June, raised nearly 50 per cent more than was anticipated, and helped provide the orchestra with vital exposure during "Dallasound Countdown 30," the orchestra's final 30-day campaign to enable it to qualify for a $2-million Ford Foundation en-dowment grant.

Key elements in the marathon's success included advance organization, enlistment of support from local leaders and business, and a simple and workable formula, in this instance the playing of records in return for contributions. Beginning at 6:00 a.m. on a Thursday morning and continuing through midnight Saturday, listeners to WRR-FM, the city-owned classical music radio station, were invited to pledge specific amounts to the orchestra and in return, dedicate musical selections to a person or an organization of their choice. For $5 unspecified selections could be dedicated; for $10 specified selections up to 15-minutes in length could be dedicated; for $20, 30 minute requests; and for $50, 45 minute requests. Those pledging larger amounts were given such extra benefits as multi-record symphonic albums or the opportunity to be guest disc jockey on the program. Single LP records donated by commercial recording firms, were offered as incentives to callers throughout.

To maintain interest local celebrities served in three hour shifts as guest disc jockeys. In addition, such special guests as the city's mayor and orchestra officials appeared.

Of the $150,000 the orchestra needed to raise during June, the three day marathon realized $7,500 and provided an extra publicity base for the month-long fund raising effort. Commenting on the marathon, Robert H. Alexander, public relations director of the Dallas Symphony said, "The station was delighted with the results, and to have your name mentioned on the air for 72 hours is worth more than any amount you actually collect in the marathon, although $7,500 is sweet to think about." (72)

Orchestra Rummage Sale Breaks All-Time Record

A well-organized rummage sale sponsored by the Women's Committee of the Toronto Symphony Orchestra netted the organization $27,000 in a single day.

The event grossed $35,000 from the sale of thousands of articles selling for as much as $95 (a mink jacket) and as little as five cents (a piece of costume jewelry). Expenses ran to $8,000, of which $3,000 went for rental of space at the Canadian National Exhibition.

An estimated 15,000 people attended. Some 600 bargain hunters were lined up in rows four and five deep hours before the doors opened at 10 in the morning. Early birds were rewarded with such bargains as a lamp for 35 cents, a pair of ski boots for $1, a suitcase for fifty cents, and a large radio priced at only $1. Yellow-smocked volunteers worked in shifts until 9 in the evening when the sale culminated with the auction of one-of-a-kind small appliances contributed by retailers and individuals.

The women's committee is responsible for raising $90,-000 of the orchestra's annual $250,000 deficit. Other means used by the committee to raise funds include a cocktail party, a large ball, and a theatre benefit. A canvas by the women picks up $40,000, and the Junior Committee this year raised an additional $5,000 by presenting Captain Kangaroo during the Christmas season.

In addition to fund raising, the committee engages in other activities. It promotes students' concerts and gives suppers for the Student Councils and music directors of the secondary schools. Also, three musicales were held in members' homes to promote younger artists. A sub-committee arranges parties for visiting artists and, in an effort to keep in touch with symphony members, a party is given for orchestra members and their wives at the end of each season.

Participation in the rummage sale—this was the tenth one sponsored by the committee—has become a social status symbol in the community. Each of the 1,000 volunteers (over and above the committee's 200 regular members) is screened and instructed carefully.

Preparations for the next sale begin almost as soon as one is completed. This gives the committee a full year to do its work. Activity reaches its peak eight days before the sale opens, when volunteers begin sorting the contributed goods. Articles for sale are picked up by trucks of major companies in the community. These companies also make warehouse space available until the time of the sale, and, as an additional service after the sale, arrange for delivery of the goods to the homes of purchasers willing to pay a $1.00 delivery fee.

At the sale, goods are placed on tables or on the floor, and the would-be customers—only 600 at a time are allowed in the building because of fire regulations—use pushcarts borrowed from a supermarket chain. They check out their purchases at cash registers manned by cashiers loaned by local banks.

The committee permits its volunteers to take first crack at the goods on sale. Volunteers may do their buying in the eight days before the sale, but pay a 50 cent premium on each item. This special privilege is not publicized, however. On the day of the sale volunteers work in three shifts.

Mrs. Arnott Parrett, organizer of this year's affair, summarizing the lessons learned, said that the evening auction created so much enthusiasm it will be extended next year. Also under discussion is the possibility of renting additional space. The sale this year occupied 20,000 square feet. (16)

Tickets to Art Raffle Party:

Taking a Chance for Art's Sake

A fund raising raffle with works of art as prizes has netted an average of $12,000 for a New York settlement house during the three years it has been held. The Collector's Choice Art Benefit, a creation of the Hudson Guild Neighborhood House, can be adapted to the money raising needs of cultural groups on a wide scale.

Key points in the successful Hudson Guild raffles are: selecting art work prizes judged as especially attractive to the organization's friends, limiting the number of tickets sold, setting the right price per ticket and organizing the ticket sale with precision.

In 1960 and 1961, the art benefit offered three prizes, both sculpture and paintings, to 200 subscribers at $100 per ticket. This year's drawing offered four art prizes to 225 ticket buyers at the same rate. The ticket admitted a couple to the gala cocktail party at which the drawing was staged.

For the three years the total price of the art works averaged $3,000, and were obtained by a committee of collectors from galleries for the best value in terms of price, quality and importance of the artist. Gross receipts averaged $17,000 per yearly raffle; other expenses (cost of the drawing party, printing raffle brochures and mailing) averaged $2,000—producing a net for the beneficiary of $12,000.

A group following the art raffle formula must determine at the outset how many tickets at a given price can be sold, and what price tickets will bring the optimum result. The Hudson Guild set up a committee of board members and friends to sell tickets. Prospects were singled out and a seller assigned to each. As the sale progressed, a publicity committee was active in the society, art and social work fields.

Meanwhile, the drawing party was planned at the home of a prominent guild member, and the point was stressed by ticket sellers that the cocktail party would be a memorable social occasion, offering buyers the opportunity to mingle with distinguished art lovers.

Initial expenditures in a raffle of this kind can be considerably reduced if one or more prizes are donated by a local art patron. The donor should be given a receipt for the value of the art work to be used as a tax deduction. (6)

————◄•►————

Unusual Gifts Increase Museum Shop Revenues

Museums interested in bringing in additional revenues can learn from the experience of the Gallery Shop in the Brooklyn Museum, New York. By stocking imaginative merchandise, closely allied with the museum's exhibits, the shop does a thriving business that requires four paid, full-time employees and many part-time volunteers. Many of the 750,000 yearly visitors to the museum stop to buy unusual toys, or original hand-crafted sculpture and jewelry, imported from 61 countries all over the world. Some of the most unusual offerings come from remote places visited by friends of the museum, who bring back arts and crafts suitable for exhibit as well as for sale.

The idea for the shop came from Carl Fox, its present manager, who was an administrative assistant in the museum's art school. Mr. Fox knew that 250,000 children visited the museum yearly, and he wanted to stimulate their interest in collecting works of art. In 1953 he organized the Gallery Shop, and filled it with toys, arts, and crafts from many foreign countries. Prices started at five cents. Today the shop still sells toys, but also carries merchandise for adults, such as hand-made jewelry and primitive African and Peruvian sculpture and masks. Prices now range from five cents to $200, but the toys still outsell everything else.

The shop is open seven days a week, 364 days a year—it is closed only on Christmas. Hours are 10-5 daily, and 1-5 Sundays and holidays.

According to Mr. Fox, other museums have tried the same merchandise formula and have been equally successful. (20)

Win-an-Orchestra Contest Builds Community Support

Radio station WRYT in Pittsburgh is known within its coverage area for its unusual contests and off-beat promotional stunts, but one of its most notable contests was a recent one benefiting the Pittsburgh Symphony Orchestra.

In effect, the listener-winner got the Pittsburgh Symphony Symphonetta for her own personal concert by writing a letter to the station and enclosing a contribution to the symphony orchestra's annual maintenance fund campaign.

The contest idea came from Bob Stevens, Program and Operations Manager of Pittsburgh's good music station, WRYT. Stevens serves on a Campaign Advisory Council for the Pittsburgh Symphony Orchestra. His scheme was to ask WRYT listeners to write letters to the station explaining why they would like to have some of the symphony's musicians play a special concert for them. Each letter was to include a contribution to the orchestra's maintenance fund campaign.

The program began in mid-summer and ended just before the opening of the fall concert season. It called listeners' attention to the fact that a symphonic concert would be just fine on a patio or in a small neighborhood. The private concert idea caught fire, and soon entire communities were sending entries through civic officials. Hospitals, schools, housing developments, churches, building superintendents and industries also sent entries with cash. One entry even asked the orchestra to play for a wedding.

Letters were considered by an impartial board of judges. A young supervisory nurse at Presbyterian University Hospital was declared the winner. She wanted the Pittsburgh Symphony Symphonetta to play a concert in the hospital auditorium so that shut-ins and hospital personnel who could not hear regular concerts would be able to enjoy a performance.

A quartet of musicians was dispatched to the Western Pennsylvania School for Blind Children to play for the youngsters there, in response to a second letter that was judged the runner-up.

In addition to raising funds for the orchestra, the WRYT contest served the very useful purpose of keeping the orchestra in the public mind through its off-season.

When the concert season began in October, residents of the station's listening area were well keyed to its activities. In consequence, campaign officials believed they were better able to approach potential ticket buyers and contributors because of the frequent spot announcements carried by WRYT. (12)

A Fashionable Evening Program Helps
Arts Groups Raise Funds

Fashion has provided an arts group with an unusual setting for a successful annual fund-raising effort. For the past three years, the United Arts Fund of Greensboro, N. C. has been the beneficiary of Fall Fashion Concert, a combined fashion-entertainment show, sponsored by the Greater Greensboro Merchants Association and presented in the auditorium of the city's coliseum.

The fashion extravaganza idea was initiated by Greensboro merchants five years ago as a means of calling attention to the city's importance as a fashion center. Although tickets were only $1.00 each, attendance was disappointing until the third year, when Merchants Association officials asked the chairman of the United Arts Fund to head the ticket sales effort. He agreed, but only on the condition that all proceeds from ticket sales would go to the arts fund. Since then, between 2200 and 2600 tickets have been sold annually, although the auditorium seats only 2400, and the arts fund has realized better than $2,000 each year.

The event itself, which comes after the arts fund has completed its own annual drive, features local personalities modeling fashions as well as music and entertainment. In addition to its monetary importance, Fall Fashion Concert ties local business to the arts and focuses attention on community arts groups. It also pre-publicizes and sets the stage for the coming United Arts Fund campaign which, this year, has a goal of $130,000.

The Detroit Symphony Orchestra is another arts group that has tied fashions into its fund-raising picture. This March, the orchestra's Women's Association in cooperation with the J. L. Hudson Company department store, presented "Fashionscope Symphorama" as a benefit for the orchestra's maintenance fund. The showing of men's and women's styles featured well known Detroiters as models, including several top professional football and hockey players. A small contingent from the orchestra performed in a musical portion of the program.

Fashions are included in still another Detroit Symphony activity, the Coffee Concert series. These very successful Friday morning programs have been presented under the sponsorship of the National Bank of Detroit since 1970, both to attract shoppers downtown and to help support the symphony. Along with the concert performance by the orchestra, each program includes a complimentary continental breakfast and a short fashion show.   (76)

Volunteers Man Parking Lots, Raise Thousands

An arts organization with a large number of male volunteers can raise considerable sums of money by following the example set by members of the Kiwanis International. Starting seven years ago, Kiwanis members took over the parking concession at tent theatres operated by Music Fair Enterprises, a commercial theatrical producing organization. The lodge members collect donations from show-goers for expediting their entry and exit from parking lots. After paying expenses, the Kiwanis clubs use the net proceeds for their charitable, educational and youth activities.

At the most recently established of the chain locations, Shady Grove Music Fair near Washington, D.C., manager James O'Neill worked out a seven-year parking contract with the Kiwanis Club of Silver Spring, Maryland. Under the agreement, Kiwanis agreed to furnish manpower to handle traffic at every performance during the summer tent season, and to repay the show company for having the parking lot paved with gravel. Kiwanis furnished uniform caps, reflective vests and signal lights for its crew.

Except for one regular, paid employee, Kiwanis adult members and boys from the Kiwanis-affiliated Key Clubs in local high schools man the parking areas as volunteers. Usually, each volunteer serves one evening a week, and is admitted to the show gratis after cars are parked. Eight to ten persons are required to handle the parking job on crowded nights.

The Silver Spring Kiwanis draws on two other neighboring clubs for manpower, as well as on the high school boys. "You need about 70 active people to do the job right in a place this size," President Thomas G. Owen of Silver Spring Kiwanis told *Arts Management*.

95

In its first (1962) season at Shady Grove, Kiwanis took in about $1,000 weekly from parking donations, over a 15-week season. The 1963 gross should be above $20,000, Owen said, because the tent seating capacity has been expanded, and the season lengthened to eighteen weeks. Owen expects Kiwanis to net $8,000 from parking this season, compared to $4,000 last year. It should go higher in 1964. According to James Hay, manager of the Westbury Music Fair, in Westbury, N. Y., these sums are comparable to the money collected at his fair.

From the showmen's viewpoint, O'Neill told *AM*: "The Kiwanis club has taken the parking problem off our hands, and is raising money for a good cause while doing it. We both benefit." (18)

Industries and Bank Aid Novel Fund Drive

A non-profit organization seeking funds, a packaging firm searching for new business, a bank eager to attract depositors and seven manufacturers looking for free publicity all combined in a new form of fund raising that can be successfully adapted by arts groups wishing to raise considerable sums of money.

When the Association for the Help of Retarded Children sought a new and effective fund raising device it turned to James J. Harris, a board member who also heads Guest Pac, a product packaging firm. He came to their aid with an idea used successfully by his organization to gain new customers for banks. As a result, depositors at any of the eight branches of the Lincoln Savings Bank in the Metropolitan New York area were offered gift sets of cosmetics and drugs worth $15 in return for contributions of $3.00 or more to the A.H.R.C.

Tying in the sources that both supplied and promoted the offer was Mr. Harris, who convinced manufacturers to contribute their products and induced the bank to advertise the offer free on behalf of the Association.

The key to his approach, Mr. Harris told *AM*, was assurances made to manufacturers that their products would receive prominent mention by name in all promotions of the offer. Moreover, it was pointed out that they would enhance the image of their companies by being linked with a non-profit organization.

The promotion was given added impetus when the bank offered to compound interest on savings from a date as much as two weeks prior to the date of deposit. Thus, potential depositors attracted to the bank's interest rate advantage, were exposed to the gift set offer in the same advertisement. This was especially important since any person wishing to receive the gift set by contributing $3.00 to A.H.R.C. had to become a bank depositor first. The promotion did not disrupt bank services since only a handful of volunteers were needed to man a single table prominently placed on the banking floor where the kits were exchanged for donations.

To attract the public to the offer, the bank placed advertisements in leading daily New York City newspapers. The Association, which did not contribute toward the cost of the advertisements, thus received valuable free publicity.

While considerable funds were expended in the drive by the A.H.R.C., the organization expects to profit by more than $200,000 from the campaign. Gift Pac, which charged the non-profit group less than $1.00 a kit for the collection, transportation, assembling and packaging of 100,000 kits, is also realizing a profit from the promotion.

Items in the sets were handsomely boxed and care was taken to acknowledge each link in the offer with stickers on the outside of each package. A thank you note enclosed in the kits read in part, "Items in this kit have been provided through the courtesy of the manufacturers. The Association for the Help of Retarded Children has paid for the assembly and distribution." By detailing the sources of the offer and the expenditures involved, contributors were quickly informed of the Association's stake in the drive.

Initial responses to the offer have been excellent and most depositors indicated their delight at receiving such a fine bargain in return for their contribution. Moreover, the Association, in addition to the prospect of raising considerable funds, has also laid the groundwork for future fund drives. Bank advertisements told the public that the A.H.R.C. is an organization having "a varied program which has dramatically demonstrated that the mentally ill can lead fuller lives." (29)

Checks from Checkrooms

Why lease checkroom concessions when a profit can be made by operating them yourself? In Salt Lake City, Utah, the Utah Symphony Debs, a volunteer service organization, staffs the checkroom at concerts. Proceeds realized from charges of 15 cents per person and 25 cents per couple, go into the sustaining fund of the symphony. (19)

Volunteers Helping Orchestra Beat Matching Grant Deadline

With volunteer help from a local advertising agency, support from business, government and service organizations, and the use of a wide assortment of fund-raising events and devices including bumper stickers, billboards, "buck bags," and auctions, a symphony orchestra is winning its race against an upcoming June 30th matching fund deadline. By March 15th, the Sacramento Symphony Orchestra had raised all but $50,000 of the $500,000 needed to match a Ford Foundation grant for a permanent $1-million orchestra endowment fund and was confident that it would reach its goal. (In July 1966 the Ford Foundation awarded $58,750,000 to 61 orchestras for endowments, with funds to be matched within five years. According to an American Symphony Orchestra League survey made at the beginning of the current season, 31 orchestras had not yet matched the funds.)

Although the Sacramento Symphony's campaign began in 1966, it was still only about half way to its goal after four years. At that point, early last summer, support was drawn together from every corner of the community for an all-out effort. Both local newspapers, the *Bee* and the *Union,* ran editorials urging symphony support and the *Bee* published a four-part series on the orchestra last August. A gala auction at the lieutenant governor's home early in September, raised $42,000.

Local business also came to the orchestra's aid. One retail furniture chain, Brandwein's, donated ten percent of the purchase price to the symphony, when buyers requested it. A department store, Weinstock's, allowed credit customers to automatically donate money to the symphony on their monthly charge account payments. In September, the Sacramento Metropolitan Chamber of Commerce took unusual steps to help the fund drive by issuing a formal resolution supporting the effort and by organizing a task force of 20 top businessmen to go out and win support for the campaign. In October, the chamber sponsored a major presentation in which it took the orchestra's case to some of the community's leading executives. Thus far, the chamber program, which continues until June, has raised over $30,000.

Less than half a year from the deadline, with the goal much closer but still elusive, a local advertising agency, Curran, Singley, Hitomi and Associates, volunteered its services for a "last six months campaign." In order to impress local citizens with the urgency of the drive, the agency selected as its theme the message, Save Our Symphony (S.O.S.). Since December, S.O.S. bumper stickers and lapel badges have cropped up all over town and the message has been flashed on billboards donated by local firms.

A widely publicized S.O.S. auction held three nights at the Florin Center, featured goods contributed by shopping center merchants and volunteer manpower provided by such local service groups as Lions, Kiwanis, Rotary and Optomists. It raised $7,000. The local Bachelor's Club made the orchestra beneficiary of its annual Best Dressed contest. Beginning this February, members of the Junior League of Sacramento and the regional arts council, the "S.O.S. buck bag girls," began popping up all over the city to collect small donations in their easily identifiable little bags. Throughout this entire period, local newspapers have been reporting regularly on the drive's progress.

Although the goal hasn't been reached yet, local leaders have no doubt of the campaign's success. Peter P. Tencati, the orchestra's business manager, points to total community involvement and the volunteer efforts of orchestra people and local service clubs as key factors in the campaign's success. Thomas Curran, whose advertising agency created the S.O.S. campaign, points with pride to his company's involvement. "The S.O.S. campaign," he told *AM,* "is a good example of what can be done if 'cultural type' people join with businessmen to get results." (70)

Fund Raising Event Achieves Social Status

The active participation of community leaders in the planning and execution of a fund raising event can transform it from an institutional function to an important social occasion. In New York City, the participation of leading department store executives, fashion editors and designers helps make the "Party of the Year," held by the Metropolitan Museum of Art's Costume Institute, an outstanding social as well as financial success.

The 17th annual party, held several months ago, drew a turnaway audience of more than 800 persons and raised more than $74,000 in net profit for the Institute. Tickets sold for $100 a person, and not a single ticket was distributed free of charge. Some persons not attending the event nevertheless sent contributions to the Institute.

A key to the success of the event was that leaders in the fashion industry, who benefit from the work of the Institute, were involved in virtually every phase of it.

Leading department store executives encouraged attendance and participation in the event. Invitations to the party were signed by John S. Burke, general chairman of the party committee and president of B. Altman & Co., and the two party co-chairmen, Melvin E. Dawley, president of Lord & Taylor and Adam L. Gimbel, president of Saks Fifth Avenue.

A highlight of the festivities, which were held at the Museum, was a show produced and mounted by persons prominent in the fashion industry, including leading editors. Top fashion models contributed their services free of charge to the show.

Funds raised at the annual function help further the work of the Institute which, in addition to serving the public, makes its resources available to the fashion industry.   (36)

Thrift Shops

Any charitable thrift shops in your community? In New York City, the Nearly New Thrift Shop accepts donations of clothing, furniture, antiques, and household items and turns over the proceeds from the resale of these items to ANTA and other non-profit organiations. Donors, who may claim tax deductions, can specify which of the participating charities should receive the proceeds from the sale of their gifts. (55)

————•◆►————

Volunteers Raise Money with Ad Supplement

The production of a special supplement about a cultural organization, published as part of a major newspaper, can effectively publicize the group while at the same time bring in substantial revenue through the sale of advertising space. In Toronto, Ontario, for example, the Women's Committee of the Toronto Symphony Orchestra Association raised more than $27,000 by selling advertising in a 20-page Sunday photo supplement on the orchestra. It appeared as part of the October 31st edition of the *Toronto Telegram,* which has a circulation of 800,000. The supplement was sold to the committee by the newspaper at cost.

In a well coordinated and carefully planned campaign, members of the women's committee sold advertisements to 100 leading businesses in Toronto. Although the women had no previous newspaper experience, they also wrote text for the advertisements, wrote feature articles on the Toronto Symphony Orchestra and participated in all the editorial functions that went into putting the special section together. In some cases, businesses made donations to the orchestra instead of buying space in the supplement.

The volunteers began selling space in the special section to advertisers about a year ago and by last January they had completed the selling phase of their work. To insure success of the campaign, the committee initially lined up about 30 leading companies as pacesetters, firms which agreed to purchase advertisements but did not commit themselves to the amount of space they would buy. The names of these companies were then used to influence other local businesses to purchase advertisements.

As an inducement to advertisers, socially prominent women and their families modeled for the advertisements. Most of the models were members of the women's committee. In a number of instances, businessmen's wives modeled for their husbands' products.

Advertisements identified the models, some of whom were photographed in their own homes with the products advertised, and told of their role in supporting the orchestra.

A totally diversified set of advertisers was featured in the section including major automobile manufacturers, radio stations, department stores, textile firms, a brewery, music publishers and a bank.

Members of the orchestra cooperated with the committee by appearing in the photographs. In one advertisement, for example, Walter Susskind, who directs the orchestra, thanked a manufacturer of concert pianos for his support.

In addition to the advertisements, the supplement also featured a number of stories about the Toronto Symphony Orchestra. Articles summarized the orchestra's history, discussed the program for the coming season and told readers about special orchestra events, the orchestra staff

104

and the work of the volunteer committee which put the supplement together.

Stressed throughout the section was the orchestra's need for funds. One article outlined the orchestra's financial picture, emphasizing the fact that $325,000 was needed for the coming season which runs from late October through mid-April.

Barbara Heintzman, who headed the committee, told *AM* that other arts groups wishing to undertake a similar project "should allow at least a year" from its inception to date of publication. (33)

Volunteers Raise $11,000 a Year Selling Books

A one-week sale of used books that nets $11,000 for a college scholarship fund depends on techniques adaptable to the needs of many arts organizations. The sale, sponsored by the Vassar Club of Washington, started in 1949 and has since become an annual institution in the nation's capital. In its early years it yielded only about $1,000 a year. But tight planning and hard work has made it increasingly profitable.

"A primary reason for the success of the book sale is its institutionalized character," Mrs. Mary Randall of the Vassar Club told *AM*. "We hold the sale at the same time every year, in the spring. People have come to expect it." But good management is important, too.

The club calls upon members to solicit book contributions all year long from among neighbors and friends. About 30 of the club's 700 members volunteer to pick up donated books and deliver them to a central storage point—the basement of a member who has willingly made this her contribution to the organization every year since the sale began. About 30 more volunteers sort and price the books. A few of the women have become "real semi-professionals" at pricing, *AM* was told. Occasionally, a member's husband is called in for advice on pricing of books in a technical field with which he is familiar. During the week of the sale itself, about 50 members turn out to help as sales clerks and cashiers.

Costs are kept to the bare minimum, making the event a low risk way of raising funds. Total expenditure for the sale is about $1200—roughly ten per cent of the gross income from the sale of an estimated 50,000 books per year. Biggest items of expense are: publicity, mailings and advertising; transportation of the books by a professional mover from the storage point to the site of the sale. Except for the one moving bill, the entire project is carried out by volunteer labor. Also vital to keeping costs down is the club's securing a centrally located, yet vacant, downtown store rent-free for the week required.

"This project has been a success not only because we have developed expertise over the years," says Mrs. Randall. "It is a project that appeals to our members, and the cause—college scholarships—is appealing to the community. But we also work consistently at publicity."

Postcard reminders are mailed to people who left their names and addresses at the previous year's sale. (Everyone leaving the sale is asked whether he wishes to be notified of the next one.) In addition, local newspapers carry publicity pictures of preparations for the sale as well as advertising. The store windows are used, too. Some of the finest bargains are displayed in the windows a few days before the sale opens.

A tribute to the quality of the Vassar book sale is the determination shown by numerous book dealers in elbowing their way to the front of the crowd that presses around the door on its opening morning. (10)

Enlarging the Garage

The garage sale is a fund-raising staple of smaller organizations with limited funding goals. If a current experiment proves successful, however, the garage sale multiplied into a series of coordinated sales may put goals of $100,000 within reach. This is the approach of the Seattle Opera which has scheduled 500 different garage sales during April and May, an average of 45 a weekend. The objective is $200 a sale and $100,000 overall. More than 5,000 opera subscribers donated sale items. (Note: The sale raised $30,000.)

(75)

Foreign Flavor

Planning a benefit program with a foreign theme? Support may be available from foreign companies or government agencies in your area. The recent Pro Arte Symphony Orchestra Ball in Long Island, used its "Carnival in Rio" theme to win support from the Brazilian Government Trade Bureau, a Brazilian jeweler, H. Stern, the Brazilian Coffee Institute and Varig Airlines. (65)

Taped Appeal

Looking to reach big contributors? Cassettes may be your answer. The Pacifica Foundation recently gave away both cassette players and pre-recorded tapes in an unusual campaign designed to reach donors in the "high gift" category ($5,000 to $100,000). Pacifica, a listener sponsored FM broadcasting service, hand-delivered to 300 patrons free players and four tapes, contributed by Lafayette Radio and Electronics, which synopsized ten years of its programming. In addition, a half hour tape narrated by Thomas Hoving and featuring several notable, discussed Pacifica and its need for capital funds to build a broadcasting center. The tape concluded with an invitation to listeners to attend a scheduled meeting.   (69)

Audience Appreciation

Looking for a dramatic and effective way to thank your contributors and members? You might consider honoring them with a performance. The Wichita Symphony, which successfully matched a Ford Foundation Endowment Fund grant by raising more than $600,000 from the community, thanked its contributors with a "Gala Appreciation Concert" this February. Invitations for the free concert were sent in advance to all donors of record. Later, tickets not reserved by contributors were made available without cost to the general public. Further recognition was given in the concert program which listed all Ford Fund donors.   (75)

Chain Party

Would you like to pyramid donations? You might try using an old fund raising idea that worked well for the Indianapolis Symphony last season—the chain party project. The initial step is to find someone to host a party and collect $1 from each guest as a donation to your organization. Each guest then hosts his own party within the next three weeks inviting one less person and collecting a $1 donation from every attendee. The Indianapolis Symphony pyramid was launched by Indiana Governor Whitcomb who held a dinner party for eight couples. Then all eight couples hosted their own parties for seven couples who in turn had parties for six couples and so on down the line. Parties ranged from picnics to teas to formal dinners. Although in theory, a party beginning with eight should eventually involve 109,600 people contributing $109,600, don't plan on the chain remaining unbroken for too long. Nevertheless, the Indianapolis Symphony was more than delighted with the $14,000 the pyramid raised. (73)

* * *

Orchestra Employs Novel Fund Raising Methods

An all-out publicity and promotion drive, which employs new techniques yearly while retaining successful ones from the past, is a vital ingredient in the continuing success of the annual fund and membership drive conducted by the Rochester Civic Music Association. The C.M.A., which supports the Rochester Philharmonic Orchestra and other community musical activities including the Civic Orchestra, Tiny Tot Concerts and radio concerts for the public schools, raised nearly $250,000 in its recently completed 1963 fund drive. While this was two per cent short of the quota, it still established an all-time record for funds raised in the regular C.M.A. campaigns dating back to 1931. Moreover, with 17,000 individual pledges, C.M.A. officials believe that among comparable organizations, it has the broadest base of support in the United States.

While emphasizing a strong and continuous public relations program through normal publicity channels, C.M.A. officials do not neglect to investigate any new approaches which come to their attention. For example, although television coverage has always been excellent, the C.M.A. went a step further this year in arranging for the local American Broadcasting Company outlet to donate a full hour program in prime evening time to the C.M.A. On a Sunday evening, just prior to the campaign's kick-off, the program, featuring filmed interviews with top musical figures who had performed in Rochester, including Arthur Fiedler and Benny Goodman, was broadcast to a large audience. In addition, major local companies such as Rochester Gas and Electric donated commercial time on the programs they sponsored.

Another new device was the use of a four-sided display booth erected in Midtown Plaza, a covered downtown shopping area built by two leading department stores. The plaza management donated the space and the telephone company donated four telephones set up inside a display which also included pictures of musical activities in Rochester. When a visitor picked up a phone he heard a recorded message urging support of the C.M.A. from Eddy Meath, one of Rochester's leading disc jockeys.

Past approaches used successfully again this year included messages on billboards donated by outdoor advertising companies, the display of posters in 900 stores throughout the city, and the use of 200 car cards in public transportation vehicles. For the fourth straight year, the Blue Boy Dairy imprinted solicitation messages on every bottle of milk it processed during the drive. The message, which appeared on more than 250,000 bottle caps read, "In Rochester there is music for everyone. Join the Rochester Civic Music Association."

As a climax to the promotional effort, thousands of notes were sent to children in Rochester schools near the end of the campaign. The notes, which were brought home by the youngsters, reminded parents that in case they had not yet given, there was still time to contribute to the C.M.A. (15)

Vacation with Profit

Seeking a fund raising device with family appeal? An arts group in Roslyn, New York, is raising funds and promoting ties with members and their families through its sponsorship of hotel weekends. Several times a year, the North Shore Community Arts Center contracts for all the rooms in a small hotel at reduced rates for a weekend, and then rents them to members at slightly higher rates. Fine arts programs are featured throughout the weekend. (46)

Movie Premieres

Premieres of major movies can be used by cultural organizations to raise funds and win wide attention. Whenever possible, however, the film should be viewed beforehand to determine its suitability. Several arts groups in cities throughout the country recently sponsored benefit opening night showings of Twentieth Century Fox's *The Agony and the Ecstasy*, a motion picture based on the life of Michelangelo. The film company arranged for the appearance of celebrities at the openings and provided publicity, advertising and promotional materials. While offering these services, the company specified that the sponsor purchase all the seats in the theater for the premiere night. In New York City, the film's opening was sponsored by the Metropolitan Museum of Art, and tickets purchased by the museum for $3.25 were sold for $100 each.   (45)

The Art Express

Looking for a unique setting for a fund raising event such as an art show? One organization in Long Island, New York, recently sponsored an Israeli art festival in three parlor cars borrowed from the Long Island Railroad. On four consecutive Sundays the trains were moved to locations in four different communities where townspeople were invited aboard to view the paintings, which were hung in the cars. The public flocked to the showings and purchased many paintings.   (31)

New Credit Cards for the Arts a Reward
to Fund Drive Donors

There's a new status symbol in the arts—credit cards. In St. Louis, a select group of arts patrons can now say "charge it" when they purchase tickets or works of art from ten local cultural organizations.

The plan was conceived by the Arts and Education Council of Greater St. Louis as a way of showing appreciation to the 1,300 people who contributed $50 or more to the recently completed united arts fund campaign, which topped its goal for the first time in the fund's five year history. The drive drew $776,584 from 10,500 donors, believed to be the highest total ever raised in any united arts campaign. The Council also hopes that the cards may help to raise standards of giving for next year's drive.

Issued in September, and valid through December 31, 1968, the wallet-sized green and white cards list the names, addresses and phone numbers of all participating organizations, which include the St. Louis Symphony, the Repertory Theatre of Loretto-Hilton and the Painters Gallery.

In a separate attempt to raise the sights of donors, the Council has, for the past two years, sent a "wheel of tickets" to everyone who contributed $25 or more to the fund. The wheel, a circular piece of paper with eight sections, each devoted to a different local organization, offers free tickets to events sponsored by the participating groups. (58)

Culture for Christmas

Cultural groups can promote subscriptions or memberships as Christmas gift items. The Buffalo, N. Y. Fine
Arts Academy suggested a gift package for $10 consist-
ing of admission to exhibitions, copies of publications, and
a discount on items sold by the gallery.   (20)

Orchestra Wins 80,000 Donors in Six Weeks

Arts groups seeking to broaden their base of support
might steal a leaf from the pages of the Sacramento Symphony's unique and succesful Roll of Honor. The orchestra,
which raised all but $50,000 of its $500,000 Ford Foundation matching grant by March 15th, went soaring over the
top in an unprecedented six-week Roll of Honor drive
which added nearly 80,000 individual donors to its roster
and $120,000 to the campaign treasury.

The Roll of Honor was conceived by Carlyle Reed, publisher of the *Sacramento Union* and an orchestra board
member, as a way of involving the total community down
to and especially including the $1 donor, in the drive. This
appeal to the smallest contributor was symbolized by an
actual book—the Roll—which contributors were told would
be inscribed with the name of every $1 and up donor and
permanently displayed in the foyer of the city's Community Center, with a different page to be spotlighted daily.

A small committee of four planned the entire campaign
and maintained control of all phases of its development.
To reach various segments of the community, seven committees were organized in advance composed of: cultural

and civic leaders; labor union presidents; college students; business leaders; military officers; representatives of men's service clubs; and officials of the state employees association. A week before the actual solicitation began, a coordinated all-out publicity drive was launched featuring donated billboards and car cards, bumper stickers, frequent broadcast spots and features, and extraordinary coverage by all three local newspapers. In the *Sacramento Union,* which sponsored the campaign and paid its costs, at least one major arts story appeared daily.

The campaign officially opened April 14th with a press conference and mayor's proclamation. During the following weeks, to the accompaniment of a barrage of publicity, large contribution envelopes with spaces for 50 names were circulated throughout the city, to stores, schools and companies, and the *Sacramento Union* distributed enrollment envelopes among newspapers.

With most letters bringing in $1 contributions, the original $50,000 goal was reached in less than two weeks and within six weeks the $100,000 mark was passed. The 78,682 names are being computerized now prior to their inscription in the Roll.   (73)

------------◄●►------------

Campaign Kickoff

Looking to add some extra interest to your season ticket or fund-raising campaign? You might select your chairman from an area not normally associated with the arts, such as sports. Try, however, to choose a personality who has had some involvement with your group. Theatre Calgary in Canada recently named its first honorary season ticket chairman, Fred James, defensive tackle for the Calgary Stampeders football team. Releases noted that Mr. James was "a season ticket holder of several years' standing." (76)

―――――◄●►―――――

Check-In

To make sure that potential contributors don't have to search for checks, the Wisconsin Youth Symphony mails them sets of preprinted checks made payable to the orchestra. Each check, in the amount of $5.00, includes spaces where donors print name, address, bank name and checking account number. As the orchestra notes in its accompanying letter, the checks are bank-approved and totally tax deductible. (79)

―――――◄●►―――――

How to "Fix" a Parking Ticket

A unique fund-raising method is suggested by the recent campaign of the Mooreville, West Virginia, Red Cross blood bank to collect 120 pints of blood.

Through an arrangement with local authorities, one 24-hour period was set aside as a day on which tickets issued for parking meter violations could be "fixed" by motorists. A violator could cancel out his parking ticket by contributing a pint of blood, in lieu of paying his fine.

The method may be adapted to a fund-raising campaign for the arts where city fathers are cooperative. It not only can bring in a sizable sum on a single day, but reap wide publicity at the same time. (8)

―――――◄●►―――――

Patrons Bid for Auction Gifts As Arts Groups
Bid for Donors

By adding a few frills to an old-fashioned American selling device, the auction, cultural groups are opening donors' pocketbooks and winning attention in their communities.

In Binghamton, New York, the Roberson Center for the Arts and Sciences, an arts council, has just completed its second annual "building blocks" campaign, an art auction of donated works for the benefit of its building fund. To assure attendance and a pre-commitment of funds, the Center sold building block certificates several months prior to the date of the event, which were redeemable in lieu of cash at the auction at twice their face value. Adorned with a special drawing by famed local cartoonist John Hart, the certificate showed the Wizard of Id and B. C., Hart comic strip characters, piling up building blocks. The cartoon was repeated in posters and in other promotional materials.

According to Roberson Center director, Keith Martin, "The building block made the purchaser aware of his participation in a building fund drive, while the promise of doubling his money made his advance commitment irresistible." The irresistibility was evidenced by the fact that last year a sales promotion team of about 40 men and women helped sell some 600 certificates before the auction took place. This year, with $10 and $25 certificates sold also, overall receipts, including auction sales, increased by 10 per cent to $6,000. A black-tie preview of the art, held several days prior to the auction for purchasers of $25 building blocks, helped spur the sale of the higher priced certificates.

Although artists donated works to the auction in the past, the success of the event will now enable the Center to guarantee artists 50 per cent of the established value of their works in future auctions.

Another successful auction with a novel twist was held in Boston, Mass., for the benefit of educational television station WGBH. This year's event, the third annual, raised $282,000, more than five per cent of the station's yearly operating budget. The auction was presented on the air for seven consecutive evenings with viewers phoning in their bids for the merchandise they saw televised. A key reason for the event's success, was the participation of top Boston area businessmen. Not only did corporations donate nearly all of the merchandise—6,000 items ranging up to $25,000 in retail price were offered this year—but their board chairmen, presidents and vice presidents acted as on-the-air auctioneers.

Meanwhile, a committee of prominent St. Louis civic, business and cultural leaders, is actively involved in finding unusual gifts for its "Cultural Auction of Many Extraordinary Lots of Treasure," Camelot, for short, which will be held on November 1st and 2nd. The auction, under the general sponsorship of Famous-Barr, a department store, will benefit the Arts and Education Council of Greater St. Louis. Among the items which have been suggested for the auction are: an African safari; a walk-on part in a Broadway play; a gold mine; and dinner with a movie actress. Similar auctions in San Diego, Seattle and Portland, Oregon, have raised more than $100,000 each for cultural groups.   (61)

Arts Group Tries "Hard Sell" and Boosts Financial Support

Faced with a growing budget and a moribund fund raising program, a Canadian arts group instituted a step-by-step "hard sell" campaign to win increased financial support. The new approach, conceived two years ago by the Royal Winnipeg Ballet, set a chain reaction of giving into motion, which resulted in greater financial assistance from government at every level and new and important support from business and industry. This same approach has provided a continuing framework for the organization's now-successful fund raising program.

According to George Coroneos, the ballet's general manager until recently, the organization had "a kind of defeatist attitude until 1964." Recognizing then, that a coordinated effort was necessary to meet an anticipated annual budget of $200,000, the group's leaders developed a program which began with a pragmatic approach to the city government.

Documenting its case with concrete information—how the ballet company helped to keep money in the city and how it promoted the city through its outside tours—the group's leaders asked for $25,000 from a city government which had given it only $3,000 the previous year. Pages of statistics were presented to the Winnipeg Metro Council, an official municipal agency. The presentation showed how the company created employment not only for its own members, but for independent local contractors, and it indicated how much money remained in the city through the purchase of goods and services by the ballet. Also, scores of press clippings demonstrated how the company promoted the city of Winnipeg nationally and internationally. The hard-hitting presentation was successful and the Ballet received a grant of $18,000.

Following the same basic approach, but broadening the case to include the entire province of Manitoba, (charts showed anticipated cultural growth with the opening of a new arts center in 1967), the ballet asked the provincial government for greater support. An increase to nearly $13,000 was granted. Next, a presentation to the Canada Council pinpointed the national benefits of the company's activities and resulted in a grant of $42,000.

Bolstered by its success in winning increased government support at every level, the ballet prepared its case for local business, which had contributed less than $40,000 the previous year. The Metro Council grant, in particular, had been well-publicized in Winnipeg and it provided the ballet company with a weapon to prod the community to give more.

In advance of any direct approach to business, the ballet's board prepared a detailed profile of corporations in the area, rating them according to their actual and projected incomes and their past giving records. Next, two-paragraph letters, "selling" the ballet, were sent to key local corporations. The letters emphasized four essential points: what the Royal Winnipeg Ballet was; what its future prospects were; how much it had to raise to achieve this goal; and how much it expected to raise from the people of the city. Each letter indicated a specific date on which representatives of the ballet would call a company executive to arrange an appointment.

Aware that many corporations thought of ballet as an "esoteric activity," the dance company selected a group of practical, business-minded board members and aggressive staff people to make oral presentations to each corpo-

120

ration. To strengthen their case, they brought a specially prepared brochure with them, which pinpointed the current and future financial picture of the organization.

A major business breakthrough came when the ballet received a grant of $50,000 from the head office of the largest investment brokerage firm in Canada, James Richardson and Sons. According to Mr. Coroneos, the brokerage house, which had contributed only modest sums to the ballet previously, was influenced by increased government support and the approval which that support implied. The business-like approach to the company also helped. "For the first time," he told *AM*, "they were clearly able to see the ballet's long-range plans."

Although the Richardson grant was not publicized in the press, it was used by the ballet in its approach to other local businesses, and it started a chain reaction of business contributions. As a result, a total of $118,000 was raised from local business. Also, the size and number of individual contributions increased.

Using the same approach in its 1965 fund campaign, and with its budget upped to nearly $250,000, the ballet company again increased the total amount of money it raised. (48)

Chapter II – Audiences and Programs

THE AUDIENCE: MEASURING AND ANALYZING IT

Key Study Shows Public Receptive to Arts

The public has a far more favorable attitude toward the arts than is generally believed and it recognizes the importance of the arts to the quality of neighborhood life and to the economic well-being of the community. In addition, an overwhelming majority of the public respects artists and views arts education for schoolchildren as essential. Moreover, if the arts were made more accessible to non-whites and people in communities without adequate cultural facilities, attendance would increase substantially.

These are among the revealing and provocative findings gleaned from a still-to-be-released trailblazing study of public attitudes towards the arts in New York State conducted by the National Research Center of the Arts, for the American Council for the Arts in Education. *Arts and the People: A Survey of Public Participation in and Attitudes Towards Arts and Culture in New York State* is believed to be the most comprehensive attitudinal study of the arts yet undertaken. Its 200 odd pages of findings are based on 1531 interviews, averaging nearly an hour and a half each, with a representative cross section of state residents over the age of 16. This large and scientifically sound sample was broken down into 26 demographic groupings —each large enough to be projectable on a statewide basis —according to geographic region, size of place, sex, race, income, education and age and also into a series of attitudinal groupings created from responses.

In answer to the question, "How important is it to you that your community and neigborhood should have a theater where plays and ballet are performed?" 39 per cent of the respondents answered Very Important (V.I.), and 33 per cent said Somewhat Important (S.I.). Only 10 per cent indicated this was not at all important. Virtually the same proportionate response held true for questions about the importance of concert halls and art museums. There was an even higher positive response to questions on the importance of cultural facilities to the community itself. Some 50 per cent indicated that the arts were very important to the quality of life and 35 per cent answered somewhat important. The importance of cultural facilities to the business and economy of the community resulted in responses of 38% V.I. and 36% S.I.

In addition to choice questions, respondents were given a series of positive and negative statements on the arts and asked to agree or disagree with each. Generally, there was strong agreement with positive statements and strong disagreement with negative statements. For example, 77% agreed with the statement, "It is important for young people to see live performances on stage" while only 33% agreed with the negative statement, "Movies are much more relevant to life than most things you see on stage." There was majority support for live over electronically reproduced programming and strong agreement that television should broadcast more concerts, operas and drama. Conversely, there was better than majority disagreement to such statements as: symphony concerts are just for highbrows (72%); it's so difficult to go to a live performance that it's not worth the effort (52%); and, I don't mind going to a concert in the park but a symphony hall makes me uncomfortable (63%).

In another kind of arts reaction check, respondents were asked to indicate their respect for various kinds of well-recognized professions and the arts won a dramatically high following. Musicians came out fourth on the list, immediately behind scientists, doctors and lawyers and ahead of bankers. Poets were next, ahead of businessmen, with 43%, or a projected 5½ million New Yorkers, according them high respect. Painters and sculptors followed businessmen by only a single percentage point. Although actors and ballet dancers were near the bottom of the list —critics were at the absolute bottom—79% accorded them some or great respect.

A key pattern to emerge from the section on public receptivity to the arts, chapter one of the report, was evidence of the strong arts interest shown by non-whites and those in the middle and lower middle range of the socio-economic scale. (It was not a surprise to discover that the upper strata scored high for the arts). The study clearly shows that the economic situation doesn't seem to change an individual's feelings as to the value of the arts or its importance to the community. Nonwhites as a whole, in fact, were more favorably inclined towards the arts than their white counterparts on a number of questions put to them, and along with women were more concerned about neighborhood arts facilities and the general quality of life. Clearly, when the arts are brought to the public and are made accessible, they receive very high interest and recognition. What this means to the arts is the demonstrated fact that there is a much larger culturally inclined coalition than had ever before been indicated and that this coalition includes good representation from the middle class. The only groups with consistently less than positive attitudes towards the arts were rural residents and those with gradeschool educations.

In addition to receptivity to the arts, the study explored key subjects in each of its other six chapters: attitudes towards children's exposure to culture; the level of individual participation in the arts; arts attendance; background of arts exposure; access to cultural events; and attitudes towards public and other funding. The highly positive reaction to education in the arts for schoolchildren was an especially meaningful finding. In spite of the fact that the majority of people think there is more arts activity in the schools than there really is, they indicated that they wanted even more exposure to the arts for youngsters. Positive interest in increasing the arts role in education was strongest among non-whites, urbanites and young people themselves. Perhaps the best indication of the overall attitude on this subject was the fact that a majority of respondents favored credits for arts subjects in grade and high schools, thus placing the arts on an equal basis with math, science and English.

Figures regarding attendance at cultural programs provided some positive and surprising results as the study, perhaps for the first time, developed a per capita rather than total attendance count. The results suggest, in fact, that previous estimates of the cultural audience are much lower than it really is. At least once during the year from November 1971 to November 1972, some 7.4 million of the states' 13 million people age 16 or older visited one art museum. Concert attendance based on at least one visit was 4.4 million individuals (34%), theatre 5.5 million (42%), and ballet or modern dance 2.1 million (16%). Even more significant was the count of multiple attenders, those who visited art museums three or more times a year or attended at least eight performances—four or more in each of two different performing arts disciplines. Over 2 million New Yorkers (25%) were multiple attenders at museums while over one million (9%) were multiple attenders at performing arts programs. According to Joseph Farrell, president of the National Research Center, "The study indicates that attendance figures are most controlled by access with the socio-economic more important than the geographic factor." He cautioned, however, that attendance figures obtained in a cross-sectional public study are rough projections, although accurate enough to indicate a general range of numbers.

The study shows some misunderstanding of the role of state and local governments in culture although the public seems to favor more government support. The prevailing opinion seemed to be that arts support is more a responsibility of the federal government that it is of either state or local government.   (79)

Reach: A New Method of Measuring an Audience

By

Bradley G. Morison and Kay Fliehr

The traditional measuring stick for audiences in the performing arts has been box office—a direct reflection of total attendance. In recent years, as producing organizations decentralized and institutionalized, a second audience statistic took on added importance: the season subscription total—a measurement of the thoroughly committed audience base.

But now, with emerging interest in expanding and broadening audiences, a third audience measuring stick must be given the same close scrutiny as the familiar total attendance and season ticket count.

This third figure is one we call *reach*. It is the measure of penetration into the total community which an institution is achieving. As we define its application to the performing arts, *reach* is the total number of different people in the community who involve themselves with an institution one or more times during the year. The figure usually differs drastically from either total attendance or season subscription.

Regardless of the year-to-year trends in total attendance or season subscription, a healthy audience development situation demands that *reach* grow steadily. Intelligent analysis of and attention to *reach* is an important key in the fight for survival of any performing arts organization.

To illustrate, let us use a hypothetical theater, assuming a five play season in which 20,000 people see each production for a total attendance of 100,000. *Reach* would be the total number of different people who saw at least one production.

If this theatre had 20,000 subscribers, each seeing all five plays, then the *reach* would be 20,000. At the other extreme, suppose that the theater had no subscribers and none of the people who attended saw more than one production. The *reach* would then be 100,000.

In a real situation, actual *reach* would fall in between the two extremes. Assume, for instance, that the theater had a season ticket sale of 8,000 and that the average single ticket buyer saw two of the five plays. The statistics would look like this:

Total attendance _____100,000
Season ticket attendance 8,000 x 5__ 40,000
     Single ticket attendance _____ 60,000
Single ticket *reach* $\dfrac{60,000}{2}$_____ 30,000
Season ticket *reach*_____ 8,000
     Total *reach* _____ <u>38,000</u> different people

The theater reached 38,000 different people in the community. If the population was one million, the *reach* percentage for the season would be 3.8%.

Why is it important to analyze *reach* figures and their trends? Because *reach* trends do not necessarily parallel total attendance or season subscription in either proportion or direction. It is possible, for instance, to have subscriptions and total attendance increase from one year to another while *reach* is actually declining.

While a slight decline in *reach* is not disastrous, it would call for increased audience development efforts to bring new people to the theater the next year, efforts which might not be made unless an analysis was done.

It is also possible to have a situation in which season ticket sales are decreasing from year to year, but where *reach* is actually increasing steadily. While a downward trend is not desirable in season tickets, the situation where *reach* is increasing is less disastrous than one where it was declining along with subscriptions. The people who make up the single ticket *reach* constitute the best possible potential for season ticket sales. Unless single ticket *reach* is substantial and growing, it is difficult if not impossible to make season subscriptions grow. In the declining subscription situation, the increased *reach* trend is enlarging the pool of prime potential for reversing the down-trend in season tickets.

The ideal, healthy audience growth situation demands that all three figures—total attendance, subscriptions and *reach*—be increasing. Total attendance is an important measure of box office success and the drawing power of a particular season. Subscription totals are a measure of hard core, dedicated base support. *Reach,* and the percentage of the population it represents, is the measure of

128

the degree to which the institution has really touched and influenced the main body of the community. It tells the institution how much it is growing in importance and meaning to the community it is dedicated to serve and which it must serve if it is to survive.

The people who comprise the total *reach* represent the institution's potential for growth. They are the word-of-mouth communicators, the receptive audience which can be educated and introduced to more adventurous theatrical experiences, the untapped reservoir for deeper commitment to season tickets, and the friends who can be called upon for help in time of crisis. This group must be kept growing.

Calculating the *reach* of an institution requires research and additional record keeping. An accurate figure on the number of times the average person is involved with the organization each year must be determined. But the institution which wants a lucid, valid indication of how successfully they are reaching into their community—and which truly wants to extend its *reach*—will find a serious analysis of *reach* figures well worth the effort.   (56)

------◄●►------

Cultural Audience in America is Identified

By

Alvin Toffler

It is safe to say that since the end of World War II there has been a sharp increase in the proportion of men in the culture public. Among readers of *American Artist,* a magazine for amateur painters, 40 per cent are male. And a recent study of the audience of the Tyrone Guthrie

Theatre in Minneapolis reflects about the same distribution: 55 per cent female, 45 per cent male. On Broadway, where theater-going sometimes comes under the heading of business entertainment, the audience is predominantly male. An American male is no longer regarded as a "sissy" if he shows an interest in the arts.

This shift toward increased male participation in the culture market has been accompanied, I think, by a drop in the average age of the culture consumer. A surprising number of professional administrators in the arts, who have an opportunity to observe the audience first-hand, report being struck by the presence of youth in its midst. Perry T. Rathbone, director of the Boston Museum of Fine Arts, says his museum now draws more people in the 20-40 age bracket than it did in years past. In Richmond, Leslie Cheek, director of the Virginia Museum of Fine Arts, calls attention to the increasing number of "young marrieds" on his membership list. Similarly, Harry Abrams, a leading publisher of art books, concludes that the largest part of his market lies with customers in the 25-45 age bracket, a group, he says, that is particularly alert to new trends.

One can hardly be dogmatic about the evidence, but it would seem that the increasing youthfulness of the culture consumer will affect programming deeply. For one thing, the younger the audience, the more receptive it is likely to be to all forms of innovation and experiment.

As far as income is concerned, the rich, of course, are still with us. However, the culture consumer is, most often, a member of the comfort class. In a country in which the national median income lies between $5,000 and $6,000 we find the lowest reported median among a group of surveyed arts audiences to be about $9,000.

Our culture consumer, it will be no surprise to learn, is

also far better educated than the man in the street. He may not have completed college, but the odds are roughly four out of five that he has had at least some exposure to higher education or that the head of his household has.

This does not mean that there are not in our country some poorly educated Italian shoemakers who nourish a passion for grand opera or some denim-clad ditch-diggers with an appetite for abstract expressionism. What it does mean is that they form a small part of the total culture public. In fact, there is evidence that education is the single most important indicator of a person's cultural status, more important even than income.

If we analyze the culture consuming public by occupation we find that families in which the head of the household may be termed a professional or technical employee form a heavily disproportionate part of the culture public. They are followed by what might loosely be called businessmen or executives and their families.

There is still another discernible characteristic of the culture consumer that is worth noting: his relatively high mobility. The class we have been describing tends, in general, to travel more, to move more often, to progress up and down the social scale more rapidly than most Americans.

Another characteristic of the culture consumer is his exposure to communications. He is, through one medium or another, more "tuned in" to the world around him than his non-culture-consuming counterpart. Being tuned in implies more than just passive receptivity. It implies active interaction with the world around him.

The popular image of the reader or culture lover pictures a sedentary, home-centered person. Quite the opposite tends to be true. Generally, he is more active in community and business affairs than his next-door neighbors. Being more active, he also tends toward community leadership.

It is clear from the foregoing that the culture consumer is a new breed. The effective arts manager must understand this new breed, must understand the interests and motives of the culture audience, if he is to appeal successfully to it.   (32)

Survey Shows When Audiences for Different Art Forms Overlap

To what degree is there a "general" culture public in any community? To what degree does the audience for opera or ballet overlap that for theatre or symphony orchestra concerts? Such questions are of vital importance for cultural leaders planning to create a new arts institution, studying ways to expand their ticket sales, or developing interdisciplinary programs of any kind. They are questions that have fascinated arts managers in every discipline for years. Yet there is a surprising lack of objective data to help one identify the kinds and degrees of overlap.

Recently an analysis of the first season audience at the Tyrone Guthrie Theatre in Minneapolis, conducted by the Twin Cities Market and Research Department of Batten, Barton, Durstine & Osborn, Inc., turned up some interesting facts about audience overlap, not merely between cultural disciplines, but between theatre and such other entertainments as baseball and football. The results indicated a substantial overlap between theatregoers and symphony concert attenders, but a relatively small overlap between the theatre audience and the audience for opera or ballet. In fact, the overlap between theatre and baseball was greater than that between theatre and opera or dance.

The survey was conducted by distributing 20,917 questionnaires to members of the Guthrie Theatre audience. Approximately every ninth seat holder received a form along with a request to fill it in. In all, 10,421 completed returns were submitted—49.8 per cent of the total. Information on the questionnaires was transferred to punch cards and later fed into an IBM computer for tabulation.

The key question in this series asked: "Last year (1962) did you attend any of the following kinds of attractions?" A total of 8,898 persons responded by checking one or more items in a list of events. The results were as follows:

Symphony concerts _____ 65.8 per cent
Pro-baseball games _____ 55.3 per cent
Operas _____ 33.7 per cent
Jazz concerts _____ 19.2 per cent
Pro-football games _____ 28.3 per cent
Ballets _____ 24.0 per cent

Results add up to more than 100 per cent because of multiple answers. As might be expected, the degree of overlap in the symphony, opera and ballet was greater among women than men. The degree of overlap in baseball, football and jazz was greater among men.

The survey then attempted to distinguish between overlap patterns among different occupational groupings in the Guthrie audience. (In the percentage tables below, the following symbols will be used: S—symphony; PB—Pro-baseball; O—Opera; J—Jazz concerts; PF—Pro-football; B—Ballets).

	S	PB	O	J	PF	B
Professionals	72.2	48.6	40.2	18.0	23.3	29.3
Housewives	62.0	54.4	30.9	11.4	27.1	23.2
Students	71.2	56.1	30.8	35.1	25.5	19.8
Business	53.2	75.8	29.4	16.9	50.0	17.9
Clerical	63.2	57.6	31.4	17.2	23.1	24.2
Technical and Engineers	55.2	67.7	22.0	18.7	31.8	18.4
Retired	70.5	39.7	48.5	4.4	18.0	34.9

In all but one of the categories the pattern of overlap between theatre and symphony, opera, ballet and jazz was exactly the same. There was the greatest degree of overlap with symphony, the next most with opera, the next with ballet and the least with jazz. The exception was among students, in which category the overlap with jazz was greater than the overlap with ballet.

These similarities suggest that the patterns are heavily influenced by the availability of the different attractions within a community. Thus Minneapolis has both a big league baseball team and a pro-football team, as well as a major symphony orchestra. It does not have a nationally known ballet, opera or jazz group. This underscores the danger of attempting to apply the Guthrie figures in another city without careful evaluation. On the other hand, the differences between the various occupational groupings and age groups (e.g., students and retired persons) may be less influenced by local factors.

The survey also attempted to show the difference in overlap patterns between season subscribers and single ticket buyers. It found that single ticket buyers were more likely to attend symphony concerts, opera, ballet and jazz performances than season ticket subscribers, but that season ticket subscribers were more likely to attend baseball and football games than single ticket purchasers. (27)

―――――◄●►―――――

Multiple Joiners in the Arts

Do symphony orchestra members also belong to the local museum, theatre, or opera?

In an attempt to discover whether people supporting one arts activity also support others, a research worker for the Adult Education Department of the University of Nebraska compared the membership lists of the seven leading cultural organizations in a Nebraska community. Out of a combined membership of over 4,000 he discovered the following:

4,000 people belonged to only one organization; 250 belonged to two organizations; 100 belonged to three organizations; 30 belonged to four organizations; 10 belonged to five organizations; and one belonged to six organizations. Not one person belonged to all seven organizations.

Many arts managers have wanted precise data on membership overlapping, but it has only rarely been produced by exact study. (10)

----◄•►----

Surveys Can Improve Programs, Reduce Costs by Predicting Size and Character of Audience

By

Duncan F. Cameron

The techniques of marketing and public relations research have applications in the cultural world that can lead to significant savings in dollars and cents, and, more important, to significant increases in program effectiveness.

Too little work has yet been done to say how great a role such research can play in the arts, but the few studies executed in recent years show promise. Audience-potential surveys have been carried out in connection with art center construction programs in the U. S. and Canada. The Minneapolis Symphony some years ago conducted a survey of audience characteristics. Some work on theatre audience characteristics has been done by *Playbill,* a magazine distributed in theatres. But it is in the museum field that the most survey work appears to have been conducted.

At Colonial Williamsburg, the educational effectiveness of exhibits has been explored; at the University of Nebraska, the value of museum teaching for biology students is under investigation; the U. S. Department of Interior is concerned about studies of the effectiveness of its national parks museums; the Royal Ontario Museum, Toronto, is studying the effects of admission prices, the value of museum orientation programs for university students, and the place of museums and art galleries in the leisure patterns of the Toronto community.

Despite this list of varied research programs, audience research in the arts is still in its infancy, and is regarded with skepticism by many arts managers. These same officials will be spending millions of dollars in the next few years on programs and construction.

Industry and commerce have learned that experience and intuition are not enough, and have come to depend on market and opinion research as valuable assets in planning. For decades social welfare organizations, community chests, civic recreation authorities, and other institutions serving the public have used social surveys as an aid to planning. Perhaps it is time for the arts administrator to take a fresh look at the usefulness of surveys.

Museum audience research is not new. In the late 1920's and the early 1930's, the American Association of Museums directed studies of museum visitor behavior. These investigations were supported by Carnegie Foundation grants. In the post-war era, analyses of audience composition have been made in Milwaukee, Washington, Toronto and a handful of other cities.

Unfortunately, the earliest workers, though competent professionals, did not have the advantage of today's sophisticated techniques. Many of the post-war studies were carried out without professional help, and an unknown number of other studies remain unpublished. It is only in the last ten years that museum audience research has begun to be treated as the domain of the professional researcher, with the obligation to publish inherent.

One of the most active programs is at the Royal Ontario Museum, where a dozen studies have examined attitudes towards admission fees, the composition of the visiting audience, characteristics of frequent visitors, the museum staff's image of the audience, convenience of public hours, orientation programs, effects of special exhibitions, etc. How much has it cost? And has it proven to be a sound investment?

The best answer is that the study of attitudes toward admission fees led to fee changes that produced more revenue in the first year than the total cost of all studies since the survey program began in 1957. Current studies at the R.O.M. are expected to produce valuable information about the most effective advertising media for the museum, about motivations underlying museum visiting, and about public interest in different museum subject areas. The largest annual budget for audience research at the R.O.M., including the cost of professional assistance and publication, has been less than $4,000.   (4)

------◄●►------

Study Shows How to Predict Museum Growth

A new, objective way to measure the audience potential of art museums is presented in a trailblazing study of museum growth patterns in 26 U. S. and Canadian cities. The yardstick is part of a 159-page report that can help museum directors and board members predict how population growth, increases in expenditures, provision of new physical facilities and other factors will affect future attendance curves. Prepared for the Montreal Museum of Fine Arts by Raymond Loewy-William Snaith, Inc., under the direction of vice-president Joseph Lovelace, the highly original report challenges the widespread belief that rising educational and economic levels in a community boost attendance figures significantly.

In a period in which museum attendance is increasing dramatically in both the U. S. and Canada, but in which there is a scarcity of detailed sociological and economic data on the arts, the report promises to become a standard sourcebook for museum management. Indirectly, its findings may also shed light on attendance factors in other kinds of cultural institutions, although the report makes no effort to generalize.

The study, which took eight months to complete, focusses on museum growth between 1946 and 1960, inclusive. The 26 metropolitan centers analyzed range in population from 253,000 to 4,418,000. Of these, two are in Canada, the rest in the U. S. Where one city boasts several major art museums, these were treated statistically as a single institution.

The report cites attendance figures as the most realistic measure of a museum's position in the community and the basis on which all future planning decisions should be made. Reviewing the composite experience of the museums in the larger metropolitan areas, it arrives at what it calls a "mean attendance ratio"—a measure of audience potential. The mean attendance ratio for a city of 500,000, for example, is given as .23. This means that an art museum in a city of that size has a potential annual attendance of 500,000 x .23 or 115,000. The ratio for a city of 1,000,000 is .18; it drops to .15 for a city of 2,000,000 and .13 for a city of 3,000,000. The reports suggests that "any museum falling appreciably below the curve is not realizing its full potential in terms of attendance."

Applying the mean attendance ratios, the report lists cities like Seattle, Dallas, Cincinnati, Cleveland, St. Louis,

Boston, Detroit and Philadelphia as performing better than average. It cited Houston, Baltimore, Buffalo, and San Francisco art museum attendance as below the audience potential in those cities.

These figures bear out a significant finding: as the population of a city increases, its per capita attendance rate declines. The decrease is quite rapid at first, then levels off. The smaller the city, the more rapid the decline.

The best way to buck this seemingly inescapable trend, the report declares, is through expansion of physical facilities as population increases. To attract visitors, it is relatively more important to have a larger museum, than to spend proportionately more on a smaller one.

The average museum surveyed increased its absolute dollar expenditures by seven per cent per year during the 1944-60 period. However, per capita expenditures declined. Per capita spending between 1946 and 1960 averaged $.1769 for the museums for which detailed financial data was available. In the 1960-1961 period it dropped to $.1560.

Museum eating facilities feed attendance figures, the report finds. Much-higher-than-average attendance ratios were found in museums with restaurants. The Loewy-Snaith report strongly urges that restaurant facilities be included in any expansion move planned by a museum. It recommends the leasing of eating facilities to concessionaires in return for 10 per cent of gross revenues. Experience of the museums surveyed indicates that 20 per cent as many meals can be served as there are visitors — a finding that suggests excellent profit potential.

On the other hand, parking facilities do not appear to be a significant factor influencing attendance. A central location, either downtown or easily accessible to downtown, is more important than parking facilities in building attendance, the report finds.

Moderately good income can be derived from a museum sales desk, the study reports. A number of museums in the sample ran their desks at a profit; one museum in a relatively small city increased its salesdesk revenue by 1000 percent in three years, boosting it well over the six-figure mark.

As to floor space, "There is a direct relationship between larger per capita attendances and larger per capita areas," the report declares. It suggests that between 35 and 45 per cent of total floor space should be used for exhibition area. A portion of this should be set aside for special exhibits since there is evidence that visitors resent dismantling of the permanent collection to make room for a temporary display. A great number of special exhibits does not necessarily hike attendance, although special exhibits of outstanding quality will.

The report, surprisingly finds that there is no established pattern to indicate that high membership results in increased attendance. It found that among museums in its sample, membership ran at a rate of beween 1.5 and 2.5 per thousand in the metropolitan area population.

The report, based on questionnaires, interviews, and documentary research, also covers costs of museum additions, service areas, the effect of air conditioning and room dimensions on operations, and other subjects.   (11)

New Audience Survey Identifies Playgoers

By

Thomas Gale Moore

Theatregoers are different; they go to the theatre. But who are they? In the spring of 1962, an audience survey conducted for the Carnegie Institute of Technology's study of the economics of the theatre attempted to learn something about the characteristics of playgoers. This article reports a few of the preliminary results of the survey which was carried out with the cooperation of the League of New York Theatres.

Since the surveying of cultural audiences is still relatively rare, the procedure used may be of interest to others contemplating audience research.

Under supervision, usherettes placed questionnaires in programs distributed to the audience at eight Broadway shows. In the case of some shows, questionnaires were handed out at only one performance. At other shows, the procedure was repeated at four performances. Large boxes were scattered around the theatres into which the audience could deposit completed questionnaires. In a trial run I tried including business reply envelopes for playgoers to mail the forms back. This did not work well. I discovered the audience normally dropped the questionnaires off on the way out. If no box was nearby, however, they simply failed to bother with the form. All told, there were 3,449 responses. These accounted for 24 per cent of the audience.

Thus, to evaluate these results properly, the reader must bear in mind that a large proportion of the audience failed to fill out and turn in the questionnaire. Moreover, to draw conclusions about Broadway patrons, we must assume that those who filled out the questionnaire did not differ in any significant way from those who ignored it. What do we find?

Seventy-three percent of those who filled out the questionnaire were married; 63 percent were males; almost 70 percent were from the vicinity of New York City. These percentages varied considerably with length of run and time of performance. Many more of those who responded at matinees were female, while a much larger percentage were single. As might be expected, a large proportion (70 per cent) of the audience at *My Fair Lady,* were from out of town.

Half of the respondents were older than 39, had a family income larger than $13,500, and had been to the theatre within the last 37 days. On average those who were from New York or the vicinity expected to spend over 50 minutes going home that night. Again, as might be expected, the audience during week nights lived somewhat closer to the theatre than the audience on week ends. The playgoers to matinees, however, reported that they expected to take on average 71 minutes to go home; this could mean they lived further away or that travel was slower in the afternoon than in the evening.

The length of time necessary to travel to the Times Square area naturally affected how often people went; the farther away they lived the fewer Broadway plays they saw. Two factors could explain this: first, the longer it takes to get to the theatre, the less frequently people will want to go; second, those who love the stage and wish to go often may choose to live close to Broadway. Thus it is possible that, if the theatre were brought closer to the suburbs, attendance from the suburban area would increase only slightly.

Sixty-five percent of local theatregoers ate at a restaurant before going to the theatre. On average, each of them spent slightly over $5.00 for a meal and drinks. On this basis, we can estimate that during the survey week New Yorkers who went to the theatre contributed about $433,000 to the coffers of local eating establishments. If we assume that the average check for visitors to the metropolitan area was the same as for local people, then, during the survey week, patrons of the theatre spent about $718,000 on food and drink. According to *Variety*, the total legitimate gross was $1,041,437. This means that playgoers paid out almost as much to restaurants as they did to theatres that week.

(23)

—◄•►—

Theatre Survey Shows 'Ice' Overestimated

By

Thomas Gale Moore

There has been much speculation recently about the magnitude of "ice" in the Broadway theatre. "Ice" is money paid by the ticket buyer over and above the regular price and the ticket broker's fee. A New York State investigation has led to charges that the amount of "ice" may reach $10,000,000 a year. This is enough to pay the production costs of 20 musicals or scores of straight plays, a matter of consequence to the entire American theatre. Is this figure of $10,000,000 realistic, however?

A survey conducted during the spring of 1962 by the Carnegie Institute of Technology's study of the economics of the theatre indicates that the figure is not. On the basis of what patrons reported on the survey questionnaire the total figure for Broadway "ice" would run between one and two million dollars—probably about $1,750,000—per season, not $10,000,000. It would   exceed $1,750,000 in a

144

season when there are several tremendous hits, and fall under this figure during a poorer year.

The Carnegie study drew 3,449 responses from theatregoers at eight different Broadway shows. It revealed that, on the average, each person going to a straight show spent $6.25 for a seat. An individual attending a musical laid out more: on average, almost $8.00 for the ticket. People on expense accounts, as might have been expected, were more lavish: the average cost of a seat was $8.20 for a straight show and $13.50 for a musical. Note that the highest box office price for straight show tickets is $7.50 and for musicials, $9.90. Thus the buyer paid, on average, considerably more than the official amount for his ticket.

A few visitors to New York were charged as much as $18.10 above list for their seats to Friday night performances of *How to Succeed in Business Without Really Trying* and *A Thousand Clowns*. New Yorkers tended to make smaller illegal payments: the highest, $17.20, was paid for a Wednesday evening performance of *How to Succeed.* While patrons from out of town made up only a small percentage of the audience, they accounted for over 60 per cent of the total receipts of scalpers.

On the basis of these figures, we find that for the top show, *How to Succeed,* the audience paid over $80,000 a week for seats; the box office received about $67,000; $12,700 was paid to scalpers; the remainder consisted of legitimate commissions.

Some brokers apparently receive more than the legal commission; 70 per cent of those who reported paying in excess of the legitimate brokerage fee for their seats claimed they bought them from brokers.

On the basis of the figures reported in the survey, it appears that total illegal payments during the week for all shows on Broadway amounted to about $34,000.

About half the people purchasing tickets at more than the legal rate paid less than five dollars above the price printed on the ticket. About one quarter paid between five and ten dollars and the remainder paid $10 or more extra. Ninety per cent of those paying over ten dollars above list were buying tickets to *How to Succeed*. Most of those were purchased for the evening performances, rather than for the matinees. In general, the percentage of total tickets that were sold at scalpers' rates was small. If our estimate of $34,000 is correct, however, ticket scalpers cannot be ignored; they exist and the sums they handle, while not huge, are substantial. (24)

Non-Newspaper Advertising Brings Few Theatregoers to Broadway Plays

By

Thomas Gale Moore

Why do people go to the theatre? How do they choose the shows they want to see? How important is advertising? Word of mouth publicity? The critic? A survey conducted by the Carnegie Institute of Technology's study of theatre economics explored these questions and cast interesting light on the motivations of the theatergoer.

The survey, conducted in the spring of 1962 among the audiences of eight Broadway shows, showed that the factors that affect the choice of shows are diverse. For new productions, critics are important; of the audience from the New York area attending *A Thousand Clowns* (which had been running only 4 weeks), almost half reported that news-

146

paper reviews had influenced them. As shows run longer, personal recommendations become more important. For *A Man for All Seasons, Gideon, How to Succeed in Business,* and *Milk and Honey,* the percentage indicating word of mouth was 61, 41, 55, and 70 percent respectively. Except for *Gideon,* which was on cut-rate tickets and doing only fair box office business, over half of those answering from the metropolitan area indicated that they chose on the basis of personal recommendations. Critics' comments played a much smaller part in the choice of shows that had been running a few months than they did in the case of *A Thousand Clowns;* even for *How to Succeed* only 42 per cent indicated that newspaper reviews had been a factor.

The only other reason local people mentioned for attending a show was newspaper advertising. While only 12 per cent of those at *Milk and Honey* and 14 per cent at *A Man for All Seasons* suggested this had affected their decisions, 20 per cent of those at *Gideon* and 23 per cent at *How to Succeed* had been influenced by newspaper spreads. Thus, advertisements in the dailies bring a certain amount of business and good reviews give a substantial boost to a show; in the end, however, these figures suggest that the success of the show will depend on how well the public likes it. If people who see it enjoy it, they will recommend it and more people will go; without these favorable comments, good reviews and newspaper advertising cannot save a production. The survey also suggests that advertising over the radio or on billboards or in magazines produces few local patrons.

The 30 per cent of the audience that were visiting New York came to a show for much the same reasons. The importance of newspaper and other advertising, however, was somewhat less. The most significant difference between local and out of town respondents concerned the role of critics. While about the same percentage attributed their choice to reviewers, about half of the visitors referred to magazine critics; New Yorkers ignored magazine critics.

A significant difference exists between those who go to the theatre often and those who do not in their expressed reasons for choosing a particular show. Over 40 per cent of those who had been to the theatre within the last week mentioned word of mouth as a factor in their decisions while only one per cent of those who hadn't seen a show in over eight months referred to it. People who go to the theatre often usually credit several sources as influencing their choice, while people who go rarely give fewer reasons. From these figures we can draw one conclusion on advertising: paid publicity probably has little effect on those who go to the theatre often; they would have gone anyway. Since some of those who seldom attend the theatre mentioned advertising as the only reason for choosing a show, we can conclude that this group can be influenced by advertising.

In the questionnaire, the audience was asked to check the curtain time they preferred. The great majority of those responding indicated 8:30 or 8:40. But among local people, the bulk of the audience, there was a substantial feeling that a slightly earlier beginning would be nice; 32 per cent of local people attending a week night performance wanted a curtain time of 8 or earlier. Only 12 per cent, however, wanted it as early as 7:30. On the weekend there were fewer requests for an early start and the number wishing a 9 o'clock beginning rose to almost ten per cent. A greater proportion of the visitors to New York preferred later curtains. In contrast, those at matinees who responded to the question about evening performances — whether from out of town or from the metropolitan area — were over-

148

whelming supporters of early starts; 64 per cent checked 7:30 or 8:00.

These results indicate that it might be profitable for Broadway theatres to experiment with an earlier curtain on one or two week nights. While 7:30 was tried unsuccessfully a few years ago, the results of the survey suggest that this was too early and that an 8 o'clock start might be a good compromise. On the other hand, there seems to be almost no support for a curtain later than the current one.

The most surprising aspect of this survey is the relatively small amount of money going to scalpers. Contrary to popular report, even for hits, over three quarters of the audience normally pays no more for tickets than the box office price, plus, on occasion, a brokerage fee.

Two practical implications can be drawn from this survey: the first is that there is a market for an earlier curtain; the second concerns the efficacy of advertising. If the responses are to be believed, we must conclude that non-newspaper advertising brings in few patrons. Radio and TV critics affect the decisions of almost no one. Frequent playgoers are less affected by advertising than by personal recommendations. Newspapers, however, have more influence on those who go casually. (25)

BUILDING NEW AUDIENCES

Offbeat Promo by Upbeat Kids Woos
Young Audience to Opera

Bumper stickers reading "Bravo Opera," buttons proclaiming that "Opera Lives," and flyers describing *La Boheme* as "four old time Hippies in an attic," are only a few of the techniques being used by the Seattle Opera Association in Washington in a campaign aimed at encouraging young people to attend opera performances.

Long interested in attracting youth to the opera audience, Glynn Ross, general director of the Association, decided earlier this year that the best way to reach them was through their contemporaries. On April 11th, he placed an advertisement in the University of Washington Daily which read: "Seattle Opera Wants Three Washington Whiz Kids. Definition: A young adult, either sex, who can make the Seattle Opera Success Trip . . . " Of the 64 who responded, Ross selected five to develop the youth-oriented promotional program.

The new program got off to an impressive start. The immediate advice of the Whiz Kids was that the Association forget old traditions and speak to young people in a language they could understand. Thus, beginning in May, scores of "What is Boheme" flyers, with copy referring to the "old-time Hippies," were distributed in the University district. Two hundred passes to a May 11th performance were given away to students, with each resident house on campus receiving two tickets. Following the performance, letters signed by Mr. Ross were sent to all the students who attended the performance, telling them about a new subscription series and suggesting they let their friends and parents know "what is really going on."

Mr. Ross's letter said in part, "As you now know, and contrary to what many people choose to believe, it is not a single star that makes opera grand. It is the blending of acting, singing, costuming, lights and music. It surpasses the popular light show as a galactic happening — a trip into the world of total art."

In June, the Opera imported an impressive 12-foot-high piece of "junk sculpture," titled *Warrior,* as its principal exhibit at the Seattle Teen Spectacular. Although the sculpture bore no relationship to opera, it was a success in two ways, according to Mrs. Erna Husak, public relations director of the Association. "First," she told *AM,* "it caused hundreds of young people to stop and consider opera as a living and dynamic thing with some sense of humor. The goal of trying to tie the general concept of opera with the youth revolution was achieved. Secondly, the rise in ticket sales during the period of the Teen Spectacular and the few days following accounted for 16 per cent of the total sales for the opera series which followed."

With this as a beginning, the Whiz Kids flew into high gear, carrying out the entire project in much their own way. Pamphlets, letters and ads were written by them and printed by the Association. Buttons, bumper stickers and posters were prepared and distributed. The message of opera was brought to students through meetings and phone calls.

Two of the Whiz Kids have already written a series of advertisements for this year's season of productions. The ad for *Don Giovanni* reads, "Well... What can you say about Don Juan—He's Don Juan-Right?! Seducer, murderer, and general rake. Seductions, mistaken identities, and a statue who invites himself to an all time dinner.

Supernatural flames and sinking palaces. A crowd of beautiful women all chasing a man who wants one thing—and gets something else—All with sounds by Mozart.''

When the campaign for fall season subscriptions was completed, the youngsters began to develop projects designed to sell opera to elementary and junior high school students. In discussing the campaign's success and the reasons for undertaking it, Mrs. Husak said, "We are continually open to new ideas, no matter how flippant or strange, that may serve to promote understanding and appreciation of opera.''

Perhaps the best justification for the campaign is contained in the flyer for youngsters advertising the low-priced Fall National Series, which suggests "an opera date for the price of a movie.'' "Why opera for teens?'' it asks. "Why not? Opera is a total experience, a cosmic happening of sight and sound. Opera is NOW...Are you prepared to dig opera? It's not for the conventional; it's for the beautiful people of NOW...people who can grasp life. Can you?''   (57)

Grass Roots Cultural Movement Accelerates

The neighborhood and ethnic arts movement continues to grow amid signs that many emerging groups are achieving organizational stability. Moreover, government agencies are beginning to pay greater attention to programs in this area.

In Washington, D. C., the National Arts Endowment's Expansion Arts Program, which was created last year to aid community-based projects, gave matching grants to 59 on-going programs and 21 special summer programs around the country during the current fiscal year.

According to Expansion Arts director Vantile E. Whitfield, official announcement of the $1-million program last December spurred nearly 1,000 requests for information and materials from non-established arts groups. In guidelines prepared for fiscal year 1973 applications, target participants are identified as "Blacks, Spanish-speaking persons, and other ethnic minorities concentrated in urban neighborhoods, as well as residents of the more remote Appalachian, Indian and rural American communities." The program's funding categories include: instruction and training programs; community-based cultural centers with multi-arts programs in operation for at least three years; arts exposure programs; neighborhood arts service organizations; and special summer projects. Guidelines are available on request from Expansion Arts Program, National Endowment for the Arts, Washington, D. C. 20506.

In New York, the State Council on the Arts' Special Programs division, which since 1967 has provided funding and technical aid to ghetto arts programs — $1.5 million during 1971-72 — has witnessed an impressive growth of neighborhood arts activity. "There were only a handful of continuing black and Puerto Rican arts groups in the state when we began," director Donald Harper told *AM*. "But each year we've had steady growth and today there are at least 100 stable and productive groups."

During the past year, Special Programs expanded its thrust into new areas. "One of our most important accomplishments," claims Harper, "is that we've taken techniques developed in ghetto communities and applied them to all culturally isolated ethnic groups."

The pilot arts program of the America the Beautiful Fund has given further impetus to grass roots arts development in New York. Under a matching grant from the state arts council and the Arts Endowment, the Fund, which since 1965 has provided seed grants and technical aid to hundreds of individuals and communities seeking to improve environmental quality, has provided funds to bring arts programs to prisons, hospitals, migrant camps, Indian reservations and rural towns. Thus far, some 72 different communities have been aided with the number expected to reach 100 to 125 by June.

Meanwhile, a grass roots program which has brought teams of humanists and artists into scores of remote communities around the country, for presentations and discussions built around specific themes, is expanding with the opening of two new regional centers. The Humanities Endowment's National Humanities Series, which has presented two-day thematic programs in 89 communities during its first two years, will now have a Midwestern Center at the University of Wisconsin and a Western Center at the University of California, Los Angeles, in addition to its continuing Wilson Center at Princeton.

Among the more ambitious grass roots projects is Aware,

a mammoth, year-round program in New York City designed to utilize artistic and other talents to promote harmony. Conceived by conductor Joseph Eger of the New York Orchestral Society, the program will include scores of street celebrations, ethnic festivals and unconventional happenings beginning May 14th, to culminate in a week-long city-wide festival on September 24th. According to Eger hundreds of volunteers including many artists have responded to the program and permanent headquarters are now being established at 355 Lexington Avenue, New York, N. Y. 10017. (75)

Community Arts Organize New National Alliance

A new national alliance of community arts groups and a separate lobbying force for community-based cultural activities are efforts in the offing. Both have received great impetus from the week-long conference on Community Arts and Community Survival held in Los Angeles this June under the sponsorship of the American Council for the Arts in Education, (ACAE). The meeting, which featured performances, exhibitions and workshops at a number of different inner-city arts centers, attracted representatives of established national arts and education organizations, foundations and government agencies as well as local community arts leaders, and focused national attention on the burgeoning community arts movement.

The idea for a national association had its genesis in mid-1971 when the Los Angeles Community Arts Alliance was organized. As unifying force and information resource center for neighborhood arts groups in Los Angeles, the Alliance was envisioned, even then, as the model for a larger organization, according to its chairman Victor

Franco. Months later, when the ACAE was formulating plans for its annual conference in 1972, its Intercultural Committee suggested community arts as a theme and Los Angeles as a logical site. Through the proposed conference, it was hoped, representatives of ACAE's member organizations, many of them arts educators, would witness a wide range of community arts programs and develop a better understanding of how community arts centers could function within the education system.

A Los Angeles steering committee, which included within its membership representatives of the Alliance, was organized and it developed the conference format and program. Later, the Alliance became a conference co-sponsor, along with U.C.L.A. and Plaza de la Raza, and it prepared two important new publications — a handbook describing the goals and program of more than 50 local community arts groups and a directory of nearly 500 cultural organizations in the Los Angeles area.

The conference was an overwhelming experience for the participating Los Angeles community groups and for the ACAE members and invited guests. At its conclusion, ACAE's board passed a series of resolutions acknowledging the significance of community arts and specifically calling on legislators, government agencies, business, the education field and funding agencies to increase support to arts organizations from minority communities. The Council also recommended that "community and neighborhood arts organizations form unions or alliances that relieve the individual organizations of many administrative and fundraising responsibilities and encourage mutual assistance and solidarity."

"The conference generated tremendous enthusiasm and good will," Franco told *AM*, "and we thought it would be a good idea to develop a national meeting for community

156

groups from all over the country." Franco, who had received a fellowship to Harvard's summer institute in arts administration, took the idea East with him several weeks later and discussed it with community arts people from Pittsburgh, New York, Boston, Cleveland, Chicago and other cities. What emerged from these sessions was the beginnings of a new organization, the National Community Arts Alliance, and a new document, a proposal for a national conference to be held in Washington, D.C. in August 1973. Conference results will determine in large measure the future structure and program of the Alliance. The American Council for the Arts in Education will work with the new organization to help find funding for the two stages outlined in the proposal, a feasibility study and the conference itself.

During the feasibility study stage, a working panel of twelve, with representation from various ethnic areas, will direct the organization. Initially they will prepare a survey of community arts associations and send questionnaires to community organizations throughout the country. "Third World" groups will be asked to indicate their purposes and needs as well as their attitudes towards the proposed conference — its structure, duration, areas of discussion, and overall feasibility. Results of this study will help determine the conference agenda and the criteria for representation at it. Several local and regional meetings would precede the national conference.

A long range goal of the Alliance as stated in its new proposal is, "To organize the community arts into an effective body, able to make its voice heard in the places of power, so that it may continue the essential development of functional arts, responsive to the great needs of its communities."

Meanwhile, another group with roots in Los Angeles,

157

whose principals were also involved in the ACAE conference, has taken the initial steps towards organizing an active lobby for the community arts movement. The Community Arts League, formally incorporated early this summer, has already had one full meeting of some 15 activist groups in Los Angeles who have agreed to work with the program. The League, which recently received firm commitments of support from community groups in Berkeley, Oakland and San Francisco, plans to organize California first before becoming national.

"We're definitely a lobby group," acting president Hazel Stewart told *AM,* "because that's what is needed now." Late this fall, according to Miss Stewart, the League hopes to have prepared a formal list of California groups with which it is involved. It will send this list along with a statement of purposes to communities around the country as a means of attracting more community-oriented groups to its program.

In a description of its goals the lobby group stated, "The League hopes to influence legislation at the national and state level to provide funding which would be directly available to community arts organizations outside of the National Endowment for the Arts and the state arts commissions. In addition, the League will be active in seeking to influence legislation on municipal, county and state levels, which can facilitate the development and funding of community arts."

If plans materialize, the community arts movement will soon be receiving increased support from the National Endowment for the Arts. In the serious discussion stage are such projects as a community arts touring program between cities, a demonstration newsletter and a training program for the administrators of community arts groups.

(76)

Student "Reps" Help Build a Theater's Audience

Arts groups seeking to attract students from nearby colleges to performances can profit from the experience of the Charles Playhouse, Boston's resident professional theater. Since 1959, the Playhouse has conducted a comprehensive student representative program, which has resulted in increased student ticket sales, widespread publicity, and has helped also to establish direct lines of communication between the theater and some 40 New England colleges.

The idea for the program resulted from the theater's inability to reach the more than 100,000 potential theatergoers at colleges in the state through normal communications channels. To find an answer to this problem, Miss Nance Movsesian, publicity director of the Playhouse, recruited a group of student representatives, eight years ago, through the drama and English departments of local colleges. The emphasis at first was on sales ability, with representatives receiving ten per cent commissions for selling subscriptions and organizing theater parties among campus groups.

Over the years, however, the program has broadened greatly and its emphasis has shifted from direct sales to promotion of the theater's productions. Although representatives still receive sales commissions, other benefits, which involve them directly with the theater and its productions, have proved more significant. Each of the representatives now receives two free tickets to every opening night performance, invitations to attend open-end panel discussions during the run of each play, invitations to attend Playhouse social events, a copy of the theater's annual journal, and special permission to attend final production rehearsals. In addition, the theater's artistic and technical staff frequently help student representatives with their theater projects. As a result, the program has attracted many students interested in theater as a career.

The functional phase of the program begins about a week prior to the opening of each Playhouse production. Student representatives, headed by their elected president, meet at the Playhouse with the theater's staff to discuss the production, exchange promotional ideas, and receive posters and other materials for distribution. Guest speakers from various areas of the theater frequently address the group. Minutes of the meeting are mimeographed immediately by the "rep" secretary, who then sends them to any representatives unable to attend the meeting.

Back on their own campuses, the 40 representatives hang Playhouse posters at key locations, contact college newspapers and radio stations to arrange coverage of productions, distribute complimentary tickets in exchange for advertising, discuss upcoming productions with department heads, and send the Playhouse any reviews or pertinent clippings which appear in local papers. In many instances, reps recruit volunteers on their own campuses to help them with their work.

During subscription campaigns, representatives distribute brochures on campus, sometimes so zealously, that the Playhouse claims to have reached every student, faculty and staff member at several colleges. Students also are indirectly responsible for increasing the number of theater parties through their collection and maintenance of up-to-date lists of all campus organizations, which are turned over to the theater's group-sales department.

According to Kenneth S. Opin, a member of the theater's publicity department, the student representative program has been highly beneficial to the Playhouse and to the participating students. "We feel," he told *AM*, "that similar programs would be equally advantageous for other cultural groups in metropolitan areas, or for arts organizations in smaller cities with sizable college populations spread out over a large geographical area." (54)

———————◄•►———————

Rock Group and Arty Party Help Orchestra, Museum Reach Youth

A symphony orchestra which appointed a rock music group, Tranquility Base, as a "resident" unit last fall, plans to continue and perhaps broaden the association during the coming season. According to Elizabeth Webster, executive director of the Hamilton (Ontario) Symphony Orchestra, the rock sextet's informal affiliation was "based on the desire to explore the musical potential of such an association, and to work together as closely and creatively as possible."

The association resulted in four well-received joint concerts — two in the student series, one in the Pop series and a free, outdoor performance sponsored by the City Council to commemorate Hamilton's 125th anniversary— which featured several new and specially commissioned works including Steven Gellman's "Odyssey," a piece for rock group, piano and symphony orchestra. Tranquility Base also appeared with Hamilton Philharmonic conductor, Boris Brott, when he led the Toronto Symphony. The audience response was excellent especially among youngsters. "Tranquility Base's participation has definitely brought out many people to our concerts," Mrs. Webster told *AM*.

The affiliation with Tranquility Base is only one of a number of efforts by the Hamilton Philharmonic to develop programs aimed at new and young audiences. This past season, in addition to its two subscription series, the orchestra has presented 450 in-school ensemble concerts and has gone out into the community to present concerts in libraries, on street corners, and in restaurants at lunch hour. One result of its educational effort is that students now comprise one third of its subscription audience.

162

Both the Hamilton Philharmonic and Tranquility Base are seeking and developing new material for the coming season. Thy will appear together in a Pop series program which will be repeated out-of-town and there is a possibility that the City Council may reschedule the outdoor concert, which attracted 30,000 people but was rained out after half the performance had been completed. Also, the rock group will perform at library concerts.

The reaction of both adult audience members and orchestra players to Tranquility Base has been surprisingly favorable. Mrs. Webster says of them, "This is a particularly attractive and talented group of highly trained musicians who have awed the symphony players by their versatility and improvisational ability."

Another arts organization which has successfully reached out for young audiences is the Seattle Art Museum. Each year during its Northwest Annual exhibition, the museum has hosted an "Arty Party" for students featuring free refreshments, music by a youth combo, and attendance by participating artists.

The party idea was conceived by museum volunteers in 1966 as a way to introduce young people to the museum and its collection and, at the same time, provide a social event for young artists and art history students. Held on a Sunday afternoon in the fall, when the juried Northwest annual is presented, the party has drawn between 1200 and 2,000 students annually.

Volunteer planning begins early with posters, designed by local artists and duplicated by a "generous" printer, distributed to schools. Local merchants provide free beverages, cakes and other refreshments. When contacting schools, the museum requests that a few students from each act as hosts during the party, and spread the word about it in advance. Publicity is usually excellent with downtown and suburban papers providing good coverage and radio stations contributing free spots.   (71)

---◄●►---

Group Sponsors Musical Picnic; Wins New Audience, New Image

A unique cultural event, presened for the first time, helped a Rochester, N. Y., arts institution to: favorably change its image; uncover a new and untapped audience; sell out the house; attract hundreds of congratulatory letters; bring its own staff, students, and performers much closer together; give the community an unforgettable evening; and reap scores of other direct and indirect benefits. The event was the Eastman School of Music's first Musical Picnic, a smorgasbord evening of activities for family groups presented last November. Billed in advance as a low-priced music/fun event, the program included box suppers, prize drawings, costumes, a children's play room, films, a music wheel, and strolling minstrels, all combined with its basic ingredient—good music and lots of it.

The picnic was conceived last July by Eastman's concert manager, Mrs. Ruth Glazer, who was seeking a way to win new audiences for student performances. Perhaps, she thought, the answer was a change in format and concert time; an event which could bring in whole families, who otherwise couldn't afford to buy tickets and pay for dinner, parking and baby sitting. According to Mrs. Glazer, a casual remark by a young Rochester mother provided the final impetus for the resulting program. "I think of the Eastman School," she had said, "as a rather forbidding place where a layman like myself has no place."

164

Planning for the new event proceeded with three goals in mind: to change the "forbidding" image that some local people had of the school; to develop a new audience; and to present a congregation of the arts in a relaxed atmosphere of fun and gaiety at a reasonable price. Although there were many performing units at the school, including student ensembles, it was decided to make the picnic a community event by also inviting such groups as the Brockport Dance Company and the Brickler Marionette Theater to participate in the program.

With banks and leading local corporations aiding in the effort, thousands of Musical Picnic brochures were distributed in advance. Recipients were invited to bring friends, dates, wives, kids, plus their love of music, their appetites and their sense of humor. "We'll furnish the parking, the music, the food, the prize drawing, the fun," the brochure promised. Tickets at $4.00 were good from 5:30 to 9:00 and $3.00 tickets were honored from 6:30 to 9:00. Children's tickets good for the entire event were only $2.00 each. More than a week in advance the entire house was sold out.

On Friday the 13th of November, an overflow crowd of better than 3,300, including nearly 2,000 children, descended on Eastman, colorfully decorated for the occasion with ribbons, balloons and toy animals. Volunteer hosts and hostesses costumed as opera characters greeted the audience. Those with 5:30 tickets sampled the marionette show, the dance performance, and the Imagination Playroom, where Eastman students entertained youngsters. At 6:30 everyone assembled in the big theater for box suppers.

The supper entertainment opened with a color movie, "The Great Concert Hall Caper," which described the adventures of two children locked in an auditorium after hours. Then music took over for the rest of the evening

165

beginning with a Philharmonia Orchestra concert, which included Saint-Saens "Carnival of Animals" narrated by Mayor Stephen May, while artist David Majchrzak also on stage, sketched the animals. Children selected the order of the next four works by spinning a giant musical roulette wheel on stage and the audience then listened to a jazz quintet, an opera aria, the school's trombone choir and its chorale. The Eastman Wind Ensemble completed the concert with three selections, the last an audience participation version of the "On the Mall March," with clapping and whistling.

How successful was the event? The low ticket cost precluded a profit, but the out-pouring of good will more than compensated for this. Here's how Mrs. Glazer described the program's benefits to *AM*. "We more than accomplished our purpose. We completely changed the image of the school from a cold, forbidding, mausoleum-like place to a warm, open-hearted one peopled by friendly, attractive students. We made hundreds of friends and most of the community suddenly woke up to the enormous contributions which the school makes to its cultural life. Best of all, the whole school — faculty, students and maintenance personnel — worked together on a creative project." The program now becomes an annual event.

Cultural groups interested in developing similar programs must be careful not to call them "Musical Picnic," "A Musical Picnic," or even "Music Picnic." Eastman has copyrighted all three versions of the title.   (69)

Holiday Party Brings Publicity, New Audiences

A Boston arts group has started to think about New Year's Eve already and with good reason. Last year, the Handel and Haydn Society's first combination New Year's Eve concert and follow-up party not only drew huge audiences, half of them first-timers at a Society concert, but resulted in outstanding publicity and good will.

According to Society manager Margaret May Meredith, the idea for the New Year's Eve celebration grew out of a desire to do something imaginative "on a night when entertainment is getting pretty mundane." What resulted was a non-subscription performance at Boston's Symphony Hall of Haydn's oratorio, "The Creation," with soloists, chorus and orchestra conducted by Thomas Dunn, followed by a bring-your-own-bottle party at Horticultural Hall, across the street. There were separate admission charges for the two events—the concert was scaled from $3.25 to $7.25 and party admission was $1.50. People could attend the concert or the concert and party, but *not* the party alone.

The concert, which drew outstanding critical notices, ended about 10:15 in the evening and about half the audience of 1800 crossed the street to attend the party. The Society discovered just how popular the event was when the crowd, swelled by party crashers, reached over 1,000. "We could have sold at least another 400 party tickets if room had been available," said Miss Meredith.

Although party-goers brought their own liquid refreshments, the Society contributed food, noisemakers, and entertainment. In the hall's larger room, donated records were played. In the second room there was live entertainment by chorus members doubling as barbershop quartets and do-it-yourself piano playing and singing by audience members. Decorations, helium-filled balloons and large tropical palms, were lent or donated. In keeping with the festive holiday spirit, advance fliers had described the party as a "do-it-yourself creation" and had invited the guests to "dare to dress as you care—White Tie to Tie-dye." Many did.

Although the event occasioned several problems, foremost among them party-crashing and high refreshment costs, the Society viewed the evening as an unqualified success and received scores of "fan" letters. "It certainly gave us a lot of publicity including television interviews and spots," commented Miss Meredith, "and helped promote the rest of our season. Also, it gave us a good focal point for an outstanding choral work and seemed to enhance our image of imaginative programming."

Planning for this year's concert and party has started already. Although the party will again be held at Horticultural Hall, there will be some changes made based on last year's experience, including higher admission prices, better security against gate crashers, and allowing the public to bring in more of the food. (76)

————————◆●▶————————

New Theater Involves Public and Scores
Box Office Success

By totally involving a community in its program, and by emphasizing sound management practices, a new resident theater will be "in the black" when it ends its first full season late this spring. Behind the success of New Haven, Connecticut's Long Wharf Theatre is the drive and philosophy of Harlan P. Kleiman, its executive director. Mr. Kleiman, who holds a combined masters degree from Yale University in industrial administration and drama, contends, "Arts groups must compete in the fiscal market." He has woven this belief into a bold program of management that strikes out into almost every avenue of audience development. Consequently, more than 85,000 persons, including 8,000 season subscribers, are expected to see the company this year.

Every step in the growth of the theater was carefully planned. Even before the organization gained its nonprofit status, it began to develop the nucleus of a resident company by starting a commercial summer theater in Clinton, Connecticut, in 1964. That fall, Mr. Kleiman conducted a detailed survey within a 50-mile radius of New Haven to determine if a professional resident theater was feasible there. The survey showed that there was a sufficient number of professionals, educated people and people with annual incomes of $6,300-$17,000, the groups most likely to support a resident theater. Based on these and other positive results, plans were made for organizing a professional theater in New Haven, headed by Mr. Kleiman and Jon Jory, artistic director.

"There are three keys to having a successful theater," Mr. Kleiman told *AM*. "Make yourself important to the community, it won't let you down; present it with good plays; and make seats hard to get.''

Relying on the strategy that by involving the community it could later approach it for funds, the theater organization asked for advice from persons in the area as to the kind of theater they desired, the plays they wanted to see and the ticket price structure they preferred.

In addition, more than 140 lectures were presented to community groups by about nine speakers trained by the neophyte organization. "You get more by talking to 40 persons," Mr. Kleiman maintained, "than you do from a half page ad."

A goal of $125,000 was set in October, 1964, to initiate the full-time theater. Pledge cards were used initially in lieu of collecting contributions. When the pledges showed that the theater was well on its way to its goal, contributions were collected. By July 4th, the goal was reached.

To prepare for its first full season which began last fall, the company first presented a summer season in New Haven. The summer theater sold out 99 per cent of its seats, with 93 per cent of the audience subscribers.

Prior to the opening of its first fall season, the theater recognized that it was virtually impossible for a new arts group to receive grants from national foundations. Therefore, it devised programs which would bring special groups to the theater through grant support from government agencies like the Office of Economic Opportunity. It also helped local schools to prepare Title III proposals utilizing the services of the company.

To pursue this program to its maximum effectiveness, Long Wharf hired a full-time director of theater development to help groups get grants to come to the theater. "She made back her salary in two weeks," Mr. Kleiman said.

170

Thus far, the theater has developed a program to bring groups of elderly persons and adult literacy students to the theater, a program to bring economically disadvantaged students to the theater, and a school program, including touring, which in its first three months, involved 89 schools from 57 towns. A new program, which would involve the mentally retarded has been proposed and is awaiting approval. It is essential to the operation of these programs that participants are not seated in a special section of the theater but are integrated with the regular audience.

The theater receives additional help from active volunteers like The Long Wharf Hands, a group of 250 women who raise money, help backstage, and were responsible for selling 25 per cent of the season subscriptions.

Advertising has helped the theater pay for much of its literature. Mr. Kleiman said, "Our playbill makes a fortune." Furthermore, a special study guide distributed to 10,000 youngsters participating in the touring program was paid for through advertising.   (46)

The Older Audience

If you offer special performance discounts to senior citizens, remember that many of these people cannot attend the theater or concert hall without a younger person providing transportation. Recognizing this fact, the Studio Arena Theatre in Buffalo, N. Y., which offers weekday reduced rate tickets to older people, allows them to purchase two tickets, instead of just one, upon presentation of Senior Citizen identification cards.   (60)

Young People are Effective Salesmen for Culture

Young people from grade school through college age are helping to "sell" the arts in communities throughout the country. In Salt Lake City, Utah, for example, a Collegiate Advisory Board of the Utah Symphony Orchestra (CABUS) was established this fall to promote the orchestra's activities among college students in the state. The board, like the University of Washington "Whiz Kids" who work with the Seattle Opera, is composed of college students who offer suggestions to the orchestra management on how to reach young people and then implement these suggestions themselves. As its first project, CABUS suggested that the orchestra's president proclaim the week of October 6-11 as Utah Symphony Week on the University of Utah campus. During the well-publicized week, CABUS volunteers manned season ticket booths at three campus locations. The student advisors also have been active in the promotion and sale of "Happy Birthday Ludwig" bumper stickers commemorating Beethoven's 200th birthday.

In a separate youth-oriented program, the orchestra invited all the 2,000 or more foreign students enrolled in the state's universities and colleges to attend an October 22nd concert as guests of the symphony, the local Rotary Club, and the Utah Committee for the United Nations. Preceding the concert, the foreign students were feted at a reception in their honor.

At a younger age level, 10,000 elementary and secondary school students in St. Paul, Minnesota, are promoting the arts council's fund drive by wearing bright green buttons reading, "I invest in the Arts and Science Fund." The buttons are left in a big barrel in the St. Paul Science Museum and youngsters can take them without contributing anything. But most of the juvenile button-takers have deposited upwards of a penny in the coin slot behind the barrel. According to arts council director Marlow G. Burt, "We view the buttons as a fun promotional gimmick which, thus far, has been extremely successful."

In Princeton, New Jersey, high school coeds helped the Princeton Chamber Orchestra reach an untapped ticket sales market and benefit an important community charity drive at the same time. The idea for a cooperative project was initiated in discussions between Gordon G. Andrews, the orchestra's manager and Martin Lombardo, head of the local Multiple Sclerosis campaign. Lombardo had organized teenage girls to work for the M.S. drive in the past, and he thought that the same girls could be succesful in selling season subscriptions, especially to the affluent new residents not being reached by the orchestra. A cooperative arrangement was established in which the girls would sell season tickets and the orchestra, in turn, would contribute ten per cent of these revenues to M.S.

The results, according to Andrews, were "phenomenal" and a check for $560.00 was presented to the health charity. "Not only were we serving a community interest," Andrews told *AM*, "but M.S., in turn, was serving a community activity. The project was so successful last season that we have already finalized plans to do it again this year." (66)

Military Post Audience

Civilian employees residing on a military post a distance
from town can be effectively reached for reserved seat performances through an on-post ticket agency. The Olney
Theatre (Olney, Md.) arrangement with the Fort Meade
personnel service, to collect money and phone in ticket
reservations, has been a gratifying success to the theatre
management.   (6)

Theater Celebrates Anniversary With Full Week
of Free Events

If your organization has a key anniversary or landmark
date coming up, you might let the whole community cele-
brate with you and reap new audiences and widespread
publicity in the process. In Winnipeg, Canada, the Manitoba Theatre Centre celebrated its 15th anniversary this
September with a carefully planned week-long series of
free events culminated by a giant all-night birthday party
at the theater, open to the entire community. Not only was
Open House Week a huge promotional success, but it helped
MTC launch a new season effectively, increased the mailing list by several thousand, encouraged new season subscriptions, and importantly, wound up costing the theater
nothing.

Following an official proclamation of Manitoba Theatre
Centre Open House Week signed by the mayor of Winnipeg
in a public ceremony at the theater, the week opened on
Sunday September 10th with the release of thousands of

balloons (some containing ticket vouchers) from the theater roof. From Monday to Friday, between one and eight p.m. the theater, manned by volunteers and staff, was open to the public for free guided tours which included costume and prop displays and a slide showing of past productions. Coffee and tea were served in the lobby. With the incentive of free single seat and season ticket drawings, visitors filled out forms listing name, address, phone, category—student, adult, or senior citizen—and whether they were new to the theater. Among the visitors were some 3,000 not previously on the mailing list.

Although attendance was open to anyone, special days were designated for certain audiences. Tuesday, for ladies, featured a fashion show of MTC costumes and a wig styling demonstration. Senior Citizens' Day, Wednesday, included bingo games hosted by a local television personality and a bake sale. Saturday morning was set aside for activities and displays for children followed by a family barbeque at noon. Later in the afternoon, an auction of MTC costumes from past productions realized $700 for the theater.

Although the closing event, the free all-night party on Saturday, was the most expensive on the week-long agenda with orchestra and food costs about three fourths of the $1,000 spent during the entire week, (posters, daily refreshments for visitors and the opening ceremonies were the other expense items), the proceeds from bar sales paid back part of the cost. In fact, because of bar and auction proceeds, contributions of prizes and equipment made by local business, and the fact that activities were manned by volunteers and staff, the week actually wound up costing the theater nothing.

The publicity value of the event was excellent according to Penelope Burk of the theater's public relations staff.

"As we run from October to May," Miss Burk told *AM*, "there is, naturally, a slump in publicity over the summer months. This week is valuable to us, because it helps, in a soft-sell sort of way, to announce that MTC is back in business again, and that people should get ready to come back to the theater." The fact that the event is free gives it an interesting twist according to Miss Burk. "For an organization which spends most of the year trying to get the public to give their leisure money to MTC rather than put it somewhere else, a turn-about, where the theater invites the public to come and have fun free of charge, (or at the theater's expense), is a welcome change for both theater and public."

Although this year's Open House marked the theater's 15th anniversary, the event was actually held for the first time at the start of last season, proving perhaps that any anniversary provides a good excuse for an effective season kickoff program.   (77)

Arts Try Cocktails, TV to Reach New Audiences

The search for new audiences has taken arts groups into such unlikely performance settings as prisons and hospitals. It is doubtful, however, if many American performing organizations have ventured into nightclubs, as the Halle Symphony orchestra in England recently did. Beset by financial difficulties, the orchestra looked for a new and untapped source of income and found it at a nightclub in Wakefield. Audience response was excellent as was the fee, and the orchestra signed for four more dates.

The cocktail audience, but in a more traditional setting,

is a target of Town Hall in New York City also. Recently, it initiated a series of Wednesday programs aimed at businessmen, which begin with cocktails in the lobby at 5:00 p.m. followed by a one-hour performance at 5:45. Tickets are priced at only $1.50, thanks to support from the New York State Council on the Arts. The varied program, which runs through the end of May, features such groups as the Paul Taylor and Arthur Mitchell Dance Companies and Jazzmobile. (74)

Using Cassettes

Pre-recorded cassette tapes sold to subscribers can be a useful tool in educating audiences. The Indianapolis Symphony, for example, recorded listening tips and program notes for each concert in its 1970-71 subscription series and offered subscribers either 16 of these programs on eight cassettes for $49.95 (for concert series A) or eight programs on four cassettes for $29.95 (series B or C). The orchestra also offered cassette recorder-players to subscribers at an announced discount price of $39.95. (71)

Opening the Circuit

With large apartment developments beginning to experiment with the use of scheduled closed circuit TV programming for their tenants, arts groups might be able to promote themselves and their activities by getting in on the act early. In New York City, the Queens Council on the Arts now pipes a regular Friday evening program on the arts, featuring live interviews, films and tapes, into some 1300 apartments in Parker Towers from an on-site studio in the housing complex. Soon, the council will start a project designed to teach individuals and arts groups how to operate video equipment. The council envisions an extra benefit from the current experience—it will be prepared to program for cable TV when it comes to Queens.

------◂●▸------

Civic Ballet Draws Huge Crowd With Free Tickets for Christmas

An unknown, pent-up desire to see and enjoy good ballet flooded over the Atlanta Civic Ballet to its delighted surprise, once the price dam was broken by the staging of a free performance on December 27, 1962.

The enthusiasm generated by the announcement that free tickets were available resulted in a rush for tickets by 15,000 people. The experience proved to certain unbelieving citizens that Atlantans really want art, and in large numbers.

The idea of staging a free performance for all comers as a Christmas gift to the city of Atlanta from the dance group, the oldest civic ballet in America, originated with Dorothy Alexander, the founder of the company. Her organization is a non-professional group of high standing.

After discussions between the ballet leaders and the mayor of the city, he agreed to donate use of the municipal auditorium free of charge for the performance. Immediately hundreds of volunteers went to work to raise the money to cover the cost of costumes and sets, payment of union scale to stage and lighting men, and rehearsal and costume rental expenses for the Choral Guild of Atlanta. Businessmen responded with an impressive number of gifts ranging from $100 to $1,000.

A grant was received from the Music Performance Trust Fund of the Recording Industry, covering 75 per cent of the rehearsal and performance costs of the Atlanta Pops Orchestra. The Atlanta Civic Ballet, from directors and staff to dancers, contributed their services free.

By December 20, a week before the scheduled performance, more than 9,000 ticket requests were received. Yet the auditorium held only 4,800 seats. Within the final week another 5,000 requests arrived at the ballet office. Hundreds of letters of gratitude poured in, many from people who said they had never before attended a ballet.

A capacity audience attended a special dress rehearsal, and the December 27th performance, featuring "The Nutcracker," played to a standing room only audience.

On the momentum of the recent success, the ballet company is already planning three "Holiday Gift" performances for next Christmas, and a fund raising effort to finance them has begun. Even in advance of this, however, spontaneous gifts had reached the dance organization. (12)

--- ◄●► ---

Educational Services Develop Interested Cultural Audiences

A Midwest arts council is offering two radio series to its audience, an Eastern drama school is sponsoring a workshop for directors of nearby community theaters, and a state arts council is underwriting an experimental program designed to help public school teachers learn how to look at art. These and a mushrooming number of similar activities are all indicative of the educational services which arts organizations are offering in the hopes of developing knowledgeable and interested audiences.

The Arts and Education Council of Greater St. Louis, for example, has presented a weekly "Living Calendar" radio series since November 1967, as a supplement to the monthly calendar of events which it publishes. Aired on station KFUO, the program highlights cultural events for the coming week and includes "in depth" interviews with cultural newsmakers. Now, in an effort to stimulate critical thinking locally, the Council has initiated a second weekly radio series, "Armchair Critic," presented over the NBC affiliate, KSD. This program is an informal discussion by four informed and intelligent laymen, not necessarily experts, who have seen four local cultural events in advance of the program. The thirteen-week series, which began on March 3rd, featured in its initial program, a discussion of the Pulitzer art collection at the City Art Museum, the film, *The Graduate,* a recent Public Broadcast Laboratory program, and the Loretto-Hilton production of *Six Characters in Search of an Author.*

In Buffalo, the Studio Arena Theatre School inaugurated a twice-weekly workshop for community theater stage directors on January 23rd, with an enrollment of 22 local directors. According to Maurice Breslow, director of the School and instructor for the 30-hour program, "the workshop represents an important step toward establishing the type of relationship that a professional resident theater should have with its community, one in which the theater and the community work together to raise the level of theater throughout the area."

Another theater group, the American Conservatory Theatre, will initiate an Advanced Training Congress this summer. From June 11th through August 18th, the Congress will provide an exchange of new ideas and methods for actor-training, and will offer 400 hours of instruction to more than 250 theater teachers, regional theater leaders and actors.

In the visual arts, the movement toward greater service to the community through the establishment of neighborhood museums continues. In mid-April, the Bedford Lincoln Neighborhood Museum, the first branch of the Brooklyn, N. Y., Children's Museum, will open in a redesigned facility which formerly housed an automobile showroom and pool hall. The new building, which will be open seven days a week, including 12 hours each weekday, is envisioned as a pilot facility to test the feasibility of establishing a series of small neighborhood museums throughout Brooklyn.

Another pilot project in New York City, started in February, is designed to help school children and their teachers respond to and enjoy art and other visual experiences more fully. Sponsored by the New York State Council on the Arts and the New York State Education Department, a "Workshop in Looking," conducted by art critic Katharine Kuh, is bringing together 52 elementary and high school teachers from all subject areas for a series of 12-weekly meetings featuring open discussions and individual experiments. Orthodox lectures and technical terminology are taboo in the meetings. (60)

———————<+●>———————

Informed Audience

Arts groups striving to develop an informed and interested audience might benefit from the experience of the Hartford Stage Company and its "Sunday at Six" program. Initiated last year, and continued because of its popularity, the hour-long panel discussion program for subscribers is held between the matinee and evening performance of a production as it nears the end of its run. Panel participants include the director, producing director, a designer, three actors, and several others, including a moderator. Since most of the audience has already seen the production, the questions are frequently provocative. Summaries of each program are included in issues of the theater's magazine. (63)

———————<+●>———————

144

Museum Offers Tour Information On
Nationwide Arts Attractions

A new information service by the Walters Art Gallery, Baltimore, Md., keeps vacationers and travelers posted on museum activities in other cities. Information on current exhibitions, displays and lectures at museums throughout the country is available from Walters.

Several months ago Geoffrey W. Fielding, Walters' public relations director, wrote to museums asking to be put on their mailing list, and offering to reciprocate. Material is now coming in regularly, from museums in more than 50 cities, on their current shows and events. All sections of the country are represented.

News of the service was publicized in the Baltimore press. Individuals were invited to call the gallery from 9:30 a.m. to 4:30 p.m. to get news of events in museums in other cities, or to stop in and consult an up-to-date file in the first floor office of the membership secretary.

According to Mr. Fielding, requirements for the service are minimal: about a foot of file space, and a few minutes of a secretary's time daily to keep the file current, and to answer phone calls. Walters plans to offer the service on a year-round basis. (18)

———◄●►———

New Study Calls for Involvement of Older Americans in the Arts

Older Americans may be more deeply involved in the arts if a soon-to-be-published study has its anticipated effect. In late September, the report, which outlines a wide range of cultural programs for the aged, will be released by a joint committee representing the Kennedy Center for the Performing Arts and the National Council on the Aging. Titled, *Older Americans and the Arts: A Human Equation,* it discusses approaches which can be utilized by community arts centers and other organizations.

"Many older people already make major contributions to the arts," said John B. Martin, Commissioner on Aging. "But this program, when developed, could involve millions more nationally."

The report suggests ways to encourage retired artists to share their talents with their peers and tells how arts groups can best utilize the resources and abilities of older people. According to Jacqueline Sunderland, project coordinator, its major thrust is "to alert arts managers to a potential rather than a problem."

Copies may be obtained without charge from Mrs. Sunderland at the National Council on the Aging, 1828 L Street, N.W., Washington, D.C. 20036. (76)

———————◄●►———————

Baby Sitters

Do you want young parents in your audience. St. Paul's Community Theater in Brooklyn, N.Y. did and to entice them into coming, it offered a special baby sitting service at the theater on selected weekend dates. Telephone reservations for the service, available at $1.50 per child, were accepted in advance. (71)

Question Mark

A lively forum can help to draw public attention to the arts. In St. Louis, a leading newspaper in cooperation with the Arts and Education Council is providing just such a forum. A regular question and answer column about the arts appears in the *St. Louis Globe Democrat* under the title "Queries on Culture." (65)

Study Groups

Cultural groups attempting to spur public interest by organizing study groups on their programs, should seek to include men as well as women in the sessions. The Seattle Symphony, which organized afternoon study groups 15 years ago conducted by university teachers and members of the orchestra, recently added Sunday evening meetings to its schedule. As a result, many men now attend these programs. (43)

Behind the Scenes

Arts groups can encourage a direct interest in their activities by initiating behind-the-scenes tours of their facilities. If the organization's work is diverse and extensive enough for an interesting tour, the group can even charge a fee for the visit. In New York City, for example, the American Museum of National History offers annual "Behind the Scenes" tours where it shows visitors how its staff simulates a natural effect in displays. The fee is $2.00 for non-members and $1.50 for members. (39)

Museum Seeks Audience Through Radio Concerts

A museum seeking to interest music lovers in its art collection introduced a special "picture of the week" service which is broadcast during the intermissions of concerts it sponsors.

In Washington, D. C., the National Gallery of Art uses the intermissions during its weekly Sunday night concert series to discuss a single great painting. To help listeners follow the discussions, the Gallery offers them reproductions of each painting printed on 11" x 14" heavy paper, suitable for framing. Individual prints are sold for 25 cents each. A subscription, which provides listeners with a reproduction a week for the entire 22 week series running from October 4th through February 28th, is $5.50. Each picture is accompanied by a short text and a check list of all the pictures in the series. The service was described in detail to listeners during the intermission of the season's first concert.

According to John Walker, director of the Gallery, a similar idea was a great success in Holland. He hopes that listeners' curiosity will be so stimulated by the discussions that they will visit the Gallery to see the paintings they have heard described.

Tying in with the discussions is an added service offered by the Gallery. During the week following each broadcast, two discussions a day are held at the museum in front of the painting described over the radio the previous Sunday. (31)

————◄•►————

187

Special Effects

A dramatic off-stage touch can help to call extra attention to an unusual event or exhibition. When Theatre Calgary in Alberta, Canada presented a production of *Dracula* this season, it had nurses from St. John's Ambulance on duty to heighten the play's atmosphere. During the production's run, however, one audience member fainted and four became hysterical, necessitating aid from the nurses and resulting in some added publicity for the play.   (70)

Happy Time

An occasional fun event can be a pleasant experience for both the arts group and its audience. This season, as part of its "Six for the Show" concert series, the Indianapolis Symphony presented "Mystery Night at the Symphony." Printed programs, instead of listing the works to be performed, asked the audience to identify them by filling in blanks or selecting from multiple choice answers. Most of the 11 works were legitimate if unusual and unfamiliar, and the program was highlighted by a performance of Malcolm Arnold's "A Grand, Grand Overture for Orchestra, Organ, Rifles, Three Hoovers (vacuum cleaners) and an Electric Floor Polisher." Guest artists on the non-traditional instruments included Indianapolis's deputy mayor, a mayoral aide, local broadcasting personalities, a soprano and the orchestra's harpist, publicist and manager.   (70)

Free Bus Lures Tourists to Cultural Institutions

By working together, cultural groups can use nearby tourist attractions to increase attendance at their own facilities. For the second straight summer, Philadelphia's Academy of National Sciences and the Franklin Institute, its neighbor across the street, have joined in the sponsorship of a free bus service bringing visitors from Independence Hall, a prime tourist attraction, to the museums and then returning to Independence Hall. The bus service is run on a regular hourly schedule from Tuesday through Sunday of every week.

The idea for the promotion was conceived last year as a means of boosting lagging attendance at each of the museums during the summer months. It was considered successful in its first season when more than 4700 tourists used the bus service. This year the Philadelphia Museum of Art joined with the Academy and the Institute in sponsoring the project, which was launched on June 16th as a climax to "Museum Week" proclaimed by Mayor James H. J. Tate of Philadelphia.

Busses are rented from Philadelphia's public transportation company and the overall costs including rental, flyers and signs are pro-rated among the three museums, based on 1963 attendance figures. Thus, between June 16th and September 5th, the height of the tourist season, the museums are sharing the bus rental charge of $50.50 per day and $44.00 on Sundays with the Academy paying 24 per cent, the Institute paying 35 per cent and the Museum of Art paying 41 per cent. While the bus also stops at the City's Hospitality Center, a starting point for the tours of many out-of-town visitors, the Center does not share in the cost of the service.

Independence Hall has been helpful in publicizing the service. It has placed a signpost announcing the tour at its regular bus stop and it displays posters and bus schedules at its information counter. Guides end their tour of the Hall by mentioning the service to tourists.

A cooperative promotional campaign by the three sponsors has included radio and television spot announcements, news releases and attractive flyers sent to hotels, motels, tourist agencies and other museums in the area. In addition, each of the sponsors promotes the tour in its own institution with posters and schedules, and guards and cashiers invite tourists to visit the two other museums. The tour bus itself is an effective promotional device with two large banners attached to each of its sides.

Although the free bus idea has great potential, Mrs. Libby Demp Forrest of The Academy of Natural Sciences noted that dealing with a public transportation company subject to union demands has also created several problems. "I would caution other institutions," Mrs. Forrest told *AM*, "to carefully study all the aspects before they institute a similar service." (29)

Dinner Stop

Performing arts groups with inadequate parking facilities may be able to arrange parking at hotels and restaurants with a free bus link to their door. To attract dinner guests, two hotels in Minneapolis offer these services to pre-concert diners later attending performances of the Minneapolis Symphony Orchestra. (39)

190

At Your Service

Is your facility located in an out-of-the-way, impossible-to-reach-by-foot area? The Long Wharf Theatre in New Haven, Connecticut, located a mile from the town's center and directly off a highway connector, worked out a way to attract those people who would not ordinarily attend performances because of the transportation problem. A limousine, rented for a nominal $15.00 an hour, shuttles audience members to and from a center city hotel and the theater. Since the distance is short, there is not much waiting, and the two to three trips necessary take under 15 minutes. The house manager coordinates loading of the limousines. (62)

Charter Bus

Attendance at downtown auditoriums with limited parking area can be increased through charter bus service provided for ticket holders. In addition, riders will be in their seats on time. The Utah Symphony in Salt Lake City runs a special bus which stops at six convenient locations to transport passengers to and from the concert. The charge is 50 cents. Advance reservations are made by phoning the orchestra office. (13)

Orchestra Invites Its Audience to Select Programs It Prefers

An arts group can gain greater identification with its public and reap publicity benefits at the same time, by inviting its audience to indicate the programs it prefers. In Washington, D. C., the National Symphony Orchestra asked the 30,000 persons on its mailing list to vote for the composers they most wanted to hear played on orchestra programs. Questionnaires were mailed in August as an insert in concert season brochures, and answers began being tabulated in September for November publication.

As a result of the survey, which drew more than a thousand responses, the orchestra received excellent local publicity at the time the poll was being taken and later when the results were published. The questionnaire was printed on a pull-out envelope which was self-addressed to the orchestra and which also contained a subscription order form for tickets to orchestra series. The orchestra received many requests for the questionnaire from persons who were not on its mailing list.

According to the orchestra, the poll was taken to enable its music director, Howard Mitchell, to ascertain the tastes and interests of his audience.

The repertory of soloists and the music to be played by guest conductors was already set at the time the questionnaires were mailed, as were the full programs for early season concerts. However, Dr. Mitchell, who instituted a similar survey ten years ago, indicated that he would be guided by the replies. He stated that for future programs later this season and next season, he will pay greater attention to the symphonies of Gustav Mahler. Although Mahler's symphonies were not box office successes in the past, there is a strong rebirth of interest in his scores, according to the survey which ranked him eighth among the symphony composers the audience most wanted to hear. Beethoven, Sibelius, Mozart, Brahms and Tchaikovsky were rated in the top five positions, in that order.

Results of the survey were tabulated by volunteers. The poll was subdivided into groupings of symphony subscribers and non-subscribers, and these groups were further divided by age into those under 40 and those over 40.

One part of the questionnaire asked "How do you usually hear about National Symphony concerts?" Among the nine answers respondents could check were newspaper advertisements, radio interviews and direct mail. Other questions asked "Which newspapers do you refer to most for music information?" and "Which radio station do you usually listen to for music information?" Results obtained from such questions will help the orchestra plan future promotional campaigns.

Questions listed specific works and composers, although space was left in the third section of the survey to write in "compositions you would like to hear." While the first part of the questionnaire asked for composers' works the audience would like to hear, the second section asked for an indication of preferences in miscellaneous orchestral works, such as overtures and suites. Dr. Mitchell said he was highly pleased with both the quality and quantity of the response. (34)

Show Tempts Audiences With a Free First Act

In an attempt to stimulate waning attendance caused by unfavorable reviews, an off-Broadway producer recently instituted a free first act policy, with theatre-goers paying for seats only if they stayed to see the concluding two acts. Bro Herrod, producer of *The Chief Thing*, at New York's Greenwich Mews Theatre, initiated the policy one week after the play opened.

Although people heard about the plan, few took it seriously and nobody took advantage of the offer. The show closed a week after the policy went into effect. Herrod told *AM* that the plan didn't work because it wasn't promoted prior to the show's opening, before the reviews were published. He intends to reinstate the policy again with a full pre-opening promotion for a new production later this summer. (17)

---◀•▶---

Audience Eats Dinner on Lawn and Stays to See Shakespeare

If visitors to your arts festival complain of crowded conditions in local restaurants, you may be interested in the arrangement which the Oregon Shakespearean Festival Association in Ashland, Oregon has worked out with a local hotel.

The hotel's management, aware of the pressures upon local restaurants during the summer festival, devised a plan by which visitors to the Shakespeare plays can eat in the relaxed atmosphere of the 100-acre Lithia Park (where the performance is held) and still attend the theatre without a last minute rush.

The theatregoer reserves a "gourmet basket" by calling the hotel, giving his seat number, the date and time, then picks up a take-along ticket. On the night of the performance, he presents his ticket at the hotel, picks up the picnic basket (priced at $2.75 each or $5.50 for two), goes to the park, selects a quiet spot and eats his dinner in the park. Then he strolls to the theatre.

Although the Oregon Shakespearean Festival is not directly involved in this promotion, Festival officials voted on the idea at the regular board meeting in April. The consensus was that the gourmet picnic would indirectly advertise the Shakespearean plays and allow visitors to take advantage of Lithia Park or the mountain forest regions which surround Ashland. (16)

The Way to an Audience's Heart

Monticello College in Godfrey, Ill., helped make the appearance there of the Sahm-Chun-Li Korean dance group a particularly memorable and gala evening by arranging with a local restaurant for it to serve a specially-prepared Oriental dinner the night of the performance. The arrangement resulted in good local publicity as well. Ticket prices did not cover the cost of the meal, but college announcements made a point of advertising the dinner menu at the co-operating restaurant. (26)

Orchestra, Audience, Meet and Eat

One way to strengthen the ties between a performing arts group and its public is to bring artists and audience together in an informal setting. An organization that does this regularly is the Seattle Symphony Orchestra which holds a Tuesday night open house at a local restaurant. The public is invited to come and meet its conductor, Milton Katims, and the guest artist of the evening. Started last fall, the program has won enthusiastic response, according to Mrs. Hugh E. McCreery, manager of the orchestra.

The symphony group takes over most of the space in a first class restaurant immediately after the Tuesday evening concert. Those who hold a ticket stub from the performance are granted a 20 per cent discount on any food purchased. The restaurant is happy to offer the discount because it receives an increased flow of business at an hour when turnover is usually slow.

No formal program is presented, but everyone has a chance to meet and chat with the artists. Attendance averages 60 to 75. (3)

Visual Device

A visual device which members of an audience may keep as a souvenir can help to arouse interest in a cultural organization's event. For example, at a lecture on ancient Greece given recently at the Walters Art Gallery in Baltimore, Maryland, a paper with a rendering of an ancient Greek sign was distributed free of charge to the entire audience. (32)

196

THE ARTS AND SOCIETY

Report Focuses National Attention on Arts

Foundations should increase their giving to the arts, the Federal Government should provide matching grants to meet the capital needs of performing arts organizations, and corporations should accept the responsibility for helping to support the arts in their communities. These are some of the key recommendations made in the newly-published Rockefeller Panel Report, *The Performing Arts: Problems and Prospects.*

The report, based on information obtained from research, personal interviews and specially commissioned papers, is expected to focus considerable national attention on the current and future needs of professional, non-profit performing arts organizations.

In a chapter on foundation support, for example, the 30-member panel suggests that local foundations provide continuing operating support to performing arts organizations in their communities, while the large foundations, at the national level, encourage experimental projects of all kinds. The report asks for flexibility in foundation giving practices and suggests that foundations which have not previously contributed to the arts can change direction if they wish. The panel urges arts groups to recognize the differences between foundations, to prepare better cases for support and to improve administrative practices before approaching foundations.

In its discussion of the economics of the performing arts, the panel indicates that earned income, including box office receipts, can never make non-profit groups self-sustaining and in fact, "the gap between earned income and total costs can be expected to widen in the years immediately ahead." It urges performing arts groups to broaden their base of support through programs of community service accompanied by energetic and skillful public education programs. United fund raising for the arts, a method now used by 14 arts councils, is suggested as an efficient and attractive means of increasing support from a community.

Corporate dollars, says the report, can be the difference between life and death to an arts group and corporations should be stimulated to use the five per cent deduction allowed them for charitable contributions. Approaches to business by arts groups should be well-documented and related to the "personality" of the corporation from which aid is sought. Increased corporate giving to the arts could be stimulated, it is suggested, if an organization for the arts, patterned on the Council for Financial Aid to Education, were created.

Expansion of the professional performing arts is a key panel recommendation. "In the long run," states the panel, "it is essential to encourage formation of resident organizations. In the meantime, there is perhaps more pressing need for regional organizations designed specifically to serve large geographic areas." Envisioned by the panel as operating on a year-round basis are 50 permanent theater companies, 50 symphony orchestras, six regional choral groups and six regional opera and dance companies, in addition to the resident and touring companies already in existence. Cooperation between communities, between state arts councils and between existing and new arts centers, which in the latter case could form regional and perhaps national networks for touring groups, is deemed essential.

198

Corresponding to the need for more performing organizations, according to the panel, is a need for a wide variety of service and information organizations in each art. As one of its key recommendations the panel urges the creation of "an independent national information center that can assume an important and continuing role in the development of the performing arts." This organization would gather data, circulate bulletins, undertake research projects and cooperate with existing national service organizations.

Stressed throughout the report is the need for better management in the arts. More effort, on a more formal basis, to provide good training for arts administrators is required, including perhaps, a special school for arts administration.

The boards of arts organizations are not as widely representative of the community as they should be and board members are recruited too casually, according to the report. It recommends careful screening of potential board members, and board rotation procedures. The report recommends that large arts organizations consider having a full-time paid president or chief executive.

Government at all levels should remove tax burdens and legislative restrictions on the arts, states the report. Local government should help strengthen community groups and include the arts in the school curriculum. The panel endorses the concept of state arts councils and their sponsorship of touring arts programs. Federal aid, it says, can be most effectively provided through matching grants to meet the capital needs of the arts groups.

Although the report continually stresses the fact that the performing arts today are in trouble it also asserts, "the potential for successful development of the performing arts is tremendous."   (36)

Culture's Role in the Community is Receiving Wider Recognition

The arts battle for recognition and status in the community continues with some positive points scored in recent months. This January, for example, in a precedent-shattering move, the Chicago Press Club awarded a plaque to the 106-member Chicago Symphony Orchestra as 1971's "Chicagoan-of-the-Year." In Seattle, the County Board of Realtors named an arts administrator, Glynn Ross, general director of the Seattle Opera, as recipient of the city's coveted First Citizen Award.

In April, the arts case for increased federal funding was given a boost by a leading national magazine, *Saturday Review*. An editorial by president and editor-in-chief John J. Veronis strongly supported the Partnership for the Arts' priority of $200-million in federal funds by 1976.

In the education field, greater recognition for the arts has come with the granting of credits to students participating in arts activities outside the classroom. Long Beach State College in California has awarded credits for off-campus dance activities and Hunter College students in New York are receiving credit for working with the city's Cultural Affairs Department. In Mahopac, New York, high school credits are being given to students participating in the program at the Belle Levine Arts Center.

A somewhat whimsical recognition of the growing cultural audience was found in a letter accompanying a mailing of South Carolina's February ETV program guide. The letter bore the simple heading, "Dear Arts Fan." Recognition came to the New York State Council on the Arts when it became the subject of a song in a professional theater production, perhaps the first government arts agency in history to earn this singular distinction. New

200

York's Equity Library Theatre, in its between-the-acts appeal for funds, held during the entire two-week run of *One for the Money,* featured an original number written by composer-conductor Fred Roffman. A cast member, lamenting the fact that the future of the Equity Library program was in jeopardy because the state council did not renew its grant, sang such lyrics as, "I've got the New York Council on the Arts blues/ Can't lose 'em/ Because the New York Council cancelled their dues." (75)

A Helping Hand

A community's better-known arts organizations might lend a helping hand to less established groups and help themselves at the same time. This past fall, Allied Arts of Seattle, an arts council, organized a Survival Series with each of the four events featuring a different small arts group in a performance followed by a discussion. Designed to widen the audiences for the less-established groups and give them financial support, the programs were planned also to give Allied Arts members and supporters an opportunity at bargain prices to see groups that they had heard of but had never seen in performance. The subscription price was $10.00 with $2.00 from each single performance price of $2.50 going to the producing group. Although there were some difficulties because of the program's newness most subscribers considered it a success. The result? An expanded series of six events is being planned for next fall. (79)

Institute in the Netherlands Studies
Sociology of the Arts

The Dr. E. Boekman Foundation of Amsterdam grew out of a realization by arts leaders and social scientists in the Netherlands that the development of a healthy cultural life could be realized best through a scientific study of the sociology of the arts.

Established in November, 1963, under the auspices of the Netherlands Federation of Artists, the Boekman Foundation includes diverse aspects of the arts in its purview. Among them are: the social position of the artist; the relationship between government and the arts; the arts audience; the formation of sociological theories of art; the function and meaning of the arts in society; and the social implications of a work of art.

Within this framework, there are four areas of concern: documentation, research, conference organization and coordination of activities.

In its two years, the Foundation has made considerable progress. It has organized an index card system listing 9,000 publications from throughout the world that relate to the sociology of the arts. It is in the process of building up a detailed library in the field, with special emphasis on statistics and research projects. Also, it is publishing bibliographies on the sociology of the arts. These are available to individuals and organizations conducting research in this area.

In the research field, the Foundation carries out investigations on its own initiative, and at the request of others, and publishes the results whenever possible. A 1964 study on the attitude of young people toward the theater in Holland, the first of its kind, was published in September.

The Foundation also organizes an annual two-day conference on a topical problem of the arts. A report of the 1964 conference, on how the contemporary artist communicates with his public, was recently published. The 1965 conference, held last month, was devoted to the changing function of public organizations and trends in the theater-going public.

In its fourth major area of concern, coordination, the Foundation seeks to avoid duplication of effort. As the central Dutch arts information agency, it collects data on developments at home and abroad.

The Foundation is eager to collect material from America on the sociology of the arts, including conference reports, research papers and published articles. It is located at Keizersgracht 609, in Amsterdam. (43)

The Pressure of Non-Art . . .

Cultural programs are now being presented under the auspices of churches, colleges, businesses and many other organizations whose primary objective lies outside the realm of art. The college wants to educate. The church to inspire. The business to profit. But how do such concerns correspond with the needs of art? Or, to raise in another way a question that will become increasingly important: does sponsorship by a non-art institution create unusual extrinsic pressures on the artist and his work, If so, what should be done about them?

Two recent events suggest the dangers. The first occurred at Baylor University in Waco, Texas, where the drama department's production of *Long Day's Journey Into Night* was shut down because the president of the university, Abner McCall, received complaints about "offensive phrases and words" in the O'Neil play. The university is operated by the Texas Baptist Convention, and McCall, in a letter to trustees, assured them that in the future the drama department would avoid plays containing profanity, or would bowdlerize them. Moreover, he said, no plays would be presented that ridicule the Christian faith. This position lead the respected head of the drama department, Paul Baker, to resign. He was joined by his wife, 11 staff members, and a mathematics professor. (The resignation does not affect Mr. Baker's widely acclaimed work with the Dallas Theatre Center, with which Baylor is associated.)

The second case is that of the artist at the University of Mississippi who was arrested after exhibiting an abstract painting having to do with the recent anti-Negro riots on the campus. Assistant Professor Ray Kerciu was

204

charged with indecency, obscenity, and desecration of the Confederate flag. Suit was brought by a law student who is running for a seat in the state legislature. Recently, the suit was dropped.

In both cases the artist has been placed in an untenable position. Who, for example, at Baylor is to decide what plays do or do not ridicule the Christian faith? Is this always so clear? Or is it open to interpretation? And in Mississippi, is the university or the state to inform the artist what subject matter he must avoid?

It is encouraging that in both cases the men under fire have received broad support based firmly on the principle of artistic or academic freedom. Mr. Baker has been snapped up by Trinity University, a Presbyterian school in San Antonio. And in Mississippi the local chapter of the American Association of University Professors has called on the school, itself, to undertake Prof. Kerciu's defense. "If this is not done," the educators declared, ". . . the individual members of this faculty can only conclude that they will be abandoned to the whims of any pressure group which may be offended by the conscientious and legitimate exercise of their academic obligations."

Seldom do cases arise in which outside pressures are so easily identifiable. But as more artistic activity comes under what might be called "non-art" sponsorship, it becomes increasingly vital to think out, in advance, the appropriate relationships between artist and auspice, and to frame these in terms that encourage, rather than hedge, the right to experiment, to innovate and to express individual conviction. (15)

Need for Arts and Society Research Cited

By

Ralph Kohlhoff and Joseph Reis

An investigation of the role of the fine arts in society raises questions about their value, viability and impact as agents of change. . . . That there is interaction between art and society is unquestionable, but the extent, the type, and the quality of this interaction in our culture has not received the attention needed.

Sociologists and psychologists, in creating their models, often tend to exclude a consideration of the interaction of what could be called aesthetic phenomena with the phenomena of human behavior. They seem to ignore the gross involvement of human beings in our culture with the great varieties of visual and audio material that are a fundamental part of our environment. Because 150 million individuals in our society are involved for extended periods of time with the works of writers and artists who create for mass consumption through television, we can no longer consider these works a peripheral influence to behavior. In modern architecture and in the design of automobiles, furniture, utensils, and clothing, we can see the pervasiveness of the artist's role in society. The enormous amount and variety of aesthetic phenomena in our environment should begin to be considered in terms of their value and impact on human behavior.

Using the research methods of the sciences and the knowledge and training of art, a new role could be created, that of the arts-and-society researcher. The techniques of information gathering would be borrowed from the social sciences, but with a background of training in the fine arts, the researcher would use his artistic insight and understanding to decide what questions would be asked and what information would be sought.

The arts-and-society approach to research is to use the methodology and techniques of pure research for influencing social change. . . . The dynamics of the interaction of aesthetic phenomena and social phenomena is such that objective description would have little validity. Unlike the physical sciences where the phenomena to be studied can be isolated and uninfluenced by the researcher, the researcher of society begins as a part of the phenomena he is studying. In this way his research when completed, and even in the process of completion, tends to influence the phenomena studied. . . . Arts-and-society research should admit its involvement in the phenomena it proposes to study and should realize its role of influencing change.

The basic contribution which arts-and-society research will bring to the field of fine arts will be the collection of organized material about the arts in sociological rather than philosophical terms. . . . Among the many questions developing out of a consideration for arts and society would be the following: What is the institutional framework for the fine arts? Who controls that framework? How does the institutional framework of fine arts differ from that which is called commercial art? Who controls the institutional framework of commercial art? Is there a justifiable dichotomy between the arts forms prevalent in the mass media, which have great impact on the broadest segments in our society, and the fine art forms which seem to be created for a cultural elite? Is there a cultural elite, and, if so, what is its nature? Is there social stratification in the arts, and, if so, what is its nature?

As is generally the case in any field of study, the more information made available to use, the greater the tendency toward developing innovations. Thus by collecting data within a framework not previously considered important as an area for inquiry, arts-and-society research very likely will stimulate many kinds of innovations. The ultimate goal of such research and the resulting stimulation for innovations will, hopefully, be the contributions which the fine arts can make to the general improvement of our society.

(50)

PART TWO: ARTS ORGANIZATIONS AND
MANAGEMENT

Chapter III – The Organization

Chapter IV – Operations

Chapter V – Facilities for the Arts

Chapter III – The Organization

THE BOARD OF DIRECTORS

The Board of a Cultural Organization: Its Structure and Its Significance

By

Richard Trenbeth

Each year an increasing number of able individuals willingly take on the responsibilities of board membership in cultural groups. A few strong institutions may be the lengthened shadow of a single man, but many more are the outgrowth of countless board and committee meetings. By working collectively, boards of trustees or directors provide a continuity and permanence to the organization, and counterbalance the effects of a single strong opinion. No matter how interminable the regime of a durable chief executive may seem, the collective control, assistance and wisdom of a strong board usually will long outlast the influence of any one person.

Broadly speaking, an organization's board is comparable to the legislative branch of government. Board members represent many different segments of the community. Because they both influence and are influenced by the groups they represent, board members, as a rule, synthesize varying points of view into broad policy which is widely acceptable. In this sense, even the most aristocratic of boards (and they seem to abound in cultural organizations) do represent the spirit of democracy at work.

One of the broad functions of a board is to interpret the organization's program to the community. A well-informed board member can tell his friends and associates how the program is going to affect the community. And in so doing he is in a position to be the most effective fund raiser for the organization and its projects—as indeed he should be, for the right to control and improve plans carries with it the responsibility for seeing to it that money is available to accomplish those plans.

The ideal board should be so constituted that its members have a wide variety of special skills, talents, and contacts that can be used for the benefit of the organization. No board should expect its members with special skills to give an unlimited amount of volunteer work in the field in which they earn their living. Board service should be a refreshing avocation rather than a way of continually contributing professional services.

Some large cultural agencies may have more than one type of board. Usually the basic unit is the controlling board of trustees or directors who have direct legal responsibility for the institution and the authority to hire the staff at all levels. Occasionally, there are functions that the controlling board cannot carry out itself; these may be assigned to specially created auxiliary boards.

Women's boards or auxiliaries are often formed to handle official entertaining or to staff projects that require constant volunteer help. Some larger art organizations also form young men's groups for specific assignments. Members of such groups get many opportunities for thorough indoctrination in the affairs of the organization. These special men's groups thus frequently become a kind of training group for future appointments to the controlling board. Sometimes the presidents of auxiliary boards are ex-officio members of the controlling board.

212

A third type can be classified as associational boards because their only responsibility is connected with the affairs of a membership group or satellite association, as in the case of opera guilds, friends of the orchestra, theater, and so on. Like auxiliary boards, these groups not only carry out specific duties but also broaden the circle of informed persons capable of interpreting the agency's program. They also broaden the base of financial support.

Why do people join boards and give freely of their time and energy? A number of studies indicate that some of the most important motivations are: a sense of civic duty, sometimes related to carrying on a family tradition; persuasion by friends or business associates (occasionally on the boss's orders); interest in the field (art, music, drama); recognition, honor, prestige, and a challenging opportunity to learn something new.

One characteristic that distinguishes cultural board members from trustees of health, education and welfare organizations, is a nearly professional knowledge of the cultural area served. Non-cultural trustees rightly feel unqualified to compare their own ideas on technical subjects with the ideas of staff professionals trained in medicine, education or social welfare. In the arts many an informed collector of art, or student of symphonic music or opera can, and often will challenge the opinions of the staff professionals. Cultural boards also tend to be higher in prestige value, especially among women, who often look upon board membership in certain organizations as a symbol of having arrived socially.

Cultural boards range from five to 50 members, somewhat smaller than boards in other fields. Arts organizations often make less effort to indoctrinate new members and to keep them informed, either because the staff is overburdened or because it underestimates the importance of such orientation.

Another rather common, and regrettable, difference between cultural boards and those of most other agencies is inadequate attention to wisely constructed by-laws and other written directives, procedures and policies. Some organizations lack even a basic statement of objectives as a basis for planning their program. (20)

How to Organize the Board of a Cultural Group

By

Richard Trenbeth

Although cultural boards vary considerably in size, scope of responsibility, and complexity, most of them follow a similar pattern in organization. At the top is the key man, the board chairman. In many cultural organizations he is called the president. Two or more vice-chairmen are common and the treasurer is sometimes a volunteer and occasionally a paid officer. In large institutions the secretary almost always is a salaried staff member.

Board business is carried out in committees, the number of which depends on the complexity of the organization. Almost all have executive committees composed of the officers and top committee heads. When physical properties are important—as they are to museums and theaters— there generally is a committee to make major decisions on managing and maintaining the property. Most agencies have finance or budget committees to plan budgets and manage endowment funds.

Cultural groups often overlook the desirability of a personnel committee to keep informed about salary scales in comparable organizations—and especially on trends in college faculty and staff salaries, permitted outside sources of income, and contributory investment plans for retirement. All organizations should have a development committee to supervise planning, publications and publicity, membership sales, and fund raising.

Functional committees may vary in accordance with the program. Museums usually have exhibitions committees, orchestral groups will frequently have a committee concerned with concert material and guest artists, and theaters generally have a committee concerned with the types of plays to be offered, guest stars, and other production problems.

Miscellaneous committees may include one on the business aspects of a museum store, another on selling advertising in programs for concerts and theatrical productions, and perhaps a library committee when that is a function of the organization. An increasing number of organizations have permanent nominating committees to keep a constantly watchful eye for potential board replacements.

The effective board, of course, is much more than an organization chart with impressive boxes connected by solid and dotted lines. It is a uniquely qualified group of people acting together in delicate balance with each other and with the needs and opportunities of the community which can be fulfilled through the skills of the professional staff.

Ideally, however, there must be clearly understood channels of operation on overall policy with some shortcuts to deal with specific problems. On broad policy matters, the chain of command must be from the chairman through the board to the chief salaried executive and thence to the department heads. To handle specific activities, the wise chairman and executive may delegate authority to department heads to work directly with board committee chairmen or other qualified individual board members. All such arrangements, however, should be subject to frequent review and direction.

A university president propounded the Rule of Three W's for board membership. The three W's are Wisdom, Work, and Wealth, and the rule states that a man possessing any two of the three characteristics is a good prospect for board membership. For a cultural board, however, something more is definitely needed. And that something more is at least a quiet enthusiasm for and knowledge of the cultural discipline in which the board member's organization functions.

Most arts organizations are fortunate in having among the most interested people in the community a number of men or women with a flair for advertising, marketing, public relations, and related promotional work. Board members with these talents must assume leadership in impressing the rest of the board with the importance of the consumer. If the agency is a small one without an adequate promotional staff, such a board member can be invaluable in directing the complex job of marketing the organization's services and perhaps even assigning his own employees to help with writing and production.

In larger organizations, however, the promotionally oriented board member must be careful to maintain his role as an effective teammate of the professional staff, but he should guard against any inclination to require all details to clear through him for final decisions.

Some boards are constituted almost by formula. Some of the factors taken into consideration include the proportion of members by sex and by age, religious, ethnic, and economic status, location of residence, special capacities for board work, experience on other boards, and potential for future board leadership. There is a tendency in older, well established cultural organizations to lean toward an aristocratic rather than a democratic board. The post-war years have clearly indicated that an above-average lay knowledge of the arts is not limited to the economically or socially favored few, nor is the willingness to work for an organization. For a truly dynamic, working board there is much to be said for including in its membership at least two or three intelligent, responsible people who have not yet "arrived" in either a social or business sense, but who show considerable promise as effective board members.

No organization whose board represents a narrow perspective or a hyperconservative approach can ever hope to win wide participation or support.   (21)

Work of Cultural Boards Needs Periodic Review — Check These 12 Points

By

Richard Trenbeth

Books can be written on the importance of adequately orienting and indoctrinating new board members and then keeping them informed and interested. The effective executive is one who cheerfully spends his time with new board members in an effectively planned, thorough indoctrination program, followed by specific job assignments.

Although boards theoretically work only on the policy level, the business, legal and fund raising aspects of the organization permit assignments which go more deeply into administration. There are other areas in which board work can and should go far beyond policy level. Some board members may be most effective in speaking assignments and public relations appearances. Others may prefer behind-the-scenes work cultivating and then soliciting prospects for large gifts.

The wise board chairman steers his fellow trustees away from attempting to take over types of work and decisions that should be handled by experienced professional executives and staff.

The work of an executive and his staff bears directly on the amount of time required of the effective board member. On some boards the staff planning, research and documentation is so thorough that committee and board meetings are brisk and businesslike, requiring only major decisions instead of endless discussion. In such fortunate organizations, a board member may be highly effective in three or four hours of actual work each month, whereas in others good board work requires 30 or 40 hours monthly.

Periodic evaluation of the work of a board is both healthy and necessary for the continuing welfare of a relatively volatile arts organization. A series of financially disastrous concert or theatrical seasons, for example, may require a drastic change in board policies and personnel that might have been avoided through a frank assessment of continuing trends.

Who should make the evaluation? In his excellent book *The Effective Board* (Association Press, 1960), Cyril O. Houle observed that the rating should be done by anyone interested, and particularly by the chairman of the board, the executive committee, any board member (especially new members) and the salaried executive. To this list could be added a qualified public relations or management consultant hired from the outside.

The rating scale offered by Prof. Houle includes the following characteristics, to be rated as excellent, good, average, poor or very poor:

1. The board should be made up of effective individuals who supplement one another's talents.

2. It should represent the interests to be consulted in formulating policy for the institution.

3. It should be large enough to carry all necessary responsibilities, but small enough to act as a deliberative group.

4. The basic structural pattern (board, board officers, committees, executive, staff) should be clear.

5. There should be an effective working relationship among the board, executive and staff.

6. The members of the board should understand the objectives of the agency and how they are achieved by the activities undertaken.

7. They should have a feeling of social ease and rapport with each other.

8. Each member of the board should feel involved in its work.

9. The board should formulate specific goals to guide its work.

10. Decisions on policy should be made only after full consideration by all parties concerned.

11. The board should maintain effective community relationships.

12. Its members should have a sense of accomplishment and progress.

In addition, the board should be willing to accept financial responsibility for its decisions. And it should approach the career problems of the agency staff with the same considerations as the board members' own companies would give to their employees of comparable rank and responsibility.

Even the most effective board is at best a fragile and fluid thing, inheriting the human characteristics of its members. But, in generating points of view which may at first be little understood, and even unpopular, boards of cultural institutions, perhaps more than any other type, can exert a deep and lasting influence on our society. (22)

For a Cool Head and Cold Feet Add a Tax Lawyer to the Board

By

Joseph L. Wyatt, Jr.

Setting up or restructuring your board? It pays to have at least one member who is a specialist in tax and estate planning.

At the very beginning, an experienced lawyer-trustee can show a new organization how to achieve tax exempt status quickly. I know of a group which was able to apply for immediate exemption (it normally takes at least a year) by altering its proposed board of trustees before it was actually set up.

Once a group is established its lawyer-trustee can guide it in drafting literature for distribution among prospective donors and to other lawyers among whose clients there may be many potential benefactors. While the best of these brochures are excellent, the worst of the lot are superficial, unimaginative and dangerously gimmicky. The lawyer on the board can avoid embarrassment to the institution—and to its patrons.

His knowledge can help an institution plan an endowment campaign, to take advantage of the latest Internal Revenue Service rulings.

For example, he can explain what is good, bad, or uncertain about recent rulings on the so-called Pomona Plan under which would-be givers transfer cash or assets to an institution and receive a contract from it to pay them income from the gift for life.

A well-trained lawyer can help in other forms of fund raising activity as well. A fund solicitation, widely publicized on the West Coast, suffered much adverse publicity recently when it appeared the group had failed to comply with local law requiring approval of such campaigns by a municipal bureau. Its future drives are now under a cloud.

Do not expect him to obtain tax exempt status, draw up articles of incorporation, or draw up a handbook of sample will clauses gratis. Pay him or his firm—or some other lawyer—for such work.

Do expect him to exercise professional judgment, to help widen the institution's circle of contacts in the community. He is there to consult, to guide, to prevent. The board lawyer's occupational disease is cold feet, and a pair of them is most useful to have around. (2)

Artists on the Board

Should a practicing professional artist be a member of a cultural board? There is no doubt that some professionals can be a definite asset, but the possibility of jealousy may offset any advantages. Some organizations get around this by electing to their boards only retired professionals—such as former actresses for a theatrical group—or older professionals whose status is so well established that the possibility of criticism is minimized.   (23)

Keeping the Board Posted

Clippings, reports, letters and other materials which may interest board members often go unnoticed because board members don't receive them. Collect and put aside all items of interest until a staff member has the time to duplicate copies for them on a copying machine. Also, maintain one copy of each item in a big looseleaf scrapbook to which board members can refer.   (8)

Getting to Know You

By giving recognition to board and committee members, you can help to keep them interested in the organization. Every month in its newsletter, Roberson Center in Binghamton, New York, highlights a different board or committee of one of its member groups. It lists every member by name and asks readers to call them if they have questions about the Center or the group.   (68)

MEMBERSHIP

Recipe for Recruiting Members Includes
Good Food, Fine Art

Good food, fine art, and an ultra-soft sell campaign for new members, are the ingredients of a successful new program presented every Wednesday afternoon at the High Museum of Art in Atlanta, Georgia. Conceived and sponsored by the museum's Members Guild as a volunteer activity, the program, which began last October, features a "petit gourmet" luncheon for members and their guests in the museum's members room at noon ($2.50 a person) sandwiched between regular 11 a.m. and 1:30 p.m. museum docent tours. In addition, visitors are encouraged to arrive at 10 a.m. to attend the weekly "Great Artist" lecture.

Because the luncheons were designed to promote membership they operated initially on an "each one reach one" principle, with every attending member bringing along a non-member guest. Attendance for the first two luncheons was slightly less than capacity, although a number of guests became members. The museum then sent 5000 members a special light-hearted mailing featuring a *Peanuts* cartoon about museums with a message reading, "Man does not live by art alone. Join us." As a result of the mailing, and a subsequent full-page picture story with luncheon recipes by the food editor of the *Atlanta Constitution,* the luncheons soon became sell outs, with reservations a must. To permit more members to attend, the guest requirement was waived although potential members still constitute about one third of each week's diners.

A key to the program's success has been the volunteer

effort. Guild hostesses, completely responsible for preparing and serving meals, take turns as chefs and cook much of the food at home first because of the tiny museum kitchen. Recent luncheons have featured such entrees as shrimp and cheese casserole and chicken in wine.

Although no formal membership presentation is made, a wine sipping preceding lunch gives members the opportunity to promote membership. Objets d'art from the museum's shop are used as table centerpieces and matches, with the museum logo and "Are you a member?" printed on them, are handed out as favors. According to publicity director, Elizabeth M. Sawyer, it is conceivable that the low-keyed recruitment approach may be up-graded in the future to include special membership programs at lunch.

The launching of the noon program coincided with the museum's initiation of a fall membership drive and helped promote it. The drive topped its goal.   (74)

----◄●►----

Turn On Brings Turn Out

Want to have a good turn out at your annual meeting? Try to make it interesting as well as businesslike. The Pro Arte Symphony Orchestra in Hempstead, New York, announced that its recent annual meeting would be "adhering not strictly to business." At the meeting, the business portion was limited to only 45 minutes and was preceded by a pot-luck buffet and followed by a piano recital.
                                                                (68)

----◄●►----

Conducting Members

The Chicago Symphony Society which uses a variety of benefits to lure new members including free admissions, ticket discounts, open rehearsals, newsletters, tours abroad, parties and a special bonus record, is not appealing to the Walter Mitty in potential members. A new benefit, especially for those "who feel moved to conduct when listening to great records," is a perfectly balanced 14-inch baton imprinted "Chicago Symphony Society." (78)

Careful Timing Can Cut Down Your
Membership Work Load

The clerical work of renewing annual memberships, which can be considerable for a large organization, can be eased at the peak period if a special appeal is made to members for early renewal.

The National Geographic Society, with nearly 3,500,000 members, has found its Summer Remittance Plan a great help in evening out the flow of work connected with membership records and dues payments. More than half of the *National Geographic* members now pay the coming year's dues by the middle of October.

Early in July the Society sends a notice to all members explaining that renewing yearly membership in the summer preceding the dues-year has helped to cut office costs and keep membership dues low. The alternatives, it points out, would be expensive overtime for the staff, or hiring a huge and costly part-time force. (26)

Membership Renewals

Getting members to renew after the first year is a constant problem facing arts groups. One renewal inducement used with great success is a plastic card case offered to continuing members by the Art Institute of Chicago. The wallet-sized case has two pockets with the Art Institute's crest embossed on the outside. One pocket holds a printed membership card and the other a card listing the museum hours and the members' room hours. Each card case costs the Institute only 7 cents. (18)

Annual Ball Helps Arts Group Win New and Keep Old Members

An annual social event is helping the Minneapolis Society of Fine Arts win new members and keep old ones. The Society is the governing and supporting organization for the Minneapolis Institute of Arts, a museum. A key to the success of the organization's Members' Ball, held in the Institute's galleries, is that tickets at half-price are offered as added inducements to both new members and to the current members who recruit them.

For five years prior to the first ball, which was held in 1963, the Society's various efforts to build new membership and reduce drop-outs proved only moderately successful. An evaluation of these methods, however, revealed that special programs were the greatest incentive to membership and that "happy members were the best recruiters of new members."

These combined principles resulted in the current Members' Ball. In 1965, for example, the price for the entire evening, including dinner and dancing to a chamber group of 14 musicians from the Minneapolis Symphony Orchestra, was $15. However, new members, and every member who brought in a new member, were entitled to purchase two tickets for the price of one. All half-price requests had to be accompanied by membership dues for the recruits.

More than 80% of the tickets sold each year were purchased at the reduced rate—an indication of the popularity of the incentive plan. Although half-price tickets have been underwritten to some extent by the membership-promotion budget, the effort has paid off handsomely in the form of increased income from the $15 annual membership dues and increased renewals.

Each year, attendance at the ball has risen, the event has become more self-sustaining, and the membership ranks have grown proportionately. Of the 458 new members who joined the Society in 1965, 358 were recruited through the ball.

Planning for each event begins a year in advance and is carried out by a volunteer committee of approximately 14 members who work under the supervision of Miss Helen M. Lethert, the Society's Director of Membership. Miss Lethert told *AM*, "We feel that this is a most successful recruiting event because not only does it bring in new members, but it gives them a gay and impressive first introduction to the museum." (50)

New Members

One way to show your new members that you appreciate their support is to plan a special function in their honor. The Art Gallery of Toronto, for example, has a reception in April which is open only to all members who have joined the organization since the preceding November. (2)

Display Your Publicity

Members and volunteers may miss seeing important articles about your organization when they appear in print. Often, these articles may serve to heighten members' pride in the organization. Establish a central location, such as the members' room, where articles may be posted regularly along with other items of interest. (23)

Film Showings

Looking for a service to institute for your membership? Try arranging free film programs on subjects relating to your organization's interests. There are many excellent motion pictures, filmstrips and slides on a wide range of topics, available free or for small rental fees. A number of directories are published annually which list free or low rental films by titles and subjects. (18)

Naming Names

Seeking better relations with patrons and volunteers? Inform them in advance when their names appear in your group's publication or newsletter. Inexpensive mimeographed form postal cards can be used for this purpose, with the page and date of the publication in which the name appears filled in by hand. (35)

Match Books

Inexpensive items featuring an arts group's symbol, and distributed free to members, may help to remind them of the organization. The Virginia Museum of Fine Arts, in Richmond, Virginia, distributes members' match books in its members' suite. (46)

Premiums Pay in Direct Mail Membership Drive

A study of a cultural institution with one of the most successful membership programs in the country indicates that direct mail has been the single most important promotion factor, by far, in achieving recent membership growth. At the Art Institute of Chicago the fiscal year ending last June was the most successful in the organization's 63 year history.

Overall, the Institute showed a record membership of more than 28,000 by June, 1963. This total was about evenly divided between annual members and life members. Total membership receipts ran to $196,000 as against $147,000 the year before.

The greatest growth was in annual memberships, with sales up 49.2 per cent over the year before. As of June 30, 1962 the Institute claimed 10,970 annual members. Among this group the renewal rate—a figure of critical importance in membership promotion planning—was 83.7 per cent. With slightly more than 9,000 of these members renewing, and with a sale of 4,665 new annual memberships, the Institute was able to boost annual membership to 13,814 by June 30, 1963.

While the overall renewal rate for annual members was 83.7 per cent, the rate for first year members was much lower—65.3 per cent. Institute officials believe this indicates the need for added concentration on making membership a meaningful experience during the first year. Once a member renews for the first time, the chance of holding him for many more years increases sharply.

The role of direct mail in the museum's membership program is highlighted by the fact that, of the 4,665 new annual memberships sold, nearly 2,600 were sold through direct mail promotion. This represented a jump of 68 per cent over the number brought in by direct mail the year before. In the words of an Institute report: "Direct mail promotion was not only the most important single factor in membership growth, but far surpassed reasonable expectations." What accounted for the difference? According to the Institute, an increase in the size of the promotional budget, a revised sales letter, better mailing lists and an excellent premium combined to make the big difference. The choice of a premium was vital.

Selection of a more attractive membership premium increased the rate of mail return by .87 per cent. This was two-and-a-half times more than the amount needed to pay for the total cost of purchasing premiums for the entire year's promotion. Ordered in the middle of the fiscal year, when supplies of a first premium were exhausted, the new premium, a remainder supply of a handsome book on Van Gogh, enabled the Institute to complete the fiscal year with a strong sales record in late winter and spring, and with enough copies remaining for the first mailings this fall. A new premium, an attractive book on Degas, was ordered for use later this year. This book, however, can be reordered in any quantity, if it proves successful, thus eliminating the uncertainty created by using remainders which are soon exhausted.

The Institute, which mailed out a total of 123,000 pieces during the year, finds it increasingly difficult to locate large and productive lists of prospects. It was helped last year by trustees and men's council members who provided it with various kinds of directories that yielded small but highly selective lists.

Among the lists used by the Art Institute were those of a radio station, several local department stores, and a magazine read by female office workers. Other significant lists included the names of book buyers, members of a university faculty, art teachers, social study teachers, and doctors and dentists.

The heaviest mailings were sent out in the fall, at the beginning of the Institute's season. Thus 57,500 pieces were mailed in September and 20,000 in October. Additional mailings of 10,500 in December, 1962, 16,400 in March, 1963 and 18,700 in June, 1963 completed the direct mail drive. In terms of responses, the September and March mailings were the best, with each drawing nearly three per cent. The worst response followed the June mailing, which drew under one per cent.

At the same time that it was scoring notable success with its direct mail campaign, the Institute was finding that a membership recruitment desk, placed in the museum lobby for more than a year as an experiment, was not proving worthwhile. The desk was discontinued when it proved to be uneconomical.　　　　　　　　　(24)

Free Gifts Win Members for Cultural Group

A free gift promotion is being used by a major Eastern arts institution to attract new members. The Brooklyn Academy of Music in Brooklyn, N. Y., which sponsors more than 300 cultural events each season, has conducted a free gift program for the past six years that offers personal and household items to new subscribers with their $20 membership fee. This has been an important factor in increasing membership.

In addition, members of the organization are offered a free gift for each new member they help to enroll. The entire gift purchase program is conducted at no risk to

232

the Academy because the items are bought on consignment. The gift promotion idea was initiated in an effort to boost lagging membership by Wm. McKelvy Martin when he joined the Academy as director in 1958. While many factors such as an expanded cultural program have contributed to a rise in enrollment, Sarah Walder, membership coordinator and in charge of the gift program, told *AM* that the promotion has significantly aided the success of the membership drive. Since its inception, membership has risen at the rate of about 500 a year, except for last year when it dropped by 500 subscribers, a decline attributed to a five dollar fee increase. Membership today stands at 3,500.

Members are entitled to discounts on special events in addition to free admission to regularly scheduled Academy programs such as lectures, films, instrumental recitals, concerts, opera, theater, folk and ballroom dancing, ballet and modern dance recitals. There is also a full children's program.

According to Mrs. Walder, the gift program has stirred many members to a concerted effort to attract their friends to the Academy. This year an initial order of 707 gifts has been placed by the organization with its supplier, Gifts for Thrifts, Inc. of Nevada, in anticipation of a large response to the promotion.

Gift items usually retail at twice the price paid for them by the Academy. They are usually name brand products and the Academy saves on their wholesale cost by buying in volume. Membership gifts cost the organization about one to two-and-a half dollars. New members as well as members enrolling one person choose from one of eight items offered including a weekend case, a chip and dish set, a scale planter, a tropical server, an eight-piece kitchen tool set, a French purse, a blanket and a multiserver. If they wish, members may accept five dollars instead of a gift for each new member they enroll.

For members enrolling two new subscribers, gifts cost the Academy about five or six dollars and include any of the following items: a salt and pepper set, a clock, a slicer knife, a three-piece luggage set, a set of steak knives and an ice chest. Those bringing in three members are entitled to one of four items including an electric coffee maker, a sugar, creamer and tray set, a pair of binoculars and a camera.

The membership drive is held from September to May, and the Academy defines a new member as anyone who joins for the first time or who has not been a member since the 1958-59 season. However, the gift offer which is made each September, expires at the end of November.

The offer is promoted by the Academy with a lobby display and in newspaper advertisements of its events series. In addition, wide use is made of posters announcing the offer in subway stations, in banks, and in churches.   (31)

―――――――◄●►―――――――

Increasing Membership

An arts center in Brooklyn, New York, is trying a unique method of boosting its membership. The Brooklyn Academy of Music, which has offered free gifts to new members for several years, is instituting a "point" system this year. Members received two points for initial membership and five more for each new member they recruit. Gifts will be distributed on a point basis with the higher the point value, the more valuable the gift. The 53 gifts range from carving sets at two points to vacuums at 25 points.   (52)

―――――――◄●►―――――――

Rewarding Members

One way to reward members of an arts organization for their loyal support is to hold a special "Two-Fer" performance in their behalf. The Old Globe Theatre in San Diego, California, allowed its members to purchase two tickets for the price of one to a "members only" performance. (43)

New Members

The discriminating distribution of free tickets to an event through existing members can be a key to winning new members. In Binghamton, New York, for example, the Roberson Memorial Center instituted a complimentary guest slip program. In its monthly publication, the Center printed a page with four guest slips so that members could share their special interest in the arts group with their guests. It advised members to fill out the slips with the name of a friend, a neighbor or a new resident in the community, and the event he wished to attend. They were told to mail the slips back to the organization, so that it could be kept informed of the number of non-paying guests to expect at a particular event. In addition, this system alerted the center to "roll out the red carpet" for the guests invited by the member. The complimentary tickets are for events for which there would ordinarily be a charge for non-members. (32)

Humorous Cards Prod Members to Renew Season Subscriptions

Membership renewal is a serious problem facing many cultural organizations. In Midland, Texas, the Midland Community Theatre, Inc., has helped to solve this problem with a humorous approach to its direct mail program. Each year, toward the end of its annual membership drive, it sends "painless prods" to unrenewed members, which according to Art Cole, the group's director, "really do the job for the person who has simply forgotten to put the check in the mail, or the person who has been on the fence."

One of the more effective mailing pieces the organization uses is a group of three-by-six-inch cards clipped together in sequence. The first card in the series asks, "Perhaps you've been . . . sick?" Each succeeding card then shows an old-fashioned drawing and asks a question relating to it, such as "Busy at the office?" with a drawing of two blacksmiths at work; or, "Been listening to your hi-fi?" with a drawing of a gramophone. The next-to-last card in the series states, "Whatever it is you've no doubt been too busy to mail your 1965 Community Theatre membership check. We need it and we don't want you to miss . . . ," followed by a card listing programs for the coming season.

According to Mr. Cole, the series usually evokes favorable comments and thank you notes, accompanied by membership checks. To take advantage of the surprise element, the series of cards is always mailed in unmarked envelopes.

Holiday greeting cards for St. Patrick's Day and Valentine's Day are other successful renewal devices used by the group. Each card features a humorous drawing and an appropriate membership reminder. The Valentine's card, for example, shows a cover drawing of an amorous swain with an arrow through him, and the greeting, "Happy Valentine's Day to you." Inside there is a membership message and a drawing of the same swain receiving a blood transfusion. This is followed by a P. S., "Don't spoil our beautiful friendship," and a second P. S., "We need your blood."

During the rest of the year, the theater conducts an ardent campaign to woo all newcomers to the community to its membership. A small brochure, "Theatre in West Texas?" which includes an exchange coupon for free attendance at one production, is mailed to new residents. For one recent production, 23 per cent of the persons using the free tickets became members immediately.

Situated in a town of about 60,000 persons, the theater attracted an audience of 30,000 persons last year, and a membership of 3,000. (38)

Date Stickers

One way an arts group can help its members to remember important dates is to send them notices typed on gummed or pressure-sensitive labels. Members can be urged to paste the labels directly on their home calendars. The organization's message can't be missed when the date of the occasion arrives. (37)

Block Membership

Arts councils and cultural groups that have a close relationship to other arts organizations in their community, might consider a block ticket and membership offer to stimulate subscriptions. This program enables a subscriber who is a member of two or more arts groups to send in one

237

check to cover dues or subscriptions to the various groups in which he is interested. The Greensboro Community Arts Council in North Carolina achieved a 33 per cent increase over the previous year in response to a block ticket mailing.
(28)

Graduation Gifts

Recently graduated students represent an excellent and untapped area of membership potential for your organization. Now is the time to begin planning a campaign to promote memberships as meaningful and unique June graduation gifts. To highlight the promotion, consider the possibility of establishing a special new membership category at slightly reduced rates for recent graduates. (25)

Point of Sale

In addition to offering outlets for sales, shops run by cultural groups can promote membership in the organization. The Art Institute of Chicago used its museum store recently to house a membership display. The group promoted membership by offering a 10 per cent discount on items in the store to its members. Many inquiries resulted from the display, and about 15 per cent of them resulted in new memberships. (38)

VOLUNTEERS

Follow Five Rules When Using Volunteer Forces in Fund Work

The volunteer worker is the backbone of most fund raising drives. Organizing a volunteer force for a campaign, enrolling the volunteers, and inspiring them to do an effective job, calls for advance planning and plenty of hard work. Here are five basic points to remember when gearing up for a volunteer effort.

First, it is important to develop a proper relationship between the volunteers and the staff. Staff professionals may guide and advise the volunteer leaders, but basic policies should be set by the volunteer organization, not handed down by professionals. In the words of one professional fund raiser, "In a fund raising campaign it is deadly when the volunteers are made to feel that the professional staff is running the show. It is important to indoctrinate and help train volunteer leaders at top levels, so that they actually lead the remainder of the volunteer forces." Volunteer leadership will feel little responsibility for policies formulated by others.

This means that the campaign chairman should be involved from the start in all planning for the drive. The chairman must offer personal leadership. He, not the staff, should speak to volunteer meetings, outlining the "case" on which the drive is to be built, and expressing his own enthusiasm for the cause. Volunteers should have an opportunity to participate fully in these meetings. The volunteer who never meets the volunteer leadership, is not likely to make an effective solicitor.

239

Second, when volunteers are enrolled, they should know exactly what will be expected of them during the campaign. If the volunteer is expected to organize a committee, or solicit in person, or carry out other functions, this should not come as a surprise to him at the last minute.

Third, during the weeks or months of the campaign, enthusiasm may easily flag. Simply reiterating that an emergency exists is not enough to keep the volunteer force working effectively. Leadership must maintain continuity of communication with the lower echelons. This means meetings, in person, with individuals or groups. It means periodic progress reports.

Fourth, meetings to which volunteers are invited should be planned carefully in advance. A dull meeting can not only kill the volunteer's spirit, but create resentment that his time is being wasted.

Fifth, it is vital to recognize and acknowledge the work of the volunteer, not merely after the campaign, but during its progress. This, too, requires advance planning.   (22)

Training Leaders

Ask your committee chairmen to train one member as a replacement before he resigns, so the new chairman will know all sides of the committee's work when he takes over. One season as trainee obviates many errors. A busy person can often be persuaded to accept a chairmanship if assured he can count on a successor after a fixed term.   (5)

Buddy System

A core of experienced volunteer solicitors can be built by using the "buddy system". An old member takes a new one first to a friendly contributor, then to at least one known to be skeptical. After seeing how the old hand deals with both types, the beginner is better prepared to make calls on her own. The League of Women Voters in Hutchinson, Kansas, has found this team system highly effective both in the amount of money raised and number of solicitors taking part. (11)

Volunteers Can Perform Highly Specialized Work

Cultural organizations have a better chance of finding and keeping skilled volunteers, if they program in advance to utilize the talents they discover. The Brooklyn Children's Museum in Brooklyn, New York, recently faced with a critical need for gallery guides, lecturers, teaching assistants, library assistants and specialists in classifying and cataloguing objects, based a volunteer appeal upon a pre-arranged program, and the results were outstanding. Little more than a month after the appeal was first issued, 19 volunteers, each with a college background and a professional skill in a definite area, were at work.

In January 1963, the museum's staff issued press releases describing the skills needed and specifically outlining the duties of volunteers. A fact sheet for volunteers had been prepared and arrangements made for training them under staff curators. More than 100 inquiries resulted from news stories about the museum's needs and 38 people turned out for the first of a series of orientation classes.

241

By the end of the orientation period 19 especially capable men and women remained. Although it was the original intention of the museum to use volunteers only on Saturdays, the response was so favorable and the calibre of those remaining in the program so high that the program was expanded to weekdays also.

Among the volunteers now being used by the museum are an anthropologist and an archeologist, a public relations executive who is cataloging the museum collection, and a history teacher who is assisting the curator of the cultural history department at the museum. In addition, because two capable volunteers are now available, children once forced to admire objects through glass cases, can take them out and handle them.

Because of the program's success, the museum is now considering using volunteer workers during the summer. In September, the entire program will be enlarged and additional skilled volunteers will be recruited.

Mrs. Nancy Paine, coordinator of special activities for the museum, delighted at the volunteer response, believes that careful planning was responsible for the success of the campaign. "I would urge that any organization facing a similar need for volunteers with special skills, have a definite idea in advance of how they would use the people they find." (15)

Hundreds of Volunteer Workers Help Make
Fund Event a Success

Viewed as either a fund raising or "fun raising" event, the annual Cast Party Festival of Young Friends of City Center is a huge success. A pre-Christmas fixture for the past four years, the festival, a combination carnival-bazaar-entertainment organized and conducted by volunteers, has increased in scope, attendance, popularity and profitability each year. Moreover, unlike many other charity events, it has achieved its success with an "open door" policy that keeps admission down to $3.00 a person. This year's event, held at the New York State Theater between five and ten p.m. on December 5th, drew over 3,000 people and raised more than $21,000—a 50 per cent increase over last year—for City Center's educational programs and member companies.

The only event in which all the Center's constituents participate, the festival is a six-month planning effort which draws on the involvement of nearly 400 volunteer members of Young Friends, City Center's supportive guild of men and women 40 and younger. The festival engenders so much excitement that this summer and fall nearly 100 people paid membership dues of $15 and up to join Young Friends and participate in the effort.

Serious planning for the December festival began June 1st with the selection of four co-chairmen and 21 committee chairmen responsible for such activities as: handicrafts; tickets; artist participation; security; and finance. Chairmen were named also for festival booths of such Center constituents as the New York City Opera, the Alvin Ailey and Joffrey dance companies, the New York City Ballet and the Young People's Theater. During the summer chairmen

243

concentrated on planning and began to solicit donations of merchandise for resale and for raffle prizes. In September, at a general meeting, chairmen explained committee work and recruited members.

Throughout October and November, committees were deeply involved in their special areas and in acquiring merchandise. The entertainment committee worked out performance plans with each City Center company and the manpower committee organized a plan to divide the 400 volunteers into three two hour shifts. Weekly handicraft sessions attracted groups of 20 to 40 volunteers who made hundreds of items for sale at the festival.

Meanwhile, as donated goods arrived at the Friends' office, volunteers assorted and priced them, generally at one third less than retail. (Goods valued at $28,000 were donated for resale and $12,000 worth was donated for the raffle.) Finally, a week prior to the event, a full meeting of all the committees was held.

On festival day—the only date in the entire year when the State Theater was dark and all the City Center companies were available in the city—a group of volunteers arrived early to set up and decorate the booths and display the merchandise. Since the theater was being readied for the City Ballet's "Nutcracker" opening in two days, the promenade floor became the main festival area complete with carnival games and booths for autographs, photographs, raffles, and each of the Center's constituents. The two balcony rings above had booths selling food, clothing, books, records, and costumes.

An hour prior to the five p.m. opening the transformation was complete and the first volunteers' shift reported to a check-in area, received identification badges and went to their booths. The Cast Party theme was visible everywhere. Instead of numbers a "Repertoire Roulette" wheel

244

of fortune featured "Manon," "Astarte," "Cry" and "Carmen." "On Your Toes" participants tried to toss rings around ballet slippers and "Hit the High Note" players threw balls through the mouths of cardboard opera characters. Performers from Joffrey, Ailey and other Center companies manned booths along with volunteers and signed autographs. Throughout the evening, entertainment floated down to the promenade from the second balcony. Occasionally an off-beat performance was presented—dancer John Clifford of the New York City Ballet delighted attendees by singing Gershwin songs.

Special care was taken to avoid problems. To keep money handling at a minimum, purchases were not paid for directly but were tallied on a list which indicated item, price and the booth at which it was bought. At special check-out desks party-goers paid for all their purchases. At locations where money was used—games, food areas and raffle booths —cash was collected regularly by authorized workers.

According to Young Friends chairman, Mrs. Stanley Nelson, the festival brought City Center performers much closer to the public. "Some artists even baked cakes and made handicrafts," she said. "Also, planning the event helped us develop a cohesive group which is involved in all our activities." (78)

National Volunteer Center Offers Arts Aid

Arts groups interested in expanding their volunteer programs or learning more about successful volunteer projects elsewhere, have a relatively new national organization ready to provide these and other services to them without charge. The National Center for Voluntary Action in Washington, D.C., which serves as a coordinating body for the field of volunteer activity, is interested in increasing its service to the arts.

"We hope the arts will regard us as a resource," David Jeffreys, the Center's vice president for organizational resources, told *AM.* "To date our organization's main involvement has been with national and local organizations in the area of social concerns. However, we've received some intriguing examples of how the arts have used volunteers. We'd appreciate receiving more."

The examples of volunteer activity are a key resource of the Center's Clearinghouse, which disseminates material and information. Some 4,000 case histories have been digested and catalogued and when requests for information are received, they are answered with appropriate samples. Because case histories are written by the organizations themselves, they vary in length and detail, although nearly all are brief.

Those wishing more detailed information, are provided with names of people to contact and published material to read. A "Green Sheet" published by the Clearinghouse includes information on organizations involved in various aspects of the human and social service fields and lists films, pamphlets and published material relating to all aspects of volunteerism. The Clearinghouse service is available free of charge to any group or individual. Requests may be made by mail, phone or personal visit to the Clearinghouse, (202-466-8444), National Center for Voluntary Action, 1735 Eye St., N.W., Washington, D.C. 20006.

The Center also publishes a free monthly newsletter, *Voluntary Action News,* and makes speakers available at no fee. Of potential help to arts groups are the local Voluntary Action Centers which are designed to identify a community's needs and recruit and train volunteers to meet those needs.   (71)

246

Building a Library

Finding it difficult to keep up with everything written about the arts? Afraid you might miss a relevant article in a magazine not specifically concerned with culture? Ask your members to help you. The resource file of Allied Arts of Seattle has grown substantially thanks to organizational members, who've volunteered to clip newspapers and magazines for articles on arts issues and on the environment. (69)

Volunteer Deductions

With income tax deadline time approaching it's a good idea to let your volunteers know that they're allowed to deduct out-of-pocket expenses incurred in helping you, provided, of course, that they can substantiate the expenses. For travel to and from meetings or other volunteer activities the IRS permits an automatic 6-cents-a-mile deduction to cover gas and other car expenses. Tolls and parking fees also can be deducted. (79)

Volunteer Support a Key to Successful Festival

An annual arts festival, which has grown in 11 years from a backyard affair attracting 1,700 visitors to an event which expects some 250,000 visitors this year, has discovered the keys to its success in flexibility, good organization and unusual volunteer dedication.

The Atlanta Arts Festival, which will be held in Piedmont Park, Atlanta, Ga., from May 24 to May 31 this year, is an eight day outdoor event which includes both the visual and the performing arts. Featured performing groups this year include the Atlanta Symphony Orchestra, three Atlanta theatre companies, all ballet and modern dance groups in the city, and the performing arts departments of three local colleges. Eminent professional artists will exhibit at an Invited Show, and amateur and professional artists alike may purchase display space for five dollars for an Open Show.

A non-profit voluntary organization, the Festival operates on an annual budget of $25,000, compared to $327 during its first year. Receipts include about $13,000 from an annual fund raising campaign, $4500 from individual and family memberships, a $3000 grant from the city of Atlanta, $2500 from a 20 per cent commission on all sales made during the Festival, and $2000 from exhibition fees and program sales. In addition, the city of Atlanta contributes the park area where the Festival is held.

Organization of the Festival is virtually a full-time project. A 45 member board of trustees meets monthly, except during July and August, to plan policy. An executive committee operates and directs the Festival activities within the framework. Committee chairmen and the executive committee are rotated annually. According to Mrs.

Alvin M. Ferst Jr., chairman of the board, "The Festival is structured so responsibilities are clear cut without being confining. By-laws, standing rules and organizational charts are guides, rather than a rigid framework."

The planning of each new Festival begins shortly after the conclusion of the old one. In June, committee chairmen report to the board of trustees on all facets of the recently concluded Festival operation and the advisory committee evaluates the Festival as a whole. During the early fall months, committee chairmen are appointed and tentative fund raising plans are discussed. By December, Festival dates are definitely set, a budget is presented and approved, and committee chairmen report to the board on progress made in such areas as art placement, scholarships, membership, fund raising, etc. The annual sustaining fund drive, held in February, has been carefully planned in advance, and by January, members are recruited to act as volunteer solicitors. From March on, after the completion of the fund drive, each of the 41 committees active in the conduct of the Festival moves at an accelerated pace until the Festival opens in May.

Because the Festival is a mammoth undertaking, conducted without paid staff, extraordinary volunteer support is necessary for it to be successful. Thus, more than 1,000 volunteers, representing every segment of the community work on it. Artists, in addition to exhibiting, often serve on committees throughout the entire year, and businessmen, who manage the organization's budget, frequently are craftsmen and amateur artists who display at the Festival. A majority of the original founders are still active in Festival work and organizational leaders estimate that well over 50 per cent of all the volunteers have been associated with the Festival for more than five years.

One volunteer leader, who has been with the Atlanta Arts

Festival for several years, attributes the success of the volunteer program to the fact that full participation in it is open to anyone. "Unlike many other cultural organizations in Atlanta," she told *AM*, "we don't attract the dilettantes and debutantes. We do attract those people who have a sincere appreciation for the arts and want to bring enjoyment of the arts to other people." (27)

Volunteers Play New Role in Fund Campaign

To ease the strain on volunteer solicitors who "ring doorbells" in its annual fund raising campaign, an arts council in Binghamton, New York, is trying an unusual experiment. The Roberson Memorial Center has enrolled nearly 100 women to serve as "secretaries" or assistants during its united fund drive which runs from April 18th through April 23rd. The campaign goal is set at $61,650.

Each of the secretaries will be working with four or five male volunteers, business and professional men, who will be doing the actual solicitation of funds. The women will confirm appointments, make sure that their "bosses" have all the necessary campaign materials with them when they visit prospects, and prepare written reports both during the drive and after it ends.

According to Keith Martin, director of the center, the new approach will not only free solicitors from routine duties, but will ensure the best use of female volunteers. "Many women never participated in fund drives because they were reticent to ask for money," Mr. Martin told *AM*. "As secretaries, they can still become totally involved in the fund campaign without ever actually leaving the office." Mr. Martin pointed out that a number of the women have previously been volunteer workers in other phases of the council's program.

Prior to the start of the campaign, the secretaries have been attending preliminary meetings where their duties have been explained. In addition, small groups of them have been meeting informally with their future bosses to establish rapport. (48)

———————◄●►———————

Summer Opera Plans Thoroughly, Starts Early

Year-round planning, the enlistment of a small army of volunteer workers, community fund-raising and tight control over expenditures are all part of the system under which the Central City Opera Festival in Colorado has become a standout summer success.

Now 31 years old, the festival in the mountain mining town an hour's drive west of Denver is held in the old Central City Opera House, an ornate relic of the gold-mining days now owned by the University of Denver. The opera program of two alternating productions lasts through July, and is followed by a Broadway play suitable for summer entertainment.

The festival is organized by a community association that involves some 500 people in the work of nearly 40 volunteer committees, in which places are filled by invitation. Because it is now an established tradition, the festival is supported by many who have learned the ropes of committee work through the years. And local business values the festival as a strong summer tourist attraction to the Denver area.

Robert Brown, general manager of the festival association, adheres to a firm policy of pegging ticket prices to production costs. Admission price is fixed on the basis that

251

a complete sellout covers 67 per cent of the festival costs, the other 33 per cent being raised by a financial drive in the greater Denver area and nearby towns. The drive is handled entirely by mail.

Brown establishes a realistic budget, allocating costs in this proportion: artists—25 per cent; orchestra—25 per cent; stage hands—30 per cent; administration—10 per cent; and costumes—10 per cent. Brown insists that he must be "ruthless about this budget" because there is very little room for maneuver on the revenue side once the total plan is made up.

The association starts early and works systematically around the calendar. Here is its schedule:

September: select production for the following season. October: close books and prepare to audit. November through January: Begin engaging cast, orchestra, directors and designers. February: engage all staff members, and begin financial campaign. March: start publicity campaign. April: get volunteer committees to work. May: open ticket sales. June: stars arrive and festival opens.

The 1962 festival features two Puccini operas, *La Boheme* and *The Girl of the Golden West,* alternating from June 30 through July 28. They are followed in August by Jean Kerr's comedy, *"Mary, Mary."* Opera ticket prices range from $3.90 to $7.75, except for an opening night scale running to $12.50.   (5)

Volunteer Recognition

Volunteers for a cultural organization's fund raising campaign should receive recognition for their efforts. One means of doing this is to send them an inexpensive gift at the end of a campaign. The Chicago Heart Association thanked its 30,000 volunteers for their direct solicitation work by sending each one a plastic bookmark. The marker was enclosed in a folder which simply said, "in appreciation," and was signed by the organization's president. (39)

Sense of Participation

Members and volunteers in a fund raising drive can be given an extra charge of interest by being invited to a private affair. For some years the National Symphony Orchestra in Washington, D. C. has invited sustaining fund workers to a rehearsal on the eve of the drive. "It makes them go out of the hall with a sense of participation," an orchestra spokesman says. (2)

Retired Executives Aid Cultural Organizations

The retired executive can perform many useful volunteer tasks for cultural organizations. However, most cultural organizations do not have a systematic way to reach these individuals and, even on finding them, have no programs that can take full advantage of their skills.

In New York City an educational program started by a college last year is not only keeping retired professionals active and busy, but is also providing cultural and other non-profit groups with the use of "students" in key volunteer capacities. At the New School for Social Research, the Institute for Retired Professionals has enrolled more than 400 retired men and women in a program of classes and cultural activities. A part of the Institute, its Community Service Committee, seeks outlets through which Institute members, retired teachers, business executives, musicians, lawyers, artists and others, may use their skills to assist others. The Committee invites requests from organizations seeking the free voluntary services of its members.

According to Hyman Hirsch, chairman of the Institute, "This kind of program is important because it taps the resources of people who are retired but who can remain culturally alert. Retired people are looking for opportunities to do something of significance, and, if they are presented with the right kind of program, they will respond."

Mr. Hirsch told *AM* that he believes that a program similar to that created at the Institute can work in other cities, provided that it begins on a smaller scale. No similar program, according to Mr. Hirsch's knowledge, has been started elsewhere as yet.   (27)

Key Programs of Junior League Now Oriented to Needs of Arts

Volunteer support, administrative help and financial assistance are the essential ingredients of a widespread program in the arts sponsored by the Association of the Junior Leagues of America, Inc. According to Mrs. L. R. Breslin, Jr., the Association's arts consultant, the volunteer organization of young women now supports more activities in the arts than in any other area. Last year it invested $668,256 in support of 538 arts projects involving 8,759 League volunteers.

In Buffalo, New York, for example, the local League is now launching an audience development program for the city's new professional resident theater company, the Studio Arena Theatre. Here, as in many of its projects, a good portion of the League's financial assistance will be invested in the salary of a professional to supervise the project. An audience development expert, who will soon begin working with the theater, will be paid from the League's $8,500 project allotment.

As part of the Buffalo project, League volunteers also will administer an annual college undergraduate production and two annual meetings involving community theater leaders and English teachers.

In Jackson, Mississippi, the Junior League organized the first Mississippi Arts Festival, held last year, and invested $5,000 in it. Volunteers helped book major attractions and promoted the festival concept to community service organizations, schools, businesses and the press throughout the state. The League supported this year's recently-ended festival as well. In line with the League's philosophy of administering a project until its support is no longer

255

essential, it will turn over the entire festival package to an independent organization of local and state cultural leaders following the 1967 festival season.

Community arts councils have been continuing beneficiaries of League activity. Since the end of World War II, the organization has played major roles in the founding and development of approximately 30 councils, including the first two in this hemisphere—in Winston-Salem, North Carolina and in Vancouver, B. C., Canada.

In San Antonio, Texas, for example, the local League helped to organize a council in 1961 and worked with the fledgling group until last year, when the council was strong enough to exist without League support. League assistance included an initial survey of the community's cultural resources, the development of a master mailing list and addressing service in cooperation with local arts groups, the publication of a calendar of events in two Sunday newspapers, and a financial investment totaling $10,000. A team of six League volunteers worked on the project over a three-year period. Further developments have included: creation of a Fine Arts Commission by city ordinance, publication of a monthly arts magazine, and plans for an arts festival.

Other League arts programs over the years have included such varied activities as providing guided museum tours for the schools, undertaking public education programs, producing booklets and films, conducting historical surveys, and initiating children's concert programs. One of its major achievements was the conception and implementation of a long-range program to establish the Arkansas Arts Center in Little Rock.

How can arts organizations take advantage of Junior League services? According to Mrs. Breslin, a cultural group should write to its local Junior League outlining its specific areas of need. "Projects are undertaken," Mrs. Breslin told *AM*, "only after comprehensive research has established the validity of a need, the best means for filling it, and the community's ability to maintain and continue to develop the new or extended service after it has been brought to maturity."   (49)

Winning Workers

A special "Volunteers Night" is one method of attracting new volunteer workers. Ask each of your present volunteers to invite one or two of their friends to attend such a session at your institution. Then, have a special program at which the work of the organization is explained by one of its leaders and each of the volunteer chairmen talks briefly about the work of her committee and answers questions from the audience. A tour of the institution or a short program of entertainment might then follow.   (25)

Men Wanted?

Want to interest men in your organization? The Junior Women's Committee of the Art Gallery of Toronto sponsors regularly scheduled special luncheons "for men only" during the normal working week. The same institution also reaches men at Family Nights which begin with supper served from 5:45 to 7:15 p.m. and feature continuous showings of art films, tours of the gallery, and informal family drawing sessions.   (28)

Men's Night

A special "Men's Night" preview of the season's musical program is held by the National Symphony Orchestra in Washington, D.C., to stimulate interest in concert-going on the part of husbands of its women's committee members. Conductor Howard Mitchell outlines the programs to be presented and explains his thinking behind the selections chosen. A crowd of 400 attended the 1962 affair. (9)

The Extra Hour

The hour saved when Daylight Savings Time ends may be put to good use by an enterprising arts organization. Tell your volunteers and members that your group would appreciate one extra hour of help from each of them so that important projects may be completed. Suggest that they donate the hour at a time when they won't miss it—after they turn their clocks back. (31)

Attracting Volunteers

One way to recruit volunteers to your organization is to reward them with free membership privileges. With this inducement, the Museum of the City of New York recently recruited more than 90 volunteer tour guides, information desk and museum shop assistants. In addition to receiving full privileges of museum membership, which includes a 10-per cent discount at the shop, invitations to museum events and previews, and discounts on tours and workshops, the volunteers are treated to a series of monthly evening programs featuring guest speakers, discussions and refreshments. (44)

Explanation for Husbands

The husband of a volunteer worker in the arts can either encourage his wife's efforts or, if he knows little about the value of his wife's work, he can object strenuously to the time she gives. An informal supper for husbands sponsored by the women's committee can serve as an occasion at which the group's work is explained and awards for achievement are given out. At one such function in Highland Park, Illinois, 200 people attended and the husbands picked up the tab. (10)

Political Clubs

A local political club may be a good source of volunteer aid or program support. In New York City, for example, the Ansonia Democratic Club formed an arts committee which has sponsored cultural events, and has helped local arts groups. (42)

Area Representatives

Do you want to attract audiences from nearby communities? You might consider appointing volunteers from these communities to serve as your on-the-spot representatives. The Milwaukee Repertory Theater recently organized a Radius Committee, composed of volunteers from 19 cities within a 100-mile radius of Milwaukee, Wisc. Volunteers provide publicity materials to media in their communities, arrange for local presentations by the theater's staff, stimulate ticket purchases, and distribute posters and brochures to businesses and organizations. (56)

Volunteer Exchange

If a volunteer project falls at a time when it's difficult to attract a sufficient number of your own workers, it may be worthwhile to suggest a volunteer exchange with other organizations. Under this arrangement, their workers may assist your organization on one project, and your volunteers will assist them on one of theirs. Aside from developing a rapport between the organizations, volunteers might welcome the change. (21)

College Students Ring Bell

Need doorbell ringers for fund raising? One group seldom tapped, is the arts oriented college student. At Brooklyn College recently, a coed organized a committee of students to engage in a fund raising campaign for a local cultural group. Chairmen of music, art, drama, or dance departments can be helpful in supplying a list of interested students and some may even make announcements in class or post a notice on the department bulletin board.   (8)

Promotional Help

Youngsters can help to promote cultural events. In New York, the Nassau County Regional Arts Center increased attendance substantially at its Sunday in the Park Arts Festival this summer by having children distribute promotional materials on the event to adults attending Little League baseball games in the park.   (42)

ADMINISTRATORS AND MANAGEMENT TRAINING

Arts Administrators May Qualify for a Tax Break

By RICHARD W. HYNSON

In 1958 Congress added amendment 403b to the Internal Revenue Code, to enable employees of certain non-profit organizations to set aside funds for their retirement with before-tax dollars. Code section 501 (c) (3, defines eligibles as full-time or part-time employees of non-profit religious, charitable, educational or other types of organizations. In many cases, the Tax Sheltered Annuity provides the only method by which employees of these organizations may efficiently save for their retirement.

Although many school systems utilize this tax-deferred vehicle, very few of the qualifying cultural organizations take advantage of it. Passed because Congress realized that non-profit organizations were usually hard-pressed to keep good management employees, that funds were often insufficient to justify substantial salaries, and that there is no tax advantage to such organizations to establish pension programs for employees, it is an excellent tool that cultural groups can use to attract and help keep personnel.

Here's how 501 (c) (3) works. There is a maximum amount that any employer can set aside each year for each employee, basically, 20 percent of the employee's annual includable compensation. The employee may request that a certain percentage of his salary be withheld and paid over to a life insurance company to be held for him until retirement. There may be incidental life insurance features for the participant if he desires, or he may elect a deferred annuity. In any event, the amount he decides to have put into a retirement plan is not declared as part of his income (other than for Social Security tax purposes). The funds continue to build up until he elects to withdraw them for retirement. The principle involved is that during his higher earning years, his income taxes are at the highest level. Normally upon retirement, his income is less; and if he is age 65, or over, he enjoys a double personal exemption. Hence, his tax-sheltered dollars work two ways for him.

An example will make the explanation more graphic. Let's assume that a production manager of a repertory theatre has a salary of $14,000 per year, that he is 38 years old, and that he is single. Using the standard deduction for simplicity's sake, his return would look like this:

Gross reportable salary		$14,000
Less personal exemption	750	
Less standard deduction		
(10%, maximum $1,000)	1,000	1,750
Taxable Income		$12,250
Federal Income Tax Payable at		
29% on the top dollars	2,702	
Total Income Tax Liability		$2,702

Now, if we suppose this same man decided to have 10 percent of his salary set aside by his employer under a Tax Sheltered Annuity, the computations would look like this:

Gross reportable salary		
($14,000 less $1,400)		$12,600
Less personal exemption	750	
Less standard deduction		
(10%, maximum $1,000)	1,000	1,750
Taxable income		$10,850

Federal Income Tax Payable at
    27% on the top dollar $2,320

    Total Income Tax Liability $2,320

This example shows that there is a savings of $382 in tax paid, or in other words, "Uncle Sam" pays that amount toward his retirement build-up.

How does this compare with another investment? Why should one who qualifies under this section go into it? If he were to put the same $1,400 aside in some other financial vehicle, being in the 29 percent tax bracket, he would have only $994 after taxes. This invested at 6.25 percent—but 4 percent net after taxes—compounded annually, would result in an accumulation of $48,674.19. Whereas, under 501 (c)(3), he would have $68,555.20. This is equivalent to an annual compound return of approximately 11 percent. On a relatively small investment each year, this is almost miraculous!

Government and industry have used and continue to use the employee pension benefit as an important drawing card to secure top people and, having accomplished that important mission, the pension plan helps keep them. These benefits are available to many arts institutions as well. Why not look into it?   (65)

Former Ford Interns Win Key Management Posts

Since the Ford Foundation initiated its Program for Administrative Interns in 1961 to help train and develop administrators for the performing arts, it has underwritten fellowships for 71 men and women as full-time on-the-job trainees with professional performing arts institutions. In some instances, the twelve-month fellowships were renewed for a second or even a third year, accounting for a total of 101 awarded.

Recently, the Foundation increased the annual fellowship stipend to $6,500. Extra allowances of $1,000 for married fellows and $500 for each dependent child are also authorized. According to Mrs. Marcia Thompson, a program officer in the Ford Foundation's Division of Humanities and the Arts, "It would have been impractical to raise the stipend earlier, because some of the fellows might then have earned more than the administrators they were working for. Happily, salaries in the field have since increased."

In an attempt to determine the program's success, *AM* recently reviewed a status report on the current activities of the 71 interns accepted into the program since it began. Thirty-nine interned with theaters, 20 with symphony orchestras, ten with opera companies and two with dance companies.

Of the 71 interns, 51 are currently employed in some capacity in the arts, including five who are still interning. Twenty-nine are presently working as administrators in the specific area in which they apprenticed, and 13 are administrators with other kinds of art groups. Four former interns are working in such related fields as theater criticism, production, and theater technology. One maintains a vicarious involvement with arts administration, through her marriage to an orchestra manager.

265

The 20 former Ford interns no longer involved in the arts include four now working in the educational field as either teachers or administrators, and six currently inactive. The employment status of ten others is unknown although several of them held positions as arts administrators following completion of their internship.

A study of the status report indicates that a little training can be a valuable asset to the job-seeker in the arts. Although 20 of the 71 withdrew from the program prior to completing internships, 17 did so to accept managerial positions with arts organizations. Currently, top positions in arts administration are held by many former interns. Ten serve either as managing directors or general managers of professional theater companies, six are orchestra managers, four are directors or coordinators of large arts centers, one is an arts council director, and one is manager of an opera company.

The intern selection process begins with the Ford Foundation soliciting nominations from arts leaders several months prior to the January 31st deadline. The number of those solicited has grown steadily each year, reaching 800 this year. Candidates are then asked to provide background information and a statement of interest for screening by a panel. Prime candidates are interviewed by Foundation representatives and by those arts groups where internship may be provided.

Interestingly, the number of interns selected annually has diminished in recent years. In 1962, for example, 22 interns were selected from 171 nominations. The figures in following years were: 1963, 99 nominations and 27 fellowships; 1964, 86 nominations and 24 fellowships; 1965, 119 nominations and 13 fellowships; 1966, 131 nominations and 8 fellowships; and in 1967, 120 nominations and 5 fellowships. Asked to explain the decline, Mrs. Thompson told *AM,* "The program has become more selective and we're now aiming for candidates who, in time, can become principal spokesmen for the arts. Also, the nature of the field has changed with the advent of many new arts organizations, all seeking administrators, and people with a minimum of experience can and do find jobs. We're interested in candidates with a deep-rooted and long range interest in the field, who recognize the value of internship training."

Although Mrs. Thompson thinks that the program has been an effective one, and will continue indefinitely, she mentioned the difficulty in selecting the arts institutions with which the interns train. "We evaluate arts groups," she added, "with the same care with which we evaluate candidates. Too few groups, however, have both the capacity and the willingness to train interns." (59)

Study Cites Need for Management Training

Strong administrative leadership in the arts is lacking, cultural groups experience difficulty in finding qualified managers, professional college training programs in arts administration are not available, and the salaries for arts administrators are not competitive with comparable positions in other non-profit fields. Furthermore, unless training and experience needs are met very soon, the administration of arts organizations and programs will stay at a doubtful status quo—or even regress.

These are among the key conclusions reached in a comprehensive study of future administrative needs in the arts, limited to New York State, but with implications for arts groups throughout the nation. Prepared for the New York State Council on the Arts by consultant George Alan Smith, the report is based on a questionnaire-survey of arts groups in New York, (189 of 338 groups responding), supplemented by the author's personal interviews with arts and civic leaders in the state's major cities. The answers to three basic questions were posed: what job openings in arts administration now exist; what openings will become available; and what were the necessary qualifications and experience for these positions.

According to report findings, there are now 58 arts administration positions open in New York State at an average starting salary of $11,157. Within the next three to five years, an additional 151 positions will become available at an average salary of about $9,000. Of the respondents who gave reasons for jobs going unfilled, 87 cited budgetary limitations as the prime factor and 23 indicated that there was a lack of trained personnel. In answer to a separate question, 79 per cent indicated that an adequate reservoir of administrative personnel for the arts does not exist.

Another section of the report, devoted to arts administration in education, revealed that within the next three to five years there will be 66 positions open at colleges and universities, including 15 now unfilled, at an average annual salary of about $13,000. Budget limitations and a lack of recognition that administrative personnel were required were cited as prime reasons for the gap. In this area also, respondents felt that there was an inadequate pool of trained administrators. Interestingly, responding arts groups indicated that they would prefer administrators without an arts background to artists with administrative potential to fill upcoming positions. Educational institutions took the opposite position.

Parallel investigations by arts consultant Smith pinpointed the national need for administrative programs. "Across the country," he said, "there are virtually no structured programs over a continuum in higher education directed to arts administration. . . . The clear and overriding conclusion, therefore, is that a sizeable commitment is needed now to attract young people to the profession of arts administration and to prepare them for it."

Mr. Smith concluded his report with the recommendations that the New York State Council on the Arts lend financial aid to organizations needing qualified administrators but lacking the resources to hire them; that the Council commission a study to define arts administration, identify criteria and develop a pilot arts administration curriculum; and that the Council provide support to universities and colleges in the state willing to offer this curriculum experimentally. (61)

Nation Now Has First Candidate For Ph.D.
in Arts Administration

The nation's first candidate for a Ph.D. in arts administration is completing his initial semester of doctoral studies at the University of Wisconsin. Twenty-four-year-old Norman Kaderlan, who holds a B.A. in biology from Massachusetts Institute of Technology and an M.A. in the history of science from the University of Wisconsin, hopes to receive his Ph.D. by June 1970, following the completion of his course work and dissertation.

The events leading to his undertaking the doctoral degree program in September 1967 were part circumstance and part design. Long interested in the arts, Kaderlan produced several Gilbert and Sullivan operettas as an M.I.T. undergraduate, and later, as a graduate student, he worked in the cultural program at the University of Wisconsin. By the time he received his master's degree in 1966, he was convinced of his career interest in arts administration. Thus, he took a summer job with an opera company and applied for and won a Shubert Fellowship in theater management for 1966-67, enabling him to join the staff of the Wisconsin Union Theater as an intern. Kaderlan then transferred to the graduate business school at Wisconsin, hoping to study for an M.B.A. in theater management. When he discovered that he couldn't undertake the kind of program he wanted within the business school, he applied to the Graduate School of the University, which approved the special committee degree program in which he is now enrolled.

The program was developed by a committee of six faculty members, including the coordinator of the University's arts council, the director of the Wisconsin Union Theater, a speech professor, and three professors of management in the business school. The committee supervises Kaderlan's courses and independent studies and formulates and administers his preliminary examinations, supervises and approves his dissertation, and administers his oral examination. The program includes credit courses in the speech department and business school, directed reading and independent study in such areas as aesthetics, labor relations, sociology and management.

As a supplement to his formal program, Kaderlan is presently serving a half-time appointment as arts and lectures coordinator of the University's Center System, where he is booking concert programs for the 11 two-year colleges affiliated with the University. In June, he will return to the Lake George Opera Company for his second summer as business manager.

Under the guidance of his committee, Kaderlan will finish most of his credit courses this year and then devote his attention to independent study. "I plan to invest a year in catching up on my reading and research," he told *AM*, "since it's difficult to find sufficient time when you're working and taking courses." In 1969, he will begin writing his dissertation on how performing arts organizations decide what to perform. Upon completion of his studies, he hopes to be involved in program development.   (59)

Theater Administrators

Information on professional regional theaters, relating specifically to administrative personnel, has been accumulated by the Theatre Communications Group, which helps non-profit theaters throughout the country. T.C.G. indicated that the greatest needs of resident theaters are in the middle management group—general and business managers, educational and school program directors, and particularly promotion and public relations directors.

Through its Personnel Research Project, which registers qualified professionals and refers them to theaters, TCG has about 300 resumes in its file, with about 100 of them administrative personnel. The average age is 33 and the average minimum yearly salary required is $9,000, compared to the average salary of $8,300 offered by professional theaters over the past 18 months. Two-thirds of those listed prefer to work in the Northeast and one-fifth prefer the West Coast. (62)

Adding Personnel

While arts institutions attempt to cope with the problem of finding and training administrators, one state arts council is helping to solve another administrative need. The South Carolina Arts Commission recently initiated a Personnel Development Program, designed to help smaller arts groups add personnel to their staff in new, permanent positions. The Commission pays two-thirds of the first year's salary and the local organization pays one-third. During the second year, the Commission pays one-half of the salary and during the third year, one-third. The program also allows financial aid to groups wishing to extend a position from part-time to full-time, with the Commission paying two-thirds of the increase. Through participation in the program, four state arts groups have recently hired their first paid administrator, and another group has extended one job from part-time to full-time. (64)

272

The Administration of Arts Programs in Australia

By

Carrillo Gantner

There is a growing awareness in Australia that increased public support for the arts, evidenced in increased federal and state subsidy, the creation of large cultural centers and the growth of national, state and regional companies, demands a new kind of trained administrator. A national survey on "Theatre Staff in Australia," commissioned by the Australian Council for the Arts, found in December 1969 that 61 full time theatre administrators were employed in this country. This figure is not definitive, both because of the frequent fluctuations of theatrical activity and because of the rapid growth of state and regional organizations in the last two years. The interesting point, however, which is stressed in the survey, is that "Of this number it may be said that none received training as administrators, but that each one reached his position through work in some other branch of the theatre. This is the traditional procedure, whereby successful or promising directors, box office men, stage managers and occasionally actors move to positions of administrative responsibility. To this procedure there may be a few exceptions, men who become theatre administrators with previous experience only in business or accountancy, but such men are rare and regarded with initial suspicion in an intensely conservative profession."

No courses in arts or theatre administration exist in Australia although introductory sessions have been introduced into the undergraduate program of the Drama Discipline at Flinders University of South Australia. The National Institute of Dramatic Art in Sydney, the country's major professional theatre training school, has no regular courses in administration or management although occasional lectures are given on related fields. Such movement as there has been towards the training of new theatre administrators has been made since the establishment of the Australian Council for the Arts in 1968. The Council is the Federal Government's policy-making and subsidy-giving body in the performing arts. One of its primary concerns is with the training of professional personnel in all aspects of the arts: administrators, directors, designers, actors, dancers, technicians, etc. As well as funding the National Institute of Dramatic Art, the Australian Ballet School, the Interim Council for the establishment of a National Film and Television Training School and opera training schemes, the Council has a provision for the specialized training of professional personnel. This allocation, which for 1971 was $60,000, is mainly used to provide in-service training for administrators, directors, designers and technicians.

Trainees are attached to the best individuals or organizations working in the area for a certain period, usually a minimum of one year. In this time they work as an understudy in most aspects of the organization's work as well as assuming specific responsibilities within that organization. In this way the Council has funded the attachment of trainee administrators with the Adelaide Festival of Arts and the Melbourne Theatre Company, and many other trainees in different fields. The Council provides the necessary financial assistance while the individual companies provide the skills and undertake to devise specific training programs which met Council approval.

As another step towards more skilled management the Council is sponsoring a Theatre Administration School in

March 1972 concurrently with the Adelaide Festival of Arts. This week-long school will cater to about forty administrative personnel from the national, state and regional performing arts companies around the country. The School is designed to expose the participants to areas of problems in their field and to encourage a sharing of skills and techniques. In the school, papers will be given by senior administrators on such topics as financial management, fund raising, law and the arts, industrial relations, touring problems and public relations. This, of course, is no long term solution but it may lead both to a greater awareness of the needs and perhaps to finding specific solutions such as annual residential courses for arts administrators or the inclusion of a full program within a university or college.

At the same time the Council is beginning to look at ways in which business and industry can be encouraged to participate more closely in the arts. Inevitably we look to the United States where so much progress has been made in this field. Australians seem to have the habit of turning to the Government to provide their every need. It is vitally important that the whole community share the responsibility for putting the arts where they belong—at the very center of our lives.   (73)

Seminar in Gallery Management to Become Continuing Program

Better management of art galleries will mean greater financial rewards for the artists represented by them. To achieve this goal and to help art galleries plan their growth, a professional management institute, in cooperation with a well-respected art organization, has developed the first national approach to administrative training in the art gallery field. The result of this effort is an intensive five-day resident seminar program, "Art Gallery Management," which was presented this May at the Westchester Country Club in Rye, New York, as the first of a continuing series of similar programs to be offered regularly throughout the country.

The concept of educating the owners and managers of commercial arts galleries in professional management techniques originated with June Wayne, the founder-director of the non-profit Tamarind Lithography Workshop in Los Angeles. The workshop, funded by the Ford Foundation since its inception in 1959, has won national attention over the past decade for its success in engendering widespread public interest in lithography. During this period, scores of artists and printers were artistic collaborators at the workshop and thousands of works of art were created there. Curators, dealers and sales personnel were exposed to Tamarind also, because of the workshop's concern with the marketing and selling of original prints.

One fact that emerged from the Tamarind experience was that well-intentioned but amateurish business practices in art gallery operations were not uncommon, and many artists, as a result, were poorly represented. Convinced that only a national program wedding professional management techniques to the fine arts could alleviate the situation, Miss Wayne and Tamarind contracted with the Executive Development Center of Sterling Institute to help develop and then present a comprehensive training program. Sterling, a Boston firm, specializes in creating advanced management programs for industry and government.

The resulting seminar, underwritten by Tamarind and

developed by Sterling in cooperation with the workshop, was presented to 13 dealers representing medium-sized galleries. Each paid $450, excluding meals and accommodations, for the Monday through Friday resident program, which utilized a specially written seminar notebook and such learning methods as role playing, video tapes, goal-setting models, and case presentations and discussions. A staff of four was headed by Charles D. Orth, director of Sterling's Execlutive Development Center.

How successful was the seminar? *AM* met briefly with three participants, gallery owners from Jacksonville, Montreal and New York City. Each praised the program's professional orientation and seemed pleased with the benefits. (65)

British Management Training Program a Success

An interesting approach to the training of arts administrators initiated five years ago by the Arts Council of Great Britain, is proving highly workable. Unlike many successful American and Canadian training programs, the British concept does not involve post graduate university study. Instead, the 11 month program alternates periods of highly concentrated classroom study at a technical institute with three different periods of residency or secondment.

Until the Arts Council developed the current program, there was little formal training available in England. However, with the Council's own grant disbursement program growing annually and with many recipient groups administered less than professionally, it became evident that proper management and financial administration was in-

deed a Council concern. (The Council's budget for the 1971-
72 season is the equivalent of about $30 million, up from
less than $1-million some 25 years earlier. It subsidizes,
directly or indirectly, 1200 different organizations.) In
1967 the Council funded and developed the current course
at the London Polytechnic's School of Management Studies.
When the program began, it barely attracted the full quota
of 18 students. Now, there is strong competition for a
program place and more than 100 annual applicants, most
having a university background and some beginning arts
experience, are carefully screened.

The program begins each September with a four-day
orientation at the Polytechnic, followed by a one-month
secondment at an arts institution. In October, students
return to the Polytechnic for an intensive training program
which lasts until Christmas. Emphasis is on finance with
Polytechnic instructions lecturing on such subjects as accounting, marketing, statistics, and economics, and such
guests as Anthony Fields, the Council's Finance Director,
discussing arts accounting and box office management. In
addition, experts are brought in to discuss virtually every
area of arts management including publicity, audience research, funding and relations with local governments. Following a brief vacation students begin their second secondment, a three month residency devoted to some special
project. They return to the Polytechnic on April 1st for
three more months of advanced classroom work and conclude their training with a final secondment during July.

The program's positive results have been evident thus
far. Of the 18 students accepted annually, about 16 become
professional arts administrators. The Council's program
responsibility includes job placement although many students find positions during the training period. This past
year, for example, 13 graduates were placed with such

organizations as the London Symphony, New Philharmonia, Contemporary Dance Theatre, Midland Arts Center, Festival Ballet, and Royal Shakespeare Theatre. In four instances, students returned to places of secondment. The experience of one recent graduate, a 30-year old woman with teaching experience and a slight background but strong personal interest in the visual arts, indicates the kind of development possible. During her first secondment, she served as assistant to an art gallery director. Her second secondment was spent with another gallery where she organized and conducted an audience survey. She took a job with a different visual arts organization prior to her third secondment.

Several months ago, a special committee completed a detailed analysis of the program. Its just-published report confirmed the success of the program and recommended its continuation with some slight modifications.   (74-

---

Administrative Training Programs Show Progress

Two events of historic and practical importance to the field of arts administration training, mark the beginning of a new year. In January, 1971, Hyman R. Faine became the full-time director of the graduate arts administration program at U.C.L.A., (he served as a visiting regents professor in the program from January to June 1970) and assumed, what is believed to be, the nation's first regular professorship in the field of arts administration. Within coming weeks, Norman Kaderlan, recently named supervisor of performing arts for Arlington County, Virginia, will receive America's first Ph.D. in arts administration, from the University of Wisconsin. Elsewhere, there are

279

other positive developments including the initiation of a new graduate training program for arts managers at Drexel University in Philadelphia.

Faine's appointment as adjunct professor of arts administration in the Graduate School of Business Administration, marks a permanent commitment to the program by U.C.L.A. The program has been strengthened additionally by a substantial grant given it by Lloyd E. Rigler, president of Adolph's, a business concern.

The fourteen students currently entered in the program, including three of its original enrollees, are averaging about 14 hours of class a quarter and supplement their three or four courses with three-month internships during the fall quarter of the second year or during the preceding summer. Interestingly, such courses as Environment of the Arts World and Programming Policies of Arts Institutions are attracting students from other university departments, and a number of young law students have suggested that law and arts administration be combined into a single four year program. In addition to its courses, the program currently has ten research projects funded and underway, and hopes to develop an arts executives training program featuring short courses for cultural administrators.

The graduate arts administration program at the University of Wisconsin, under the direction of Professor E. Arthur Prieve in the School of Business, is also making considerable progress. In addition to the Ph.D. to be awarded Kaderlan, at least two students should receive arts administration M.A.'s by this June. Last semester, the seven enrolled students gave special attention to publications in the arts and this semester, with several new students added, the seminar program will focus on such areas as contracts, promotion and fund raising. Currently students are interning with such groups as the Milwaukee Repertory Theater, the Wisconsin Arts Council, and the University's own office of arts programs.

Arts administration training with a more commercial orientation, is proving successful at the University of Miami. The School of Music offers an undergraduate program leading to a degree in music merchandising, a field encompassing publishing, recording, copyright, teaching, performing, musical promotion and musical instruments. The program, in which 21 students are currently enrolled, provides internships for all students during the final semester of their senior years. According to Alfred Reed, the program's director, "every intern thus far has been hired by the firm in which he worked, and I have more calls for interns than I can possibly fill in the immediate future."

(69)

◆●▶

Chronological Developments in Administrative Training

Among key developments in arts management training are the introduction of new programs and the continued growth and development of existing ones. Harvard Universtiy's second annual Summer School Institute in Arts Administration for example, held this July, again attracted capacity enrollment including a number of students from Europe and Asia. Just published is the Institute's *Cases in Arts Administration*, ($17.50) available from the Institute at 75 Sparks Street, Cambridge, Mass. 02138.

Programs to be initiated this fall include New York University School of Education's one-year M.A. in performing arts administration and Southern Methodist University's

ARTS MANAGEMENT HANDBOOK

two-year M.A. program in arts administration, a combined effort of its School of Business and Meadows School of Art.

Elsewhere, business school interest in arts administration continues. At the University of Utah, the College of Business is cooperating with the theater department in offering an M.F.A. program in management and at Rollins College the theater arts department and Crummer School of Finance and Business Administration are offering an M.A. in performing arts management. At the University of Santa Clara, the School of Business initiated a new undergraduate course in management and the arts last quarter as a precursor to a possible program.

An important spur to the arts management training movement was a two-day conference at York University in Ontario, Canada, several months ago, when brought together representatives of programs at York, U.C.L.A., Harvard, Yale and the University of Toronto. Commenting on the meetings, D. Paul Schafer, the director of York's arts management and administration program said in part, "It was felt that case study research was necessary at one level but that some of the research should be directed towards broader issues, such as international and continental cultural policies, shifts in arts patronage, and trends in the arts. It was felt that attempts should be made to relate the development of programs in arts management and administration to the general trends and changes that are taking place in the arts in North America today." (71)

In Toronto, Ryerson Polytechnical Institute introduced a four-year arts administration program this fall as one of the major areas in its newly-established theater department. Elsewhere, new university courses being introduced this semester include: performing arts management in Ohio State's theater department; arts administration at Amer-

282

ican University's business administration school; and business problems of the film and entertainment industries at the New School for Social Research in New York. (74)

New programs at the graduate level have been launched at several universities. At Golden Gate University in San Francisco, the program in Arts Administration is offering the first of its six, three-credit, graduate level seminars this semester within the University's Graduate School of Business Administration. At Drexel University's Institute for Urban Management in Philadelphia, the graduate arts administration program announced last fall has finally gotten under way. To be eligible for either of the above programs applicants must have an accredited undergraduate degree. (77)

The Banff Centre's new Cultural Resources Management Program in Banff, Canada, becomes fully operational this March when George Moore assumes its direction. Beginning with a two-week-long executive development course in March, the program will conduct a continuing series of short courses and symposia throughout the year. Upcoming events include three-day seminars on cultural resources marketing in April and financial matters and taxation in May. Two-week programs in commercial art gallery management and performing arts management are scheduled for June and a six-week program in festival management will be held this summer. As the program develops, 500 to 600 people annually are expected to participate in some aspect of it. (79)

SERVICE ORGANIZATIONS
Service Organizations Expand Programs, Reach

Growth and program expansion loom ahead for several important but relatively young arts service organizations. The National Art Workers Community, for example, which was organized early in 1971 to provide key services and a collective voice for the individual artist, is on the verge of a major thrust forward. A recent recipient of its first grants from the National Endowment for the Arts and the New York State Council on the Arts—they totalled a modest $17,000—NAWC opened a permanent office on April 1st to house a full-time staff of three and scores of volunteer workers.

In behalf of artists NAWC has initiated a fair practices agency, a discount prescription and optical supplies program, and an exhibition space project. It will soon launch a medical/dental insurance plan. To receive NAWC newsletters and materials write the group at 32 Union Square East, New York, N.Y. 10003.

Geographical expansion is on the agenda for several organizations. Thanks to a grant from the National Arts Endowment, Hospital Audiences, Inc., which has provided arts programs for over 300,000 individuals in New York State hospitals and prisons since mid-1969, is now helping groups elsewhere to develop similar programs. As a result, HAI chapters have recently been established in Long Beach, Calif., Fort Wayne, Ind., and Hartford, Conn., with several more to be operational by year's end. Volunteer Lawyers for the Arts whose program began in New York in 1969, has since helped organize VLA-type groups in Chicago, Los Angeles and Washington, D.C. and has established relationships with correspondent attorneys in 11 other cities. Since its inception, VLA has found volunteer lawyers for nearly 200 artists and arts groups in New York and its roster now lists 135 attorneys.

Another expanding New York-based program, Theatre Development Fund, whose ticket purchase program has helped scores of theater and dance groups in New York and provided low-price tickets for thousands of people (200,000 tickets are being distributed this season) will branch out to Philadelphia next year and provide moderate ticket subsidy for theater, dance and musical programs there. TDF is exploring possible operations in Chicago and Washington, D.C. in coming seasons and an expansion of the New York service to other art forms including opera and concerts.

The Council of National Arts Organization Executives, a group which has been meeting regularly for more than a year held its first inter-organizational conference late this February with representatives of 15 organizations attending. The Council, now in a program development stage, plans to enlarge its membership beyond the current 10 national arts groups represented.   (75)

New Service Programs Respond to Arts Need

Two pioneer service programs, one national and one limited to New York State, are helping to meet important financial and administrative needs of cultural institutions. Since early this year, the New York Foundation for the Arts has been developing an experimental program, including the establishment of an interest-free revolving loan fund to state arts groups. In time this effort could influence the creation of similar programs on a national scale. Opportunity Resources for the Performing Arts, which launched its national program in July after months of preparation, is the first centralized inter-disciplinary personnel service for administrative and technical positions in the arts.

The non-profit New York Foundation was organized to help state arts groups out of the financial morass created by late-arriving grants and to help the New York State Council on the Arts solve an administrative problem. With a $13-million program of direct aid to state arts groups to manage during the past two years, the Council found it difficult to administer its ongoing programs as well.

Since February, however, efficient and economic administration of ongoing Council programs has been provided by the Foundation, which is not a state agency, but an independent Council grantee. During the current 1972-73 fiscal year, for example, the Foundation will administer Council funds of $536,000 for such programs as: technical assistance; touring performances; exhibitions; special programs pilot projects; information materials; and community informational services. The Foundation, which has no grant-making functions, utilizes Council staff members as program consultants and concerns itself strictly with administrative matters.

In its revolving loan fund program, the Foundation has answered a major need of the cultural group which learns it has been awarded a grant and then waits months to actually receive it. During the period of waiting, the arts group is frequently hard-pressed to meet its existing budget and finds it difficult, if not impossible, to obtain interim financing from conventional lending institutions. The new program has filled this breach by making interest-free loans to grantees, who, as a condition of their loans, assign to the Foundation the grants they eventually expect to receive. When the loan is repaid in full, the total amount of the grant is released to the organization. Using available funds, the Foundation made 65 loans totalling $257,050 to cultural groups through July 31st. According to director Richard d'Anjou the program has worked extremely well thus far and the default rate has been zero. All but $112,500 has been repaid and that total isn't due until November 15th. To continue and expand the program the Foundation is now seeking additional funds. "We'll accept money in any amount and on virtually any basis," d'Anjou told *AM*, "as long as we have the use of the funds at no cost."

Having established its two basic programs, the Foundation is now exploring its involvement in other areas. "We're a flexible instrument," commented d'Anjou "and we can respond to needs fast and efficiently. Having created our structure, we have the potential to undertake programs which nobody else can provided that sufficient funding is available."

The other new organization, Opportunity Resources, already has enrolled nearly 200 individuals seeking managerial or technical jobs—full and part-time as well as seasonal—and it is currently working with 24 arts groups seeking personnel. Arts administrators using the service pay an annual $10 registration fee while organizations pay $25. For each candidate referred by Opportunity Resources that it employs, the enrolled organization pays a small percentage of the first year's salary.

Individuals seeking positions fill out three-page forms provided by the service to indicate general skills and qualifications, employment background and long-range goals, and then are interviewed personally by director Gary Fifield or an assistant. Following each interview the Opportunity Resources staff member personally records his impression of the applicant. When positions are available, qualified applicants are contacted and if they are interested, their resumes and other data are forwarded to prospective employers. To reach applicants unable to come to New York, Fifield will visit several cities this fall to set up two or three day regional interview centers.

Organizations seeking personnel are entitled to submit an unlimited number of requests during their year's enrollment. When openings occur they are asked to provide Opportunity Resources with job descriptions. Profiles of suitable candidates are then forwarded to them, usually within several days.

Although it's too early to pinpoint definitive trends, Fifield indicated that 90 per cent of the job openings thus far were administrative rather than technical. "We've noted a great need," Fifield added, "for publicity people and fund-raisers with organizations outside of New York. Also, a number of groups have been seeking experienced stage managers." Individuals and organizations interested in registering with the non-profit service should write Opportunity Resources at 130 West 56 St., New York, N.Y. 10019. (76)

Community Arts Councils Move in New Directions

Community arts councils, a leading force in the decentralized, grass roots arts movement of the 60's, but somewhat overshadowed by state arts councils in recent years, are beginning to explore new methods of organization and new areas of interest.

In Hoboken, N.J., a densely populated community directly across the river from New York City, a Model Cities Agency is leading the drive to organize a new arts council to serve inner city residents. By May 1st, the Hoboken Model Cities Agency expects an affirmative response from the Housing and Urban Development Agency in Washington, D.C., to its request for seed money to establish the council. The request was part of an overall fund submission for the second year of a five-year program. If demonstration projects prove successful, the Agency plans to request larger sums in subsequent years.

Model Cities involvement with the arts began last summer, when it provided office space and facilities and helped fund small projects and street festivals for a pilot inner city arts project sponsored by New Jersey's state arts council. "From the local point of view," claims Robert C. Armstrong, principal coordinator of the Hoboken Agency, "our involvement gave legitimacy to the project. People didn't know the arts but knew us."

During the summer program, local talent in both the visual and the performing arts was discovered but there was no framework or organization for developing this talent throughout the year. That's when Armstrong and Phillip Danzig, the project director, began to shape the concept of an arts council. "The important thing," added Armstrong, "is that we don't want it to be an elitist council. Model Cities wants to help it with seed money, but we don't want to run it."

An action with great implications was recently taken by the Winston-Salem, N.C. Arts Council. According to new by-laws, effective July 1st, the council will be governed by a 15-member board of trustees including five officers, drawn not from the council's member groups, but from the community at large. The decision by the nation's oldest arts council to place leadership in community hands, will be watched with interest elsewhere.

Across the continent, an already established arts council has expanded its area of concern to include environmental issues affecting the community. Allied Arts of Seattle, through its committee on urban development, recently issued a widely publicized report, months in preparation, which concluded that the Port of Seattle Commission "has shown an indifference bordering on arrogance toward the city's total environment."

The report contained a series of specific recommendations to the Commission, suggesting ways to safeguard the city's shoreline. It also urged Allied Arts to take an active interest in future Port activities. The council adopted the report's recommendations. (70)

Chapter IV – Operations

MANAGEMENT TECHNIQUES

Management Expert Advises Long Range Planning

By

Dr. H. Lawrence Wilsey

Established arts organizations are noted for their ability to stave off financial disaster and organizational collapse year after year. Newer arts organizations lead a more tenuous existence, with enthusiasm often being their basic asset. In view of the relatively insecure and unstable life of an arts organization, there are compelling reasons for imaginative, yet practical, long-range planning.

A long-range plan for any arts organization calls for basic decisions at each of seven planning levels. The following are examples of questions that should be considered and answered in order in planning:

Philosophy. What should the role of arts organizations be in meeting the cultural needs of society and the individual? What knowledge, skills and interests need to be developed to meet the needs of society and the individual? (A simple, brief statement of philosophy sets the perspective of the organization and provides the reason for its existence.)

Objectives. What are the cultural expectations of the people of this community? To what extent should this organization strive to meet or modify them? Which are the publics that this organization should interest? Are the cultural needs of these publics being satisfied by other arts organizations? If so, should the broad objectives of this organization be extended or modified? What are the levels of audience exposure for which this organization should strive in future years? What should be its membership goals?

Programs. What should be this organizations type and range of programs in order to achieve its objectives? What should be the optimum frequency of arts events? In what locations should such events be held? What program effort should this organization direct toward school age children to assure future audiences? What effort should be directed toward groups with extensive leisure time?

Organization. What human abilities are required to execute this organization's programs? What boards, committees, professionals, and administrative positions are required to plan, conduct, and evaluate the work of this organization? What functions and responsibilities should be assigned to each board, committee and administrative position? What working relationships and reporting responsibilities will help conduct the organization's work most effectively? How should external relationships be conducted?

Staffing. What numbers of people with what qualifications and characteristics are required to provide effective board, volunteer, and professional staff leadership for this organization? What kinds of incentives can be given to volunteer workers? What type of classification, salary, and professional development program is required?

Facilities. What numbers, kinds, quality, and location of facilities are required to serve program needs, as previously defined? Are the proper types of facilities being planned for future expansion, programs, flexibility, and economy?

Finance. What operating and capital funds will be required to support the agreed-upon arts programs and to provide necessary staff, facilities, equipment and supplies? When will these funds be required? From what sources can they be obtained? What financial programs can be modified? Which can be extended depending upon levels of support? Is federated giving appropriate to this organization and its objectives?

The effort involved in the planning process is demanding. However, the results may far outweigh the time and mental stress involved in its development. Benefits that can realistically be achieved include:

1) Better definition of the organization's objectives, with assurance that its goals are in reasonable harmony with the community's expectations.

2) More effective arts programs.

3) A higher level of morale and enthusiasm by those who feel a part of the organization and its future.

4) A sounder approach to financing arts programs, with financial goals keyed to achievable and desirable program levels.

5) Greater assurance that the organization is contributing effectively towards meeting cultural needs of the community. (18)

Save Time and Money by Weeding Out Old Records

By

Eleanor Oshry Shatzkin

Every modern business and organization recognizes the need for written records, but too few of them recognize the need for their destruction. The larger the organization, the more it needs a systematic program of record retention and disposal. Such a program can increase the efficient use of records which are retained, and also result in saving money that would otherwise be spent on filing cabinets, space and clerical time.

To control the growth of files, one must control first the creation of new records and second, the destruction of old records. The most effective way to limit the paper work problem is to practice "birth control" with respect to the creation of new papers. Unless new forms and reports are limited to those that satisfy a proven need and unless the number of duplicate copies of each is controlled, files will overflow an office.

Even if a report is necessary, its useful life may be limited. Certainly if it has been issued in many copies, it need not remain in the permanent files of each of the individuals who received it.

When a new report is approved, the ultimate disposition of each copy should be determined. At this time, too, plans should be made for the consolidation of data which may be needed only in summary form after a given period of time. In this way the removal from active to inactive storage and the destruction of papers which have outlived their usefulness will be automatically controlled.

Almost every inventory of an organization's files will turn up papers which can be destroyed without further consideration. For the remaining ones, each group should set up destruction schedules based on its individual needs, considering legal requirements, degree of risk in not having the record and frequency of reference to the record.   (9)

———————◄●►———————

Make Financial Picture Public;
Free Auditing Services Available

By

George M. Schaefer

One of the most essential but most frequently overlooked requirements for good business management of cultural institutions is an annual certified audit of its accounts. Yet it is remarkable how many such institutions, some of them with full-time professional directors, will go for years without a proper investigation of their finances, in spite of the fact that audit services are often available free of charge.

If for no other reason than that of self-protection, boards of directors and administrators should be eager for a yearly statement to confirm the honesty and accuracy of their stewardship.

I do not mean to suggest that the audit would ever reveal a misappropriation of funds. No one with a talent for embezzlement would waste time in a field that suffers from a chronic shortage of cash. It is this same shortage that often forces directors, business managers and curators to add bookkeeping to their workload or to depend upon volunteer, amateur, part-time help. Mistakes are inevitable, but generally honest, and of a nature that a CPA can correct in a matter of minutes. If, however, they go uncorrected and are carried forward year after year, a hopeless jumble results.

Normally museums, symphonies, theatres, and similar institutions operate on budgets that can bear the expense of audit fees, and accounting firms are usually quite modest in their charges for services to such agencies. However, if the budget will not bear even this amount, the National Association of Accountants is extremely cooperative and will request one of its members to do the job as a public service. If approached far enough in advance, the NAA will also schedule a member CPA to audit a fund-raising campaign.

Most cultural organizations receive a large part of their support from public contributions and some from tax revenues. Both sources automatically authorize large numbers of people to know how their money is being handled and spent and there is no better way to answer an inquiry regarding finances than by producing a neatly bound, certified audit for the most recent complete fiscal year. In short, anyone responsible for the operation of any organization who does not pay every cent of its costs from his own pocket should insist on an annual audit. (8)

Insurance Lowers Risks for Cultural Groups

All the activities, and the properties, of cultural groups add up to one word—risk—for the organizations involved. Arts groups are in constant contact with the public and employ a variety of workers, volunteer and paid, who could suffer injuries on the job.

Arts groups are frequently the custodians of priceless works of art, expensive musical instruments, costumes and scenery. They may own a variety of equipment, from showcases to typewriters, and it is not uncommon for them to have large amounts of cash on hand, as money comes in from advance ticket sales, benefits and so on.

Every arts manager, and every cultural group should therefore be aware of the risks incurred, and the kind of insurance protection needed.

One of the first things to consider is the extent of the group's liability. This varies depending on whether or not the group is incorporated and what state it is in. There are legal questions involved, and they should be settled by a lawyer.

Once liability is determined, it is necessary to ask: What kind of insurance is needed? Each group will have to decide on the basis of its activities and its budget. However, there are several kinds of insurance that should be part of a good insurance package.

The following description of the policies is meant not to be definitive, but to provide some guide lines.

Liability: Public liability is almost a must for any group which deals with the public. It can be short term (special events) or long-term, depending on the need. When thinking of it, bear in mind that the group deals with the public not only in the concert hall, or theatre, but also in elevators,

297

on the grounds, and in the parking lot. Liability also includes employees, some of whom may be covered by compensation laws. These vary considerably from state to state and should be checked.

Bonding: Anyone who is responsible for large sums of money should be bonded. If many persons handle the money, it is possible to get a blanket bond, or a position bond which, within a fixed time limit, allows for the theft to be discovered and reported to the insurance company. This is important in situations in which an inventory (of costumes, for example) is not made frequently.

Fine arts policy: An all-risk policy covering all kinds of losses—fire, theft, breakage, water damage and so on. It can cover property (usually paintings and sculpture) belonging to the group, and property on loan, either to them or by them. It can be short term—as little as one day—to long term—up to three years. Payment may be a flat fee decided on in advance, or it may be a monthly fee that varies, depending on what valuables are on hand at the moment. A similar policy can insure costumes and sets.

Floaters: There are two types of floaters of interest to arts groups—the theatrical floater, designed for an acting group, both while traveling and on location, and an instrument floater, which offers protection on an individual or an orchestra basis. (Rates decline as the number of instruments insured goes up). These floaters insure against fire, theft, accidents, etc.

Equipment, including office equipment: It should be protected against the usual hazards, both natural and manmade. The policy might include an all-risk office contents clause. In some states vehicle liability insurance is compulsory, but if any vehicles are rented, the kind of coverage the leasing agent provides should be looked into.

Where can arts groups go to get good insurance advice? Most groups include some individuals who either sell insurance themselves or can recommend someone reliable. Another possibility is the agent who handles insurance and bonding for the local school district. Many of the problems are similar, so that the agent comes to the arts group with a good idea of what is needed. He is also familiar with local laws and can help guarantee that there are no gaps.

It is part of an insurance agent's job to give insurance advice without fee, although of course he hopes it will lead to a sale. It is also his job to plan a policy which gives maximum coverage for minimum cost.

When considering coverage, a committee should evaluate the proposals before making recommendations. Keep in mind that there are two kinds of insurance salesmen, those who work for a mutual company and can sell only the insurance of their company, and independent agents who represent many companies and choose among them.   (19)

Outdoors Affair?

Rain insurance is issued by all leading underwriters as a financial umbrella over outdoor affairs. Premium rate is around $13 for each $100 of protection, against 0.1 inch of rain or more.   (7)

Card Files Keep Tabs on All Facilities in Community

Two unique filing systems are helping community cultural organizations in Yakima, Washington, to discover, in an instant, the availability of all local facilities that can house arts presentations, the names of local instructors in the arts, and the name of every performing artist and group in the city.

In a file titled "Auditorium Space," the Allied Arts Council of the Yakima Valley, a year-old organization, lists more than 80 available locations in Yakima with seating capacities ranging from 25 to 4,000. Each separate card lists information on seating capacity, stage facilities, kitchen facilities, the person to contact for rental of the space, the fee, and any special data which might be useful such as, the availability of classrooms or extra space which might be used for exhibitions.

In researching the information for the file, a committee of five women worked for nearly a year, visiting the facilities and checking on their possible use for meetings, rehearsals, exhibitions and performances. Among the kinds of structures listed are auditoria, churches, clubs, granges, gymnasia, hotels, lodges, school facilities, and theatres.

The second file compiled by the arts council, contains the names of several hundred instructors, artists, performers and exhibition groups from every artistic discipline. Instructors' cards, for example, list such details as the kinds of classes they conduct, their fees and their educational background. The file is cross-indexed so that in addition to being listed by name, each instructor and performer or group is listed by the art he specializes in.

According to Mrs. Robert Busse, who headed the council committee which worked on the project, the list is assumed

300

never to be complete because the city and its residents is constantly changing. Thus, additions and subtractions must be made frequently. (21)

What Do You Sound Like?

The voice that answers the telephone for you is more than an important cog in the machinery. It is an important part of the image your institution presents to the public. Telephones left unattended, or phones that are always busy are annoying to the public. Curt replies or "holds" by your operator can lose ticket sales or offend the audience. The operator who can answer elementary requests for information without shunting the caller to an extension not only makes friends, but saves others in your institution valuable time. (4)

Tip on Group Structure

The way an organization is structured can have great impact on its effectiveness. Voluntary groups like orchestra associations or theatre patron societies can make better use of their members' energies by taking a tip from management experts. Dr. Rensis Likert, director of the Institute for Social Research, University of Michigan, suggests one technique art managers might bear in mind: Says Dr. Likert:

"The organization should be built into highly effective groups linked together by persons who hold overlapping memberships in at least two groups. For example, a superior of one work group is a subordinate in the work group

301

at the next higher echelon. Organizations built on this principle can achieve higher motivation, better coordination, better communication, greater confidence and trust, higher productivity, and lower costs than those relying on a man-to-man pattern of organization.'' (6)

————— ◂•▸ —————

Skilled Leadership Key To Good Group Meetings

Meetings of arts groups need not be a bore or chore. They can be creative and satisfying. Skilled leadership is the key.

''Discussion leadership is becoming a science,'' says University of Michigan psychologist Norman R. F. Maier, noted for his studies on group problem-solving. According to Prof. Maier, the skillful leader uses certain principles of group behavior, derived from research in various fields of psychology. What are they and how can they serve to improve problem-solving discussions?

The starting point of a problem is richest in possible solutions. Partial success in moving toward a goal makes people reluctant to start all over again, but a fresh start is the only way to increase the variety of solution possibilities.

Encourage the group to be more problem-minded. The first prerequisite for reaching agreement on a solution is reaching agreement on what the problem is.

Avoid dead ends. Stick to ''surmountable'' obstacles. All too often ''a particular obstacle is selected and pursued despite the fact that it cannot be remedied.''

Disagreement can lead either to hard feelings or to innovations, depending on the discussion leadership. The leader ''must not only prevent the suppression of disagreement, but also encourage a respect for disagreement and

302

thereby turn it into a stimulant for new ideas."

The idea-getting process should be separated from the idea-evaluating process. The latter is the practical side of problem-solving and involves the testing and the comparison of solutions in the light of what is known. Idea-getting requires a willingness to break away from past experience and search for something different or new.

Problem situations should be turned into choice situations. "The fact that one solution is found does not preclude the possibility that there may be others, yet people frequently behave as though this were the case."

"Solutions suggested by the leader are improperly evaluated and tend either to be accepted or rejected." Thus he must "refrain from introducing his views or passing judgment on the ideas expressed by participants. His job is to conduct the discussion."

Maier examines these principles in his book, *Problem-Solving Discussions and Conferences* (McGraw-Hill). (23)

Check Your Security, Detective Warns Arts

By

E. R. Kessler

A rash of art thefts in recent years have made international headlines. The stories about them make exciting reading, but for the arts managers whose institutions have suffered, the theft of a valuable painting is not at all entertaining. The fact is that, sooner or later, almost every artistic enterprise needs to take a look at its security program. This applies as forcefully to theatres, orchestras and other performing arts groups as it does to museums, although, of course, the problems of each kind of institution may differ.

For many years Pinkerton has provided protection for theatres and music halls, museums and galleries, carnivals, fairs, conventions, exhibits, and special events of every description. From this experience has emerged a set of guidelines that arts administrators, responsible for the safety of people and property, should bear in mind.

For many institutions, the box office is the most vulnerable point. The prudent theatre or orchestra management makes sure that the box office staff is locked in to avert a surprise entry. The cubicle should be equipped with an audible alarm, with concealed button, to alert the public and the nearest police station in the event of emergency.

The backstage areas of arts facilities should be carefully policed, and unauthorized persons kept out. A stage doorman must never leave his post to summon a performer; he should deputize someone for such an errand. Backstage help and the regular stage crew should be instructed to protect the personal property of the performers on stage.

Ideal backstage planning permits but one exit to the street and one to the front of the house from backstage. Both should be under constant surveillance. Temporary openings—for carting scenery, properties, trunks, instruments—also may require guarding against unauthorized entry.

Performers and musicians should be cautioned against leaving money and valuables backstage. The concert hall or theatre, however, should provide lock-up storage for portable musical instruments and lockers for street clothing and personal property.

"No smoking" rules must be enforced with reasonable and safe areas provided for smoking. Watch out for cleaning fluids, faulty wiring, and electrical appliances which are potential fire hazards.

Although it is best for museums and galleries to get advice from a professional security agency and follow it, there are several general rules to be followed. Uniformed guards should be stationed to command constant surveillance of all valuable exhibits. Electronic and supersonic devices can insure protection from loss or damage. In some cases, close public inspection must be prevented by roping off sections. All areas, including washrooms, should be patrolled to prevent concealment after hours. Building security should prevent entrance through the roof, shaftways, or windows.

When large crowds are anticipated for special exhibits, plainclothesmen should circulate among the public. Wherever possible, however, visitors should be limited to a number that can be readily watched at all times. Of course, good door, lock and key controls are essential.

Festivals and other arts programs held in the open air, should have a minimum number of entrances and exits which can be easily watched. The use of uniformed guards and close cooperation with local police will minimize thefts, arguments, disorders and diversions.

Take security seriously. Don't let artistic temperament or a genteel atmosphere result in haphazard security or relaxed protection.

Remember that you are not only leaving yourself open to management's losses, but you must also protect the public, your public. (6)

Thanking the Speaker

Letters of appreciation should be sent to guest speakers immediately following their appearances at meetings of your organization. The letters are not only good ways of thanking them for their efforts, but may help also to insure their return. (45)

Addresses on Publications

When sending out published material, be sure to put the address of your organization within the publication. *Arts Management* recently received an eight page newsletter which was handsomely produced and well written. However, nowhere within the newsletter was an address given for the sponsoring institution. (21)

Answering Service

If your organization uses a telephone answering service, be sure that it is equipped to give simple routine information such as the name of your production or presentation. A well-informed answer service operator can make friends for your arts group. (17)

Answering Letters

Letters to a cultural organization should never go unanswered. If an executive of your organization will be away from his office for a definite period of time, a system of acknowledging his mail should be instituted. A reply should be mailed immediately to the letter writer stating that the official is away and giving the date of his return. The reply should also indicate whether the matter referred to is being discharged by another member of your organization's staff or if it must await the executive's return for further action. (32)

Monthly Reminder

Organizations publishing a monthly newsletter might have increased response to their programs if they include in it a detachable, easy-to-read calendar of events. The Huntington New York Arts Council's "Month-At-A-Glance" newsletter insert lists events and times and can be posted for easy reference. (69)

Brown Bagging

Lunch hour may be a convenient time for meetings but group sessions at restaurants often prove unproductive because of noise and table clutter. You might try holding meetings in an office instead and invite participants to bring their own sandwiches. Allied Arts of Seattle holds brown bag committee meetings in its office and the N.Y. Board of Trade's Art & Business Cooperative Council, which holds regular "bring your own lunch" meetings each month, has discovered that busy participants appreciate the informal, yet businesslike sessions. (72)

Inadvertent Humor

Every letter or document which leaves the office of an arts organization contributes or detracts from the image of the organization. Although proof-reading is tedious, the good administrator can't afford to sign his name to a letter or a proposal which he hasn't carefully read. Seems obvious? The following quotations were taken directly from material mailed by arts groups. "We would like to begin a new *pogram* in the arts," said one. A second organization requested "matching *fun* grants." (65)

FREE GOODS AND SERVICES

Save on Office Machines By Free, Discount Deals

Non-profit cultural organizations can sometimes get needed office equipment free or at a discount from the manufacturer. A recent *Arts Management* check of leading companies making typewriters and other office equipment reveals the conditions under which arts groups can save money on this merchandise.

Remington-Rand, for example, will give used office machines free to non-profit organizations, depending on the availability of the equipment and the worthiness of the institution. Interested groups should apply to the local Remington office which in turn will submit recommendations to the company's national Contributions Committee. This body determines which applicants receive free used typewriters, adding machines, computers and desk calculators. According to Gordon Smith of Remington's public relations department, a group has a far better chance of receiving equipment if a Remington employee is involved in its work. Remington does not offer discounts on new equipment.

Underwood has a policy of offering non-profit organizations discounts on new typewriters (including portables, standard machines and electric models), accounting machines, calculators and small computers. Cultural groups interested in buying new machines should apply in writing to the nearest of the 125 Underwood branch offices.

Smith-Corona, although it does not offer equipment to cultural institutions, has a policy of making cash contributions to foundations and organizations as it sees fit.   (7)

———————◄●►———————

Textile Mill Remnant Bargains Slash Set and Costume Costs

Theatre and opera companies can slash production costs by buying material for costumes and draperies directly at the mill as remnants, rather than through local retail outlets.

One East Coast community opera company told *Arts Management:* "We saved about 90% on our material costs for our last show. The bill could have run to $600 or even $700."

In the textile industry, mill remnants are frequently on hand in lengths of a dozen yards or more, and in a variety of styles and shades. Mill managers are glad to turn such remnants, too small for commercial sale, into cash-and-carry deals. A Pennsylvania mill opened its plant on a Saturday recently to show its wares to a theatre director. The latter made a 500-yard bargain purchase.

In the immediate vicinity, textile mills can be found through city directories and classified telephone books. For the larger surrounding area, a quick way to locate mills and determine the types of fabric they produce is to consult *Thomas' Register of American Manufacturers.* (2)

Free Office Furniture Available

Office furniture, used, but in good condition, is often available to arts organizations at no cost. Business firms moving to new quarters frequently refurnish them completely. Some are willing to give the older furniture to non-profit groups. One college recently received over 2000 pieces of office equipment left by a business on the move. (10)

------◄●►------

Schools Can Get U.S. Surplus for Arts

Paints, canvas, pianos, electronic sound equipment and other materials useful to arts managers are among the thousands of items the U.S. government is trying to give away as surplus. Arts managers who know how, and whose organizations qualify as educational institutions, can obtain such equipment and supplies. But, according to J. Wendell Gray, chief of the Surplus Property Utilization Division, U.S. Department of Health, Education and Welfare, a surprising number of those who qualify don't know it, and don't make use of their opportunity.

The merchandise available is decidedly not junk; about 30 per cent of it has never been used. Moreover, the range of goods is amazing. "We have distributed more than 30,000,000 running yards of canvas," Gray told *AM*. "We know that in some cases it has supplied art classes with canvas for easel painting. We have given away paints, sheet plastic that can be molded, paper of all types, materials for soundproofing auditoriums, vehicles, and all kinds of equipment for stage sets, even pianos and other musical instruments."

Unfortunately, there is no master list of materials available at any given time. For this reason, arts managers who wish to draw from the $400,000,000 surplus pile must use their imagination and know the right procedure.

Actual distribution of surplus is made by state, rather than federal, agencies. Each state has a surplus property administrator (titles vary) who oversees the whole opera-

311

tion. If you are interested in receiving surplus materials, the first step is to determine whether anyone in your institution has already been authorized by the state administrator to procure surplus. If no one has, a permit should be obtained from the state, and one individual in the institution should be appointed to take charge of the program.

This official should keep the state office informed in detail of the needs of the institution so that when state personnel draw supplies from federal sources, they can keep their eyes open for the items wanted. In turn, he should be kept informed by his own department heads of their requirements.

There is no guarantee that appropriate supplies will be available at the time of the visit to the state warehouse, inasmuch as goods move in and out constantly. But close liaison with the state agency, combined with visits and a flair for adapting materials to needs, can result in a harvest of supplies for the institution.

Recipients must pay a service charge for handling and storage, but this averages only 3.8 per cent of the original government purchase price, *AM* was told. The institution must also carry away its selections.

All questions, Gray emphasized, should be sent to state officials for surplus property at the state capital — not to Washington. (4)

Good Buys on Vehicles

Motor vehicles are sold or exchanged periodically by a number of public and private institutions that must have new ones. An organization can save the dealer's commission and be sure of a sound buy by keeping in touch with them. One local Red Cross chapter last year sold eight 1958 station wagons in excellent condition at more than $150 below the standard used price, on a first-come basis. Such organizations, not being in the used car business, are mainly interested in finding buyers promptly who can pay the full amount at once. (5)

VISUALS: FILM AND AUDIO

Artists Lay Down Rules For Promotional Design

A panel of artists meeting to consider the graphic quality of printed materials circulated by health and welfare groups in New York has come up with a series of guidelines broadly applicable to the problems of cultural organizations as well.

In planning brochures, pamphlets, and other literature, they agreed, the first step is to know what general style or tone will appeal to the target audience.

Illustrations and text should both be used sparingly, allowing ample white space. In general, they found, a few large illustrations are more effective than a great many small ones.

The inside of the folder or brochure should be just as carefully planned as its cover, and should be just as well designed.

Color—an expensive extra—should be used with economy. A little bit can go a long way. Many two-color jobs are more striking and effective than far more expensive four-color productions.

Work closely with the designer and printer, giving both enough time to do a good job.

Do not try to cram too many ideas into a single piece of literature. Keep it simple and direct.

According to J. K. Kansas, chief of press relations for Esso Research and Engineering, and a member of the panel, basic decisions must not be left to the designer or printer. "The public relations man must make all decisions relevant to his materials, since he alone fully understands what he hopes to accomplish with the specific printed piece." (7)

Effective Charts

A chart in your printed materials can often dramatize a point better than a thousand statistics. But it can also confuse. An effective chart must be uncluttered and simple. Use brightest colors for most important points, duller hues for subordinate ideas. Avoid cliches like the fund drive thermometer. (20)

Child's Play

Planning a production involving numerous costume changes? The Arena Stage in Washington, D. C., preparing for the premiere of *The Great White Hope,* devised a scheme to help actors keep track of the more than 200 complete outfits and 1,000 individual costume pieces used in the production. The Arena's costume designer prepared sets of cut-out dolls carefully dressed to look like the actors. Each of the 62 actors then received his own set of dolls dressed with all of the costume pieces and changes used by him in the production. (58)

Local Artists

Performing arts organizations can highlight their printed materials by showcasing the work of local artists. The Oklahoma City Symphony Orchestra, for example, features a different three-color abstract print by local artist Harrison Taylor, on the cover of each of its new programs. In addition, the orchestra displays the entire series of prints in its auditorium lobby and offers them for sale. (35)

315

Charting Progress

An arts organization with an impressive record of growth can effectively dramatize it by using charts and graphs in its publications to tell the story at a glance. In a recent issue of its newsletter, the Art Gallery of Toronto showed its growth from 1935 to the present with a bar graph. Next to the graph, three columns of figures compared the growth of its programs in numbers and percentages. A quick look at the illustrations was better than words in telling the story.   (36)

------- ◄●► -------

Film Makes Dramatic, Versatile Promotion Aid; Arts Groups Can Get Free Help From Cinema Clubs

Can your organization use a motion picture film to display its activities? The recent rapid growth of cinema clubs in all parts of the country may provide the means.

A 19-minute color film made by a club of skilled amateurs, accompanied by original music and commentary on tape, has preserved the highlights of a 1961 community arts festival and helped in building an arts council in Williamsport, Pennsylvania.

Mrs. Barnard C. Taylor, executive director of the Greater Williamsport Arts Council, outlined for *Arts Management* how the novel film-making project was carried out and how it has been used to promote the cultural development of the city. Costing only $900 to produce, because almost all work was donated, the picture and tape would have cost about $9,000 had it been made commercially.

"We offer it to anyone who wishes to see what we did,"

Mrs. Taylor said. "There will be a fee for postage and handling."

Original sponsor of the project was the Junior League of Williamsport, which contributed $500 of the originally-estimated cost. The vital film-making talent came from members of the Susquehanna Cinema Club, who volunteered time, equipment and filming services, and from Hugh MacMullan, a former Hollywood director who had also previously directed a film for a Williamsport welfare agency.

MacMullan directed the script writing, building it from scenes and groups participating in the festival. Much of the recording was done months after the festival ended in early May 1961. Titles were painted by Mrs. Taylor's husband, a graphic artist, commentary was delivered by a local radio announcer, John Archer, and music for the film was composed by Dr. Glen Morgan of the Lycoming College Music Department.

The film was first shown at a dinner attended by 250 people who had participated in the 1961 festival. Mrs. Taylor took this occasion to present plans for the 1962 arts festival. Since opening night, the picture has been shown to 23 organizations that had taken part in the filmed festival, and to schools. No fees were asked. Cinema club members ran the film.

"Three groups that had not been involved the year before were introduced to the idea of the festival through the film," Mrs. Taylor told *Arts Management*.

The picture also served the broader publicity interests of Williamsport. It was run twice on local television covering several counties and was shown to the staff of America House and to a representative of the Museum of Modern Art, both in New York. Congressman Herman T. Schneebeli has asked that the U. S. Information Agency consider making use of it.

Mrs. Taylor told *AM:* "The Junior League members, who underwrote it, feel very good when they see the film as a record of the events presented under their financing. The clubs enjoyed seeing friends and neighbors perform and the sections of performances they missed. Others were sorry they missed the 1961 festival after having seen the film.

"To other communities planning a similar venture, I would advise holding a planning session with the film makers to reach conclusions on the emphasis the arts group wishes for its future educational use. To show what has evolved, and how it will develop, is difficult for one who has not been knee-deep in the process, and this should be discussed until a definite approach can be decided upon." (7)

Theatre Films

Do you have any high quality films about your organization that might be suitable for showing in movie theatres? Here are some tips. Theatres prefer color to black and white and require that all prints be 35 millimeter. As a rule, running time of each film should not exceed 10 minutes. Also, the films offered to theatres should not have appeared on television previously. Finally, films, although informative, should have some entertainment value and the material in them should not be dated. Such films are distributed to theatres by national agencies. (28)

Color Slides

Color slides taken by members of a cultural group on one tour can do double duty in illustrating a lecture and in indirectly promoting the next tour. On October 1 the Walters Art Gallery in Baltimore presented an illustrated lecture on English art, using pictures taken by members last April during a two-week charter flight tour of English galleries and private collections. The program, open to the public, was held two weeks before the deadline for joining the Walters gallery in order to take part in its charter flight art tour of Southern France next April.   (9)

Supermarket Slides, LP Records Potent Arts Promotional Tools

Arts groups, often with the help of local corporations, are developing unusual promotion devices for use in raising funds, reaching new audiences and promoting programs. In St. Louis, where the Arts & Education Council's annual united fund drive has a $1-million goal this year, flags, slide showings and phone recordings are among the devices currently being used in support of the campaign.

A staple of the Council's annual promotion diet and a very effective one, is the tape-slide showing prepared with the voluntary help of Batz-Hodgson-Neuwoehner, a local advertising agency, for dissemination to civic groups and other organizations. Focusing on the activities of the fund's 10 beneficiary cultural and educational groups, the showing features 140 slides and a 20-minute taped narrative.

With business assistance, the sight and sound of the fund reaches thousands of people daily during March and April. Flags, imprinted with the fund logo, fly from business offices downtown and in the suburbs. The time and temperature phone service sponsored by the First National Bank of St. Louis has an added taped message during the drive, "Support the Arts and Education Fund. The time is now." At 43 locations of St. Louis's largest food chain, Schnuck's, shoppers waiting in check-out lines are treated to slide showings from special rear projection machines. Although the machines have been installed mainly to flash commercial messages, at the rate of one every six seconds, some 20 slides in each carousel of 100 are devoted to public service spots, with about 5 to 10 at each store promoting the Arts and Education Fund. Another slide show, this at member banks of Mark Twain Bancshares, features six slides in each of eight projectors devoted to the drive. Slides alternate pictures of the fund's participating agencies and a title reading "Another reason to give to the Arts and Education Fund."

In Philadelphia, Franklin Concerts, Inc., an organization which helps young professional musicians begin their careers, is using a long-playing record, "Stars of Tomorrow," as one of its prime promotional tools. Underwritten by Sears Roebuck last year, the demonstration stereo LP features performances by five Franklin ensembles and six artists. It has been used successfully in introducing potential concert buyers and foundations to the artists and as a gift to donors. (75)

Go-Go Logo

Logos, the visual organizational symbols which appear on letterheads, programs, etc., can reap extra publicity—in advance. If your group doesn't have a logo or needs a new one, you might turn to the community for help. The new Cleveland Area Arts Council held a well-publicized logo contest among local design students with all entries exhibited in the lobby window at the Cuyahoga Savings Association. The bank also donated a cash award for the winning design which has since been adopted as the permanent symbol of the council. In Seattle, the Arts Commission recently approved a $500 award for a design contest to find a new Commission logo. (77)

PRINTED MATTER AND DIRECT MAIL

Four Methods for Building a Mailing List

Directors of arts groups are in a unique position to build mailing lists, according to one of the most experienced authorities in direct mail work.

"Because these directors are conducting ventures that will benefit the whole community, they can hope to enlist the support of sources for names that would be closed to the ordinary profit-making organization," declares Milton Smoliar of Names Unlimited, a New York list brokerage firm. Smoliar made this statement when asked by *Arts Management* about the most efficient methods to build a mailing list. There are several basic ways:

Establishing personal contact with local sources of names, as Smoliar suggests, is advisable when a relatively small, selective list is needed. For example, when a museum or educational institution wants to reach prospective patrons, the local civic clubs, college alumni groups and business associations may very well be willing to furnish their own lists.

Personal contacts may be supplemented by research in directories. The best are the city directories published by R. L. Polk, Social Registers, and the *Guide to American Directories for Compiling Mailing Lists.*

By collecting recent programs of events staged by local organizations, cultural and otherwise, you can obtain lists of officers, board members and benefactors, printed in the programs. The society page of the newspaper is another source of names of patrons or active volunteer workers. A good typist familiar with the city in question can search and type these names and home addresses from the phone book at a rate of 30 an hour or faster.

The telephone book itself, is the best source from which to compile a so-called saturation list. When the aim is a large response this is by far the most efficient way to start. A home typist can reproduce a list from the directory at a cent a name or less.

The third method of building a mailing list, using a commercial list compiler, is more expensive. There are list compilers in almost every sizeable town, but their fees range from $10 to $15 per 1,000 names, and some specialized lists cost much more. Moreover, commercial list houses sometimes provide lists which are essentially duplications of the phone book.

List brokers—not the same as list compilers—are helpful when an arts group is planning a mailing of national dimensions, but quite ineffective for a local project. The broker is a middleman who knows what lists are available from publishers, mail-order houses, industries and compilers.

List brokers charge at least $15 and sometimes as much as $50 per 1,000 names, and this fee generally covers rental of the list for one-time use only. (3)

How Experts Use Direct Mail to Raise Money

By

Sidney Green

Soliciting funds by direct mail is one of the most expensive ways to bring in contributions. Moreover, for direct mail activity to yield good results it must be tried over a period of years, and with expectation of losses at first. Nevertheless, if an arts organization is committed to a long term fund raising effort and can meet certain preconditions, this technique can prove highly successful. Moreover, tests and experience indicate that once a prospect has contributed through a direct mail drive, he usually remains a contributor.

Institutions that have employed this fund raising device with success enjoy a large following. They must, inasmuch as mailings to fewer than 50,000 possible patrons seldom prove very profitable. Second, these organizations have concrete, simply expressed needs, and their needs are related to broader social or cultural issues. That is, while they may be asking for money for a new music building, they are able to argue convincingly that support of the campaign would help advance the cause of music in general, or help revitalize downtown or serve some purpose over and above the organization's own. Finally, they have money to invest and they are in a position to buy, create or obtain through exchange the necessary mailing lists of potential donors.

Let us look at the development of a recent direct mail campaign conducted successfully by a relatively small but financially sophisticated national organization. This group mailed an appeal to 280,000 prospective givers. It drew up this extensive mailing list by renting some lists from professional list sellers, and by exchanging its own lists with other groups. Thus its overall list was a composite including lists of subscribers to various magazines, members or contributors to parallel organizations, and names compiled from *Who's Who* and other directories. About 10,000 of the names were on the group's own list of past contributors— always the best source of fresh donations.

Individuals should be on the list only because their past record in some way indicates they are likely to respond to the appeal. There is, for example, no reason to believe that a subscriber to *Field and Stream* magazine would respond to an appeal for funds sent out by an art museum. Nevertheless, this same subscriber might be an excellent prospect for a conservation organization. The success of any organization's direct mail campaign depends most heavily on how skillfully the lists are selected and compiled.

For reasons of economy and brevity, the customary mail appeal consists of a letter—running to no more than two pages—and a postage paid reply envelope. Sometimes these are supplemented by a printed folder describing the sponsoring organization in more detail than the letter. The appeal letter, carefully composed, should, if at all possible, be signed by an individual of national reputation. This individual need not necessarily be connected in any way with the sponsoring organization, but must, of course, be willing to permit the use of his or her name in this way.

The appeal letter may be printed by any of a number of processes, but the least expensive and therefore the most commonly used are photo offset or multigraph. A typical printing bill for 100,000 two-page letters produced by a large printing establishment in a major city might run $1200 to $1600 for photo-offset or multigraph, with the latter method the more expensive. The same letter printed by letterpress would cost about $5000. And if the letters were individually typed by automatic machine, instead of printed, the bill would zoom to an astronomical $27,500—which is, for all practical purposes, out of the question.

Other costs now come into play. Addressing and stuffing the envelopes—unless done by the group's own volunteers—costs between $10 and $20 per thousand. Postage costs can be kept to a minimum by sticking to third class.

The total cost of the 280,000 letter campaign described above was $30,000. Of this, roughly $10,000 went for supplies and printing. About $18,500 went into mailing, addressing and similar expenses. And approximately $1500 went for the rental of lists.

This, obviously, is a big investment for a cultural institution—or for any other kind of organization. Is it worth it? The organization that carried out the above mailing of 280,000 letters thinks so. It drew contributions from 2.5 per cent of those mailed to. The average contribution ran to $15.00. Thus this campaign brought in slightly over $100,-000 or nearly $3.50 for every $1.00 spent.

Another recent mailing by the same organization drew 3.4 per cent returns with an average gift of $15.85, yielding over $5.50 for every dollar spent.

These unusually good responses indicate how useful direct mail can be, and are a tribute to the care and professionalism displayed by the sponsoring organization. This care continues long after the last check has been received, for, after each mailing, lists must be carefully analyzed and culled. Those yielding poor results must be set aside. They should not be discarded, however, but should be tested at least three times, since very often a fresh letter over another signature sent to the same prospect, can do what an earlier letter failed to accomplish. Work must begin soon on the next mailing, for the direct mail campaign depends on continuity to help it succeed. Appeals should go out at about the same time each year, preferably during the last three months of the year, when potential givers are thinking about their tax situation, and are often receptive to the letter that tells them their contribution is tax deductible. (10)

———————◄●►———————

Right Word

Wording can make a difference on direct mail appeals for funds or members. The Community Gallery of the Brooklyn Museum in Brooklyn, N.Y., seeking donations in three different categories, ranging from $5.00 to $25.00, tried a different approach by renaming the categories. The lowest gift category, $5.00, remained Friend, a traditional membership designation, but $15.00 givers became Good Friends and $25.00 givers were identified as the Best of Friends. (67)

———————◄●►———————

Coding Responses

By coding reply forms, groups can determine which of several mailing lists used drew the best response. One unobtrusive and inexpensive coding system, successfully employed by a number of arts groups, has a series of letters in alphabetical order printed in small type on reply forms. Before mailing to each list, the printer removes one or more of the letters. The last remaining letter in the series represents the list to which the mailing is directed. For example, a response with ABCD on it indicates that it came from the D list. One reading AB, came from the B list.　　(41)

Surveys

Planning a mail survey? Experts say that the rate of return on questionnaires is greater if a stamped, self-addressed envelope is enclosed with the survey form. Also, accurate typography on good quality paper, they claim, will bring higher returns.　　(42)

Hitch a Ride

Is there a dignified business firm in your community that conducts an active direct mail promotion program? It may be possible to enlist its backing for your ticket sale campaign or fund drive. In New York, Channel 13, the educational television station, lined up the support of the Book-of-the-Month-Club, which sent a special mailing to its subscribers in the TV station's market area urging them to contribute to the station. If the business will not do a special mailing, it may be willing to permit your organization to "piggy-back"—i.e., enclose material along with one of the company's own mailings. Make sure that the company's mailing list is appropriate, however.   (26)

Novel Mailing Pieces Make New Friends and Money

A striking mailing piece can spell the difference between a successful fund raising campaign and a poor one. The Equity Library Theatre, a non-profit showcase in New York affiliated with Actor's Equity, completely redesigned its mailing piece this year. The new look not only increased revenue substantially, but also aroused tremendous public interest.

An amateur rendering, the new mailer was conceived by David Lunney, the ELT tour coordinator. Aware that previous annual mimeographed letters were unsuccessful, he designed a folder which solicited money by entertaining rather than cajoling. It was produced and mailed at a cost of $300 for 1,600 and the initial response alone brought in almost $2,000, double the best past result.

The new mailing piece, an accordion fold, printed on one side in sepia, tells the story of a fictitious ELT actress, Heliotrope Fenwick, and humorously suggests, in original sketches and text, the costs of mounting a production. It concludes, "And here is the envelope (gummed, self-addressed and stamped) that holds the check (a large sum) that supplies the cash that pays the bills that support the theatre that showcases the actor . . ." and tells how Miss Fenwick was hired, "all because she was seen at Equity Library Theatre, the theatre that you built."

According to Lunney, letters and telephone calls have come in to the fictitious Miss Fenwick and many contributors have turned the piece over to friends, suggesting that they contribute to ELT. (13)

Mailing Piece

Promotional mailing pieces must capture the reader's interest if they are to be retained and referred to. Often, an unusual visual device can accomplish this. In New York City, for example, a flier for a children's show, mailed by the Paper Bag Players, featured black brush stroke outlines of a face against an orange background. To gain reader attention, two holes were cut in place of the eyes, without significantly adding to the cost of the piece. (42)

Attracting Attention

Looking for a unique way of attracting attention? The Dramatic Arts Center in Ann Arbor, Michigan, mails packets of wallet-sized picture cards to promote its programs. The front of each card shows a different and unusual photograph of a live action scene. The back of each card carries specific information on tickets, programs and the performing group. (36)

——————◄•►——————

Direct Mail Brings In Members and Money

Promotion of membership by direct mail brings both immediate and long range cash results, leaders of the Arts Institute of Chicago were told in a special report. The report includes percentage response figures that other cultural institutions may find useful.

Richard P. Trenbeth, supervisor of development and membership, submitted the memorandum to the Institute's Committee on Development in support of a plea for greater emphasis on direct mail activity. He pointed out that although figures needed for a comparison with the experience of other leading museums are lacking, the Chicago Art Institute's rate of return and actual profit compare favorably with those of the Automobile Club of Maryland, an organization held up as a model by a leading direct mail trade publication. "At practically every point of measurement our record of selling memberships . . . is at least two or three times better," Trenbeth declared.

Last year Trenbeth's department mailed 115,352 pieces of membership solicitation material. This brought in 1,809 memberships at $12.50 each. This is a return rate of 1.6 per

331

cent. The auto club, selling memberships at $17.50, drew a response of slightly under .5 per cent.

The museum's cost per new member enrolled this way was $3.21, leaving a profit of $9.29 each. Cost is thus slightly over 25 per cent. In contrast, the auto club's memberships cost the organization $14.69 each, or roughly 84 per cent of the amount brought in.

The high cost of initial enrollments is compensated for by membership renewals after the first year, the report points out. First year renewals, universally the hardest to achieve, run about 65 per cent for the Art Institute, Trenbeth said, compared with 60 per cent for the Maryland organization. The overall renewal rate—i.e., including the first and subsequent renewals—runs 82 per cent for the Institute.

The report points out that: "Our average annual member renews for four more years, adding $50 of profit to the $9.29 of the first year. If we spent even one-half of our first year income, we could offer a much more expensive and attractive premium (to new members) and enroll many more than we do now."

Long an ardent advocate of direct mail techniques in membership building, Trenbeth told *Arts Management:* "I am convinced that major museums, theatres and other arts groups could do far better with direct mail than they now imagine, especially where there is a strong record of renewal." (6)

———◄●►———

List Exchange

Need additional lists? Before the summer season ends offer to exchange lists with any special summer festival series in your area. Their lists will be current, and may add a few names for your next fund raising drive. On the other hand, your lists, lent to them after your drive is completed, may be helpful to them as they begin their promotion before the start of next summer's season.   (19)

Summer Mailings

Summer is generally a poor time for direct mail campaigns because many people are on vacation. If, however, your organization sponsors performances during the summer, you might substitute direct audience appeals for letters. Remember that audience appeals must be gentle and should never interfere with the performance or delay it.   (16)

Save the Stamp

An organization with a large and loyal following that it solicits regularly by mail can save some of the mailing cost by adopting an idea used successfully by a number of colleges. Suggest to your donors that they put their own stamp over the prepaid marker on the return envelope.   (22)

Over and Out

Don't carry a good thing too far. A prominent West Coast cultural group which used its postage meter stamp to advertise a special arts week, was still using the announcement on its envelopes 11 days after the special week had ended! (69)

Stamp Schedule

An idea used by colleges to promote their football teams might be applicable to arts groups interested in promoting upcoming productions. The University of Bridgeport, for example, used postage meters to print this year's entire ten game football schedule on its envelopes next to the metered stamp. Included in the miniature advertisement, which although small was still readable, was the date of each game, opponent and starting time. An eight play season or concert series might just as easily fit on the envelope. (78)

Showing Off

Picture post cards can be effective promotional mailing pieces, if you have a message with visual appeal. The Studio Museum in Harlem, New York City, used attractive cards with pictures of African masks, figures, and musical instruments to invite viewers to its recent *Impact Africa* exhibit. (68)

Visual Impact

Brochures must make a visual impact on the recipient or often they'll go unread. The new brochure of Hospital Audiences, Inc. won't suffer that fate. Its covers are pieces of plain tan corrugated cardboard featuring only a button popping through the front cover, reading HAI in logotype. Inside the 8½ x 11 inch brochure are ten pages, printed on stock the same color and general appearance as the cover. Four of the pages feature very brief descriptions of the group's program while four others feature offsets of handwritten letters sent by audience members. The only picture is on the inside back jacket. The design and printing was a gift from business—a contribution to HAI from Standard Oil of New Jersey. (77)

Breezy Report

The Province of Ontario Council for the Arts Fifth Report 1968/1969, is a bright, breezy, colorful, irreverent and highly effective brochure printed on blue, yellow, and white stock. Its message is brief yet complete, and its language is non-traditional. In describing its innovative five year plan for the arts, the report says in bold, black letters more than three fourths of an inch high, "Huzzah for the program grant," followed by a statement reading, "You cannot foster the arts, or anything else for that matter, on a kind of cultural welfare. For five years we've fussed over symptoms, trying to patch them up with operating grants. Now we're after cures." The "Huzzah" sentiment illustrated with a bright and colorful full page drawing. (66)

Effective Brochures

Eye-catching program brochures need not be expensive. At the University of California in Santa Barbara, entertaining yet low-cost brochures are helping to promote the arts and lecture series. The format, developed last fall, utilizes graphics and pictures from very old books and magazines, (there is no copyright problem) to illustrate, page by page, arts events in fanciful and frequently amusing style. The brochures themselves are printed in booklet form on news presses using paper one grade above news stock, thus accounting for considerable savings.   (76)

Soft Soap Donors

Looking for instant recognition to attract donors for its annual united fund drive the United Arts Council of Greensboro, N.C. recently kicked off its campaign with a brochure whose cover bears a marked resemblance to an easily recognized household item—a detergent box. Printed in red and yellow on a blue base, with the words virtually leaping off the page, the cover extolls "New! Improved Greensboro Arts," (the latter word in giant red letters) as "loaded with action!" Its active ingredients" are listed as: Arts Festival; Crafts For All; More Music Theater; New Headquarters Building; Youth Symphony; and E.M.F. Project Listen. Once the cover has enticed the reader to open the brochure, the approach is anything but tongue in cheek. In direct fashion pictures and text tell potential contributors about the many new community arts activities in Greensboro, which now cost more than ever before to support. The approach may be unorthodox but the stakes are high. The campaign goal is a record $130,000.   (74)

TICKETS AND SUBSCRIPTIONS

Arts Groups Experiment With Subscriptions

Greater flexibility, extra benefits to subscribers, and monetary savings are some of the features of subscription ticket plans being tested by performing arts groups throughout the country. In New York City, for example, the Shakespeare Festival has introduced a new Public Theater pass for $15 ($7.50 for students and over 65's) which admits holders to one performance of each of the productions planned for this season, a minimum of eight. Each time a subscriber exchanges his pass for a ticket, either in person or by mail, one of the 12 dots printed on the pass is stamped to indicate the specific performance for which it is used. Because the Festival has four performance facilities, the subscriber can visit the theater without making prior arrangements, and be fairly certain of getting tickets for one of the productions. When the idea was conceived, the theater set its goal at selling 5,000 passes. By the first week of October more than 10,000 had been sold.

Across the river, the Brooklyn Academy of Music has introduced its first flexible subscription program. The $25 coupon book—$20 each for two or more—guarantees subscribers orchestra or mezzanine seats to up to 14 different events. Subscribers redeem coupons for any performance of a particular event on a first-come, first-served basis. In New Haven, Conn., the Long Wharf Theatre is giving audiences the option of purchasing either traditional season subscriptions, with performance dates for all eight productions specified in advance, or flexible admission cards. The cards, at $27 for eight admissions, are exchangeable for any weekday performance and can be used singly for each performance or all in one night. The Indianapolis Symphony, in response to what it terms numerous requests for greater flexibility, has given Thursday night subscription series audiences the option of purchasing either a winter or spring "half series" subscription.

Theaters elsewhere are wooing subscribers with a variety of extra benefits. In San Francisco, the American Conservatory Theater is offering subscribers a $5 "Bonus Benefit Package" featuring inexpensive parking, special dining privileges from several nearby restaurants and discount coupons for extra tickets to ACT productions and special events. Thus far, about 20 per cent of the subscribers have purchased packages and $4,000 of an anticipated $10,000 has been realized. Buffalo's Studio Arena Theatre is offering its season ticket purchasers free Subscriber Discount Cards with these dividends: 10 per cent discounts on additional ticket purchases and on bar tabs in the theater's lounge; a 15 per cent discount on performance nights at six top restaurants; and a 30 per cent discount on parking.

One of the more interesting and apparently successful experiments is the Guthrie Theater's "Five Plays for the Price of Six" season subscription. The new plan, conceived by the theater with the help of Arts Development Associates, reverses the usual policy of offering extra productions as a bonus and asks subscribers instead to contribute the price of an extra ticket to the theater. "Subscribing members" receive five tickets for the price of six and "investing members," who pay $125 for two subscriptions, not only purchase five for six but also subsidize student memberships. According to a spokesman, "the response has been extraordinary."   (72)

Ticket Campaign in Store Window a Success

With the cooperation of a local store, arts groups can increase ticket sales by staging a telephone "marathon" promotion. In Atlanta, Georgia, volunteers made telephone calls from the window of one of the country's leading department stores, Rich's, and sold over $2,500 in season tickets for the Atlanta Symphony Orchestra in a matter of hours. Only subscriptions to the entire 12-concert season were sold.

"More tickets were sold than on any previous single day in the orchestra's history," Mrs. William Robertson, Jr., the orchestra's publicity director, told *AM*. Sales during the marathon were bolstered by a 16,000-piece mailing that went out to new ticket prospects prior to the marathon date.

Volunteers, including members of the orchestra's board of directors, women's committee, and local celebrities, sat in the department store window during the promotion. Manning six telephones for three-hour shifts, the volunteers called prospects and aroused their interest by opening the conversation with the provocative sales line, "You won't believe this, but I'm sitting in a window at Rich's selling tickets to the Atlanta Symphony."

Mrs. Robertson told *AM*, "The marathon was a great success and one that can be highly recommended to other communities. Even then, it takes the proper combination of enthusiasm, timing and people."

The only expense incurred in the marathon was the cost of local telephone calls. While this was the first time such an event was held, its success has spurred the group to plan another one next year. It is planned to run for two or three consecutive days instead of only one day.   (35)

Telephone Blitz Sells Season Tickets for Theatre

A gigantic telephone blitz campaign, undertaken by more than 300 volunteers on behalf of a year-round legitimate theatre in Canada, resulted in the sale of more than 5,000 season ticket subscriptions this year.

In Winnipeg, Canada, the Manitoba Theatre Centre, a non-profit organization, begins its intensive fall ticket sale campaign during the summer. Brochures describing the productions to be presented during the coming season are mailed to a list of about 30,000 prospective customers in August. About a week later this is followed by a reminder letter.

Shortly after Labor Day, the week-long telephone blitz campaign begins. The Theatre Centre's women's committee recruits between 300 and 400 women as volunteers and sets up a switchboard and more than a dozen telephones in the theatre's lobby. The women then make personal phone calls urging the purchase of season tickets to every prospect on the list who has not responded to the previous mailings. In the evening, members of the organization's board of governors often relieve women at the phones. In one instance, an enterprising board member sold two season tickets by bringing together a man and woman over the phone who both claimed they wanted to buy tickets but had nobody to go with.

According to Lucile Fleming, the publicity director of the Theatre Centre, the telephone campaign is tied in with an intensive advertising drive in all media. In addition, a comprehensive publicity program, which includes the airing of radio spots made by actors scheduled to appear during the forthcoming season, insures total saturation in the community. (24)

Installment Buying

Cultural organizations may increase season ticket sales by offering subscription purchasers the option of either paying the entire price at once or buying tickets on a time payment plan. The St. Louis Symphony Orchestra allowed buyers of season tickets to make a one third down payment in September. The balance is payable in equal installments in November and January. (31)

Last Minute Changes

Last minute program changes in a previously announced season series can cost a performing arts organization ticket renewals the next season. After a series is announced in print, every effort should be made to adhere to the schedule. Otherwise, ticket subscribers may be disappointed and lose confidence in the organization. They will be cautious when renewing, remembering that the program to which they subscribe is not necessarily the one they will attend. (43)

Return Stub

Arts groups can ease the way for holders of season tickets to renew their subscriptions. Stage Centre of the Manitoba Theatre Centre in Winnipeg, Canada, issues season tickets in strips. A renewal stub is included between the penultimate and last ticket in the strip. The stub can be mailed or handed in at the box office, assuring subscribers of automatic seat renewals for the next season. Should subscribers prefer a different seat location, they merely notify the box office when sending in renewal stubs.

(38)

Program Change

A mid-season change of program is often confusing to season subscribers, unless the change is clearly explained to them. To inform subscribers that the order of two productions had been switched, the Long Wharf Theatre in New Haven, Conn., printed little four-page folders titled, "There've been some changes made . . ." Inside, the new performance schedules were noted. (54)

Daytime Numbers

Ask for a daytime telephone number from ticket buyers on your mail order blank; with it, you can talk your way out of many a ticket snarl. Without it, you may have no way of reaching the purchaser during working hours to straighten out misunderstandings or other difficulties. Orders arriving in a rush frequently impose arbitrary decisions on the box office staff. Sending tickets for alternate performances, price classes or separate seats can lead to ill-will and empty seats. Quick phone contact helps arrange a full house to everyone's satisfaction.   (2)

Explaining Subscriptions

If the logistics of season subscriptions are confusing to your audiences, then take the trouble to explain your policies to them. Late this summer, the Studio Arena Theatre in Buffalo, N. Y., in response to inquiries from subscribers who wondered if the theater was attempting to oversell the house, issued a release headed, "Once again—the subscription dilemma." The release explained in detail how a 509-seat theater could accommodate 14,000 season subscribers, the announced goal of the organization, and still sell single tickets. "Scrutiny of the mechanics," it stated, "will show our goal to be mathematically viable."   (58)

Flexible Subscriptions

Performing arts groups seeking to attract new audiences with flexible and convenient season subscription plans, might be interested in the Guthrie Theater's Hot Line membership. Under the plan, subscribers purchase a membership for two for $20 and receive in return 14 coupons, two for each of the season's five plays and four "free choice" coupons for use at any play. Each coupon is worth $2 toward the purchase of one ticket in any of the theater's three price categories. A key selling feature of the plan is the members' special Hot Line phone number. When subscribers select a performance date they call Hot Line, give their membership number and reserve tickets in any price category they wish. On performance night they bring their coupons to the theater's new Members' Window, pay the difference—"with a $2 coupon, the lowest priced ticket will cost only $1.45 in cash," states the brochure—and pick up their tickets. In promoting the program, the theater stresses its advantage to subscribers. They save money by paying only $20 for $28 worth of tickets; they have flexibility in being able to purchase tickets at different prices for different plays; they are able to bring friends with free choice coupons; and they have the convenience of attending the theater when they wish without going to the box office in advance or paying the total price in advance.   (71)

—◄●►—

Seasonal Calendar

Although most performing arts seasons coincide with the academic year, September through June, most printed calendars cover the year from January through December. Why not help your subscribers see your season at a glance with seasonal calendars. The Seattle Opera distributes handy little plastic cards featuring on one side, a 1971-72 calendar running from a mid-year to mid-year. On the reverse is a smiling soprano and the legend, "Season's greetings from Seattle Opera."   (73)

Satisfaction Guaranteed

What happens when a performing arts company offers a money-back guarantee to its audience? The Atlanta Symphony, which has offered such guarantees occasionally, most recently for its Sunday afternoon concert series this spring, has never yet been asked for a refund. Another group, the Saint Paul Opera, took a half-page ad in the *St. Paul Pioneer Press* this October, offering money-back guarantees to two performances in the hopes of attracting new audiences to its "new era in opera" performances. The result? No requests for refunds, the largest single ticket sales in the company's history for one of the two performances, and greatly increased corporate support for group sales.   (66)

345

Arts Gift

Promoting tickets as gifts? You might try selling gift certificates which offer purchasers discounts on events. The Fort Wayne Fine Arts Foundation sells "handsome, parchment-like Gift Certificates" for $10. Each certificate contains $10.50 in discount coupons which can be redeemed for a variety of arts activities in Fort Wayne. Seven of the detachable coupons offer $1.00 discounts and seven offer $.50 discounts. To promote the gift idea, certificates are personally inscribed to whomever the purchaser designates and bear his name also as the donor.   (72)

Season Subscriptions

Want to increase your sale of season subscriptions even after the first performance in a season series has already been presented? Single ticket holders may be your answer. In Winnipeg, Canada, the Manitoba Theatre Centre invites non-subscribers to take their ticket stubs to the theatre box office where they may apply the cost of a used single ticket toward the purchase of a subscription membership. The savings to be realized—15 per cent over single ticket purchase—is emphasized in the promotion of the plan. (25)

Theatre Offers Trading Stamps as Box Office Bait

Trading stamps, most commonly used to promote patronage in grocery stores and filling stations, have been extended to the arts. An off-Broadway theatre producer in New York City, faced with the loss of audiences due to the extended newspaper strike, offered trading stamps with the purchase of tickets. His audiences increased by 25 per cent.

Ned Hendrickson opened his production of "The Wide Open Cage" at the Washington Square Theatre shortly after the New York newspaper strike began on December 9, 1962. Because normal advertising and publicity channels were closed, he turned in desperation to the E. F. MacDonald Company, distributors of Plaid Stamps. Since January 14, every ticket buyer at Hendrickson's theatre has received 30 Plaid Stamps with the purchase of a $3.00 ticket. Some people have even come to the box office specifically requesting stamps.

In addition, Hendrickson arranged for Plaidland redemption centers to distribute coupons entitling purchasers to receive a bonus supply of 500 stamps by presenting the coupons at the box office.

Although Hendrickson pays $15.00 for each pad of 5,000 stamps, he believes that the increase in his audiences following his offer of trading stamps proves that the stamps are paying for themselves. He therefore intends to continue using Plaid Stamps even after the newspaper strike ends. In spite of Hendrickson's apparent success and the fact that he recommends stamp programs to other theatrical producers, it should be remembered that he issued stamps as a desperation measure in an unusual situation.

A check by *Arts Management* of several leading trading stamp companies indicates that the use of stamps by cultural organizations is a rarity. An official of S&H Green Stamps, one of the oldest and largest companies, is pessimistic about their value to the arts because, he said: "Stamp plans work best only where there is a very high volume of trade."

H. T. Goodenberger, a district manager of E. F. Mac-Donald in the New York area, is more optimistic about the possible success of stamp programs in the arts, although he cautions that plans work only if there are a large number of outlets in one area which offer the same brand of stamp.

Companies which issue stamps generally do so under a licensing arrangement. They provide identification signs and other promotional materials boosting the stamp they distribute. The Plaid Stamp organization will also on occasion design and print mailing pieces at their own expense for a customer's use.

Plaid Stamps, as an example, cost $15.00 per pad of 5,000, and $12.50 for each pad after the first five. Stamps must be paid for on delivery, although the MacDonald company guarantees to refund any leftover stamps at the price paid. Stamps must be issued by the user at the rate of one stamp for each ten cent purchase, although bonus arrangements similar to the one used by Hendrickson are permitted. (14)

Tickets on Consignment

To help build audience, some organizations send tickets to lists of potential buyers with a request that they either pay for them or return them by a given date. Because most recipients feel a sense of personal responsibility, and respond one way or the other, the system can be quite effective. But it must be employed with discretion. Use lists of names who have proven interest in the organization. Always record both address and phone number of recipients. Set the deadline for payment or return early enough to follow up with those who fail to respond. (11)

Bulk Ticket Sales

Looking to sell blocks of tickets? The college student union in your area may be a good outlet. As part of their programs, college unions often arrange student visits to nearby cultural attractions. The University of Delaware union, for example, purchased large blocks of tickets for monthly concerts at the Academy of Music in Philadelphia. The Trenton State College union in New Jersey arranged student bus trips to off-Broadway theaters in New York City. (48)

Alumni Groups

College alumni groups represent a generally untapped market for block purchases of tickets. Many are looking for cultural programs to offer their members. In New York City, the Wisconsin Alumni Club recently sent a mailing to its members informing them they could obtain preferred seats for summer concerts by the Metropolitan Opera at Lewisohn Stadium if the group purchased a block of 20 tickets. (39)

Taped Promotion

Arts groups faced with an upcoming program and lagging ticket sales might try a technique used successfully at the University of Indiana in Bloomington. With a concert for the benefit of Czechoslovakian relief less than a week off, and tickets moving slowly, the school's concert office asked a group of distinguished local citizens for their help. The community leaders taped 30-second phone interviews in which they explained why they were attending the concert. A Bloomington radio station then aired the tapes as public service spot announcements. The result? Local interest was engendered, and the concert was a great success. (64)

New Ticket-Selling Techniques Winning Audiences for Culture

Arts organizations throughout the country are experimenting with a variety of ticket distribution methods in an attempt to increase attendance, develop new audiences and attract members. In many instances, the approaches used are variations of techniques which have proved successful elsewhere.

In Dayton, Ohio, the Miami Valley Arts Council recently introduced a Membership Privilege Book in an attempt to enlist new members. The book, similar to the "two-fers" used by Broadway theaters, offered members a set of coupons, which could be exchanged for two tickets at the price of one. The book's attraction was that it included coupons redeemable for programs presented by 14 diverse cultural groups, including the Cincinnati Symphony Orchestra, Playhouse in the Park, the Dayton Civic Ballet, and the University of Dayton's Arts Series. The purchase value of the tickets was about $40.00.

All 14 participating groups combined their mailing lists for the initial direct-mail campaign. Within three weeks of the first mailing, a successful ten per cent return had been achieved, and 500 new members, at $5.00 a year each, were enrolled. According to the arts council, the campaign achieved three important results: the $2,500 raised through new membership dues enabled the council to expand its services; coupon redemptions helped to sell tickets which otherwise might not have been sold; and by offering a variety of performances in different disciplines, a cross-fertilization of arts audiences took place.

Coupon redemption was the key also to the Corporate Coupon Program, designed to win business support for the

Alley Theatre in Houston, Texas, when it opened its season in its newly-built theater last fall. A similar program, initiated the previous year by the Tyrone Guthrie Theatre in Minneapolis, resulted in the sale of 2,000 corporate subscriptions to 37 Twin Cities corporations.

Under the program, Houston firms were offered the opportunity to purchase as many books of five coupons as they wished, with each coupon redeemable for one ticket to each of the five plays presented during the Alley season. Books were priced at only $13.75 each, or $2.75 per individual ticket, although the normal single ticket price ranged from $2.80 to $6.90. When redeeming coupons for tickets, coupon holders were guaranteed seats in the best locations available for the performance they chose.

There were two keys to the campaign, both carefully outlined in a detailed brochure mailed to 140 selected local firms prior to the season's opening. First, corporations were told that they could use the coupons successfully in their employee relations programs by either selling them to employees at cost, or a discount. In either instance, employees would purchase tickets at the lowest price possible. The second key aspect, was the group of services offered by the theater to coupon holders including: special box office attention when calling for reservations; free Alley posters for corporate bulletin boards; free payroll envelope inserts; photographs and news material for employee publications; theater staff help in selling tickets to employees; and a free coupon book for every 25 purchased by the company.

To promote the concept to corporations initially, seven young bank executives, under the direction of Lewis A. Brown, vice president of the Texas National Bank, and the program's chairman, personally visited all of the corporations which received brochures. The results were impressive, with 1500 coupon books sold to 40 corporations. According to Paul E. Stroud, the theater's director of board relations and special events, the program will continue next year, and hopefully, the services offered to business will be broadened to more fully involve corporations.

Elsewhere, the old question of which is more effective—selling season subscriptions or individual tickets—was explored by the City Center Joffrey Ballet, and the results, although not conclusive, proved interesting. When the dance company mailed brochures for its upcoming spring season, it suggested in the same mailing piece that purchasers could buy individual tickets for any performance or they could purchase subscriptions. The responses, when analyzed, showed that subscriptions and individual ticket sales were almost evenly divided. (64)

Family Night

Parents can be induced to take their children to performances if the ticket costs aren't too high. The Great Lakes Shakespeare Festival in Cleveland, Ohio, sets aside several evenings at a special price for families. Single admissions are $3.00 and $3.50, but a family, regardless of the number of children, pays only $6.00 total. On family nights, all seats are reserved on a first-come, first-served basis. (62)

Sell Tickets in Suburbs

Organizations seeking to increase ticket sales or promote membership in suburban areas might consider the use of a "ticketmobile." Libraries, museums, and commercial enterprises have had great success in serving hard-to-reach groups of people through mobile units. A symphony orchestra, for example, might send out a truck or station wagon equipped with orchestra recordings, pictures, programs, and ticket and membership information. Notify, in advance, neighborhood publications in the communities you are visiting to insure maximum publicity. If shopping centers are visited, arrange for distribution of posters announcing the visit or notices to be placed in shopping bags.
(8)

Ticket Sales

Selling tickets? Make it easy for the audience to buy them. The Arts Council of Greater St. Louis recently bound a ticket order form into the center of its monthly calendar of events, offering readers the opportunity to purchase tickets to 39 performances sponsored by nine different arts groups during a single month. With one order form, and with one check, purchasers could buy tickets for any of the programs. (53)

Apartment House Tickets

Apartment buildings seeking new tenants may be good outlets for the purchase of tickets in bulk. In Washington, D. C., for example, the Park Plaza Apartments is offering an inducement to new tenants—a pair of complimentary tickets for Arena Stage's 1966-67 season. The offer extends also to current lease-holders who bring in new tenants. (49)

Birthday Gifts

Giving tickets to a performance as a birthday present has become a popular solution to an annual problem. Performing arts groups can sell more birthday gift tickets by putting out an occasional reminder of this way to mark a family milestone. (7)

Pocket Promotion

Would you like to have your audience in your pocket? Then put yourself in their pockets. The Old Globe Theatre in San Diego, Calif., has developed a wallet-sized promotional piece, printed on both sides of a 9½ by 3½ inch sheet, which folds twice into a convenient 3½ by 2½ inch card. When folded, the front page lists box office information, subscription and single ticket prices, and performance times. The middle pages detail information on each of the nine productions offered in the eight-month season, and the full 9½ inch-long reverse side contains a calendar listing every performance. (63)

Attractive Tickets

One way to promote the sale of tickets is to enhance their appearance. In Woodstock, New York, when the Woodstock Artists Association, Inc. was planning an art raffle, it arranged for artist Bernard Steffen to execute an original drawing for the tickets. The drawing was printed on a detachable portion of the tickets. (41)

Symphony Sells Seats With a Coloring Book

An unusual promotional device, a Symphony Coloring Book, is helping to attract young couples to concerts of the Atlanta Symphony Orchestra. Published by the Junior Committee of the orchestra, the eight page booklet describes in whimsical fashion, the 11 special concert evenings sponsored by the Junior Committee. Each of these evenings begins with cocktails at a leading Atlanta country club at six p.m. Dinner, at a cost of $3.00 per person, follows at seven. At eight o'clock, waiting buses whisk diners from the country club to the concert auditorium for fifty cents. The Committee reserves an entire section of the auditorium for each of the 11 subscription concerts, ($23.18 for each season subscription) so that couples who eat together can also sit together at the concerts.

The theme of togetherness is emphasized in the coloring book. The first page has a cartoon depicting a couple slumped in front of a television set. The caption underneath says, "See the dreary people. They never go anywhere. They never eat out. They are missing all the fun. Color them bored.'' The next page, which shows an unhappy couple driving a car, suggests that traffic will detain the couple and that they will be unable to find a parking space. Opposite this page is a cartoon of smiling people seated at the concert. The caption reads, ''See the smiling people. They are at the Symphony. They are with their friends. They ate dinner with their friends. It was good. They cleaned their plates. Yum. Yum. The nice bus brought them right to the door—on time. Color them happy.'' (21)

———————◄●►———————

Give Music Now, Pay Later

From now on in Washington a Christmas gift of good music will be chargeable to accounts in any of five major stores in the capital city, thanks to a successful innovation by the National Symphony Orchestra during the 1962 holiday season.

During the six weeks before Christmas the symphony sold gift certificates to be used for tickets to all orchestra concerts. The orchestra box office is conveniently located in the heart of the Washington shopping district, where Christmas shoppers congregate. For those who did not want to pay cash, the orchestra arranged for the certificates, ranging in amount from $2 to $200, to be charged to accounts at Garfinckel's Hecht's, Jelleff's, Lansburgh's and Woodward & Lothrop.

For some years past the stores had been charging National Symphony season subscriptions bought by their charge account customers. Mrs. John Hoover, a volunteer orchestra worker, originated the idea of extending this store service to the Christmas gift certificates, which were attractively decorated in the form of a Christmas tree bearing a picture of the orchestra with Conductor Howard Mitchell at the apex. (13)

Seating Plan

At the orchestra hall or theatre box office, both ticket buyers and sellers save time when the seating plan is prominently displayed at the point of sale. People can decide on their preferences while standing in line. Seating plans should also be included with mailings soliciting advance purchase of tickets, and given to newspapers for publication at the season's end. (5)

Chapter V – Facilities for the Arts

Planning a New Arts Building? Pick Your Architect Carefully

The possibility that more than $375,000,000 is in the cultural pocketbook for building activities means that cultural groups must learn how to collaborate with architects on a scale not seen before. Many have no experience along this line.

After the functions of the building are decided, the next step is selecting precisely the right architect. Just finding a "good" architect is not enough. The right architect for an arts building must not only understand the community's tastes, traditions and cultural patterns, he must have a thorough knowledge of the rather special technical and mechanical requirements of theatres, museums, or concert halls.

He must be able to estimate construction costs realistically. He should know the business side of his profession— the best supply sources, the time to solicit bids and the responsibility of contractors.

For these reasons the best bet is an architect who has had definite experience with the special needs of arts groups. The local chapter of the American Institute of Architects can often recommend one.

When several candidates are found they should be invited to make their presentations individually to a screening committee. They will show pictures of buildings they have completed, letters of commendation, perhaps brochures explaining their services. Frequently they offer to arrange field trips to examples of their work. At these meetings the client has an opportunity not only to see the work but to assess the individual. Since the relationship between client and architect is a close one lasting months, it is important that they be able to work together amicably. Candidates for the account should not be asked to submit free sketches.

After the choice is made, however, the architect prepares a preliminary schematic design for discussion. This should be modified or expanded until both client and architect are satisfied. At this critical stage both sides must be understanding and willing to make needed compromises.

Next the architect submits preliminary drawings of both interior and exterior, and should explain the reasoning behind them. He should understand the technical problems involved, local and state building codes and inspection requirements. When he recommends building materials and equipment clients have a right to know his reasons for his choice in terms of price, durability and ease of maintenance. He should also provide samples of materials so the client can make a choice.

All the work is not on the side of the architect, however. A good client helps him do the best possible job. For example, the arts group should, if possible, consult the architect before selecting the site, because one with difficult terrain can add to the cost.

The architect should be told the financial limitation that may affect it. If there are fixed limits the client should put these in writing.

The arts group will, of course, try to negotiate the best possible fee, but it is wise to be wary of a bid which is considerably lower than the others because it may mean that the bidder does not understand the problems involved. On occasion an architect may give an arts group the best possible price because its cultural aims interest him.

360

Fees vary widely. The A.I.A. chapters in each state have established a recommended schedule of fees for various categories of building, and this schedule can be a point of departure. The fee also depends on such variables as size, time limits, the complexity of the building and its equipment. (11)

———————— ◄●► ————————

Student Architects Aid In Planning New Theatre

A unique project that joined a cultural institution with a class of college architectural students, resulted in excellent publicity for the arts group and also provided it with valuable research material and a 143-page documented report containing many useful ideas.

The project began after the Mummers Theatre in Oklahoma City, Oklahoma, recipient of a $1,250,000 grant from the Ford Foundation and $750,000 from local contributors, announced plans for the construction of a new theatre building. In spite of the fact that the actual building and theatre were to be designed by accomplished professionals, architect John Johansen and theatre designer David Hays, the senior architecture class in design and working drawings at Oklahoma State University offered to undertake the design of a new Mummers Theatre. It was understood that none of the working drawings submitted by the class would be used for construction of the new theatre and the effort would be viewed strictly as a class project. It was felt, however, that the results of the student project might contribute valuable ideas for the actual construction.

The Mummers Theatre presented the basic concept of the building and the kind of theatre desired to the class. Jointly, a building program was drawn up and the class of

44 students, under the supervision of professors, was divided into an executive committee and nine working committees in the following areas: sociological conditions; site selection; physical conditions; code requirements; technical investigations; acoustics and lighting; theatre equipment and stage design; finance and project planning. The project was completely realistic, with students interviewing persons who were concerned with the new building and gathering detailed information in each of the committee areas. In addition, several technical consultants were called in and the students worked with actual building sites under consideration in Oklahoma City.

The result of these efforts was a detailed, carefully documented, 143 page report which was complete enough to allow for the actual construction of the theatre building. The report, completed early this year, was accompanied by working drawings and elevations prepared by each of the students. According to David Lunney, Ford Foundation administrative intern at the Mummers Theatre, the student contributions were greatest in the areas of audience, shop and office space.

The Mummers received excellent publicity as a result of the student project. Just last month, one of the leading banks in downtown Oklahoma City presented an exhibition featuring some of the outstanding working drawings prepared by the students. The exhibition generated community excitement, focussed attention on the forthcoming new building and the theatre itself. (27)

Steps in Planning an Arts Building Project

By

Welton Becket

The pronounced increase in cultural awareness is resulting in great interest in the construction of new facilities for the performing arts.

Many cities have only now begun to examine the possibility of building new stages, concert halls, museums or art centers. The first step is usually to seek expert help in analyzing the feasibility of the project. Such help may come from specialized research organizations or from architectural firms that have research capabilities—or from a combination of the two. In Tacoma, Wash., for example, such a study is being made in conjunction with a research organization, whereas, in Nassau County, N. Y., we have just completed a sizable study ourselves.

A feasibility study is concerned with the potential demand as indicated by socio-economic characteristics of the area, and by availability of facilities in adjoining communities; potential use, as indicated by the wishes of the citizens and availability of attractions to be staged; and financing, based on available and potential public and private funds. In addition, the study may concern itself with selecting a site if none has yet been acquired, or with determining the suitability of an already acquired site from the standpoint of location, traffic and cost of development.

Most communities today realize that they will require a multi-purpose building, as opposed to New York City's Lincoln Center concept in which a separate building is being erected for each use (at a cost of over $160 million). The question that must be resolved is: how multi is multi?

363

Smaller communities with less means tend to group as many activities within a single structure as possible. For example, Winter Park, Fla., is planning a theater, concert hall and museum in a single facility to cost between $1.5 and $2 million.

One of the most flexible facilities we have designed is the Santa Monica, Calif., Civic Auditorium. As a performing arts facility, it accommodates the entire spectrum from symphony and dance to light opera and drama. But a feature of this structure is that the entire floor tilts, so that it can be leveled for use as a sports stadium as well as for consumer shows and banquets.

Financing of an arts facility can be accomplished in one or a combination of several alternative methods. These include revenue bonds, in which the bonds are backed by revenue from the facility; a special tax, which ranges from pari-mutuel tax to a hotel bed tax; general funds, where a municipality has such uncommitted funds available; general obligation bonds, a popular method but one that requires passage of a bond issue; grants-in-aid, either from the state or federal government; and contributions from private donors, corporations and foundations. Several combinations of the above are possible, including matching funds, in which the government unit and the citizenry both contribute.

Prior to entering into an arts building project, all concerned should be aware that a facility of this type must be considered in the same light as a school or a park. That is, it will need continued fiscal support and should not be regarded as being able to pay for itself.

Following determination of the size and scope of the multi-use structure, the architect is ready to begin actual design.

Falling within the average architect's scope of work are site planning, internal circulation and public facilities, and the aesthetic design of the exterior and interior.

Most architects will have to retain consultants, however, in such fields as acoustics, which has a strong influence on interior design and even on sight lines; seating; staging; stage lighting; air conditioning; and traffic, including circulation and parking. Of these all-important items, the public will usually be most critical of acoustics and air conditioning.

The multi-purpose structure is not without problems. Adaptation to a variety of uses must always mean some compromise. Operating cost elements such as setting up and taking down movable chairs and a concert shell, for example, must be considered.

However, with proper care in planning and design, and reliance on specialists when a firm itself does not have special capabilities, even the most multi-purpose buildings can result in near-optimum conditions for enjoyment of the performing arts.   (28)

------◄●►------

Audience Invests in its Theatre, 1,000 Buy Building Fund Bonds

By

Thomas C. Fichandler

Early in its life, almost every growing cultural organization faces the big decision whether to rent, buy or build new quarters. Although rental is sometimes the solution, often the answer lies in raising capital funds with which to buy and remodel an available building, or, even more costly, to build a new one.

Arts managers in various fields may find something of value in the unusual experience of the Arena Stage in raising $225,000 toward its building fund through a bond drive. Our success in selling bonds bearing interest at six per cent was a key factor in financing the beautiful new theatre that we opened last October.

When we decided in 1959 to build, there were several reasons why we decided to borrow money through a bond issue.

1. Generally speaking, people are not used to the idea of giving money to a theatre. They are accustomed to fund drives for the symphony orchestra, but not for the stage.

2. Washington is a city without industrial fortunes rooted in the community.

3. We needed funds quickly, because we were soon to lose our rented property. We had no established fund raising organization, nor time to build one.

4. Our big asset was the following Arena Stage had won through nine years of life. This included nearly 5,000 season ticket subscribers.

5. The general economic climate of the times had led many middle-income people to become modest investors, when offered the prospect of a reasonable return for their money.

Our decision, therefore, was to raise the $225,000 we needed by asking our playgoing friends to buy six per cent sinking fund debentures at $100 face value each. Thus they would be helping a cultural cause and at the same time getting a better return than they would from most other investments.

We announced our bond drive in the fall of 1959, issuing two mailings to our own list of more than 10,000 Arena theatregoers. We explained in detail the purpose and method of the bond offering and asked our friends to send back pledge cards for the interest-bearing loans. Between the acts of our first play of the season the bond campaign was announced and bond literature was available at the theatre for several months.

We found the bond sales campaign a relatively painless way to raise a large sum (though admittedly the repayment process will be felt somewhat). The main expense was for printing and postage. After the mailings were prepared, the bond campaign required little manpower.

While our main effort was in getting individual loans through bond sales, we did, of course, accept gifts to the building fund. At the same time, foundation support and business gifts were actively pursued. Various methods of recognition of both donors and loaners were spelled out in our literature, such as listing names in the theatre lobby and placing individual nameplates on theatre seats. In each category of recognition, bond money counted just half the value of outright gifts.

Altogether, close to 1,000 individuals bought $225,000 worth of bonds. Single purchases of $100 each were most common. About 75 per cent of the people participating bought in lots of either $100 or $200. The number of pledges not honored was minuscule—about one per cent. We could tell by the end of January 1960 that our effort was going to succeed, and the bulk of the money was in hand by late April.

We now put aside seven per cent of our total loan annually for interest payments and debt retirement. We draw lots yearly to determine which bonds will be paid off; the entire list is to be liquidated in 35 years. We were happily surprised to find that some bondholders, when sent their six per cent interest in 1961, mailed it back to us as their gift to Arena Stage. (3)

Real Estate

Arts groups may be able to purchase property at a considerably lower figure than its current appraised value, by emphasizing the special tax benefits available to the potential seller. If a taxpayer sells property to a non-profit, tax exempt organization at the price originally paid, and the current assessed value of the property is higher than that price, the taxpayer can deduct the difference between the two prices, without having to pay a capital gains tax. (61)

Donors "Shingle" Roof

Arts leaders in a small West Texas community, faced with the prospect of raising $2500 to begin converting an historic hotel into a museum, resorted to a "model sales" program to reach the goal.

When the heirs of Annie Riggs, the owner of the oldest hotel in Fort Stockton, Texas, donated the building to the local historical society, the organization found itself without funds to remodel the building. Since a new roof was necessary before additional restoration could be undertaken, the initial fund effort concentrated on the roof.

A local carpenter constructed a model of the building without a roof. The model was displayed throughout the town—in store windows, in the leading bank, and in local schools. When not circulating, the model was kept on the porch of the museum building. Small shingles were sold to townspeople for any amount they wished to donate, and the shingles were then inscribed with the name of the donor and lightly tacked onto the museum model. When the shingles completely covered the top of the model, they were removed and new shingles were sold.

The drive captured the imagination of the community. Grade school students donated small amounts so that a shingle could be bought in the name of their class. Local businesses gave larger amounts. Following the success of the initial drive, additional remodeling was undertaken.

(58)

———— ◄●► ————

Arts Facilities Throughout the Nation Make News

Not since the opening of Lincoln Center have arts facilities commanded as much public attention and controversy as they have within recent months. While the big newsmaker by far has been the $70-million Kennedy Center which opened September 8th in Washington, D.C., other facilities—new theaters and renovated ones, theaters for sale and for razing—in an incredible diversity of settings, have vied for a share of the spotlight.

The Washington, D.C. area, in addition to the Kennedy Center, gained two new arts facilities this year, the Arena Stage's 500-seat Kreeger Theater and Filene Center, the $2-million concert auditorium in Wolf Trap Farm Park in Virginia. New facilities elsewhere include Midland, Michigan's $7.8 million Center for the Arts which opened in May, and several campus arts centers including the University of Pennsylvania's $5.7-million Annenberg Center

369

for Communication Arts and Sciences which opened this spring. The University of Michigan just unveiled its $3.5-million Power Center for the Performing Arts and earlier, Simpson College in Iowa opened a $1.25-million center.

Renovated structures have been important additions to the scene in several large Eastern cities. A former movie palace in Pittsburgh has been completely renovated and opened in September as Heinz Hall for the Performing Arts, the glittering new home of the Pittsburgh Symphony. In Philadelphia, a $2-million interior renovation and facade restoration enabled the nation's oldest theater, the Walnut Street, to reopen in October as Philadelphia's new cultural center. The Boston Center for the Arts, which will eventually provide performing, rehearsal, storage, office and studio space for over 200 artists and arts groups, is being carved out of a group of seven old buildings at a cost of $5-million. The buildings were to be destroyed, but arts leaders led a successful effort to have the Boston Redevelopment Authority designate them as the site of the new center. In Rochester, N.Y., a grant from Eastman Kodak will help to pay for the $2-million renovation of the Eastman Theater where the Rochester Philharmonic performs while in Detroit, Orchestra Hall, which was scheduled for demolition, has been saved thanks to a $30,000 gift from David Elgin Dodge last month. On a less happy note, a facility built in 1965 to house the now defunct Theatre Atlanta Repertory, was listed "for sale" in a recent magazine ad.

Meanwhile, in New York City, a plan under which the city would acquire Lincoln Center's Vivian Beaumont Theatre for $1, remodel it at a cost of $5.2-million to accommodate three new movie theaters and a relocated Forum Theater, and turn over its operation to the City Center

370

erupted into a major controversy. Several cultural leaders organized a committee to save the Beaumont and its Forum Theater, and apparently, their effort has been successful.

New York also has new arts facilities under construction, including four legitimate theaters to be housed in office buildings. Two of them, the new homes of the Circle in the Square Theatre and the American Place Theatre, are scheduled for completion this season.   (72)

————◄●►————

Amateur Company Turns Professional in 40 Days

The purchase of a downtown nightclub in Buffalo, N. Y. last August signaled the start of a new era for one of the city's oldest amateur theater groups. In an unusual display of local cooperation and support, the nightclub was transformed into a theater within 40 days, in time for the Studio Arena Theater to present its first professional performance in its new home. Assistance from the New York State Council on the Arts helped bolster the local effort.

It was the ambition of Neal Du Brock, executive director of the Studio Theater, to turn the 38-year old community group into a top professional performing company. When a local nightclub, the Town Casino, was put up for sale, he saw it as an ideal site for a new theater. He asked his trustees for support, and, although funds were not on hand, they backed the project.

In mid-September, the board, headed by two local bankers, started an ambitious fund-raising drive for the new theater. Since then, more than $100,000 toward the goal of $175,000 has been raised. In addition, a campaign to sell memberships, seat dedications and subscriptions for the fall season, has been highly successful.

In the meantime, an architect and a construction company began renovating the old nightclub. Members of the company and volunteers helped ready the theater.

The State Council provided the theater with technical assistance. Milton Lyon, head of Equity's program to extend professional theater, and Marvin Kraus, general manager of Guber, Ford and Gross, a producing company, advised the group, and helped it locate and hire a front-of-house staff. In addition, the Council provided the theater with support to hire Rod McManigal, an expert in audience recruitment, for three months. Commenting on Council aid, Mr. Du Brock said, "The New York State Council on the Arts has virtually guaranteed our life."

On October 7th, the new three-quarter-round theater with 550 seats opened with Eugene O'Neill's, *A Moon for the Misbegotten,* directed by José Quintero and starring Colleen Dewhurst and James Daly. The new production was critically acclaimed, and attendance since the opening has averaged more than 80 per cent of theater capacity. In its first professional season, the company has presented three productions and four more are scheduled through next spring.

Members of the old amateur group are appearing in the new company, and new actors and directors have been hired. Next year, the theater hopes to have its own resident group of Equity players.   (44)

Let The City Build Your Cultural Facility

By

William A. Briggs

If grants and campaigns can't give you your tailor-made theater or concert hall, has it ever occurred to you that organizations like the Biscuit Bakers' Institute or the Ambulance Association of America might be the key to your own stage door? Last year such groups spent over a billion dollars at conventions.

Most conventions were held at civic centers in cities that are desperately seeking this foreign dollar and are willing to spend capital funds to secure it. High on their budget list is the facility to house the arts because entertainment is a paramount part of the pitch used in booking conventions.

Cities with civic center theaters and auditoriums due for occupancy by 1970 include Amarillo, Birmingham, Fort Worth, Lexington, Norfolk, Phoenix, Roanoke, Tucson and Wichita, with many more either on the boards or recently completed. Ranging in size from 600 to 3,000 seats, most are equipped to accommodate trouping and repertory productions. Although local arts groups are usually considered, your building *can* be tailored specifically to your own requirements if your cultural groups cooperate instead of compete and voice their needs in the Council Chamber. Understanding the background can help your project.

The nebulously named civic center has finally shed its cocoon of all-purpose auditorium-arena and is nestling profitably into an equilateral triangle whose base is convention money. Sports and spectaculars comprise one leg of the triangle and the other legs are reserved for live performing arts and conventions.

Due to the new "Triangular Concept," groups can now plan meetings not just in New York City, Chicago or Miami, where there is more than scenery to look at after the business sessions, but in scores of cities all over North America. Businessmen can bring their families and be assured of comfortable lodging, good food, sports, and top cultural events. This is one way the convention base helps support local arts. Extra performances mean bigger box offices because you're playing to a new audience—an audience not even approached by your season subscription.

The new Triangular Concept was inevitable. It jelled in the minds of progressive civic leaders and talent promoters eight or ten years ago when they realized the old "civic auditorium" (usually a "multipurpose" coliseum with portable or fixed stage at one end) just didn't fulfill the new needs of local cultural groups or sports-oriented citizens; nor did it begin to satisfy the demands of the tourist or conventioneer.

The forward lookers knew the answer—bricks and mortar to create suitable settings for the talent that baits the convention. But new buildings cost taxpayers' money and few politicians would risk re-election on a platform that promised much beyond patching streets and sewers. However, pressures were bearing down on the City Fathers. The downtown merchant found his customers straying off to new shopping centers. Local industry was losing key personnel to cities offering recreation and cultural programs in facilities properly designed for the purpose. As more and more businesses evacuated downtown for better surroundings, the once sparkling show-window lights dimmed. The city population dwindled and took with it the tax dollar. The city that wanted to live had to act, and the City Fathers had to take off their blinders. Their motive was no altruistic effort toward aid for arts or sports; rather, they had to find ways to garner foreign funds for elevating the tax base and reviving the central business district.

The civic center seemed to be the answer. Federal and state grants, planning loans and other sources of financial assistance were available if they knew where to look. They looked and found ways and acted—some with commendable cohesiveness of effort resulting in bright new architectural beauties that quickly increased interest and activity in the arts and sports. But due to expediency, and an understandable lack of experience in the design of such long-forgotten building types, some of these gems were myopically envisioned, functionally inadequate or just plain wrong. There were few guide lines and almost no appropriate prototypes. In the rush to get the house built, little study was devoted

375

to specific local needs and there was no long range programming.

Now, however, guided by the new Triangular Civic Center Concept, great strides are being made. Here's your cue! Capitalize on the strength of a concept which doesn't drain the budget. It can build the two things you need most—the right facility and the large foreign (not alien) audience. To get into the act, first get together. Then get the merchant's ear, the manufacturer's eye and the City Father's voice and you may soon be helping the architect design your home in the civic center. Today's civic centers can't thrive without culture! Don't worry about the audience—the chamber of commerce will have extra performances booked long before the show can be mounted. (60)

Mix Business With Pleasure

Cultural groups can provide their members and contributors with a pleasurable social experience while educating them to the organization's needs. The Montgomery County Arts Center, in Maryland, which is planning to build a theater, gallery and educational unit, recently sponsored a visit to an arts center with facilities similar to those it is planning for itself. The Center chartered a bus to the Goucher College Art Center in Towson, Maryland, to see how the performing, training and exhibiting facilities at the school are operated. A champagne supper was served aboard the bus, and a quartet in residence at the college performed for the visitors. Those unable to take the trip were urged by the organization to visit Goucher on their own. Arrangements were made for future visitors to be shown the facilities by college officials. (30)

Cinema Becomes State Arts Center in 14 Months

An unusual set of circumstances has, in 14 months, returned a seedy movie house to a semblance of its former glory as a leading legitimate theater. In the process, the theater, acquired without cost, reopened on February 1st as Delaware's first performing arts center.

Built in 1871 by the Masons of Delaware as both Masonic Temple and theater, the four-story-high Grand Opera House was one of the handsomest buildings in Wilmington with an imposing cast iron facade and one of the largest stages in the country. However, following decades of use as a legitimate theater, the house declined along with the surrounding downtown area and became a second run movie theater. The Masons, who continued to use the building's top two floors as club and meeting rooms, were concerned with the deterioration and were interested in restoring the theater to its former state. They recognized however, that the tax situation and financial problems would prevent them from undertaking the task.

The building's centennial anniversary year provided a group of concerned leaders, including members of the Delaware Arts Council and Greater Wilmington Development Council, with a springboard for direct action. On the 100th anniversary of its opening, December 22, 1971, the Delaware Governor and Grand Master of the Masons presided over a gala held at the opera house to mark the beginning of the cultural center campaign. Then the wheels began to turn. A new non-profit corporation was formed and immediately set up meetings with Mason officials to determine how the building could be transformed into a cultural center while allowing the Masons rent-free use of meeting facilities.

After months of discussion, a plan was worked out under which the Masons gave building title without cost to the City of Wilmington which, in turn, immediately conveyed title to the newly created Grand Opera, Inc. The roundabout maneuver not only formalized city recognition but served a more practical purpose. As building owner the city waived the real estate transfer tax saving Grand Opera thousands of dollars.

In a matter of months, the 1100-seat theater was readied for its new role. Foundation grants paid for cleaning and theater renovation, Dupont donated carpeting and furniture for offices and Delaware Power and Light donated box seats and orchestra chairs while also offering the Opera House the free use of its adjacent auditorium for receptions. Immediate income was available from the rental of two street level stores and a patronage campaign was launched concurrent with the announcement of a six-event inaugural season running from February through May. In its first 20 days the drive snared 130 grand patrons at $100 each and won 400 season subscribers. According to Lawrence J. Wilker, a University of Delaware faculty member who donated his time to serve as theater director, "It really snowballed."

As opening night neared, Wilmington business rallied to support the new center. Virtually every local store promoted the Opera House with fliers and window cards, nearby parking lots offered discounts to ticket holders and ten area restaurants offered special "grand opera dinners" at reduced prices. The opening night Delaware Symphony concert drew an enthusiastic overflow audience.

With its initial season a reality Grand Opera, Inc. is now turning its attention to long range development and fund raising. A professionally booked season of 12 to 15 events is being planned for next year and several leading state cultural groups may move into the building.

"We've got the theater painted and cleaned," said Wilker, "but it will take $3-million to restore it to what it was." With its recent designation as an architectural landmark, however, the possibility of federal funds for restoration exists. Also, theater leaders hope to turn the vacant second floor into a mini-mall of arts-oriented shops to produce additional income. (79)

College Combines Culture and Athletics in New Campus

The first college "Theatron"—a $2,000,000 cultural and physical education center on the campus of Monticello Junior College, Alton, Ill.—will open in October with a full program of cultural events for students and the community. The dedication takes place just two years after Monticello's president, Dr. Duncan Wimpress, persuaded the board of trustees that a proposed physical education building, with a stage at one end of a gymnasium, should be, instead, a cultural center for the college and the community with physical education facilities.

A new physical education building had been suggested in 1961 by Mrs. Spencer T. Olin, an alumna of Monticello, and her husband, who planned to donate the funds. After accepting Dr. Wimpress's suggestion that the gift was an opportunity to serve the cultural needs of both community and campus, a committee was formed to choose an architect. The administration and the faculty then worked with him to integrate the needs of the 325 students with those of the community of about 80,000. The result was Hatheway Hall,

379

called a "Theatron", the Roman term for a building combining facilities for games and the arts.

The building includes two gymnasiums, a pool, a 1,000-seat theatre and an art gallery large enough for permanent displays and traveling exhibits.

Before invitations to bid were issued the architect estimated costs on the basis of "quantity take off." This involves tabulating each quantity in the building—concrete, glass, steel, floor covering and others—and then judging costs based on the quantities involved. This type of estimate, in the opinion of the college, provides a much more accurate basis than a square foot or cubic area basis.

(20)

Cultural Building Boom Biggest in History

(This concludes a two-part series based on Arts Management's 1962 survey of chambers of commerce.)

Rising public interest in the arts has created a boom of wholly unprecedented proportions in the construction of new buildings to house cultural activities, *AM*'s latest survey reveals. The survey, which drew detailed replies from chamber of commerce officials in 147 cities, asked a series of questions about construction of new arts facilities. The results are dramatic evidence of the scope of the cultural upsurge.

Some form of building activity in connection with the arts was reported to be planned or under way in 69 communities, virtually half of those replying to the construction questions. The projects mentioned in the survey represent a budgeted or contemplated expenditure of at least $120,000,000. The survey results suggest that the total national building bill for the arts (including Lincoln Center in New York, and others not covered in the survey) may run around $375,000,000. This means that for the first time in history the nation's cultural establishment has become an economically important market for commercially-produced goods and services. This is a historic development that can have a deep impact on the long range relationship between business and the arts in America.

Within the construction boom can be seen the increasing influence of the inter-disciplinary movement in the arts. Combined facilities—art centers sheltering a number of different kinds of cultural activity—are being planned or built in 40 of the 147 cities covered in the survey, 27.2 per cent.

These range in size from the ambitious plans for the National Cultural Center in Washington, estimated to cost $30,000,000 (only Lincoln Center will be bigger) down to the estimated $10,000 for an art center in Key West, Florida. Peoria has engaged Victor Gruen Associates to design a new $700,000 center. Syracuse, N. Y. reports plans for a center to be part of a community plaza development to be built as part of its urban renewal program.

Winter Park, Florida, is planning a theatre, museum and concert auditorium in a single facility to cost between $1,500,000 and $2,000,000. Laramie, Wyoming, Trenton, N. J., Hartford, Conn., and San Leandro, California all report plans for combined arts facilities, and plans are in the talking stage in cities like Odessa, Texas, Gadsden, Alabama, and Tenafly, N. J., to mention a few.

A breakdown of the kinds of facilities planned shows that museums are running slightly ahead of theatres and concert halls in terms of numbers of cities now building or planning them.

Fully 34 communities, 23.2 per cent of the total, reported new museums going up. Washington's Board of Trade estimates that $25,000,000 will be spent there on new museum construction. Milwaukee is spending $5,500,000. New museums range in type from Oklahoma City's $400,000 combined arts and science museum, to Tampa's children's museum, and the museum of American Indian artifacts planned in Quincy, Illinois.

In 30 of the cities covered by the survey, 20.4 per cent of the total—new concert auditoriums are either rising or being blueprinted. A number, like the ones in Baltimore and St. Petersburg, Florida, are part of civic centers. Others, like those in Hartford, Conn., and Lakeland, Florida, are connected with colleges.

Theatre construction is indicated in 28 of the reporting communities. Framingham, Mass. for example, is building a permanent theatre in the round. Ypsilanti, Mich. is spending $400,000, Asheville, N. C., $500,000 and Salt Lake City, $1,250,000.

The survey results also indicate that a great deal of money is being spent on remodeling and enlarging existing facilities in every area of the arts. Savannah, Georgia, and Beckley, W. Va., are remodeling theatres. Tampa, Florida's concert auditorium is being remodeled at a cost of $350,000. The arts center in Tacoma, Wash., is being altered and furnished. Museums in Greensboro, N. C., Grand Rapids, Mich., and Colorado Springs, Colorado, are being expanded.

The long range significance of this hectic activity is hard to interpret, But, inevitably, the increase in physical facilities will bring with it the need for greater than ever numbers of trained arts managers to man the bigger, more complex arts "plant." In turn, the growth of the arts management profession is likely to have profound consequences on the content and character of the arts of the future.   (5)

Urban Renewal Spurs Arts Building Activity

Urban renewal programs are playing an important role in the cultural building boom, a nationwide survey just completed by *Arts Management* reveals. Although cultural facilities in urban renewal areas are mostly on the drawing boards today, the next few years should produce new arts structures in every area of the country.

The survey, believed to be the first of its kind, drew replies from urban renewal agencies in 95 cities, ranging in size from New York with its eight million persons to Edinburgh, Texas, with a population of 15,000. Responses to *AM* questionnaires came from 31 states and the District of Columbia.

In the urban renewal program, Federal funds are used to purchase land which is then cleared, and developed, rehabilitated or conserved. While the Government must approve the urban renewal plans of local agencies, it does not provide construction funds. In the majority of instances, private developers construct the facilities.

Of the 95 cities surveyed, 43 or nearly half, include the construction of arts facilities in their urban renewal plans. Of these cities, some have more than one urban renewal project involving the arts. In some instances, there are several arts facilities included in a single project. Of the projects reported, 14 are under construction, 26 are in the planning stage, 4 in remodelling and 4 have been completed since 1960. In addition, four other cities in the early stages of urban renewal planning are leaning towards the inclusion of arts facilities. A preponderance of these arts facilities are theatres, with arts centers and museums receiving the next greatest emphasis.

Of the major cities surveyed, most include the arts in their urban renewal programs with the exceptions of Minneapolis, Minn., St. Louis, Mo., Los Angeles, Calif., San Antonio, Tex., and Buffalo, N. Y. New York City has the largest project, the Lincoln Center complex, as well as the Washington Square theater. However, other metropolises like Philadelphia, which is planning the expansion of its Academy of Music and College of Art, and the possible creation of a cultural center around existing institutions, also have ambitious programs.

Chicago's program includes cultural facilities on a new University of Illinois campus, a theater and two cultural centers. Atlanta will have an auditorium to replace an existing city auditorium, and an exhibit hall. Washington, D. C., has its Arena Stage completed in its Southwest renewal area, and Pittsburgh is building a theater, and a center for the arts which will house its Symphony Orchestra. In Baltimore, one urban renewal project in the planning stage calls for additions to the Peabody Institute of Music and the Walters Art Gallery, and another calls for a new theater to replace Ford's Theater.

In San Francisco, arts facilities are planned in several urban renewal areas. Two commercial theaters, a museum and a Japanese cultural and trade center will be built there. Although a site was sought for the city's Actor's Workshop, the renewal agency said, "the project is likely not to materialize in view of the departure of the principal members of the organization to the Lincoln Center Repertory Theater."

Detroit is considering the inclusion of theaters in two of its urban renewal projects. Its agency reported, "It is entirely possible that in the future there will be a cultural center urban renewal project in the vicinity of our Institute of Arts, Main Library and Historical Museum."

384

In medium-sized cities, those with 200,000 to 500,000 persons, 6 of 10 agencies include the arts. Providence, R. I., has proposed in its master plan, "Downtown Providence 1970," that a center for the performing arts of Rhode Island be included. Miami, Fla., which has recently submitted an application to the Government for its first urban renewal project, has proposed a large community center to include theater facilities.

In Rochester, N. Y., an urban renewal program in the planning stage calls for the construction of a performing arts theater in the downtown business district within 5 to 10 years. In Norfolk, Va., an adjunct to the Norfolk Art Museum is being restored, in San Jose, Calif., a theater is planned, and in Tulsa, Okla., a theater will be included in a civic area.

Urban renewal also appears to have sparked the construction of arts facilities within project boundaries but not on land cleared with urban renewal funds. Based on such land usage, an arts center is planned in Springfield, Ohio; Tulsa, Okla., will have a new theater; and Little Rock, Ark., has built an arts center. (37)

Arts Facilities Uplift Urban Renewal Areas

Arts facilities included in urban renewal projects are tending to uplift their surrounding areas, and early indications are they will also raise real estate values and increase business volume. This was concluded by *Arts Management* from its recent survey of urban renewal and the arts, to which 95 cities responded.

Of the 43 cities which included the construction of arts facilities in their urban renewal plans, 23 had advanced far enough in their projects to venture estimates as to the effect the facilities would generally have on the city as well as the project area.

In answer to the question, "What benefits will your city realize from new or improved cultural facilities?" all cities responding indicated generally positive effects, while five specifically cited an anticipated increase in attendance at cultural events.

Pittsburgh, Pa., reported that its planned center for the arts will develop its downtown area as a cultural center, strengthen the prestige and financial position of its symphony orchestra, and attract visitors to the city. In Washington, D. C., construction of the Arena Stage has "added enormously to the cultural vitality of the city."

Of the small number of cities in a position to estimate the effect that arts facilities in urban renewal projects will have on real estate values, 11 reported rising values. In addition, five cities indicated increased traffic and three cities reported heightened business volume in the urban renewal area. No cities, however, reported a drop in any of the above.

As reported in *AM* previously, the majority of cities with populations exceeding 200,000 (61 per cent) include arts facilities in their urban renewal programs. In contrast, only 38 per cent, or 27 of the 71 smaller cities responding to the survey, include the arts. Four other smaller cities report they are considering structures to house the arts as part of their urban renewal plans.

New Rochelle, N. Y., has submitted plans for a legitimate theater to builder-developers and hopes for responses in the near future. A theater center is planned in Hartford, Conn., a performing arts center is being built in Binghamton, N. Y., and a museum is being constructed in Lansing, Mich. An auditorium is planned in Cedar Rapids, Iowa; Fresno, Calif., is modernizing several theaters in its cultural center; and White Plains, N. Y., is considering construction of a county-wide arts center.

Several cities with populations under 50,000 have ambitious plans for the arts in their urban renewal programs. An arts center and museum are planned in Brunswick, Ga., and Williamsport, Pa., plans a theater for the performing arts. Potsdam, N. Y., with less than 10,000 persons, plans the relocation of its Village Museum, and has already completed concert halls at the State University College, Clarkson College of Technology and the Crane School of Music.

More than a quarter of the surveyed cities that included arts facilities in their urban renewal programs are being aided in the planning of these facilities by arts organizations. But the types of organizations vary. In New York City, Lincoln Center aids the city's Housing and Redevelopment Board in plans for its urban renewal area.

Rochester, N. Y., has a Committee for the Performing Arts to help it plan its urban renewal projects. Pittsburgh works with various organizations interested in the arts, such as the Heinz Foundation, the Mellon Charitable and Educational Trust and the Allegheny Conference on Community Development. San Francisco consults with its Museum Board, the city's Symphony Foundation and its ballet company. San Jose, Calif., works with its Fine Arts Commission and Symphony Association.   (38)

———————◄•►———————

Visual Arts Seldom Featured In Local Urban Renewal Plans

Urban renewal projects are making limited use of painting and sculpture. In only a few instances are specific proposals for art works written into the project; occasionally they are included without being stipulated in plans. And competitions appear to play a small role in the selection of art works, and in the design of cultural facilities.

These were the conclusions drawn by *Arts Management* from its recent survey of urban renewal and the arts, to which 95 cities responded.

In answer to the question "Does your city program include any stipulation that builders must set aside a percentage of contract dollars for the purchase of art?" only five of the 47 cities responding answered "Yes." In each of these cities the total amount budgeted for visual art is one per cent of the overall construction figure.

In its four urban renewal areas, San Francisco will have sculpture by such artists as Henry Moore, Marino Marini, Seymour Lipton, Jacques Overhoff, and Duane Faralla; paintings by David Simpson and Keith Boyle; a mosaic by Mark Adams; and a pagoda in its Japanese Cultural and Trade Center by Yoshiro Taniguchi.

Baltimore anticipates sculpture in addition to a fountain in its Charles Center Project. Murals, statuary and fountains will mark Washington, D. C.'s, Columbia Plaza urban renewal area. Bethlehem, Pa., has selected a citizens' committee to recommend how $90,000 should be spent for art, sculpture and murals in its Civic Center. And Asheville, North Carolina, will also beautify its renewal projects with art work.

While making no specific provisions for it, three other cities include art in urban renewal projects. Chicago reported it includes art "indirectly" by basing awards of contracts to builders on criteria which state the desirability of including art and sculpture in building plans. Los Angeles says it encourages art work in design criteria. Hartford, Conn., has a "permissive" policy; one per cent of construction costs may be devoted to art.

Five cities, Kalamazoo, Mich., Springfield, Ohio, Stamford, Conn., Chester, Pa., and Portsmouth, New Hampshire, indicated that while no stipulation exists for art work in urban renewal projects, such a requirement is being considered.

Meanwhile, six cities have conducted competitions for design of structures, or for works of art as part of their urban renewal programs. Except for Rochester, New York, these are the same cities stipulating a one per cent budget figure for art works in urban renewal projects.   (39)

Cultural Building Boom to Continue, AM Chamber Survey Reveals

(This is the second part of AM*'s 1967 survey of chambers of commerce. Part one was based on 181 responses. An additional 40 chambers, who responded to questionnaires later, are included in the current study.)*

More new buildings for the arts have been completed in the past five years than in any other period in history. This bricks and mortar boom will not only continue, but seems likely to accelerate in the next five years, *AM's* survey of chambers of commerce reveals. The survey, which drew detailed responses from chamber of commerce officials in 221 cities, was undertaken to determine the number of cultural facilities completed since 1962 and the number of new buildings underway or planned.

More than two-thirds of the responding chambers, 141 of 221, listed some form of arts construction activity in their communities since 1962. Seventy cities completed a total of 100 new arts structures in the past five years. This list includes 36 museums, 34 theaters, 23 arts centers, and seven concert auditoriums. The costliest of these projects (New York's Lincoln Center was not included in the survey) was Los Angeles' $33.5-million Music Center.

Facilities now underway or planned outnumber those completed, according to the survey, with 98 cities reporting 126 projects in various stages of development. Cost estimates, which are given for 66 of these projects, totaled nearly $220-million. If a similar amount were projected for the 60 other projects, and if we assume that another 60 facilities were not included in the survey (colleges which are experiencing an arts building boom were listed infrequently), the national arts building bill for the next five

390

years would easily exceed $600-million. Translated into economic terms, the building of facilities to house arts activities represents a market of considerable significance.

Motivation for many of the new facilities appears to have come from chambers of commerce. Ten chambers listed themselves as motivators, and eight other chambers claimed to have played key roles in the planning of new structures for the arts.

Two trends were evident from survey results. First, more communities are thinking about building arts centers, facilities which house several kinds of arts activities, than any other kind of structure. Of the 126 projects listed as underway or planned, 49 were arts centers. Second, many multipurpose centers are being built by municipalities and financed through bond issues and special taxes. These centers house not only facilities for the arts, but facilities for such income-producing, non-arts programs as trade shows and conventions. Norfolk, Va., for example, has broken ground for an $18-million cultural-convention center which will include an arena, theater complex and museum; Wichita, Kans. is constructing a $12.6-million municipal auditorium complex including a theater, music hall, auditorium, convention rooms and exhibit space; Saginaw, Mich. will complete its $6.5-million civic center, housing a music hall, arena and auditorium, in 1969; and Richmond, Va. will break ground for its new $20-million coliseum in 1968. Other cities now building civic centers combining the arts and commercial activities include Denver, Colo., Charleston, S. C., and Monroe, La.

Centers limited strictly to arts activities range in size from Atlanta's $13-million Memorial Cultural Center and Milwaukee's $10-million County War Memorial Center for the Performing Arts, both scheduled to open in 1968, down

391

to Cincinnati's $400,000 Contemporary Arts Center, which will be completed in 1969. Brockton, Mass. is planning a $5-million center; Tulsa, Okla., a $4.5-million center; San Jose, Calif., a $3-million center; and Memphis, Tenn., a $2-million center. Colleges planning or constructing arts centers include Millikin Univ. in Decatur, Ill., Akron Univ. in Ohio, Washburn Univ. in Topeka, Kans., and the Univ. of Idaho in Moscow, Ida. New cultural centers are being considered as part of core area redevelopment programs in Boulder, Colo. and Providence, R. I.

A breakdown by types of facilities indicates that theaters are running ahead of museums and concert auditoriums. Responding chambers listed 30 theaters now underway or planned. Those to be completed this year include the $750,000 North Shore Theatre in Beverly, Mass., the $300,000 Spokane, Wash., Civic Theater, and a $150,000 theater in Cheyenne, Wyo. Theaters scheduled to open in 1968 include those in San Jose, Calif., ($5-million); Houston, Tex., ($3-million); San Antonio, Tex., ($2.5-million); and Oklahoma City, Okla., ($2-million). The University of Michigan hopes to complete its $2.5-million theater in 1969, and New Orleans plans to open its $4-million theater by 1970.

New museums were listed by 29 chambers with projects ranging from Columbus, Ohio's $10-million museum, scheduled to open in 1969, to Albion, Michigan's $40,000 historical museum, which will be completed this October. An $8-million museum will open in Oakland, Calif. in 1968 and a $3-million museum will open in Pasadena, Calif, in 1969. Later this year, new museums will open in Clovis, N.M., Bartlesville, Okla., Juneau, Alas., Colorado Springs, Colo., and Williamsport, Pa.

Only 18 new concert auditoriums are underway or planned according to the survey. These include facilities now being constructed in Cincinnati, Ohio, Amarillo, Texas, Jackson, Miss., Macon, Ga., Portland, Ore., Roanoke, Va., and Estes Park, Colo., each costing more than $1-million. Huntsville, Ala. is planning a $6-million auditorium and New Orleans, La. hopes to have its $4-million auditorium built by 1971. Orlando, Fla. approved a $1.6-million bond issue for an auditorium in 1965.

In addition to new construction, the survey results indicate that large sums are being spent to remodel or enlarge existing facilities. (56)

Button Boom

Buttons are becoming a new promotional tool for arts organizations. The Arena Stage in Washington, D. C., engaged in a fund drive for a second theater building costing $1.5-million, distributed handsome brochures to 35,000 potential contributors. Included in the brochures were buttons reading, "Be An Angel." (60)

PART THREE: PUBLIC RELATIONS IN THE ARTS

Chapter VI-Press and Publicity

Chapter VII-Promotion

Chapter VI – Press and Publicity

PUBLICITY TOOLS AND TECHNIQUES

Arts Organizations Must Reach Many Publics

By

A. H. Reiss

Many arts groups gear their public relations program to a single undifferentiated audience. Yet the fact is that every cultural organization, regardless of its size or the extent of its program, serves many different publics. For its public relations program to be fully effective, an organization must consciously identify the publics it wishes to reach, then attempt to determine the attitude of each toward the organization. Only then can a comprehensive program be planned that will influence not merely the "public at large," but also each of the organization's constituencies.

A public can best be defined as any group, organized or not, that shares certain interests or whose members bear roughly similar relationships to the institution or organization.

Let's analyze the publics of a typical cultural institution. Starting with the organization itself, and working outward the first public is the institution's own staff and its policy making bodies. This includes all paid employees, the board of directors, and committee chairmen. Does every staff member fully understand the goals of the organization? Are board members up-to-date on its activities? Before an organization attempts to conduct a systematic external public relations campaign, it should put its own house in order.

Next come the volunteer workers. This large and important public is frequently neglected in overall public relations planning, but, especially because volunteers have direct contact with the broad outside public, their importance should not be minimized. Special events and publications should be utilized to guarantee that volunteers understand the long range aims of the institution, as well as its immediate problems.

A third public is, of course, the audience that attends performances or exhibitions of the institution. This, being a more diffuse public, is harder to analyze. But the more that is known about the tastes and socio-economic characteristics of this audience, the more effectively will the institution be able to serve it, and the more effective will its public relations program be. Some institutions have learned the value of audience research, and make use of it. Is the audience satisfied with the institution's programming facilities and services? Should changes be made to eliminate dissatisfaction? Positively, what elements of programming or service should be emphasized in public relations efforts to reach this audience? Because this public is larger and more diffuse, methods for reaching it necessarily differ from those used to reach your internal publics.

Similarly, members and contributors represent two additional publics. Although few institutions neglect these publics, few take enough pains to study the differences between them. Analysis of reasons for giving or for joining should be the basis for any public relations effort directed at them. This analysis will suggest the kind of services or programs to provide for them. It will also suggest the ''tone'' and character of communications directed at them.

Still another public is the business community. No public relations effort aimed at this public will be harmed by a bit of simple ''research'' consisting of half a dozen personal
398

interviews with business leaders to sound out their attitudes toward the institution. Such interviews with businessmen who have no connection with the institution may reveal much about widespread community attitudes. Remember, too, that businessmen, especially if favorably inclined toward the organization themselves, are powerful levers for influencing the opinions of others in the community. It is wise to discover what important services your institution may be able to offer to them, or to their constituencies, and then to center the business-oriented public relations program on such services.

Government at each level is still another public. The story of your institution's work with schools, or at hospitals and similar institutions, can help favorably influence this public. Other cultural institutions, too, may require special attention. Their attitude toward the work of your institution helps condition the attitude of other publics.

This does not exhaust the list of constituencies that a well-refined public relations program takes into consideration. The degree to which the public relations program reflects the differences between them is a good measure of its overall effectiveness.   (18)

Hiring a Publicity Firm: Pros, Cons, Costs

In recent years cultural organizations have made increased use of professional public relations firms or consultants. While the majority of arts group still rely wholly on their own publicity departments, composed of volunteer workers or staff members, many organizations, including the Indianapolis Symphony, the Whitney Museum, the Philadelphia Chamber Orchestra and the National Cultural

Center, to name a few, are or have been represented by outside public relations counsel.

What are the advantages and disadvantages of this practice?

A volunteer amateur publicity director may get his group into the local papers, and see that its posters are distributed. But he often has no idea of the way to induce a national magazine, a wire service or a network television producer to take a look at his organization. He may not know the name of a single out-of-town editor or writer. His effectiveness is thus strictly local, as a rule, and the picture in *Life,* the story in *Look,* the appearance on a network show are beyond his capability.

The professional outside publicist is not a miracle worker. He cannot automatically ''deliver'' an article in a national magazine or an appearance on radio or television. Arranging this takes considerable time and effort, and a really firm promise of delivery should make the client cautious. But the professional public relations counsel should know how to accomplish this, and he should have the necessary contact with editors, writers and producers.

He should know how to present news, and even create news that reflects favorably on the client. He should know how to find free lance writers likely to be most interested in the client's story. He should know how to help them prepare the story, how to dig up appropriate facts and anecdotes. He should know where the story is best told, and when. He should know how to set up a press conference—and when not to. Above all, he should know how to shape a campaign to fit the objective of the organization, whether the objective is to build audience, recruit volunteers, attract out-of-town visitors, or boost contributions in fund raising.

These talents are not necessarily limited to outside publicists. Some cultural institutions employ full-time staff professionals who are thoroughly qualified, too. But for the smaller institution that cannot afford the salary, administrative cost and overhead of a full-time inside public relations operation, for the group that is geographically isolated from major press, radio and television centers, for the group that needs help for only part of the year, or for a special campaign, or for institutions with unusual requirements, the sensible answer may be outside representation.

Some cultural institutions, of course, do not need an extensive public relations program. They may be reaching their audience, filling the house, and suffering no financial pangs. But for those not in this enviable position, professional public relations can provide an important boost. Each cultural organization should analyze its own situation carefully, to determine first of all, if it needs outside help.

The main objection to professional representation is cost. Not all groups can afford it. Even the smallest public relations firm will hesitate to take on a full program for an organization paying it less than $300 monthly. While it is difficult to name an average fee (such figures are generally confidential), the range is usually between $400 and $800 a month. For large organizations, however, with heavy requirements, the fee may exceed $1200 per month.

If a group has made the decision that it can afford the fee, it should not necesarily assume that it will receive the constant, around-the-clock attention, that it might from a member of its own staff. On the other hand, some public relations firm may place a representative on the premises. There should be a clear understanding in advance of the firm's availability and the time it is prepared to give to the client.

An additional difficulty is that many public relations firms are not equipped by experience or instinct to serve a cultural account. Their entire experience may have been commercial, and they may have neither an interest in, nor an understanding of, the arts. Representation by such a firm may prove ineffective or undignified or both. Other firms, capable of serving a cultural group effectively, may not wish to, since such accounts are rarely as lucrative as straight commercial work. (5)

———— ◄•► ————

How to Choose and Sign Up a Public Relations Firm for an Arts Campaign

Before an arts group decides to hire an outside public relations firm, it should first determine what its primary objective is. Is it to increase audiences at performances? Is it to attract out-of-town visitors? Or to gain members? Or to win national recognition for excellence? Or perhaps to bring in financial support? What, in addition, are its secondary objectives?

Once the institution has thought these questions through and agreed upon the need for outside help, it should invite letters of application from as many public relations firms as possible. Board members should be polled for names of agencies they know, and it is wise to ask others close to the organization to make suggestions. Firms may be local, they may be in a nearby city, or they may be in New York where access to the national publications and networks is easiest.

Applicants should be asked to state their accomplishments, their specialties, their past and present clients, and record of activity in the cultural field. Replies should be carefully screened by a committee that narrows the list down to the most appealing applicants. These can then be invited to a personal meeting, one at a time, to discuss the client's specific needs.

After the public relations firm representatives have been briefed on the objectives of the organization, the latter has the right to ask for a written presentation listing services the firm proposes to furnish, its suggestions for an overall program, the proposed fee and expense schedule. The organization also has the right to meet and talk with a client already served by the agency.

Before making a final choice, the client should get the answers to several questions:

Is the firm equipped to handle a cultural organization? How much time will the agency give the account? Who will work on the account? Will the supervisory personnel and heads of the firm contribute their talents, or leave the job to subordinates? Does the agency have regular and intimate access to press, radio and television at a national as well as local level?

The arts group should be wary of a firm that tries too hard to impress outsiders with the size and magnificence of its office. This sort of thing does not mean results. Of twenty people in a firm, only two or three may be actually working on the account. The new client should be especially skeptical of the firm that claims to have certain free-lance writers or staff editors "all sewed up." Although a few unscrupulous firms indulge in excessive gift-giving to writers and editors, a good firm does not buy contacts. It is, instead, sufficiently creative to do constant research and thus learn what kind of stories particular editors and writers are looking for, and offer them leads appropriate to their editorial interests.

When the organization is satisfied with the presentation, all questions are answered, and the staff who will work on the account are known, a contract must be drawn up. Contracts do not have to be complicated legal documents. Many firms use simple letters of agreement which specify, among other things, the length of the contract, conditions for terminating, the fee, and the restriction on expenses. A client should not expect a contract to state the actual publicity placements to be made, since no ethical firm can state this in advance.

Most public relations firms prefer to work on a year-long contract, with fees payable monthly, in advance. The minimum period for most firms, particularly where national representation is important, is three months. This is so because the placement of a story in a national magazine may take months to accomplish, inasmuch as the magazine may work on issues long in advance of publication. For the client's protection, it is wise to limit a first contract to a trial period of three months, before committing the organization to a longer term.

Expenses to be paid by the client over and above the monthly fee should be carefully limited. These normally include only extraordinary costs, such as out-of-town travel, long distance telephoning, printing, art work, photographic costs and modest entertainment for the press. The contract can be written to fix a monthly amount, say $50, which the firm can spend at its own discretion, with the stipulation that all expenses over that amount must be approved by the client in advance.

The outside public relations program costs money. But a dignified and imaginative one, carried out with professional skill, can prove itself in prestige gained, and more than pay for itself at the box office or in the fund raising campaign. (6)

How to Cope with Controversy—and Survive

At some point in the life of almost every organization it must face the problem of public controversy. This may arise because of its programming or because of the failure of a major fund raising effort, or as a consequence of personality differences, or for many other reasons. Whatever the cause, public controversy presents special problems for the institution's public relations staff.

Should cultural organizations avoid controversy? The temptation is to answer "yes." But many experienced arts managers and public relations experts agree that avoiding "hot" issues in an effort to sidestep controversy is not necessarily wise. Some issues must be faced head-on, even at the cost of becoming unpopular with sectors of the public. But whether the institution consciously adopts a controversial policy, or finds itself embroiled in a controversy not of its own making, it should be prepared for criticism at any time and know how to cope with it.

An institution that has carried out a thoughtful and continuing public relations effort emphasizing its services to the public will, of course, be in a far stronger position when a "crisis" arises than one that has neglected its public relations. Community understanding and respect for the organization, once developed over the long haul, will help immeasurably in its time of trouble.

Here are some suggestions that may make coping with controversy easier.

1. Anticipate it. Not everything is predictable, but sophisticated organizational leadership will only rarely be caught by surprise. In setting policy, or in programming, bear in mind local sensitivities, the policies of other cul-

405

tural organizations, the traditional "image" of the institution.

2. Discreetly avoid it, if possible, by meeting in advance with potential critics, trying to win them over, perhaps even inviting them to serve on a committee to help solve the problem in question. But do not necessarily retreat if you fail.

3. In making a decision that may spark controversy, the organization should know exactly why it is doing so. The reasons should be cogently hammered out in advance, and communicated to all levels within the organization, board, staff, and even, when possible, members and volunteers. The institution whose "family" is united will be far less vulnerable than the one that enters a controversy with its own house divided or confused.

4. Clearly define authority and responsibility for the duration of the "emergency." Decide on a single spokesman to present the institution's positions.

5. In statements, be brief, clear, but not truculent. Anticipate objections and attempt to meet them.

6. Act quickly to disseminate information or to answer charges. An announcement of an unusual or controversial policy, or a reply to public criticism, may call for a press conference to which all interested news media are invited. Exclusive interviews or statements to a single press outlet should be avoided, unless it clearly is the only one of importance.

7. In replying to charges, it is usually best to maintain a tone of moderation, but there are times when indignation is justified. Reply quickly, or not at all, since delay weakens the effect. But do not attack individuals. Address the re-

sponse to issues, not personalities. Avoid sounding defensive, but do not be afraid to apologize, if the institution has, indeed, made a mistake.

8. Finally, remember that losing a battle may mean that the organization deserved to lose it—that the position it adopted was wrong. Clear away the debris and get back to constructive work.

Controversies may be unpleasant at times. But a good, healthy, spirited public debate over clearly defined issues can be a great boon to the cultural institution that is not afraid of it. (15)

———————◄●►———————

Know Media Before Advertising or Promoting

Cultural organizations rely heavily on publicity to promote their performances, membership and fund raising drives. The arts manager who understands the media for publicity and advertising and can differentiate among them will be able to do a more effective job than the one whose knowledge of them is haphazard.

An important first step in systematic publicity or advertising work is a survey of the media serving the community or region in which the arts institution operates. Usually the newspapers (morning, afternoon and weekly) and the radio or television stations are the most important media. But it is important not to overlook local or regional magazines, business publications, the newsletters of other organizations and similar specialized outlets.

The public relations or advertising staff should determine the circulation and territory covered by each publication. It should likewise learn the wattage and coverage of radio or television stations, as well as something about their equipment (e.g., can they cover a live performance, can a cameraman film an interview outside the studio?)

Next it is important to analyze each medium—its policies *vis a vis* cultural groups, its editorial point of view, its standing in the community, its special following among different sectors of the public, the age, income and educational characteristics of its readers, viewers or listeners.

It is important to know, too, how, where and at what time readers, viewers or listeners are likely to receive your message, and how the medium is geared into the work habits of the community.

If you decide to buy advertising space or time, remember that media managements and their representatives respect the buyer who tries to get full value for his money. Most media see that their rates are published and respected, and they have standard quantity discounts that are well-known.

Print publications will usually establish a discount schedule based on how much total space is contracted for over a 12 month period. Radio and TV stations offer similar reductions. Some media offer cash discounts that are worth looking into, if you are in a position to pay cash. A published rate card that differs markedly from the actual prices charged is often the sign of a weak medium.

Some of the best sources of information—apart from published directories like *Standard Rate and Data*—are local media representatives and salesmen. They are usually well-informed about local markets, and can often provide considerable statistical data about the audience of the media they represent. Remember that media representatives are interested in making your program a success inasmuch as their livelihood depends on the continuing use of their media.

Tell them, as completely as possible, what your problems are and what your resources are. Get their recommendations on size and frequency of ads, and time and length of radio and TV announcements. Then use your own judgment.

(20)

The Art of Holding a Profitable Press Conference

The press conference is perhaps the most misused of all publicity techniques.

Before calling a press conference, an arts manager should answer two questions affirmatively: Are there enough news reporters and photographers within reach who would be interested in attending? And is there an announcement important enough to justify calling them?

If there are only two or three persons who might attend, the organization's needs can be served better by giving the story directly to them without calling a press conference. A "press conference" at which the hosts outnumber the few newsmen present in a room of empty chairs is a humiliating experience for the group calling it.

To be worth calling in the press, an announcement must be important and question-provoking. The list of programs for the coming season, for example, can be adequately announced in written form alone. But if an orchestra has chosen a new conductor whom the press has not met, a conference permits him to discuss his background, plans for the season and anything else about which the press is curious.

The press conference should be held during newsmen's normal working hours. In practical terms, this means between 10 a.m. and noon, or between 2 and 4 p.m. If held

409

during lunch hours, the press conference may be resented. If it starts after 4 p.m. there is danger some newsmen will have to leave before it is finished. If there are both morning and afternoon papers in town, alternating the starting time of each conference will give each paper its chance at printing the news first. Try not to choose a day when a major scheduled event may compete for the attention of the press.

An up-to-date press list is the first requirement for calling a conference. Each newsman should be notified either by phone or a mailed announcement a few days in advance. He should be reminded by phone on the day of the conference. In cities with a news ticker service, notification to wire service clients should be made over the ticker the day before the conference.

Still photographers should first be given the chance to get posed pictures so they can leave to develop them. The conference host should cooperate fully with professional photographers by agreeing to pose as they ask, within the bounds of propriety.

Reporters, meanwhile, should have been given a duplicated statement summarizing the main purpose of the conference to prepare them to ask informed questions. Every detail the host wants to appear correctly in print, such as exact spelling of proper names, dates and amounts of money, should be in the duplicated release.

The person holding the conference may make an oral statement supplementing the release, or he may invite questions at the outset. It is essential that he be well informed and articulate. Sometimes the president of an organization can best make the announcement with the manager or executive secretary at his side to reply to questions he cannot answer. No question should be slighted.

If the organization wants to get a certain point emphatically across to the public through the press, it should pre-

pare in advance a colorful way of putting its point in a few words. This precise wording should be used both in the written statement and orally through the spokesman. In on the story appearing in the papers.
this way it can often guide the headline and lead paragraph

The conference should be decisively ended rather than permitted to drift along with some reporters impatient to return to their offices, yet afraid to leave for fear of missing something. The spokesman should remain available, however, to answer afterthought questions or make further arrangements for pictures or additional data. A complete list of those present should be compiled for future reference and follow-up. (10)

———◆●▶———

Press Conference Sent By Mail A Convenience to Busy Editors

Arts groups with important news to communicate can effectively reach the press in distant areas by holding a press-conference-by-mail. The technique is particularly suited to the needs of small organizations with resources too limited for holding large and costly press conferences. But all groups can benefit from it because editors are grateful to receive important news gathered without the burden of long and time-consuming trips to press conferences.

A press-conference-by-mail is actually an expanded press kit which contains all the material usually supplied in a press kit, such as news releases and photographs. It should also include, however, two other items. One is a prepared question-and-answer interview with your organization head that provides general background on your group. It should

411

state your organization's purpose, its recent activities and details of the event you are promoting.

In addition, a form addressed to your organization's head along with a pre-stamped, addressed envelope should be enclosed. The editor should be invited to submit his own questions on this form with the promise that they will be promptly answered.

When preparing such kits remember that they are not a substitute for a press conference that keeps editors informed of fast-breaking events, and they must be disseminated well before the date of the event you are promoting. Mail them not only to cultural editors and critics, but also to other editors who might be interested in some phase of your activities.

In addition to reaching far away press sources, the kit may be used as a convenient way of disseminating information in your hometown when news of no immediacy is being made by your group. Editors will be more inclined to use a short story about your event when they do not have to leave their offices to obtain answers to their questions.

The kit also has the advantage of giving a group time to ponder and effectively answer questions that in a press conference might receive an off-the-shoulder reply which would not serve an organization's purpose. The editor, on the other hand, has the advantage of conducting a press conference at his desk and at his convenience. It permits him to zero in on questions of import to his own readers without "tipping his hand" to his competitors.   (30)

————◄•►————

Press Calendar Aids Organization and Editors

Cultural organizations planning for the start of a new fall season are wise to include in their advance efforts the preparation of a yearly or bi-annual press calendar for dissemination to all press sources prior to the season's opening. Press calendars not only help editors plan coverage in advance, but also serve to remind an organization's public relations staff of the work to be done during the year.

Press calendars differ from the ordinary calendar of events sent to the public in that they include, in addition to performances and exhibitions, the dates for all special events, such as the opening of a fund drive, an annual banquet or ball, a rummage sale, the scheduled arrival of a noted personality, and the dates of any other organizational activity which might interest the press. Next to the chronological listing, include a brief description of the event and a comment on its story and picture potential, along with a notation as to the exact date when an editor will receive a detailed press release or other material. If you plan to send pictures, mention this, too.

For example, a museum planning to publish an annual report in January, should include the approximate date of the report's issuance. Similarly, if an important staff member is to assume his position in the late winter, list the effective starting date along with brief background information. Although a publication may have announced the appointment previously, it might consider interviewing the appointee just before he takes office.

Obviously, many organizations will not have a complete list of the year's events confirmed by the end of the summer. However, even an approximate date, if it is so identified, can be helpful advance information to a busy editor, who must sometimes plan for Sunday supplements and special sections weeks or even months in advance.

When preparing press calendars remember that they are merely a prelude to press releases. Keep each item short and to the point. Mail mimeographed calendars not only to cultural editors and critics, but also to editors of other sections who might be interested in some of your activities. Send copies to the program and news directors of your local radio and television stations. Be sure to include the name, address and phone number of an official of the organization who may be reached, if additional information is needed.

For the public relations director of an organization the press calendar is of great value in helping him to assess, in advance, the work to be produced during each month of the year. Moreover, it serves as a constant reminder to send press releases and photographs out on time. Similarly, the journalist confronted with an immediate need for an item or story may refer to the press calendar for ideas. (17)

From the Source

Arts organizations should avoid the temptation to use published material, whether copyrighted or not, in their own publications without obtaining prior written approval from the publisher. Unauthorized use of such material can lead to law suits. However, the right of fair use permits you to quote a short portion of a published article, provided you attribute it to its source. If in doubt, ask your attorney. (44)

WORKING WITH THE PRESS

Editors Critical of Publicity Effort in Arts

Communications between arts organizations and newspapers have improved over the past six years, although they are still far from ideal. Moreover, the publicity efforts of cultural groups are less than professional, ranging in most instances from fair to good. These were among the conclusions emerging from *AM's* recently completed survey of newspaper cultural editors throughout the nation, which drew responses from 27 editors in 23 different cities. In a similar survey undertaken by *AM* in 1962, there was near-unanimous agreement by editors that cultural groups did a third-rate publicity and promotion job.

Although 18 of the editors noticed an improvement in communications, eight noticed no change since 1962, and one, Harold V. Cohen of the *Pittsburgh Post-Gazette*, thought that communications had actually deteriorated. According to Conrad Wolfson of the *Jersey Journal*, "There certainly has been an increase in volume, but as far as I can determine, no increase in quality." Barbara Funkhouser of the *El Paso Times* noticed a vast improvement but added, "There is still much to be done."

How well do arts publicists do their job? Asked to estimate what proportion of local cultural groups worthy of news coverage take the initiative to inform newspapers of their activities, 23 editors replied "almost all" and four indicated that only about half do. However, the arts scored poorly in regard to the quality of their informational program as indicated from responses to the question, "Of those that do keep you informed, what percentage do it in a manner that you would judge excellent, good, fair or poor?"

415

More than 35 per cent of the responses listed fair, 31 per cent good, 19 per cent poor and only 15 per cent listed excellent.

In substantiating the contention that cultural publicists are still less than expert in their work, 24 of the 27 editors indicated that major groups often did not receive coverage because they failed to submit materials, and 23 of the editors said that big organizations received less space in print than their activities warranted because their publicity work was faulty. In contrast to the opportunities missed by large groups, 24 editors claimed that small arts groups had received maximum coverage by virtue of their excellent liaison with newspapers in their communities.

Although time is a precious commodity to editors working against a deadline, nearly half of the respondents spend a fourth of their work week or more pursuing cultural groups to get facts which should have been sent to them. Hamilton B. Allen of the *Rochester Times Union* and Harold V. Cohen of the *Pittsburgh Post-Gazette* claim that whatever time they spend is "too much." Several editors echoed the view that they can't spare any time and groups who wanted stories "must come to us."

Editors were frank and frequently brutal in listing the most common faults they found with arts publicity material sent to them. Words like "overblown prose," "flowery," "verbose," and "arty" were liberally sprinkled through the questionnaire responses, and the lack of "know-how" and amateurish approach of many groups was severely criticized. Robert Jennings of the *Memphis Commercial Appeal* said, "The organizations attempt to dictate what, when, and how the material dealing with them is displayed, often without any knowledge of news value, mechanical limitations and courtesy. The professional publicist is no problem. The volunteer for the myriad of other endeavors is often a hellish individual interested only in his or her conception of the job." Sharing this feeling was E. B. Radcliffe of the *Cincinnati Enquirer*, who faulted groups which "try to do a big job with low-cost amateur workers."

High on the list of faults noted by most editors were such obvious errors as the omission of facts, failure to adhere to deadlines, inaccuracy of material, poor organization of material, lack of consideration, inferior photographs, and what one editor termed, "lack of comprehension of what is worthy of copy and what is pure baloney." Norman Nadel, cultural writer for the 16-paper chain of Scripps-Howard newspapers, said that most of the material he received "is unimaginative, incomplete, banal and not directed at any particular requirements."

A continuing problem which plagues almost every editor is the fact that few arts publicists know how to write a press release. Irving Lowens of the *Washington Evening Star* objects to "puffery," while Mal Vincent of the *Norfolk Virginian Pilot* takes to task the publicist who is "much too flowery and too 'arty' with too many superlative adjectives." Harold V. Cohen of the *Pittsburgh Post-Gazette* claims that releases are "so poorly written for the most part that they have to be rewritten. When there is little time for this they lose out completely."

Not the most frequent, but certainly the strongest criticism that editors have of arts groups is that they often try to "pressure" a publication into using a story. Barbara Haddad of the *Denver Post* referred to two different kinds of pressure situations. "One," she said, "is the attitude that 'our story is the most important story of the year,' resulting in unrealistic and unfair demands for photographers, space and follow-up stories. The second situation is that of the organization with a board of directors which includes the so-called socially prominent. Paid or volunteer staff often have no compunctions about letting these members (often rather badly informed ones) descend on the publisher or managing editor to seek special treatment or to right imagined wrongs by the staff. This does not endear the group to employer or employee, although it may produce temporary results. It is a weak and dangerous ploy in the long run and does a disservice to the organization.''

A consensus among editors indicates that they are looking for help from arts publicists but too often fail to find it. According to Rolf Stromberg of the *Seattle Post Intelligencer,* the result is that ''most of the cultural news is deadly, dull as a corpse. It should be stimulating, which seems easy enough when one considers all the startling ideas being utilized today.'' (63)

------- ◄●► -------

Be Factual, Terse and Controversial, Say Editors

An awareness of what makes news, the accurate and terse presentation of facts, proper timing, and the ability to develop off-beat or even controversial angles, are the chief ingredients of the arts stories that editors most want to publish. These conclusions were drawn from part two of *AM's* survey of 27 cultural editors in 23 cities throughout the country.

Asked to advise arts publicists on ''the story I will print,'' an overwhelming majority of editors cited the need for a brief, factual presentation of material which they could then evaluate themselves. ''Give us everything and let us decide what's worth printing,'' suggested Dudley Saunders of the *Louisville Times.* ''Avoid adjectives,'' advised both Dick Wooten of the *Cleveland Press* and Glenna Syse of the *Chicago Sun-Times.* ''Present the facts without bally-hoo," added Barbara Haddad of the *Denver Post.* In addition, nearly every editor stressed the importance of knowing newspaper deadlines and adhering to them. "Don't wait until the last minute" was a refrain echoed by many editors.

Not enough arts publicists are aware of what legitimate news is, according to the editors. Phrases like "interest our general readers," "include facts the public wants to know about," and "find a local angle," cropped up repeatedly in questionnaire responses. Robert Jennings of the *Memphis Commercial Appeal* found some cultural groups using press books nearly three years old and deplored their "country weekly attitude" in dealing with metropolitan daily newspapers. E. B. Radcliffe, of the *Cincinnati Enquirer* summed up his requirements for the good story briefly. "One that shows knowledge of the paper's style, space conditions and news sense."

Nearly all the editors cited their continuing interest in receiving feature story suggestions with strong human interest angles. "Unless the story has news value of sufficient interest to stand by itself," said Peter Bellamy of the *Cleveland Plain Dealer,* "it should have an off-the-beaten track feature handling or an eye-catching picture." Duane J. Snodgrass of the *Omaha World-Herald* recommended that arts publicists "be alert to bright, feature ideas and attempt to find something unusual that will attract readers," while Mal Vincent of the *Norfolk Virginian Pilot* called for stories that have "an angle grounded in news value."

Two of the editors strongly urged arts publicists to be more adventurous and even controversial in their story suggestions. Rolf Stromberg of the *Seattle Post-Intelligencer* gives preference to "groups that lend themselves to controversial issues in the arts or attempt something out

419

of the ordinary.'' Del Marbrook of the *Winston-Salem Journal and Twin City Sentinel* cited a problem shared by many other newspapers. ''We continue to receive too many routine announcements,'' he said, ''when, in almost every instance, there is some interesting aspect involved that has been ignored. We are glad, as a public service, to publish announcements, but we should be happy if publicity people, and they are almost always volunteers, would be more alert to the off-beat, more willing to risk what they might consider controversy, when, in fact, it might merely lead to a good story and good publicity. There is too much second-guessing, too much image-worry among the arts groups. We expect to find it in industry and government; we are always a little saddened to find it in the arts.''

Gerald Ashford, of the *San Antonio Express and News*, who claims that the material he receives from art publicists has ''all the possible faults in about equal proportions,'' has taken a positive step to correct these errors. He's recently written a 25,000 word book on publicity in the arts, which is being published. (64)

Publicity Aid

A simple guide listing essential publicity information can be an invaluable tool for public relations directors and volunteers. The Winston-Salem Arts Council recently published an inexpensive handbook for publicity chairmen which included such practical data as media contacts and deadlines and listings by name of outlets for placement of billboards, banners and posters. Also included were instructions for preparing publicity and advertising materials. (77)

Critic Advises Arts Groups on Press Releases

(When Gail Stockholm, music critic of the Cincinnati Enquirer, was asked by a leading local arts group what, from a newspaper's viewpoint, constituted a good press release, Ms. Stockholm responded with a detailed six page letter which included examples to illustrate her points. Although every arts organization presumes to know how to prepare and use press releases, many received by AM demonstrate that this presumption is often erroneous. With this in mind an excerpt from Ms. Stockholm's response, excluding portions relating to the rudiments of form, is reprinted below.)

By

Gail Stockholm

It is a good idea to check with the newspaper before you write the release—to find out exactly how far ahead they need the release and to check on which aspect of the program may interest the paper most, the musical or entertainment, the civic, or the society aspect. Most papers today will not use the same story in two or three sections, so the release should be aimed toward one particular section in hopes that that section will give the event special treatment. If in doubt on the matter of which section is most appropriate, the best thing is not to decide yourself, but to ask the features editor or the women's editor where he would recommend you submit the story. This serves two purposes, to alert one of the more important editors that the story is coming and to get your release to the person who is most likely to be interested in it. Most papers are glad to advise you on such matters and would prefer that you consult them rather than turn in your release in an incorrect way.

Always imply that you think your music story would interest many people.

In the release itself, try to attract the reader's attention with a short, snappy first paragraph that tells why the event merits attention, and include its Who, What, When and Where. Next in order, for all amusement and entertainment pages and for the purpose of selling tickets as well, the complete musical program and the major performers should be listed, identifying the performers as you go along with their official titles.

Ideally, the basic information and the program information should be in the first two paragraphs of your story. If you wish, you may simply list the program in the second paragraph and then add the identification of the conductor or soloist in the third paragraph. If you then wish to add some further background about the area artists series or about the orchestra's history, this should follow the listing of the program and soloists. After this basic information has been presented, go on to mention local support of the event (full committees need not be listed unless the paper or society editor asks for it).

Some papers have a policy which prevents printing ticket prices or ticket information. But put it in the release anyway, so the newspaper can give the details to interested persons who may call the newspaper with questions about where to get tickets for the concert. Be very specific about full names, including for each, Miss, Mr., Mrs., Jr., and III and such details. Most papers also prefer the middle initial and the full street name. Addresses won't always be used, but papers need them for identification purposes.

An important point of courtesy: Do not try to force your newspaper to use the story, to run it on a certain date, to use a picture of the women's group, etc. This is their decision. After waiting a day or two for mailing time, it doesn't hurt to follow up your release with a telephone call to the newspaper. But don't say, "Well, are you going to run our story Sunday?" Say, "I called to make sure you received our release and that it included all the details you need. Is there anything else we can do for you?" Be sure to stress that you feel this is big news for the community—that both young and old will be interested, that people may come from miles around to attend, etc.

It is advisable to give your first story to the newspaper before running an advertisement or announcement anywhere. If the public doesn't know about it yet, it's a better news story. As soon as it appears, you can distribute posters and run ads if you wish. Also, give the release to all papers, TV and radio stations at the same time. A paper won't use the story if it has been broadcast by local stations before you give it to them. This sometimes means the paper should get it sooner than the stations, because it takes the paper longer to prepare the announcement. Some papers prefer exclusive releases—this means giving first to one paper only. If you do this, you must ask them for a commitment that they will run the story and give it thorough coverage. This usually is best done in person by a visit to the reporter.

Finally, whatever coverage the paper provides, however small, call and thank them for it. Some papers have a very hard time getting cultural news printed and a reporter may have to fight for even a few inches. For additional stories you should come up with a new angle to give the reporter— "Record-breaking 1000 tickets sold" or "Musicians will talk personally to our students while visiting," etc. Remember, when in doubt, ask the paper. They know the answer! (78)

Immediate Release

Arts groups sending stories to editors marked "For Immediate Release," should be sure that the releases indicate the date on which they were sent. Editors will often put releases aside if they can't use them on a given day. On picking them up a day or two later, they'll have no way of knowing how old the news is if releases are undated and they'll probably discard them. (37)

Colorful Releases

What's in a color? Perhaps a negative reaction by an editor to a press release. According to a survey of editors conducted by the Luce Press Clipping Bureau, over half those polled said they disliked receiving press releases on colored stock. One editor pointed out that the use of colored stock made the work of typesetters more difficult. (51)

Dual Interest

Although a single story on your organization may be of interest to several newspaper departments, avoid the temptation to send it to more than one editor. Should the story appear twice in two different sections of the newspaper, you may have two angry editors on your hands. If you think that more than one editor may be interested in the same release, it is proper to send duplicates, only if you clearly indicate on the releases that this is being done. (45)

Clean Press Releases

Press releases should be presented as clear, clean copy. Recently, *AM* received a release from a major Eastern cultural institution containing six penciled strikeovers, deletions and additions. Newspaper editors will not take time to read such a poorly presented release. Remember your arts group is in competition with other news sources for precious editorial space. (29)

Swiss Cheese Releases

Local names make local news. If you're planning an event to be attended by important people from a number of different communities and you wish to send press releases to the home town newspaper of each of the attendees, you may use a "Swiss cheese" press release which has a blank line in place of a name. The individual name can then be typed in on the blank line, although the rest of the release remains the same. (28)

Press Kits Handy Tool — But Use with Caution

Organizations planning events of major importance frequently use press kits to supplement the releases normally issued. A press kit, depending upon the event, may include all or some of the following: photographs; news releases; a general fact sheet or backgrounder; biographies of principals; feature stories; and booklets or other printed material.

Because press kits are far more expensive to compile and mail than press releases, a number of important questions

425

should be answered affirmatively before a cultural group commits itself to their use:

Is your story so complex that it demands additional information which cannot be provided in a press release? For example, if your institution is planning a ground-breaking ceremony for an important new building, architect's plans, pictures of the site, biographies of figures associated with the undertaking, background on your institution, and a chronological history of the building effort, would all be vital components of a press kit. If you are simply announcing that a study is under way to prepare for a building program, a press release is probably enough.

Is your story important enough to warrant the detailed coverage? The appointment of a concertmaster to an orchestra for example, is an important news item, but does not ordinarily require a kit. A simple release is preferable.

Is the event you are planning of interest to editors outside your immediate community? If your story is strictly a local one, a press kit is unnecessary. Invite local editors to your institution and discuss it with them.

Do you have the time and the personnel to organize and issue a press kit? Because there are many components to a press kit, it requires considerable time to assemble. A competent person should supervise the entire project. Try to allow a month.

Finally, do you have the finances to undertake the preparation of a press kit? Material must be inserted into the pockets of a heavy folder and a large envelope is required for mailing. Before preparing a kit, you must decide on the total number to be mailed, the number of inserts needed, the cost of photographs, and the weight of the entire package. Measure the cost against the kit's potential usefulness.

(3)

Small Publications

Large arts institutions frequently ignore the needs and requests of smaller publications while wooing the major ones. In doing this, they often antagonize editors and writers who, in the future, may be in a position to help them. (15)

Weekly Newspapers

Weekly newspapers, frequently ignored in publicity programs, are an excellent source for promoting arts events. There are thousands of weeklies throughout the country, and their editors are constantly searching for stories with local interest and color. If, for example, a member of your organization resides in or is a native of an area served by a weekly newspaper, prominent mention of his name in a press release may insure publication of that story. However, because the publishing schedules of weeklies vary, make sure that you know each paper's deadline so that your event can receive proper editorial consideration. (30)

To Tell the Truth

If your organization's building is old and unattractive, don't be ashamed of it. In fact, by contrasting vibrant activity inside the building with its facade, you may be able to turn the structure's appearance to your advantage. One arts institution recently sent out a mailing which informed the reader that its building's exterior was admittedly weather-worn and architecturally dull. However, it went on

427

to say that inside the building there was bustling activity. To prove this point, a long list of activities sponsored by the institution accompanied the letter. (29)

———◄●►———

Giving Awards

The granting of awards to notable persons who have made some contribution relating to an arts organization's field of interest can provide the group with a springboard for publicity. Care, however, should be exercised in making such awards. An impartial and respected panel of judges should choose the winner. (34)

———◄●►———

Quid Pro Quo

When planning an announcement of an exhibition or event, bear in mind the special needs of monthly publications. Because their columns must be closed long before the weekly and daily press, they appreciate receiving advance notice of future events. In return for this favor, monthly editors will usually cooperate in avoiding disclosure of your announcement before your chosen release date. (6)

———◄●►———

City Please

Are you sending event notices or invitations to a national press list? Be sure to include the city where the event is taking place. As hard as it is to believe, *AM* received a concert notice which named the participating group, the works to be played and other details including the street address of the concert hall, but failed to indicate the specific city.   (75)

———————

Fact Sheet

You may have a good story for the business page or another non-arts section of the paper, but you must make sure that the editor you're dealing with has the necessary background data on your group. Prepare a simple one or two page fact sheet which contains key information and figures on your group in easy-to read fashion. He'll appreciate that much more than pages of material.   (72)

———————

News Series

A newspaper feature is always welcome, but a four or five part series is even nicer. Remember, however, that the subject must have sufficient scope and interest to keep readers "hanging" until the next installment appears. You may have better luck with an editor if you suggest a cultural subject much bigger than your own group, but one in which your group could be featured. Recently published local series have included a four-parter in the *Boston Globe* on survival of the arts, and a four-parter in the *Seattle Post-Intelligencer* titled "The Huckster," about Glynn Ross of the Seattle Opera. (70)

Foreign Language Newspapers

In many communities, ethnic groups are an untapped potential audience and may be especially interested in exhibits or performances that deal with their countries of origin. Foreign language newspapers, of which there are 600 in the United States, including 70 dailies, provide you with the means for reaching these groups. Although it is ideal to translate publicity material into the language of the newspaper, if this is impossible, send short and simply written releases and avoid colloquialisms. (8)

Contest Brings Publicity

A contest, specifically related to a performance, can help to win publicity for an arts group. The Old Globe Theatre in San Diego, Calif., recently crowned "Miss Juliet" at a special Teen Night performance of *Romeo and Juliet*. Prior to the actual crowning, a publicized search to find the titleholder was conducted among teenage girls. (50)

Favorable Reviews

Arts groups that present performances of the same program over and over again should capitalize on favorable critical response. One way to do this is by collecting a series of critical quotes and immediately circulating them through direct mail. In Washington, D. C., when the Arena Stage received praise from critics for its presentation of Jean Anouilh's *The Rehearsal,* it quickly mimeographed highlights from the reviews and sent them to persons on its mailing list as well as to the press.   (34)

Quoting the Critic

When quoting a critic in an advertisement or promotional mailing piece, be sure not only that the quotation is accurate, but also that the critic's name and publication are listed correctly. A Midwestern theater sent out a promotion piece quoting a review by a *New York Post* critic, Richard Watts, and erroneously identified him as a writer for the *New York Mirror.* Discerning members of the audience quickly catch such mistakes, to the embarrassment of the sponsoring organization.   (14)

Advance Notice

Is your organization planning to issue a major study or report? If so, it is wise to let the press know about the report in advance of its actual release date. Send the press a simple mimeographed announcement several weeks beforehand telling them when they will be receiving a copy and when information about the report may be released to the public. In this way, publications may plan to hold space for a story about the report. (25)

Pruning a Press List

Cutting down on a press release mailing list may often be a more difficult task than building one up. One way to make sure that interested people receive your material is to adopt a system used by the University of Michigan News Service. On the outside of envelopes containing their press releases, three lines of reduced size copy are printed in the lower left hand corner. They read, "If you do NOT desire to continue receiving material of this type, please check here and return in a separate first class envelope." (25)

Critical Disagreement

Disagreement among critics can sometimes be turned to the advantage of an arts group. In Washington, D. C., for example, the Arena Stage capitalized on the difference of opinion aroused by its production of Thornton Wilder's still controversial play, *The Skin of Our Teeth*. The Company sent out publicity releases titled, "23 Years of Controversy Erupts Anew at Arena Stage," followed by nine published reviews of the play—five in praise of it, four panning it. (45)

The Right Name

Many people whose names are not of English origin go through life hearing them painfully mispronounced in North America. Increased use of local radio announcements by arts groups magnifies the effect of improper pronunciation. Announcers are much more likely to get a name right if the correct pronunciation is added in parentheses in every press release in which a non-English name is used. For example, if a symphony orchestra was listing the conductor Jorda in a radio release, it should read: the Spanish conductor Jorda (Hor DAH). (14)

Weekly Arts Supplement

Arts groups wishing to reach a larger audience might benefit from the experience of the Nassau County Office of Performing and Fine Arts in Long Island, New York. Although the office had published an arts calendar ten times a year in cooperation with Hofstra University, it was "comparatively useless to those organizations it was trying to serve." Seeking to broaden its audience and promote the arts on a wider and more regular basis, the county arts office joined with Hofstra and an area newspaper, the *Long Island Daily Commercial Review,* in the publication of a weekly supplement to the newspaper, a leisure guide. Costs are shared by the three participants. Published since last November, the weekly supplement provides extensive coverage of the local arts scene and a greatly expanded cultural calendar of events. It reaches twice the number of people the calendar did, including all of the newspaper's regular subscribers. (55)

———— ◆●▶ ————

Feature Stories for Newspapers Expand Possibility of Coverage

The newspaper feature article, which emphasizes the background of a personality, event, place or institution, rather than spot news, offers excellent publicity opportunities for an arts organization. A straight news story, pegged to a definite date, has to compete with "hard" news on that date, and may be crowded off the page if important news stories break. But the feature article, the colorful or anecdotal story that can appear at anytime, may prove to be a boon to a hard-pressed editor.

434

Because few organizations are able to present news of real importance frequently, the imaginative public relations director of an arts group should try to develop the kinds of feature articles, and possible picture layouts, that editors look for. How can a feature article be developed?

1. Examine your organization and its experiences carefully. Have you reached a significant milestone in your history? Are any of your activities unique? Has an orchestra, for example, acquired a rare instrument? Has a theatrical company historic costumes in its wardrobe?

2. Look at the background and job responsibilities of your staff and performers. Is a woman doing an unusual job, such as managing an orchestra, or handling the business affairs of a museum? A recent feature story in the *New York Times* described the work of the woman who managed the physical arrangements for the Lewisohn Stadium concerts.

3. Initiate research for possible features. What buildings, for instance, occupied the site you now use? A check into the records might reveal a fascinating history. Perhaps a museum has recently acquired a painting by an artist who lived in the area in the past. His background might uncover some little-known information about his life and work which would interest an editor.

4. Create features by initiating your own surveys. Interesting statistics seldom fail to captivate an editor. A theatre might survey its audience on the contemporary playwright it most admires. What kind of arts training are the youngsters in your community receiving? (An orchestra might survey its own members to get the answer to this question).

5. Look beyond your immediate "family" to the outsider who has been involved in your work. Perhaps a local

business man has presented concerts by your orchestra for his employees. Why has he done this and what is his estimate of the value of fine music for his employees? Perhaps a museum art class has an entire family—father, mother and children—all taking a course together.

When presenting a feature story idea to an editor or writer, it is wise to establish the special story and picture layout value of the suggestion in your lead paragraph. The remainder of the letter should be used to provide additional background information. Remember, too, that feature suggestions are not news releases. In most instances an editor will assign a reporter, and if needed, a photographer, to follow up on the suggestion, if he thinks it has merit. Therefore, when suggesting a feature story by letter, be concerned only with presenting your suggestion briefly and with clarity, and with convincing the editor of the merits and picture possibilities of the story. If you have pictures that illustrate your suggestions—even snapshots—be sure to enclose them. (19)

Editorial Fillers

By preparing material that busy editors can use as "fillers" your organization may increase its press coverage. Several lines of editorial copy, giving a single significant fact on your arts group, can fill an empty space in a newspaper. They also may spark a full-sized feature story or be filed for later use as background on an interpretive story about your organization. The Utah Symphony in Salt Lake City, recently issued a press release, "Just a few facts about Utah Symphony musicians," which contained a wealth of filler possibilities. (43)

436

Updating the Press

Press books are important publicity tools. They must be updated annually, however, or their value is negated. The Indianapolis Symphony Orchestra, for example, recently sent revised press books, featuring background on the orchestra, biographies of the conductor, associate conductors and concertmaster, plus quotes from recent reviews, to its press list. Attached to the folder was a note from the orchestra's public relations director, reminding editors to discard any old press materials on the orchestra that they might have in their files. (62)

New Publicist

Although it is not particularly important to the public, the appointment of a new publicity director by a cultural group is of special interest to those in the news media who cover the arts. A printed announcement card mailed to reporters will alert them to the change. It may also stimulate those who know the new publicist personally to take the initiative in getting in touch with him about writing a feature story or discussing the long range aims of the organization. (23)

Special Stories

Editors are constantly looking for pictures and stories for use in conjunction with a special day or national holiday. Now is the time to start planning newsworthy ideas for upcoming holidays such as Labor Day, Columbus Day or Thanksgiving. Also give some thought to such special dates as the birthday of a famous composer, the anniversary of a noteworthy event or the last day of summer. (18)

Events Listing

If your organization is planning a major event which is open to the public, such as an annual art exhibition or an arts festival, be sure to release this information to the press well in advance of the date the event actually takes place. Newspapers and magazines, for example, which publish special listings of important events, may need such information weeks ahead of time, since this kind of news is frequently collected and edited before other sections of the publication are. (27)

Helping the Editor

Small organizations of similar type can all get guaranteed space in the newspaper by uniting to compile their program information and deliver it to a busy newspaper editor in one package. Otherwise, the individual announcement can be lost. Community theatres in the area served by the Long Island (N. Y.) *Daily Press* have delegated one person to get their week's programs to the paper, where they appear under the heading Long Island Playbill. In addition, the newspaper guarantees to allot one photo to each theatre per season, with the theatre group arranging the schedule of pictures for the paper.   (9)

Too Much Too Soon

Advance publicity for arts events is premature if you are not prepared to meet the interest it arouses. Announcement of a recent music festival, for instance, including an exciting schedule of events with time, place and the ticket price scale, stirred great local interest. But the first and most eager people to respond found tickets not yet printed, and the staff unsure of how many seats there would be in each price class, nor even where they would be in the hall. Then the place of several concerts was shifted, and later the location of auxiliary ticket sales points was announced before they were ready to sell tickets. Annoyance caused would-be patrons could have been avoided by proper timing of arrangements and announcements.   (5)

Free Press Directories

Some national clipping services publish directories listing newspapers by state and city. These directories often are available to customers or potential customers at no charge. Check the classified telephone directory for the names of the clipping services in your area.   (17)

Motorist Magazines

You may be missing a good publicity outlet if you bypass the motorist magazines, published by many state branches of the American Automobile Association. These publications, some of which have circulations in the hundred of thousands, are interested in material of use to motorists. For example, the Connecticut Motorist carried a detailed story on the Connecticut Opera Association's 1965-66 season.   (44)

House Organs

Looking for new publicity outlets? House organs, magazines published by corporations for their employees and stockholders, some with circulations of hundreds of thousands of readers, are constantly on the look-out for newsworthy stories. For complete listings of over 4,000 corporate publications, see the Gebbie House Magazine Directory which is available at many libraries.   (61)

Photographers and Writers

Looking for a top free-lance writer or photographer to help tell your organization's story to a national magazine? There may be one living in your area. The American Society of Magazine Photographers, at 60 East 42nd St., New York, N. Y. 10017, publishes a directory which lists more than 500 members, both alphabetically and geographically, and includes their addresses and phone numbers. A directory of leading free-lance, non-fiction writers is available from the Society of Magazine Writers, 123 W. 43rd Street, New York, N. Y. 10036. Each annual edition lists members' addresses and phone numbers, their present and former connections, writing specialties, and magazines to which they contribute. (54)

Financial Pages

In publicizing your organization, don't overlook the non-arts sections of your local newspapers. The Seattle Opera in Washington, for example, benefited from a detailed article titled ''Non Profit Opera Profits Seattle'' which appeared on the financial pages of the *Seattle Times,* next to the stock market report. The story, written by a member of the newspaper's business staff, outlined the Opera's fiscal picture and indicated why private contributions were necessary. (50)

441

Well Laid Plans, Many Helpers Needed
For Festival Publicity

Careful planning and enlistment of the aid of others, are important factors in the success of publicity campaigns for festivals or community-wide arts projects. This was the experience of Mrs. Leona Flis, volunteer publicity chairman of the Tri-City Ballet Guild, which hosted the 1962 Northeast Regional Ballet Festival.

Mrs. Flis' committee established early contact with the Downtown Merchants' Bureau, an organization of 250 Schenectady businessmen, which agreed to publicize the festival at its own expense. The merchants printed, distributed and displayed store window posters, cardboard table tents for restaurants and a huge banner on the prominent railroad over-cross in midtown.

Ten cultural organizations in Schenectady and the nearby cities of Troy and Albany helped publicize the ballet festival through their own channels and sold tickets to their own members.

Special events that called attention to the ballet festival included a visit (with photographers) to Governor Rockefeller of New York by leaders of the Tri-City Ballet Guild to receive a proclamation. The mayor of Schenectady declared a local Ballet Week during the festival, and a department store carried a week-long window display in its honor.

Newspaper publicity was planned with the five daily papers in the area to avoid conflict and duplication. Mrs. Flis and her aides set up an advance story schedule, listing all the news possibilities by subject matter and date. This was broken down into five lists, one for each paper, the first story going out in mid-March.

The system was so effective that each paper used an average of two stories or pictures a week, increasing the

442

pace to one daily during the week before the ballet festival opened.

Ten radio stations in the Schenectady-Albany-Troy area used more than 500 spot announcements. Television programs featured festival posters and interviews. One station filmed a dress rehearsal, which it put on the air twice.

"It was a wonderful experience," Mrs. Flis told *Arts Management*, "but it was very hard work. If I were to do it over again, which I don't think I could, I would start planning even earlier than I did." (6)

Tell the Truth

Maintaining good press relations is a key to the success of an organization's public relations program. One sure way to rupture these relations is to place the same kind of feature story with two rival publications at about the same time. If an editor approaches you with a story idea similar to one already planned by another publication, tell him about the article which is in the works, and suggest a completely different story. Your honesty will save you embarrassment later and pay off in the long run. (27)

Praising the Press

If good press coverage has helped to fill the house, let writers and editors know that you appreciate their support and interest. One organization, the Little Theatre of Alexandria, Virginia, sent a thank you letter to people on its press list last month, following the successful run of one of its productions. The letter read, in part, "Your unstinting response resulted in an unprecedented full house for each night of the production. Thus, we are eager to share plaudits with press, television, radio. . . ." (31)

Press Passes

Press passes issued by an arts group can help develop good relations with editors. The Academy of Natural Sciences in Philadelphia mails such passes to the press, admitting editors and their guests to the Academy, its lectures and its special events. The passes are signed by its public relations chairman who in a covering letter invites the press to "stop by the P.R. office whenever you're in the Academy." Included with the pass is a list of Academy events. (39)

New Information

Often, the material gathered by an editor in an interview is not of sufficient interest to warrant its publication. If this happens, don't bother the editor constantly to check on the story's status. Wait until you have some important new data and send it to him. It may result in the story's use. (30)

------◄●►------

Off the Record

In dealing with the press much confusion can be avoided if you understand the distinction between "off the record" and "not for attribution." If a member of your organization is merely giving information to a reporter as private background and does not wish that information published at all, then the conversation is "off the record." On the other hand, if an interviewee wants the information to be printed but does not wish to be quoted as the source then it is "not for attribution." (22)

------◄●►------

Keeping the Editor Posted

If you have promised written material or information to an editor, and learn that you will have difficulty in obtaining it by the deadline date, let the editor know the true situation as soon as possible. By warning him in advance, he may be able to reschedule the story for a later date. If you wait till the last minute, however, he may never use the story and will be reluctant ever to call your organization again. (17)

------◄●►------

Good Press Relations

Want to remain in the good graces of local reporters and editors? Keep unannounced visits to them to a minimum, and never drop in to their offices at deadline time. Learn the copy deadlines of local publications and honor them.

(41)

Thanking the Writer

A thank-you note to a writer or editor who has featured your organization in a story lets him know that you appreciate his interest. While notes may be short, even handwritten, they should be sent immediately after a story appears. Such a gesture of courtesy may encourage the writer or editor to look to your group as a source for future articles.

(14)

Museum Perks Press With Novel Present

An unusual Christmas greeting sent by a museum to the press achieved a resounding critical reception.

In Philadelphia, Mrs. Libby Demp Forrest, chairman of the public relations department of The Academy of Natural Sciences, was looking for a pleasant, yet inexpensive, Christmas greeting to send last year. Because she had hundreds of fossilized sharks' teeth, inexpensive items sold at the Museum's sales desk, she decided to affix a tooth to each of several hundred specially printed letterheads and send them out as Christmas cards. A note on the card said "Unequivocally, this is the oldest thing you'll get for Christ-

446

mas.'' The card ended by inviting the recipient to visit the Museum and see many more fossils and specimens.

The card was greeted with favorable letters and local publicity. But during the year, Mrs. Forrest was continually asked what she would send out this Christmas. When this year's card arrived, it said, ''Many people wanted to know what we were going to send this Christmas. In the back of our mind was the thought how could we surpass a single superb shark tooth. This Christmas we send you two.'' (24)

Good Humor

Humor can be used effectively by a cultural organization, especially if it is closely related to the objectives of the group. Philadelphia's Academy of Natural Sciences consistently promotes its function as a natural science museum in its mailings to the press. Last year, the museum sent Christmas cards containing two fossilized sharks teeth. This year it sent amusing cards which featured a hand-drawn ''autographed'' footprint of Dolores—a dinosaur. (34)

Deadline Calendar

Publicity directors will find it useful to post a calendar carrying the deadlines of every publication to be serviced with news and pictures. The calendar should be divided into two columns covering copy and picture deadlines for each of the following outlets: radio and TV stations; daily newspapers; Sunday editions of newspapers; weeklies; monthlies, and annuals. The calendar should be referred to regularly so each outlet will be served on time. Of course, the special deadline requirements of any outlet varying from the general pattern should be noted on the calendar.   (13)

Pictures for the Press

Planning to send photographs to illustrate a story? Here are some tips to keep in mind. Editors want glossy prints, preferably 8-by-10 or 5-by-7 inches in size. Pictures, other than "head" shots, should show action by having the subjects informally doing something. Generally, no more than four persons should be included in the picture, with two or three the best number to be shown. Also, be sure to attach an identifying caption to each picture. When mailing, place cardboard around the photographs to protect them.   (36)

Photo File

Whenever possible an arts group should maintain a file of photographs for use of the editor who finds last-minute space for a picture story. In addition to "mug shots"—i.e., portraits—of leading performers or staff, the file should include action shots, preferably candid, of your people at work. Pictures of cornerstone layings, award presentations and other formal ceremonies are of far less interest to a good editor, as a rule, than shots that portray spontaneous activity or emotion. It helps to keep a file of negatives, too.

(3)

Photo Enclosed

When placing a newspaper story about a personality associated with your organization send his picture to the editor along with the story. A recent poll of managing editors, conducted by the Luce Press Clippings service, noted that 92 per cent of the editors wanted a photo with the personality story. However, only 51 per cent of the editors polled felt that photos should accompany news stories about events. If you send a picture, be sure that it has an identifying caption attached.

(19)

How to Get Help in Guest Artist Promotion

An effective publicity campaign for a visiting artist need never be a solo performance. There are organizations and businesses in each community ready to help arts managers by putting their publicity resources at their disposal. Cultural groups using guest artists can draw on others to achieve maximum publicity results.

Many businesses and organizations outside the cultural field have public relations representatives or people responsible for sending out releases, distributing pictures to newspapers, or arranging interviews. They are seeking press attention and if your guest can somehow be linked with their interest, they may prove eager to cooperate.

Of course, it is important not to damage the prestige of an organization (or of the artist) by participating in stunts of dubious taste or by allowing it to become too closely connected with individual commercial enterprises. But it is possible to work well within the bounds of simple good taste and still draw valuable assistance from these outside publicity experts.

Arts groups can work effectively with railroads and airlines, hotels, retail stores, service organizations, record companies, church groups, businessmen's clubs, restaurants, athletic teams, ethnic groups, women's organizations and many others.

The first step in conducting a cooperative publicity campaign is to learn as much about the visiting performer as possible. A letter to his management firm or to the individual himself will often answer questions about the groups of which he is a member, his hobbies, personal interests and general background. It is also wise to find out early in the game how much time he is willing to give to publicity activity.

Top ranking artists may not have the time or need to give much effort to promotion. But most secondary performers, including many with familiar names, are eager or willing to cooperate in publicizing their visit.

After carefully checking the artist's background, notify as many organizations as may be interested in his appearance in your community—consistent, of course, with the time he has available. For example, if an actor who is a member of Kiwanis is due to appear with a theatre company, Kiwanis may be interested in honoring him at one of their luncheons.

Checking the guest in at a local booster club, chamber of commerce or advertising club meeting not only exposes him to many potential ticket buyers but can, if there is time, lead to retail store tie-ins—such as window displays devoted to the artist and his local appearance. If the artist makes recordings, the local record store can arrange for window displays and a token appearance. In many cases the store will take ads in the local paper announcing the event.

Hotels are an excellent source of free publicity. Those that are members of a chain generally employ a publicity director who is eager to make news of the fact that the celebrity is staying at the hotel in question. He will often take pictures, make calls to newspapers and arrange interviews. In smaller hotels without a full-time public relations person, the sales manager may frequently be of help.

Robert Windt, publicity representative of Pepsi Cola, has won a great deal of favorable publicity for his company from this kind of cooperative local effort, particularly through the use of Joan Crawford as his visiting star. He counsels cultural organizations to use the same sources.

Most newspapers devote sections to the activities of hospitals, religious organizations and society groups. The per-

451

former's appearance, however brief, at a function of one of these groups can result in an excellent story. A visiting dancer photographed with a bedridden child who has dancing ambitions of her own makes a pictorial feature. A huge basso eating chicken legs at a church supper may have human interest value to a photographer.

An artist can throw the first ball at a game, appear at a fashion show, have a special dish named for him at a restaurant, have his photograph placed on the wall, or can do any of a number of other things that require little time but which all mean free newspaper space.

Working with others to mutual benefit requires imagination, planning beforehand and efficient follow-up. Successful publicity not only gives your event the immediate coverage it needs, but also sets up a working relationship with people who can help you in the future. **(2)**

RADIO AND TELEVISION

How to Arrange Guest Interviews on Radio

Radio interviews offer excellent publicity potential for cultural organizations. However, before suggesting a possible guest, it is important to understand the specific needs of the program you are approaching.

To find out which programs use guests and which staff people affiliated with these programs book guests, check with the program director or station manager of your local station. Then listen to two or three broadcasts of the programs to determine their guest requirements and orientation.

What special factors must then be considered? It is important to know what kind of audience the program appeals to. Generally, daytime programs attract housewives and evening programs appeal to the entire family. Within the framework, programs may appeal to narrower audiences, such as the intellectual woman or the businessman. Which audience does your organization want to reach? Who is the person within your organization best equipped to speak to this audience?

Next, how long are the interviews? Some programs interview two or three guests within a fifteen minute period while others feature extended interviews with one guest lasting half an hour or more. The guest you suggest must be able to tell his story within the allotted time.

Before approaching an interview program, it is wise to ask a whole series of questions. For example, is the program consistent with the dignity and image of your organization? A symphony orchestra might not want one of its members interviewed on a disc jockey program which

453

features rock 'n roll music. How frequent are the commercial messages? Are they used in the middle of an interview?

Who is the host and how large a role does he play in each interview? Some hosts dominate interviews and barely allow guests to develop their thoughts.

What is the program's format? Are interviews only a small part of the program? Do listeners phone in questions?

Lastly, is the program live or taped? Taped programs are often edited and important remarks can be erased. Some guests, however, give a better interview when they know the program is being taped and erasures can be made.

After analyzing a program and determining who your best guest possibility is for that program, write to the specific person who books guests for the broadcast. Relate the contributions your guest can make to the program's needs. Be explicit in listing the topics the guest is prepared to discuss and include biographical information about the guest. If you do not receive a reply within a week, follow up with a phone call.

Once an interview is scheduled, make sure that your guest speaker is familiar with the program and is completely up-to-date on the activities of your organization. Ask him to listen to the program first and brief him on the length of his interview and on the topic to be discussed on the program. If you have written a letter about him to the program, be sure that he reads a copy of that letter before going to the interview, so that he will know precisely what the interviewer knows about him and what he expects him to talk about. (21)

Publicize Radio Appearances

Many hosts of radio and television programs regularly send out pre-printed postcards on which they fill in the names of their guests. If a member of your organization is to appear on a program where the host follows this practice, obtain enough cards from him in time to do a thorough mailing. The host will cooperate because he wishes to reach as wide a listening audience as possible.   (29)

Personal Approach to Stations Results in Broadcast Publicity

Many cultural groups plan publicity campaigns with undo emphasis on newspapers, leaving other communications outlets, such as radio and television, stepchildren of their efforts. However, an energetic approach to broadcast media publicity, such as employed by the Seattle Opera Association in Seattle, Washington, can result in interviews, spot announcements and special features.

Recognizing the importance of maintaining a well-rounded publicity program, the Association has established a special four-member women's volunteer committee devoted exclusively to radio and television publicity. The volunteers work under Mrs. Erna Husak, the organization's publicity director.

The committee divides its labor so that three of its members each are responsible for covering one of the combined radio—television stations in the Seattle area. A fourth member covers 10 other radio stations as well as the University of Washington's educational television facility.

By establishing individual relationships with broadcast

officials, the volunteers "put the publicizing of the Association on a person-to-person basis, and they get much better results than we could by mail and telephone alone," Mrs. Husak said.

After Mrs. Husak provides the stations with background material on the opera company, its productions and its stars, the committee members visit station personnel to see if they are interested in an interview or feature. Members maintain virtual day-to-day personal contact with station personnel during each stage of a publicity effort, providing additional information for interviews, attending the interviews and following them with thank you notes to broadcasters and program directors.

This personal approach has resulted in widespread radio use of free spot announcements on the opera which committee members hand-deliver to the stations.

The publicity program has paid off with intense and varied coverage of opera productions. In the week before this season's opening, 13 interviews with company members were broadcast on radio and television. Television news announcements were aired frequently.

As a result of the committee's work, a 20-minute television program highlighted opening night at the opera. Later productions were also spotlighted with interviews and news announcements. The most recent production was sold out a month early.

Mrs. Husak told *AM*, "Members never push anything; they try to be available at all times. It's a soft sell and is growing more effective." (37)

Guest Artist Publicity

When arranging for a visiting artist to speak before a group or to appear on radio or television, plan to have the public relations officer of your organization accompany the artist. This serves as insurance in case last minute emergencies throw the plan off schedule. In a pinch, the public relations staff person may even have to fill in for a guest who fails to show up at the appointed time or place. The staff person should be adequately briefed to take this possibility into account. (26)

Educational Television Key Force on Arts Scene

Educational television, a powerful cultural force in its own right, is providing significant support to arts groups through its programming (often produced in cooperation with local and national arts organizations) and through its promotion of cultural events and activities. Although educational television (E.T.V.) stations have faced continuing economic problems, the size and scope of the field has broadened considerably in the past four years. The number of E.T.V. stations has grown from 79 to 112, and their signals now reach 90 per cent of the homes in America. Weekly viewership is estimated at 14 million, and monthly viewership at 20 million.

Despite the limited availability of funds, up to now, E.T.V. programming in the arts has been substantial and significant. Many of these programs have been provided to local stations by a central source, National Educational Television in New York City, which produces about six new programs a week. Although E.T.V. stations may use

457

these programs at their discretion, Curtis Davis, director of cultural programs for N.E.T., estimates that stations carry about 96 per cent of the material offered them.

Among the cultural programs produced by N.E.T. and aired by local education stations have been *USA: Arts,* a 1965-1966 series of 80 programs featuring noted artists and composers, and several series spotlighting leading symphony orchestra and professional regional theater companies. *The Creative Person,* a series of half hour programs exploring the work of noted figures in the arts and literature, was originally presented in 1965. This year, a new series of 50 programs has been produced by N.E.T. for airing by local educational stations.

N.E.T. has developed programs in association with leading companies in every artistic discipline, including such groups as the American Place Theater, the American Conservatory Theatre, the Jose Limon Dance Company, and the New York City Opera. This season, N.E.T. introduced one of its more ambitious cultural projects, the *NET Playhouse,* a regular weekly schedule of outstanding plays and films, which includes eighty new productions.

Of importance to arts organizations is the fact that both N.E.T. and local stations are receptive to program suggestions. Often, however, stations interested in producing community-based programs have difficulty in finding people who are knowledgeable as to community resources. "Get acquainted with the head of your local station," advises Davis, "and if you have a program idea, then present it to him. The acceptance of the idea does not depend on the ability of the local station to produce it, since N.E.T. will help the station if the idea has merit."

As examples of locally stimulated television programs, Mr. Davis cited a dance concert filmed in the Museum of Art of the Carnegie Institute in Pittsburgh, and *Touch*

Clay, a program dealing with ceramic artists in Milwaukee. The latter program was produced by Milwaukee station WMVS, and then distributed nationally by N.E.T. "This program was a great shot in the arm for the Milwaukee Art Center and for the community," he said.

Some educational stations, such as those in San Francisco, New York, Boston and Pittsburgh, according to Davis, do a great deal of programming with local arts groups. Often, they televise segments of upcoming productions and help to attract audiences to local arts events. (55)

Video Series Boosts Local Cultural Groups

An imaginative television series, conceived by a Washington, D. C. station, helped sell season tickets and gave a major promotional boost to three of the city's leading performing arts groups immediately prior to the start of their current seasons.

On four successive nights early last month, Washington's station WTOP-TV pre-empted one to two hours of network programming in prime time to present its "Pageant of Performing Arts." The first program on Tuesday, September 6th, featured the National Ballet in performances of *Swan Lake* and *Con Amore,* which were videotaped by the station earlier in the year. This was followed on the next two evenings by videotaped performances of the National Symphony and the Opera Society of Washington. The final program in the series was a concert by guitarist Charlie Byrd. During program intermissions, host Roy Meachum interviewed representatives of the arts organizations and discussed their forthcoming seasons.

The series was conceived by the station earlier in the year as a means of providing excellent programming for its viewers while, at the same time, motivating them to purchase tickets to regular performances by the groups. In announcing the series George F. Hartford, the station's general manager, said that the series would "dramatically point up the fact that these organizations, year in and year out, are available to Washingtonians throughout the season at their regular performances. I am certain that thousands of people who will see these televised productions have never attended a single performance of these groups."

Presented as a public service, the series cost the station a considerable amount of money. In addition to bearing all production costs, the station, by pre-empting network programming, lost income that it normally received from the network. WTOP also publicized the series, and included in its series of releases, background on each of the participating organizations and information on their plans for the forthcoming season.

Although there was no direct solicitation for tickets on the programs, Robert M. Adams, the station's promotion director, told *AM* that the series acted as an important stimulus to the viewer. "The response was excellent," he said. "We received approximately 200 letters and 240 phone calls from viewers, following presentation of the series. Some were from people who had never before seen the groups perform, but who now planned to attend programs. The National Symphony had 8 or 10 calls from viewers interested in obtaining season concert tickets. Some of our letters indicated that the writers had never been to an opera, but after seeing *The Magic Flute,* they were planning to get season tickets to the opera." (52)

Make Use of Free Broadcasting Announcements

With radio and television broadcasters coming under fire for poor program content, stations are becoming more public service-minded and more art-oriented than they have been. This means that much free time for spot announcements is available to arts groups for the asking these days. Such announcements call attention to programs and events as well as lay the groundwork for fund raising campaigns. Health and welfare organizations have long made use of opportunities for using the airwaves.

An outstanding example of a successful spot-announcement campaign is that of the Jewish Chronic Disease Hospital in New York, carried out by its public relations counsel, Edward N. Mintz. Spots varying in length from 10 to 60 seconds were sent to East Coast stations in a drive to honor the hospital during September, 1961.

One hundred forty-five stations in seven states used more than 12,000 announcements in the month, and some stations are still broadcasting them. Although the hospital is local, it was able to extend its message outside New York because the work it is doing has national significance. At a conservative estimate, the cost of these free spots, if purchased, would have amounted to $120,000.

The first step in seeking free radio or TV time is to consider the audience to be reached, and the message appropriate to it. Decisions on these points will also determine whether to aim at local stations only, or to include others, too.

The next step is to get up a list of the stations selected and the names of their directors. Directories with such listings are available at most libraries.

Then prepare copy for the spots. They may take the form of short scripts to be read, recordings to be played, or pictures or visual cards for display on television. As a rule, spots are in 10, 15, 20, 30, 45, and 60-second lengths, with the minute and half-minute lengths used most often.

In wording copy, be terse and crystal clear. Read the message and time the reading to make it fit the appropriate length. It is a good rule to make up at least six different messages for each time length, so that a station preferring a single length can deliver your message many times without deadly repetition.

After this they are ready to be mimeographed. Each spot should be marked "public service announcement" and should include name, address and phone number of someone the station may call for additional information. Then clip, do not staple, all the spots of the same length together, each marked as to time, and send them in a flat envelope to the station. (To help check on results, include a self-addressed return postcard on which the station director can indicate the number of spots he has used.)

If you are dealing with one or a few local stations, phone or meet the station managers or directors personally, if possible. This will help assure their cooperation.

Some stations prefer recorded announcements to scripts. These should be on 33⅓ r.p.m. discs, not tape, although to make a disc it may be necessary to first make a tape, since it can be edited. Studio time for making the preliminary tape and the disc may run to $20 an hour, an AM check of studios indicates. The cost of making each record varies from $5.00 to $7.50, depending upon its playing time, and the number needed. A 10-inch record can carry two 20-second spots, one 30-, one 40- and one 60-second message with adequate spacing between each of them.

The record label should be marked with the name of the organization, the person reading the message and the length of each spot, so that station engineers can tell at a glance what each record includes. (Incidentally, if the institution can get a celebrity to deliver the message, it will increase both its acceptability and its impact.)

The "telop," an inexpensive means of putting a message on TV, may also be useful. This is a picture—usually three inches by four—made on matte paper so it will not reflect light. The cost of making a telop varies according to the photographer's fee. A telop may contain a written message —in effect, a sign—or it may show a picture of some activity at the institution to be shown while an accompanying announcement is read.

Non-profit cultural institutions, even those which charge admission, can reach vast potential audiences by getting on the airwaves free. (2)

Broadcasts Help Build Audiences for Arts

Radio or television programs created by arts groups can help to build audiences and support yet cost little or nothing to produce. Such programs play an important role in the promotional campaigns of cultural organizations in Washington, D. C., Binghamton, New York, Greensboro, North Carolina and Fort Wayne, Indiana, among others.

Groups queried by *AM* devote relatively few hours to the production of a series. The programs can be sponsored either commercially or supported by radio or television stations. In the latter instance, stations may welcome such programs since they attract listener interest while helping stations meet a Federal requirement that a portion of air

463

time be devoted to public service programming. And program formats can be simple, consisting of discussion or commentary on cultural themes.

In Washington, D. C., the Arena Stage, a theater group, used its current season as a springboard for 13 weekly half hour shows entitled, *The Sounds of Theater,* presented on Sundays on an AM and FM radio station. Programs featured music, biography, discussions and dramatic presentations tied in to the group's productions.

Each show cost about $105 to mount, and was paid for by a sponsor, the Savile Bookshop of Washington, which linked commercials to program content. Programs took about 5 to 12 hours each to produce, including preparation, recording and editing time. Audience reaction has been good.

A simple format marks a weekly hour-long television program reaching 750,000 persons. It is produced by the Roberson Memorial Center in Binghamton, New York, an arts council. Air time is donated to the Center by the station, and the series costs the group $200 to $300 annually to produce.

The Center has produced radio and television shows since 1956 when it featured a five minute daily cultural calendar, a format now used by the Greensboro Arts Council in North Carolina.

Speaking of his television series, Keith Martin, director of the Center, told *AM,* "It does not have to be scholarly or probe deeply, but it should be authentic and informal. Often you can improvise when on the air."

Another approach to radio programming has been taken by the Fort Wayne Fine Arts Foundation, another arts council. Its program, *Adventures in the Arts,* is heard on four different local AM radio stations each week. Air time is donated by the stations.

464

Programs include announcements of cultural activities in the city and recordings with commentary on them. Nat Greenberg, business manager of the Fort Wayne Philharmonic, conducts the series, and is paid by funds from a local foundation.   (39)

Chapter VII – Promotion

PROMOTING ORGANIZATIONS and EVENTS

How a Symposium Can Help a Cultural Group

If your organization is new or little known, or if it is embarking on a major change in its program, or if it is seeking to shift from a local to a regional or national base, it should consider the advantages of presenting a symposium. The symposium can be an excellent fund raising event. Equally important, it can lay the basis for a major shift in the "image" of your organization and in its sources of financial support.

These uses of the symposium are best illustrated by the experience of the Manhattan School of Music which is now pressing an $8,500,000 capital fund campaign and is trying to establish itself as a national institution rather than a local one.

The event, held last November, presented a panel of prominent speakers including Supreme Court Justice Arthur Goldberg, former White House Arts Consultant August Heckscher, critic Kenneth Tynan and Secretary of the Interior Stewart Udall. Held at the new New York Hilton Hotel, it attracted a glittering audience of potential contributors. It also received widespread press coverage. Among its results: a perceptible improvement in the public image of the school; the recruiting of a top New York executive to head its business division in the fund drive; and new financial support. Although no fund solicitation took place at the symposium itself, a single contributor who until then had made only a $100 gift to the school stepped forward with a gift of $50,000.

One prerequisite for a good symposium is careful selection of the subject matter. The Manhattan School chose as its theme *The Quality of Life in This Technological Age.* This permitted the School to relate its own private needs to those of society at large. In effect, the School was saying that by contributing to its cause the patron would be helping all of society.

Typically, a symposium will last one day and consist of morning and afternoon sessions and a wind-up dinner. The institution's case is usually presented at the dinner. Guests should be encouraged to participate in the event through panel discussions or question and answer periods.

Planning for a major symposium should begin six months to a year in advance. Since success depends heavily on the prominence of the speakers and their willingness to say something new or controversial, it is essential that great care be employed in their selection. Invitations should be tendered by prominent community leaders from four to five months in advance.

About three months ahead of time a committee of prominent local figures should be enrolled as sponsors of the symposium. The Manhattan School listed 60 distinguished sponsors for its event. Their names should appear on all mailings and programs.

Approximately two months in advance an informational mailing should be sent to a carefully selected list of potential donors announcing the event. Five weeks in advance the R. S. V. P. invitations should be sent out. A good rule of thumb is to send out 10 times as many invitations or announcements as the number of guests desired. No other public invitation should be made until results of this mailing are determined. It is best to fill the hall with pre-selected

467

potential donors rather than with the general public. However, if returns indicate that not all available places will be filled, the general public may be invited through a public announcement a week or so in advance.

Whether or not guests are charged for meals or admission will depend upon the local situation. In a small city where the event can be scheduled at a time when it will face no competition for audience and where name speakers ordinarily "pull" well, it may be possible to recoup part of the cost of staging the event by charging admission or for meals. The Manhattan School charged for luncheon; dinner was free.

Total costs for a symposium may run from a few thousand dollars to as much as $50,000, depending on its scale. Chief cost items are honorariums for noted speakers (these may range from $250 to $1,000); travel expenses for speakers; meals; printing and mailings.

Smaller organizations can keep costs down to a bare minimum by using their own facilities and volunteers, and, perhaps, by eliminating the dinner. Often, speakers who are convinced of the worthiness of the institution will waive the honorarium. Similarly, local businesses may be asked to contribute space, goods or services.

It is important that the event is smoothly run. Thus lighting and sound technicians should be paid to stand by and the registration desk should be manned at all times. A press room should be provided, if possible. One person should be delegated to work with radio and television reporters if the event is to be broadcast. A telephone should be installed at the registration desk and in the press room. It is important that such details not merely be left up to the hotel or school at which the event is held. Volunteers should be available for last minute assignments.

468

By working carefully, with adequate time, and by choosing the right speakers, the right mailing list, and the right theme, the sponsor can reap long term benefits from the symposium. It can raise levels of support measurably and attract wide attention. (25)

————————◄●►————————

Speakers are Essential in Good
Public Relations Program

Organizations lacking a pool of experienced speakers should seek to develop them from within the ranks of their volunteers. Very often, opportunities to address small but specialized segments of the public, who may be difficult to reach in any way other than through a direct talk, are wasted. Organizations without volunteers to address these smaller groups cannot continually ask their business board members or executives to assume these assignments. However, volunteers who profess not to be speakers can often be very effective in addressing smaller groups, if their confidence is not destroyed at first attempt. The following points should be considered by the neophyte public speaker.

Know your audience and know what it is interested in. Be sure to address yourself to those interests.

It's better to cover one subject well than to ramble across a whole series of undeveloped subjects. Find your main theme and then develop it. If you have charts, slides, or other visual aids, use them.

Address your audience in a natural conversational style. If you're writing your speech in advance, write it in the way you normally talk. Keep sentences short.

Speak more slowly than you ordinarily do. A rate of about 120 words a minute is normal for speaking before an audience. Time yourself in advance to make sure that you don't exceed the pace.

Know what you're talking about. Do some basic research on your organization first. Use facts and statistics. They aren't dull if they're presented in the right way.

Enjoy the experience of speaking before people. If you do, the chances are that the audience will enjoy listening to you.   (22)

———◄●►———

Long Distance Talk

If one of your speakers misses travel connections because of bad weather, he might try using the telephone. Director Alan Schneider did, when he was grounded in New York City on the night he was scheduled to discuss the Ithaca Festival before a gathering of 100 people in a Rochester, New York home. Local sponsors of the event had the telephone company connect the phone lines to two speakers. Schneider then talked for about 40 minutes, explaining the festival and answering questions. The telephone call cost $72.   (48)

———◄●►———

Special Theater Week is Useful Promotional Tool

Official proclamations which honor local arts groups seldom result in dramatic increases in either ticket sales or contributions. Effectively merchandised, however, they can be useful promotional tools which help a group to reach difficult markets, publicize its programs or revive flagging volunteer interest.

Earlier this fall, the mayors of Hartford and West Hartford, Conn., proclaimed the week of September 7th through 13th as Hartford Stage Company Week, and urged all citizens to support the group. The special week followed a very slow ticket selling summer for the Stage Company, with the first phase of its subscription campaign lagging far behind the previous year's, due in part to increased ticket prices. "It was necessary to jolt our volunteers into action," said William Stewart, the theater's managing director. "A kick-off party for Phase II and the proclamation of Stage Company Week seemed the most effective method."

The kick-off party which opened the week was a gala champagne and pizza "turn-on" at the Hartford Insurance Group's Tower Suite, attended by the city's top business, educational and cultural leaders. Special guests included playwright Robert Anderson and his wife, actress Teresa Wright and actor Morris Carnovsky. Later events that week included a series of in-school programs in nearby communities featuring company members; talks by company representatives before service clubs and business groups; subscription parties arranged by the women's committee; and a series of radio and television appearances by the Stage Company's staff and board members.

Publicity on Hartford Stage Company Week was excellent, and the theater was able to win coverage in news-

471

papers and on radio and television which, without the impetus of the proclamation, it would not have received— like a special article on the Sunday business page. The company also was able to present a strong case for support to local business through speeches delivered at Rotary Clubs.

Asked to evaluate the effectiveness of the week, managing director Stewart told *AM*, "I think the week succeeded. We had excellent coverage and cooperation from the newspapers and radio and T.V. And, we revived a rather tired and sagging group of volunteers and created a climate to generate renewed interest from many people."   (66)

Promoting to Business

One cultural organization struck a unique blow for widespread recognition recently with a promotion aimed at businessmen, sports fans and other non-arts audiences. Thanks to a contribution from one of its board members, Young Concert Artists, Inc., a non-profit organization which helps talented youngsters launch their musical careers, placed full-page advertisements in regional editions of eight leading magazines during March and April. The ads, which featured a picture of 11 young artists beneath the heading "Let them be heard . . . Before they've been heard of" appeared in such publications as *Fortune, Time, Sports Illustrated* and *Newsweek*. According to director Susan Wadsworth, the response has varied from the receipt of contributions to requests for information on booking artists.   (75)

Publicity on Speeches

Is an executive of your organization delivering an important speech before a key organization in your community? If so, by sending mimeographed copies of the speech to the press in advance, you may receive publicity on the speech immediately following its delivery. Be sure to include, along with the copy of the speech, pertinent background material as to its time and place. Also send biographical information on the speaker. Mark your material for release after the speech is given.   (21)

Speakers Kit

Members of an arts organization's speakers bureau will perform more effectively if they are given printed materials from which to prepare their talks. The Studio Arena Theatre in Buffalo, New York, has prepared an extensive speakers kit. Included are such materials as a schedule of events, subscription applications, theater party discount rates, an industrial sales plan, flyers, posters and a 10-page outline of the organization's activities and its history. (47)

Arts Win Applause and Dollars From Some Unexpected Sources

Arts organizations are discovering that funding and promotional help may be available from totally unexpected sources, like "pop" disc jockeys and non-classical music stations. In Philadelphia, The Pennsylvania Ballet has won new audiences and received tremendous local publicity due to the promotional efforts of Tom Brown, one of the city's most popular "deejays."

Brown, who played records for Philadelphia Metromedia station WIP until July, when he moved to station WPEN in the same city, first became interested in the dance company early in 1968, when it was preparing for its debut week at the New York City Center. Along with the station, he promoted a tour for two busloads of Philadelphians, including many who had never seen ballet before, to see the company perform in New York. Later, Brown and the station promoted a raffle, with the winners receiving free tickets to ballet performances and a reception hosted by Brown at a leading local restaurant. This summer, he promoted excursions from center-city Philadelphia to ballet performances at a suburban music festival. During this entire period, Brown publicized every ballet performance on his radio show.

According to Eugene Palatsky, the dance company's publicist, Brown's efforts as the unofficial radio voice of the Pennsylvania Ballet have won new subscribers, including some of the bus excursionists and raffle winners, and have attracted great local attention. "A blast on the radio from Tom," he said, "and our phones promptly go roaring off the hook."

How does Brown feel about his help to the ballet company? While at WIP, he engineered the preparation of a flyer describing his activities, which was sent nationally to all Metromedia stations and personnel. And although he's now at a different station, he's continued to promote the Pennsylvania Ballet. His real interest, however, can be summed up by the fact that several months ago, he joined the dance company's board of directors.

Another prominent Philadelphia arts group, the Philadelphia Orchestra, was the indirect beneficiary of an unusual gift from an elderly spinster to the State of Arkansas. Miss Lily Peter of Marvell, Arkansas wanted to do something important for the state's territorial sesquicentennial celebration this past June, so she commissioned Norman Dello Joio to compose a new work, "Homage to Hayden," and hired the Philadelphia Orchestra to perform it at two gala sesquicentennial concerts in Little Rock. Miss Peter mortgaged one of her two farms, and paid the entire $53,000 program cost herself. (66)

The Light Touch Helps Sell Cultural Programs

A light or humorous touch can help promote cultural programs, according to the experience of several arts groups. In Indianapolis, Ind., for example, the symphony orchestra has used a series of 16 one-minute radio spots, irreverently titled "Symphony A-Go-Go," periodically since late 1965 with considerable success.

Written and produced for the Indianapolis Symphony by local radio station WATI, the spots feature dialogues between a husband and wife. Each begins with the same narration, "Now we take you to the living room for another traumatic episode of Symphony A-Go-Go." The background sounds of a football game on television are heard as the wife, Martha, attempts to convince her very reluctant husband, John, that he should attend a Sunday afternoon concert with her instead of watching football on television. As the dialogue ends, with John still a holdout, the voice of the television sportscaster is heard. A typical spot ends with the announcer saying, "Will the Packers lose? Will John go to the symphony concert? We think so, but tune in tomorrow for another exciting episode of Symphony A-Go-Go."

The Arena Stage in Washington, D. C. has applied its light promotional touch to print media. Early this summer, the theater ran a series of newspaper advertisements in the *Washington Post* and *Washington Star* aimed at selling subscriptions for the 1967-1968 season. Each of the ads featured a production photograph with the words of the characters emanating from a balloon, comic strip style. One ad, for example, showed an austere-looking man saying, "A season of plays to amuse me?" The copy below the picture read, "Yes, even you . . ." and then briefly described the coming season, including "three of the funniest plays in the theater."

Another ad in the series, showed a character about to be run through with a sword saying, "All right . . . all right . . . I'll subscribe." The copy below read, "If a thrifty Scotsman like Macbeth can see the value of subscribing to Arena Stage's 1967-68 season, need we say more . . . except to urge you to subscribe."

In direct mail promotion, the Something Else Press, a company of artists and writers devoted to publishing avant-garde materials, recently mailed a balloon along with its catalogue. When inflated it read, "Concrete poetry is something else." (58)

A Vote for Theater

Civic interest in Election Day triggered a recent tie-in promotion by the Southwark Theatre Company in Philadelphia. Season subscription forms, printed to resemble campaign fliers, with an order "ballot" at the bottom, were sent to the organization's mailing list. The flier read in part: "Defeat inflation . . . Subscription ticket guarantees 10 per cent savings . . . Conservative ticket prices . . . Liberal exchange policy." In addition, the theater sent a "campaign" truck around the city with a message on its side asking citizens to vote for the subscription ticket. The announcements noted that advertising was paid for by "The Philadelphia Citizens for Better Theatre." (53)

The Light Touch

Issuing a calendar of events? Perhaps a light and humorous approach to this routine and practical kind of publication may increase its readability. The Greater St. Louis Arts Council, in its first monthly calendar of events, urged readers that, "a calendar is to tear," should they become fond of a particular feature in it. It also made a key point in a light manner by requesting, "tell us at the end of the month whether the paper is tough enough to withstand vigorous daily wear." (22)

What's In a Name?

Issuing promotional material? Sometimes a name, a person, or some special element in your organization's program will lend itself to effective and imaginative promotion. For example, the Paper Bag Players, a children's theatre group in New York, took advantage of their name by sending out their program announcements printed on small brown paper bags a little larger than a letter-size envelope. The low cost mailing not only drew attention and reinforced the image of informality that the group wanted to emphasize, but also helped underscore the name of the organization in visual terms. Caution: make sure promotional efforts are in character with the general tone of your organization. (26)

Special Month-Long Promotions Can Bring Arts a New Audience

Cultural organizations performing an outstanding service for the community and seeking recognition by a wide segment of the public might consider establishing a special "week" or "month" for that purpose. Although advance preparation and careful coordination are necessary, such promotions may yield great benefits.

Special weeks and months have been highly successful public relations and fund raising vehicles in the health and welfare field, and many of the techniques employed there can be adapted for use by non-profit cultural organizations. For example, the Jewish Chronic Disease Hospital in Brooklyn, New York, has sponsored such a program for a number of years. Under the direction of its public relations counsel, Edward N. Mintz, the hospital's special month promotion has been a model of what may be accomplished in a carefully planned campaign.

The first step in such a program is to get official approval for the desired week or month. The Chronic Disease Hospital, for example, receives a proclamation from the mayor of New York each year designating September as "Chronic Disease Hospital Month." Once this approval is obtained, the sponsoring institution can then request the support of city agencies and key private groups. Thus, the hospital has received permission from the licensing authority in New York to place more than 5,000 stickers in local taxicabs proclaiming the month. It has also placed free advertising car cards in more than 1200 New York City buses and posted free announcements on city billboards.

The selection of a chairman to head the week or month is another important step which should be taken well in advance of the actual campaign. The hospital, for example, generally names a leading celebrity from the entertainment field as chairman. It then features his name and his picture in announcements, correspondence and publicity. Other key entertainment figures are asked to donate their time to record radio announcements and film television spots.

The support of prominent national and local political figures and leading private citizens should also be solicited, and letters and telegrams from them can be cited in direct mail campaigns or they can be read aloud at dinners and other special events. In response to letters acquainting leaders with the problem of chronic diseases and the role of the hospital, the institution received assurances of cooperation and best wishes from the White House, the Governor of New York, the Secretary of Health, Education and Welfare, both New York senators, and many other top leaders.

Special committees composed of people prominent in a particular field should be formed early. In 1962, the hospital's radio and television committee for Chronic Disease Hospital Month was headed by the vice presidents of New York's two leading television stations. In addition, officials of more than 200 radio and television stations in New York and eight surrounding states, the bulk of them solicited by mail, agreed to serve on the committee. This kind of cooperation resulted in the use of more than 100,000 written, recorded and filmed announcements on radio and television during the special month and afterwards which reached an audience in the millions. Many of these announcements featured top personalities, who contributed their time and services.

Although a special week or month can reap widespread benefits and be helpful in raising vast sums of money, it need not be an expensive undertaking, if it is carefully organized and if maximum cooperation is forthcoming. In one of its most successful special months, the Chronic Disease Hospital spent only a little more than $3,000 on the entire program. Included in this amount were the costs of making recorded and filmed announcements and in printing material for car cards, taxi stickers and billboards. Space and time were generously given by advertising media, and celebrities contributed their services. (28)

Outdoor Artists

Your local outdoor advertising company may give you the use of a white billboard on request. Get a group of volunteers to paint a message on it, with some first-rate artwork if this is possible. Not only will the billboard publicize your activities, but the work of the volunteers may make news as well. (14)

Publicity in Match Books

Local companies who advertise on match covers may be a source of free publicity. Often there is additional space in a match book for a message about a cultural organization. A Swiss cigarette manufacturer, Rio, includes a picture and message about the Museum of Natural History in Berne in its match books. (15)

Your Schedule Makes Good Copy

Schedules of cultural events are eagerly sought by editors of the many weekly and monthly magazines distributed free in the hotels, restaurants and taxicabs of many cities. These periodicals, addressed to travellers, tourists and others, reach large numbers of readers, who are looking for events to attend. Harried editors may not have time to seek out your schedule. But if it is delivered to them on time, they are likely to welcome the assistance and insert it in their what's-on-around-town columns. To get names and addresses of these publications, check a few hotels or major restaurants on your next trip downtown. (4)

Arts Kiosk

Looking to attract attention in your community? You might follow the example set by arts groups in Winnipeg, Manitoba. Five of Winnipeg's leading cultural organizations, the Royal Winnipeg Ballet, the Manitoba Theatre Centre, the Winnipeg Symphony Orchestra, the Winnipeg Art Gallery, and the Rainbow Stage joined in sponsoring a 12-foot-high cylindrical structure which stands at the corner of Portage and Main Streets, one of the busiest intersections in the Canadian city. The kiosk, similar to those found throughout Paris, is decorated with colorful posters promoting the activities of all five groups. To heighten interest, the kiosk will be moved to a series of new locations throughout the year. (64)

The Telephone Directory

The covers of local telephone directories frequently feature pictures of places of interest in the community. Arts groups using one physical facility throughout their season, thus have a unique publicity outlet which is seen throughout the year. Competition for this space may be keen, so get your request in to the community relations director of your local telephone company at least six months prior to the publication date. (16)

Promotional Tool

An interesting promotional device, designed to keep editors alert to the activities of a cultural group, has been developed by the National Citizens Committee for Public Television. The group recently sent to its press list a book-like file 12" high by 2½" wide, filled with information on the organization, and bearing its name on the spine. When new material on the N.C.C.P.T. arrives, an editor can slide the inner container outward and easily insert it. (61)

Eye-Catching Kits

Looking for an unusual way to capitalize on a successful season? The Seattle Opera Association in Washington sent out eyecatching kits about twice the size of those usually used. They contained a variety of materials on the organization, including copies of press reviews, articles, brochures and even a poster. When opened, the kits, with a cover photograph of the opera house, measured 26 inches wide. They were 16 inches long.   (46)

————— ◄●► —————

Museum Highlights Major Show With Series of Related Events

Arts institutions planning a major event can dramatize its importance by building an entire program around it. The Art Gallery of Toronto, for example, highlighted its exhibition of the 18th-century Venetian landscape painter, Canaletto, with a full program which featured special guests, luncheons, a lecture series and gallery talks. It altered its usual schedule of events to arrange most of its fall calendar around the exhibition which was held from October 17th to November 15th.

The comprehensive Canaletto showing, the first of its kind, contained more than 140 paintings, drawings and etchings assembled from England, Germany, Switzerland, the United States and Canada.

To focus public attention on the event, the Gallery arranged for Sir Philip Hendy, director of England's National Gallery, to appear at the museum and officially open the exhibition.

484

For this exhibition, the Gallery charged a special admission price of $1 for adults and 25 cents for children. However, regular members were given special free tickets to admit them and their guests. It was hoped that such an offering would help to attract new members. To accommodate the extra visitors expected, the Gallery remained open on weekdays until 10:00 P.M., except on Wednesdays when it stayed open until 10:30 P.M. The usual closing time is 5:30 P.M.

An unusual promotion used to highlight the exhibition was a series of special luncheons organized by volunteers and featuring Venetian dishes. The museum area surrounding the dining room featured displays of art books on Canaletto. An admission price of $1.50 was charged for the luncheons.

To lend greater significance to the exhibition, a series of three monthly lectures was scheduled. An international group of speakers was selected to present the talks, whose scope was wider than the exhibit, but nevertheless related to it. Admission to the lectures was 50 cents.

Gallery tours of the exhibit were presented by a member of the institution's staff four times each weekday during the period of the show and twice on Saturdays. In addition, a different Canaletto painting was analyzed at the museum each Wednesday evening by an expert.　　　　　(32)

Milestone

Passing an important milestone in attendance can be turned to publicity advantage by an arts organization. The Walters Art Gallery in Baltimore recently called public attention to the fact that sometime between 2 and 3 p.m. on December 6, the 100,000th visitor of the year entered the gallery. The Walters announcement noted that 1963 was the first year in which attendance had reached six figures, and pointed to its exhibition of King Tut-ankh-amen Treasures as the big attraction of the year. Local publicity resulted from the announcement. (23)

Happy Anniversary

Anniversaries can mean extra publicity for cultural organizations, particularly if they are marked by some special event which calls attention to them. For example, the Brooklyn Children's Museum in New York City recently highlighted the celebration of its 65th anniversary with a program of special events including a sale of dolls and toys from all over the world, and two special shows. (36)

486

Fashion and Film Help Promote Art Exhibit

Cultural events with a specific theme can often provide the basis for unique publicity tie-ins with businesses and other organizations, if public relations directors are alert to the many possibilities.

A recent exhibition of the works of Vincent Van Gogh at the Nelson Gallery of Art in Kansas City, Missouri, resulted in several unusual and important joint promotions. A local movie theatre, the Rockhill, reissued the film *Lust For Life,* a fictionalized biography of Van Gogh, in conjunction with the opening of the museum's exhibition. Advertisements and publicity for the movie in local newspapers called attention to the exhibition.

A major department store in Kansas City, Harzfeld's, used the occasion to introduce a new high fashion color to its customers. Women's dresses, coats, shoes, handbags, and hats in a yellow often found in Van Gogh's works were featured in half page color newspaper ads which also prominently showed a Van Gogh farm scene in yellow.

An editorial in the local daily newspaper, the Kansas City Star, also stirred additional interest in the exhibition. Accompanied by a Van Gogh drawing, the editorial discussed Van Gogh and his work and urged readers to attend the exhibition. (15)

Place Mats Tell Diners What's Cooking —
Until Dinner is Served

An unusual way to publicize your arts group is to print your message on place mats used in restaurants. Many restaurants and lunch places use paper place mats printed with descriptive messages on a variety of topics. If you can prepare an interesting mat promoting your organization, you may find new patrons for your exhibitions or performances.

A check of printing houses by *Arts Management* reveals that paper mats in quantities of 5,000 or more can be printed in one color in standard 10" by 14" size on 16-pound bond paper for as little as $8.50 a thousand. Though many printers prefer not to take orders below 5,000, those who do will print 1,000 mats or fewer at a rate of about $13 per thousand.

A second color generally costs a dollar or two extra per thousand. Art work, based on one price for an entire order, also costs extra.

One representative New York firm charges an additional $15 for art work on a minimum order of 5,000 provided that they are given simple sketches from which to work. A number of the printers sampled by *AM* will accept mail orders and state that if they are given all the materials they can have a place mat job finished within 48 hours.

Arrangements for printing place mats and the exact cost can be checked with local printers. It is essential, of course, to discuss the place mat promotion with one or more restaurants first. The operators who agree to use your printed mats with your message may be able to tell you what kind of message is most appropriate for their patrons.

(11)

Theatre and Manufacturer Join In Unique Promotional Venture

A theatre producer has joined with a candy manufacturer in a unique promotion which is winning wide publicity for a drama now playing off-Broadway in New York City.

Nimara Productions, aware that *Do You Know The Milky Way?* incorporated the name of a well-known candy bar, wrote to Mars, Inc., manufacturer of Milky Way candy. An agreement was concluded under which the confectionery firm displayed 10,000 cards paid for and printed by Nimara Productions, advertising its production on candy counters throughout New York City, in time for the March 14 opening of the play. In return, the theatre's management gave free tickets to its production with the presentation at their box-office of a Milky Way wrapper and the purchase of one ticket at regular prices ($3.50 top week days; $4.50 top week-ends)—in effect, a "two-for-one" sale of tickets to bearers of the wrapper.

Mars, Inc., which publicized the promotion in its trade press, also set-up a display in M. H. Lamston Inc., a large five-and-ten cent store. Similar displays were planned by Mars in cigar stores in the downtown area.

To date, only 55 wrappers have been presented at the box-office. However, the publicity director of the show believes that the free publicity the play has received was well worth the $210 spent for printing the signs.   (16)

Arts Homecoming

When old grads think of homecomings it usually means one thing—football. At Rice University in Houston, Texas, however, the theme for this year's homecoming was "The Arts at Rice." The program for Saturday, October 28th included a concert, play, film shows, and art exhibitions. While the idea is worth adopting at other colleges, perhaps community cultural groups as well might be able to convince former residents and supporters to return for an arts homecoming. (77)

Reverse Psychology

A new promotional idea in Seattle, Washington, is attracting city-wide attention. The Seattle Opera Company which distributed "Bravo Opera" bumper stickers several years ago has now come up with backwards opera posters. The black and white 17″ x 22″ posters bear the twin messages, "Opera is Alive and Well in Seattle" and "Opera Lives," but the type is reversed. Viewers have to look carefully to read the message—which probably helps them to remember it. (65)

Alumni Promotion

College alumni groups may be good audiences for your programs. The Columbia University Alumni Executive Committee of Atlanta and the Members Guild of the High Museum of Art co-sponsored the second annual "Columbia in Atlanta" program, with an arts theme: "The Arts in the Age of Anger." The University of Wisconsin Alumni Club in New York City sponsored an "Evening at the Metropolitan Museum of Art," for $1.00 a family, featuring a private gallery tour. (68)

Cable TV

According to F.C.C. regulations, cable television operators in the top 100 markets must, within the next five years, offer one or more channels for public use without charge. Arts groups interested in taking advantage of public access channels and preparing programs for them can receive technical assistance from several organizations including the Alternate Media Center, 144 Bleecker St., New York, N.Y. 10012, and Open Channel, 222 W. 42 St., New York, N.Y. 10036. (76)

Seeing the Light

The small fliers which frequently accompany the monthly electricity bills mailed by public utility companies, can be significant publicity outlets for cultural organizations. These pocket publications, which reach virtually every home in a given area, regularly feature public service information. A recent flier from the Public Service Company of New Hampshire, for example, was devoted to summer theaters in the state, while Con Edison in New York promoted this summer's Lincoln Center Festival '67.   (57)

Local Libraries

Your local library can help stimulate interest in your programs. In Washington, D. C., the Arena Stage published a small flier in the shape of a book mark, which listed the seven productions in its season. On the reverse side it printed a list of "Suggested background reading on Sixteenth Arena Stage Season by the D. C. Public Library." Included in the list were 10 books written about the plays' authors, or their subject matter.   (43)

Promotion in Airports

Travelers in and out of airline terminals often have time
between planes. Many enjoy spending some of this time
looking at rotating collections from local museums or at
photographic displays featuring local performing arts
groups. The displays promote the institutions to local residents and to travelers and help to encourage attendance.
(20)

State Listings

Many state Departments of Commerce issue calendars of
events designed to lure tourists to the state. Since material
from cultural organizations may be used in these publications, it is suggested that you write or check the Director
of the Travel Bureau of the Commerce Department in the
state capital. (17)

Local Directory

Business associations that compile an annual local directory to promote the town or area usually want to list
arts organizations because they are a community asset.
Check to see that your group is included and its activities
listed. (11)

Tourist Displays

Visual displays at tourist attractions can be useful in promoting the programs of arts groups. For example, in New York City, 20 of the city's museums, religious and educational institutions are represented in a display case on the second floor of the Empire State Building. The display catches the eyes of the many visitors who pass through the building each day. (40)

Ticket Envelope

The little envelope in which tickets are distributed at the box office can be useful in promoting future performances, as well as in advertising a restaurant near the theatre or hall. The ticket envelope used by the Coliseum in Washington, D. C. carries a restaurant ad on the back. The front is used to promote four upcoming events at the Coliseum. With each new printing as the season progresses, outdated events can be removed from the top of the list and fresh material inserted below. (14)

PUBLICITY AND PROMOTION CASE STUDIES

Arts Group Wins New Audience Through House Party Program

By sponsoring "house parties," where its representatives can meet the public face-to-face, an arts group can engender interest in its work, while laying the foundation for such future activities as fund raising and ticket sales. Although house parties have been successfully used by many established cultural organizations, they also can be extremely helpful in launching a new organization or a new project.

In Ithaca, New York, The Ithaca Festival, preparing for its first season of repertory theater, mounted an extensive house party campaign to win support for the project.

Volunteers recruited by the group have given over 100 parties in their homes for more than 2,000 friends, and the guests they were asked to invite, since the program was started in January. Parties, attended by 25-to-30 persons, served the dual purpose of promoting the festival concept in the community in advance, while conditioning guests for fund solicitations later mailed to them.

Two devices were employed to spark parties and vary programs. First, an amateur speakers bureau of local citizens was organized and trained by the Festival. J. Wesley Zeigler, managing director of the group, told *AM*, "The use of volunteer speakers has been successful because party guests appreciate being approached by members of the community whom they know and to whom they can relate. The personal approach puts guests at ease, and volunteers are encouraged to answer questions from guests, but only on those aspects of the festival with which they are familiar.''

Second, visual aids played an essential role in heightening party success. Until summer, slides of the festival site were shown at the parties. During the summer, parties were held on patios, and attracted large numbers of guests. To spur guest interest, a 40-minute film on the Shakespeare Festival in Stratford, Ontario, a small Canadian city the size of Ithaca, was shown. Departing guests were also given literature on the festival.

Success of the parties in Ithaca sparked an expansion of the program to neighboring cities. Since May, half the parties sponsored by the group have been held in nearby New York cities including Olean, Elmira, Watkins Glen, Geneva and Cortland.

The parties also spurred publicity. Newspapers reported on them, and a local station televised a staged party. The television show attracted additional volunteers who offered to give parties for the Festival. (42)

New Residents

One way to introduce new residents in the community to its cultural activity is to distribute free tickets through the Welcome Wagon organization, which is maintained by local merchants. In addition, lists of addresses of houses in newly built middle and upper income subdivisions can be obtained from the builders or from the telephone company. (11)

How to Plan for Specially Proclaimed Week

Careful step by step planning, selection of a newsworthy honorary chairman, good use of volunteers and several promotable feature events were among the ingredients which helped the New York City Chapter of Young Audiences, Inc., reap widespread benefits from a week officially proclaimed in its honor.

Last summer the New York chapter decided that a week honoring Young Audiences would provide a good promotional prelude to organizational fund-raising efforts. Letters were sent to New York's Mayor Lindsay and Commissioner of Cultural Affairs, Dore Schary, requesting proclamation of the week of November 30th as Young Audiences Week in New York. Accompanying the letters was detailed information on the organization with special emphasis on its benefits to the city's schoolchildren. Later that week several key board members phoned the Commissioner's office to offer additional background.

When city confirmation of the honor and date came within a week, the organization was ready. Immediately, each of its volunteer committees was notified and asked for promotion and program suggestions. One volunteer came up with the idea for one of the feature events, a week-long exhibit of children's art inspired by Young Audiences concerts. Her husband won a commitment from the prestigious Seagram Building to house the exhibit in its lobby.

On October 5th, Miss Marian Anderson agreed to serve as honorary chairman. Her early acceptance was crucial since letters and invitations to events could be signed by her, she could be prominently featured in printed material, and her testimonial to Young Audiences could be incorporated into upcoming announcements and releases.

By mid-October, the suggested wording for the official

proclamation had been prepared and sent down to City Hall. Also, Commissioner Schary had agreed to appear at the opening event, a Young Audiences demonstration concert at an elementary school, to present the Mayor's proclamation to Miss Anderson. Letters were sent to broadcast media to prepare them for later releases.

Special attention was given during the first weeks of November to the three events which would highlight Young Audiences Week. For the opening Monday event, the official presentation, a list of 40 top dignitaries was prepared, invitations were mailed and volunteers followed up with notables they personally knew to insure attendance. At the same time, arrangements were made with the city school system's art superintendent for the second event, "What Color is Music?" the week-long exhibit of schoolchildren's are scheduled to open on Tuesday, December 1st. With cooperation from the superintendent, chapter volunteers worked with local schools to get paintings for the exhibit. The third event was a week-long series of in-school Young Audiences demonstrations.

By mid-November, the publicity machinery was in full operation. Some 400 posters were mailed to contributors and friends to place in prominent locations. Press releases were sent to weekly newspapers for use in "What's happening" columns. National magazines received long letters describing the week's activities and the organization's program. When it was discovered that Young Audiences Week coincided with National Children's Art Month, it gave chapter publicists a national angle which they turned into an ABC network television feature.

A week prior to the event, full attention was given to daily press sources. Radio and television spots were prepared and mailed. The city itself sent press releases to dailies on November 23rd, followed two days later by more detailed releases from the chapter.

The official week opened on a wave of pre-publicity including Young Audiences store windows in Lord and Taylor and Creative Playthings and advance stories in leading dailies. The special events received excellent coverage in the papers and on television news programs, public service spots were used frequently, and feature interviews with Marian Anderson were aired on television. National magazines who couldn't do stories on the Week, became interested in the organization.

One unexpected yet important blessing also resulted from the program. Young Audiences was able to purchase ABC news films featuring Miss Anderson and have them converted at minimal cost into an excellent 60-second television spot. Prints will soon be distributed to all Young Audiences chapters.

In assessing the week's benefits, national executive director, Gerry J. Martin, said, "Both city officials and media people know us much better now and so do many potential supporters. Considering the benefits the costs weren't great, since many of them fit into the normal promotional budget." He added one word of caution, however. "Don't go into the week thinking of immediate and direct fund-raising rewards. They may come, but over the long run."

As evidence of its success the Week will become a national event this fall with all 40 Young Audiences chapters participating. (70)

————◄●►————

Press Clubs

Social affairs and entertainments held by press clubs in various cities provide an advantageous showcase for local performing arts groups. A performance at the press club is not only noted in the local papers but also makes and cements friendships that can help in the future. Press clubs can be found in most big U. S. cities as well as in such smaller centers as Anchorage, Charleston, W. Va., Fort Wayne, Las Vegas and Madison, Wis.; and in the Canadian cities of Montreal, Ottawa and Toronto.   (6)

Scholarship Program

An arts organization can focus public attention on its efforts to raise artistic standards in the community by offering scholarships to outstanding young artists in its area. By establishing an endowment fund for scholarships, a group may often receive extra financial support to help it develop the program. The Winston-Salem Arts Council in North Carolina, for example, now in its second year of a scholarship program, recently gave three cash awards to students of music, dance and art. It has received local publicity as well as a number of individual contributions to the program.   (31)

Theatre Offers Patrons Discounts on
Local Movie Tickets

Cooperative programs with local art film houses offer cultural organizations an excellent promotional device.

In Oklahoma City, Oklahoma, a legitimate theatre has worked out a cooperative promotion with a motion picture house specializing in foreign films. The program provides an extra service for theatre patrons and helps to increase the size of the audience at the movie. The Mummers Theatre offers its ticketholders a 25 cents credit, good anytime, for films being shown at the Trend Theatre. The discount is made available upon presentation of a Mummers ticket stub at the movie box-office. Although the promotion is still quite new, the response to the offer has been excellent so far.

According to David Lunney, a Ford Foundation administrative intern at the professional repertory theatre, the promotion is tied in with an inexpensive advertising campaign conducted by the theatre at the movie house. The Mummers runs a three phase trailer between films. The first phase is a theatre announcement. Next is a clip on the current Mummers production and third is an announcement of the ticket stub credit plan. Each clip costs $7.50 with the Mummers paying for the first two and the art film house paying for the third. (25)

————— ◄●► —————

Gallery Spurs Interest With City Tour Series

The affinity between interests in art and architecture has been used by the Washington Gallery of Modern Art to attract the public to its programs.

Earlier this year, the museum began a series of lecture and demonstration tours of the capital city, under the general title of "Washington Architecture." The first tour was devoted to the topic: "Urban Design—Southwest."

At $2 a ticket, it was the first guided tour under the leadership of experts in architecture and city planning that was open to the public. It concentrated on the Southwest Redevelopment Plan, which is transforming an old slum section of the city into a complex of modern apartment buildings and town houses, with shopping and recreational facilities. The plan has come in for much discussion and criticism.

To attract Washingtonians who might never have set foot in the modern art gallery, folders promoting the tours were printed in traditional design, with no hint of the sponsoring group's taste in art. The folder asked such provocative questions as:

"What is city planning? What is urban renewal? What has the planning of Southwest Washington produced? Do the buildings and projects relate to one another, and does the total environment create a neighborhood as part of the federal city, or a town within a town?" (30)

Art Exhibit

Interest in a performing arts organization can be attracted by an exhibit of graphic or plastic art works executed by members, subscribers and contributors. Such an art exhibit mounted in the lobby of a concert hall or theatre will make news in the local press. The Boston Symphony Orchestra presents an annual exhibition of paintings by subscribers to the Boston and Cambridge concerts.   (13)

Guest Artists Help Festival

Setting aside a section of a festival art exhibit for the work of a special group of guest artists can be good community relations. While the main body of an exhibit may be imported, a section devoted to local work offers an appeal to community pride and an opportunity for comparison.   (20)

Now Is Time to Prepare Summer Promotions

Cultural organizations, planning for their summer programs, should give careful attention to their printed promotional materials. Descriptive brochures can be highly effective if they contain specific information of a service nature for the potential audience.

In Ashland, Oregon, the Oregon Shakespearean Festival sends out brochures which, in addition to program and ticket information and background on the festival, contain special sections on dining, travel, area sightseeing, and lodgings. Each of the service sections, although tersely

503

written, contains specific information which will be helpful to festival visitors.

The lodgings section, for example, lists twenty motels in the surrounding area by name and includes information on their precise location and the facilities they offer. In addition, the brochure points out that transportation from each of the listed motels to the festival is available nightly on special "Bard's Evergreen Busses" which run on frequent schedule directly to the theatre.

Another promotional device, particularly well suited to the institution or festival which has a steady stream of visitors and which can be captured visually in an attractive photograph, is the picture postcard. Inexpensive to print, cards can nevertheless be an effective means of calling attention to an organization. Arena Stage in Washington, D. C. for example, has published its own black-and-white photographic postcard, which theatre patrons may pick up free from display racks in the lobby. The attractive exterior view gives a striking impression of the modern theatre building designed by Harry Weese, distinguished Chicago architect. The sign "Arena Stage" above the glass doorway can be clearly read.

Although no one knows how many of the cards have actually been mailed, Arena Stage told *AM* that 15,000 of the cards were taken from the racks in the first four months of the current season. An average of about 100 cards per performance are taken by playgoers. The theatre seats 775.

The previous season, when the postcards were left in unattended racks with a sign stating they were on sale for 5¢ each, only 5,000 were taken in more than six months. *AM* was told that money for only about half the missing cards was deposited in the slotted coin boxes. The theatre concluded that the cards did more good as giveaways in promoting Arena Stage than on a paid basis, since it was not economical to have an attendant collect nickels. Before special performances for high school groups, the cards are withdrawn from the racks.

Cost of the postcards is less than 1¢ each. Arena Stage found that local printers could underbid large houses doing a national business; it paid $7.50 per 1,000 in an order of 100,000 cards. The theatre had considered a color postcard, but found the cost prohibitive.

"Although we can't measure the result exactly, we think the picture postcards have been a good investment for publicity," an Arena Stage spokesman told *AM*.   (26)

Put the Arts on the Map for Summer Vacationers

When summer approaches millions of families begin planning vacation trips and deciding where they will go and what they will do while there. One way to attract such tourists is by making certain that the arts enterprise is properly listed in tourist guide books and on oil company maps. This publicity is completely free.

The leading guidebooks for North America are those of the American Automobile Association, which publishes thirteen regional tour books annually.

To be listed in an A.A.A. tour book, an organization should first notify the local or regional auto club affiliated with A.A.A. Consult the tour book entry for your city to observe the facts included and the space limits into which your item should fit. The local auto club reviews the proposed entry and then forwards it to the A.A.A. national office in Washington.

As a backstop, send the information directly to the National Touring Bureau, A.A.A., 1712 G Street, N.W., Washington, D. C. 20006. A field representative may call on the institution to see if it meets A.A.A. tour book standards. The primary concern is that it be of genuine interest to the touring public, and that it be fairly represented. The tour books distinguish items of special worth with a star (*).

One can also write to the national editor asking to be included in the A.A.A. Calendar of Events. This is an internal bulletin used by affiliated club travel counselors, who advise their own members on attractions in other regions, and guide out-of-town visitors on what to see locally.

The way to put an organization on the maps published by oil companies and distributed free to millions of motorists at service stations is to insure that the local chamber of commerce knows all about it. Do not write to the oil companies.

Most maps are published by three large map-makers: General Drafting Company, Convent Station, New Jersey; Rand McNally, Chicago, Illinois; and H. M. Gousha, San Jose, California.

The editorial departments of these map-makers collect their data from local chambers and from national and regional organizations of various kinds. They prefer not to be solicited for listing by individual organizations, unless the listing would be quite new or changed, or if notifying the chamber has brought no result.   (2)

Museum Tells Public How it Chooses Art Works

How does a museum decide what to exhibit? Among the factors museums may consider are the institution's early history, its original purpose and the nature of its collection, the type and size of the community, and whether the institution is the only one of its kind in the area. Although most museums rarely attempt to explain publicly how they weigh each of these different factors, the Art Gallery of Toronto recently did so in an unusual display of frankness.

The Art Gallery separates its exhibition functions into the exhibition of its permanent collection and the exhibition of temporary shows. Its policy is to balance the two. Except during large loan exhibitions, approximately 40 per cent of the building is hung with the permanent collection at all times. Last summer the whole building was devoted to non-Canadian works in its growing collection. This coming summer a Canadian hanging is planned for every room except one.

Of the Gallery's collection of 3600 works, only about 150 can be seen at any one time, thus creating pressure on both exhibition and storage space. Therefore, temporary shows must be considered carefully. The Art Gallery tells its public that temporary shows should be based upon an appraisal of the community which the gallery serves. "Before the appearance of so many commercial galleries in the city the Art Gallery of Toronto rightly felt an obligation to show the work of promising young Canadians in a number of three- and four-man exhibitions. The exhibition gallery used for this outgrown need is now devoted to prints and drawings in the hope that some day we may have a graphic department. Policies must change with changing conditions," the museum reported in its newsletter.

In addition to its own temporary shows, the Gallery also provides exhibition space to five artists' societies. Thus, during two to three months out of every year at least one third of the Gallery is hung with works which have been chosen and installed by outside organizations.

The Art Gallery strives to maintain a balance from year to year between old masters and contemporary artists, alotting almost half its space and time to the display of old masters. Thus in 1961, 51 per cent of all art displayed was work executed before 1900, 23 per cent the work of artists born in the 19th century but executed after 1900, and 26 per cent was work done after 1900 by artists who were born in the 20th century. In 1962 and 1963 the differentials between the groups remained almost the same.

A year to year balance between contemporary and historical works has also been maintained by the Gallery in its purchase of works of art. Here, as the Gallery tells its public, the percentage of spending on works of artists before 1900, on works after 1900 by artists born in the 19th century and after 1900 by artists born in the 20th century has remained nearly the same in each year from 1960 to 1963. In the last three years, however, the greatest emphasis has been upon the acquisition of old masters with 67 per cent of a total of $292,683 spent on the works of artists before 1900.

The Art Gallery's report to the public concludes by telling the membership that they own a share in the Gallery and are responsible for its welfare. (26)

Arts Win Friends and Funds With New Promotions

Gas stations, liquor agencies and professional basket-ball and football players are among the new groups and individuals helping the arts to promote programs, sell tickets and raise funds. In Seattle, Washington, where student "Whiz Kids" helped the Seattle Opera success-fully woo young audiences several years ago, it is now gas pump operators who are selling the Seattle Opera-going idea to family groups. During August and September, all Union 76 service stations throughout Western Washington have been promoting the October 2nd performance of *Madame Butterfly* to their customers. Motorists pull-ing into the stations can't miss seeing large orange and blue posters proclaiming, "Opera's a Gas!" and attendants wearing buttons reading, "Join the Opera Union." Along with gas and oil, attendants dispense opera ticket order envelopes.

As part of the cooperative promotion which runs until September 30th, the Seattle Opera is supplying station operators with weekly humorous reminders for posting. These have included "Come to the opera and bring Ethyl" and "Opera moves your inner tube."

Throughout Pennsylvania this summer, liquor purchas-ers have been reading all about community arts festivals. Featured on the front and back of one of the state's best scanned, if not best read publications, the State Store Price List, Number 107 of the Pennsylvania Liquor Con-trol Board, are striking color photographs of Pennsyl-vania's arts festivals, "where the arts and the artists meet the people in a grass roots cultural explosion." Fol-lowing 12 pages of price listings for whiskies, wines and cordials, the inside back cover includes information on and listings of Pennsylvania arts festivals during 1970, plus an order blank for a 74-page report on state culture published by the Pennsylvania Council on the Arts.

The professional athletes making their contribution to culture are four Carolina Cougar star basketball players. At a September fund-raising benefit for the United Arts Council of Greensboro, N.C., sponsored by the Greater Greensboro Merchants Association, the athletes modeled as well as entertained. Earlier this year, quarterback Bill Nelsen of the Cleveland Browns participated in a televised fund appeal for the Cleveland Symphony Orchestra.

Elsewhere, other cultural groups are using novel methods to win friends and raise money. Theatre Calgary in Canada introduced a Wall of Fame this spring, (four plywood panels seven feet high by four feet wide) which lists the names of contributors. Business donors can have their names inscribed or their logos printed on the wall for donations ranging from $25 for a 2″ x 4″ space to $100 for a 4″ x 12″ space. Used initially as part of the group's television auction, when hundreds of viewers phoned in donations to have their names listed, the wall has now become a permanent part of Theatre Calgary's home.

In New York City, museums, which have funding problems like arts groups everywhere, are trying new techniques to win new friends. Several now waive their admission and special exhibition fees every Monday, and the Museum of Modern Art has opened its gardens to the public for free entry nightly, except Sunday. The most unusual plan, however, has been initiated by the Metropolitan Museum and its Cloisters branch. Although visitors to the Cloisters and to special exhibitions at the main museum must pay to enter, they may now pay whatever they want, even a penny. According to the museum, the plan seems to be working.   (68)

Publicity Licks Costs Of Small Town Musical

A school musical needn't hit a financial sour note—even if total production costs approach $3000.

To stage *The King and I* recently, Hutchinson Senior High School, Hutchinson, Kansas, paid $1000 for production rights alone—royalty was $600 and music rental $400. In addition, the school laid out $1000 for professional costumes. Total costs ran to $2864. Profit from two performances: $182.

Director Gary Siemens credits overall success to numerous factors. But good publicity was a major element. The school received two weeks of free radio spot announcements, several free announcements on television stations, and stories in the local daily. Siemens reduced poster printing costs by having posters printed by the school's department of printing. This was professional work. Some 8000 posters costing $90—$100 were displayed in schools and business houses within a 50-mile radius of Hutchinson. Siemens also had some 500 bumper stickers made up at a cost of $48. He passed them out to high school students who put them on their own cars, friends' autos, and neighborhood cars.

The high production costs were so unusual to Hutchinson, a community of 40,000, that many people turned out just to see what nearly $3000 looked like on stage.

The show ran two nights in Hutchinson's Convention Hall, with 1500 to 1600 in attendance opening night, and a capacity audience of 2500 the second night. Tickets were $1.25 for reserved seats, $1.00 for general admission, and 75 cents for students.

Last year, in contrast, the high school staged *The Pajama Game* in a smaller auditorium, playing three nights with a capacity crowd of 600 for each performance. Tickets were $1.25 for all adults and 50 cents for students. Total production costs: $1000. The school broke even. Siemens thinks the quality, polish and investment in production helped put *The King and I* over. (3)

Dial 'C' for Culture

A telephone service, believed to be the first of its kind, is helping to build attendance at cultural events and institutions in Tucson, Ariz. The technique, readily adaptable for use in other cities, provides the public with a single telephone number to use in finding out exactly what cultural performances or exhibitions are scheduled that evening.

One call to 327-4909 in Tucson not only gives the caller a list of four or five scheduled events, but also the address, phone number, time, admission price, if any, and box office location.

Called *Tucson Tonight,* the service was initiated recently by the Tucson Festival Committee to aid non-profit cultural institutions. Every day a message giving the information described above is read into a machine, leased from the telephone company that records the message and plays it back to callers. During its first month, *Tucson Tonight* received 2,300 phone calls.

Monthly cost of the leased equipment is $10.00 to $15.00, depending on location. (1)

Foreign Flavor

Planning an arts evening with a foreign theme? You might try a technique used successfully by the Boston Swiss Club to sponsor its Swiss music festival. Several weeks prior to the event, everyone on the organization's mailing list received an artistic post card directly from Switzerland reminding him of the event. Because of the promotional value, foreign tourist services and overseas airlines may be helpful in supplying your group with free post cards or handling the mailing. For added flavor, interesting foreign postage stamps, with arts motifs, can be used on the post cards. (50)

Foreign Festivals

Arts organizations sponsoring festivals with a foreign theme can create additional interest in the events by working with officials of the countries represented. In some instances, foreign officials—eager to promote their country's arts—may be helpful in obtaining materials for the occasion. Often, dignitaries of the country may enhance the event by attending its opening. The Roberson Memorial Center, an arts council in Binghamton, New York, is holding a Danish Festival of the Arts featuring a touring art exhibition sponsored by the Ambassador of Denmark. The festival preview was attended by the Consul General of Denmark. (40)

To Sell for Christmas Plan Card Program Early

The sale of original art Christmas cards can be an effective way of promoting your cultural organization and, in some instances, a source of income.

However, many art groups throughout the country who are in the Christmas card field warn that it is an extensive and expensive proposition, begun when the preceding year's sales figures are in and ending when the holiday season is over.

In view of this, it might be wise initially to purchase slow-selling cards in bulk quantities at a trade discount from larger institutions already in the Christmas card field. (Presently, about fifty museums buy their cards from other organizations).

Whether you plan to buy and sell, or to print your own and sell, the following guidelines may prove helpful.

Form a committee to select a number of cards for your collection. The number in any collection may vary, of course, but a dozen or more designs may be needed to provide buyers with an adequate choice of price and type. The Museum of Modern Art, which runs an extensive Christmas card program each year, offers 28 different cards. Museums may draw on their own art collections for card designs. Others may buy designs from museums, or commission original designs from artists. (Some artists are willing to donate their services). In either case, vary the subject matter to include some religious, some non-religious, some non-wintery and some humorous cards. Keep legends simple. Offer some cards with no legend at all. Divide the collection between color and black-and-white. Remember that inexpensive one-color cards are usually the biggest sellers.

514

Once cards are selected and purchased or printed, promotion begins. Since card promotions tend to be expensive, it is often wise to use the same promotional material for other purposes as well. Some institutions link the card drive with membership recruitment, by offering members special discounts on cards.

Promotion should begin in September with a direct mail effort. The organization's subsequent mailings of schedules, calendars and other material should carry card advertisements as well.

As Christmas approaches try to display the cards and other seasonal material where it will get the most attention. Make sure employees or volunteers are on hand to run the over-the-counter sale efficiently.

A Christmas card sale is only slightly better than a break-even proposition at best, many institutions report. It can, however, yield non-financial benefits in terms of service to members and publicity for the organization. Every original card mailed out by a purchaser carries the organization's name. A tasteful design helps create a favorable image of the institution. (16)

Sticker Sale

If your organization has a "cause" to publicize, it can do so at a profit through the sale of stickers. The Allied Arts of Seattle, an arts council in Washington, initiated a campaign several years ago to halt the construction of highway billboards. To publicize its aims, the association sells small, colorful stickers that read, "Protect America's highways, Fight Billboard Blight." The stickers, which were designed by one of the organization's trustees, cost 12 cents per sheet of 21 to produce and sell for 25 cents per sheet. Members of the organization are encouraged to buy and use the stickers on their mail. (47)

Floating Conference

If you're planning a convention, perhaps the program for the 1966 annual conference of the American Community Theatre Association may provide you with some lively thoughts on keeping the conference moving. The A.C.T.A. meeting was billed as "the newest established floating conference," since the program took place in five different Minnesota cities. Thus, attendees had the opportunity to see eight performances and tour nine different theater buildings. Seminars on such practical topics as fund raising and audience development were held aboard busses going to and from conference sites. (51)

ADVERTISING

How Orchestra Profits from Program Advertising

Programs, distributed free of charge at performances, can bring in substantial revenue through the sale of advertising space, while, at the same time, providing arts groups with effective and handsome informational tools. In Salt Lake City, for example, the Utah Symphony Orchestra publishes 16 attractive issues of its program magazine for distribution at concerts each season, many with four color covers, and realizes a net profit of $500 per issue.

The key to the success of the Utah Symphony's program is the organization's approach to local advertisers. All advertising is solicited from the office of the symphony by a member of the staff who works on a flat salary basis. According to Herold L. Gregory, manager of the orchestra, advertisers seem to prefer knowing that the full amount of the ad goes to help the orchestra and that no portion of the fee is paid as a commission to a salesman.

In selling space, the orchestra's representative emphasizes the fact that it is good business to advertise in the program because there is full advertising value for each dollar spent. No program advertisement is ever considered a contribution to the orchestra. It is pointed out that 5000 leading citizens read and save the program.

This approach has been so successful that every program is brimming over with advertisements, many of them from repeat advertisers. In spite of this heavy schedule, however, the publication has a strict policy of never burying an ad under other ads. "Every ad in the program," says Mr. Gregory, "is adjacent to editorial copy. We maintain a general ratio of advertising space to editorial space and although this fluctuates somewhat, we keep the general rule of thumb in mind at all times.''

Advertising page rates in the program, of course, depend upon frequency of use. A full page ad is $80 in a single issue and $60, if taken in all 16 issues. Ads are also sold in half page, quarter page and eighth page sizes, the latter costing $25 a single issue. The center spread is $150 and the back cover is $75 on a 16 issue basis. With this rate schedule, the program realizes advertising revenue of $1300 per issue. The complete cost of production, including the pro-rating of staff employees' salaries is only $800 per issue.

Editorially, while the program promotes the orchestra and events sponsored by the organization, it also includes special features of general interest and articles on current topics. Generous space is also given to the activities of the Utah Symphony Guild and the names of active workers are frequently listed. As an editorial policy, the orchestra does not invite contributions of articles from the general public. In this way it avoids any chance that key donors or members may feel slighted because articles by them were not published.

At concerts, one copy of the program per couple is generally distributed, although requests for extra copies are never refused. Special efforts are made to provide individual copies to the section in which advertisers are seated. ''They must never feel we skimp on the printing of programs,'' said Mr. Gregory. ''There is no worse public relations blunder than to run out of programs.''

It is orchestra policy never to permit the use of a stuffer or advertising insert in the programs. ''Why,'' says Mr.

518

Gregory, "should any firm or organization upstage our regular advertisers and clutter up the program with extraneous circulars?" (24)

———— ◄•► ————

Arts Stretch Ad Dollar

Arts Council members in Winston-Salem, North Carolina, are getting more advertising space in their local papers, at less cost, through a new service set up by the Council office.

The Arts Council has signed an advertising contract with local newspapers, guaranteeing a minimum of one column inch of advertising weekly. Council members, who had been paying the transient rate, now get the benefit of the reduced contract rate. The savings range from 34 per cent on a Sunday-only basis, to 38 per cent on a combination of Sunday and Monday, or Saturday and Sunday advertising. Members still get their 6 per cent cash discount in addition.

The newspapers keep the names of the member organizations and use their ads when they receive the insertion order and ad copy. They bill the Council monthly. The Council adds this additional billing to its regular quarterly statement to members, pro-rating each organization on the basis of space used.

In the weeks when no one buys advertising space the Council authorizes the papers to use, in rotation, one of its standing ads featuring several members.

The Council and the newspapers have set up several rules to make the operation work. The papers insist on filled-in insertion orders with the ad copy. Duplicates of these orders and copy go to the Council office, and must arrive at least 24 hours before the newspaper's deadline. This notifies the Council that one of the members is buying space. If no order is received, the Council specifies that a standing ad is to be used.

According to William Herring, executive secretary of the Council, "None of the organizations is spending less money for advertising, but they are getting more for their money in the medium which I personally consider the most effective for the cost involved." (13)

———————◄●►———————

Advertising Aid

Local advertising agencies may provide aid to community arts groups which are planning advertising campaigns and do not have experienced staff members to implement them. In New York City, for example, the Fred Wittner Company, an advertising agency, prepares and places advertisements for the Westchester Symphony Orchestra. The agency does not charge the arts group its usual service fee. As a means of saying thank you, the orchestra gives the agency free concert tickets. (34)

———————◄●►———————

Special Newspaper Supplement Promotes Museum's Collection

A special Sunday newspaper supplement, paid for by "non-commercial" advertisements, has helped the Wichita Art Museum in Wichita, Kansas, promote its collection and its membership program. Called *A Sponsor's Tour of the Wichita Art Museum,* the section featured photographs of its "advertisers" viewing works from the museum's collection. Credits were limited to a line identifying advertisers, who were business and community leaders. The section, which was published last September, was devoted entirely to the collection, exhibits, facilities and programs of the museum.

The idea for the 32-page supplement, which was published by *The Wichita Eagle and The Wichita Beacon,* was conceived last May by Paul Miner, assistant advertising director of the newspaper. He worked in cooperation with Sebastian J. Adler, Jr., director of the museum, on developing the project.

After the museum approved the concept of the supplement, test layouts, promotional material, and presentation letters asking for advertising sponsorship were prepared. Writing, editing and laying out the issue was performed by the newspaper's staff, working closely with Mr. Adler. In cooperation with the museum, Mr. Miner sent out 300 letters to prominent members of the community suggesting they advertise in the issue.

The letters elaborated the details of the projected issue. They included a copy of the section's proposed layout, and information concerning the basic theme and the goals that the section would achieve. Cost information was also included. Advertising sponsorships were offered at the rate of one-third of a tabloid-sized page for $116, one-half for $170 and two-thirds for $250. Prospective sponsors were informed that they could select an art object from the museum's collection with which they would appear in the issue.

A typical "ad" reads, "Edgar E. Turner, Jr., partner and general manager of Head Shoe Co., stands before John Singleton Copley's oil portrait, 'Mrs. James Otis,' one of a pair of Copley portraits owned by the Museum." The rest of the ad is devoted to a description of the painting.

To maintain good relations with sponsors of the issue, after it was published, a thank you note was sent to each

521

along with a copy of his photograph and a copy of the section.

In addition, about 3,000 copies of the section were sent to museums throughout the country and abroad. "Community reaction was tremendous," Mr. Miner told *AM*. "The museum received numerous congratulatory phone calls, and I personally received dozens of letters and phone calls." (47)

◆●▶

TV Commercials Used by Museum To Increase Exhibit Attendance

Television and radio advertisements are being used to boost museum attendance in Virginia. With paid commercials, the Virginia Museum of Fine Arts in Richmond, a state institution, is attracting record numbers of visitors to its Artmobile II, an art exhibition mounted in a trailer which travels throughout the state.

One indication of the campaign's success is that following the commercials, 2,197 visitors saw the artmobile during its one-week stay in Martinsville, Virginia, compared to only 517 persons who saw it during the same period last year. David Hudson, the museum's public information assistant told *AM*, "We believe you can sell art the way you sell anything else."

Throughout the artmobile's 13-year history, the museum has relied on free public service radio and television spot announcements to promote its tours. However, although these announcements gave the artmobile excellent exposure at no cost, there was no way to guarantee when or where they would be aired.

When the museum staff conceived the idea of using paid commercials, it obtained approval from its director and

522

its board of trustees, with the stipulation that a private source underwrite the cost of the campaign. An anonymous donor contributed $26,000 to cover all production and time costs. The commercials, produced locally in Richmond, were written and narrated by a member of the museum's staff.

During Artmobile II's present tour, which runs from September 1st to January 22nd of next year, some 300 television and 1,000 radio commercials will be aired on 10 television stations and 17 radio stations in Virginia, in areas which the artmobile visits.

For television, 60-second and 20 second commercials are being shown about three times daily for a week prior to the artmobile's arrival at one of the 21 towns and cities of the museum's chapters or affiliates. Then, two different commercials, of the same duration, are substituted during the artmobile's week-long stay in a community. About 60 radio spots are used in the same two weeks.

Television time cost ranges from $500 to $3,500, and radio time from $100 to $300 per station. Interestingly, most of the stations have matched the purchased time by also using the commercials free, as public service announcements.

One of the 60-second television commercials used during the artmobile's residency in a community says, ". . . Walk into the spacious air-conditioned gallery-on-wheels and 3,000 years of art come alive in a magnificent collection. For example—stand before the glowing masterpiece by the incomparable Rembrandt. . . . Truly a Blue Ribbon Artmobile collection from the galleries of America's most exciting museum—the Virginia Museum." A special slide announcing the artmobile's location in a community is inserted into each commercial. (44)

Culture Woos a New Audience With
TV Commercial Campaigns

Cigarette commercials on television are gone forever, but cultural commercials may be here to stay. Next month in Chicago, arts and business leaders will sneak a preview of the first two completed TV spots in the soon-to-be-launched public service promotional campaign on behalf of the arts, conducted by the Advertising Council with the assistance of the Business Committee for the Arts (See *AM*: No. 67). At a February 16th luncheon hosted by *Newsweek* Magazine, the 60-second and 30-second spots, based on the themes "Art is not a luxury, it is a necessity" and "Art for man's sake," will be shown and a print lay-out for the campaign will be introduced. The commercials, made by Edward H. Weiss & Company, a Chicago ad agency, will be offered to stations throughout the nation later in the year.

In North Carolina, meanwhile, an unlikely "sponsor" has been promoting culture. The North Carolina Arts Council, seeking ways to broaden the state's cultural audience, conceived the idea of producing and presenting a series of television spots. With actors and announcers donating their services and a top Charlotte film company contributing much of its time, the council was able to produce five sound-on-color commercials for only $5,000. Last October they began distributing a different commercial every month to each of the 15 major television stations in the state. Stations have since used them frequently as part of their public service commitment and the public response has been excellent.

A key to the success of the commercials has been their light and somewhat irreverent approach to culture. In one 60-second spot set in a diner, a truck driver is about to begin eating when a voice-over says, "If everything has become just a matter of routine, it's time you let yourself go and grabbed hold of something real." The truck driver then tries to squirt some ketchup on his French fries but hits his shirt instead. Enjoying the result, he squirts ketchup on himself, the waitress and all over the diner. The scene changes to show the truck driver at an easel painting. As the voice-over says, "You need a new way of living—North Carolina, the State of the Arts," the logo of the state council appears.

Another 60-second spot shows a muscular man exercising in a locker room. As a voice says, "Gyula Pondi is one of the greatest athletes in North Carolina," the athlete puts a towel around his neck and walks out. In the next scene, done in slow motion, he is shown in dance movements and acrobatic leaps. "He works hard to master his profession," says the announcer, "and it's no easy business either. But who cares—North Carolina, the State of the Arts." Again the council's logo is flashed on the screen.

The commercials, which will run through February, also include another 60-second spot titled 'the writer," a 30-second spot called "all the arts," and a 20-second commercial with a rock music background, no narrative, and a series of quick-changing scenes showing people enjoying many different arts forms.

A light touch has proved equally effective in print advertising for some cultural groups. The Cincinnati Zoo Opera, in an attempt to entice new audiences, used bold and different types of ads. One, headlined, "Why I hate opera," portrayed four "hate opera" reasons, including "opera is fat ladies with horns." The copy then proceeded to refute each of them.

In New York City, the Hunter College Concert Bureau for the second consecutive year ran a series of quarter-page ads in the Sunday *Times* featuring cartoon drawings and boldfaced headlines to call attention to its special programs and ticket policies. One of its six ads, used to introduce its avant garde New Image of Sound Series, showed a pianist fending off a thrown tomato. The headline read, "They laughed when I sat down to play the piano, Ludwig van Beethoven." The text explained that "to the squares of 175 years or so ago, Beethoven was not considered to be such hot stuff . . . a little wild . . . a little outre. But somebody gave him an opportunity to be heard." (69)

———————◄●►———————

Insurance Firm Finds Music Broadcasts Pay

A business entering its sixth consecutive year as sponsor of a series of televised symphony concerts looks upon its sponsorship as good community relations and as a means of providing a high level program "in keeping with the image of our company we wish to present."

In Hartford, Connecticut, the Aetna Life Affiliated Companies presents a series of four monthly, one-hour concerts by the Hartford Symphony Orchestra over local television station WTIC and local radio stations WTIC-AM and FM. Each of the performances reaches an average audience of 220,000 persons in Connecticut and Western Massachusetts. It costs the company approximately $50,000 each year in time and talent fees to sustain the series.

Tied in with the series is a $1,000 music scholarship contest for state high school students. From nearly 300 students competing for the prize, a panel of judges headed by Fritz Mahler, the conductor of the symphony, narrows the group to three finalists, each of whom performs on one of the programs. The winner appears on the last program to perform and accept his prize.

According to Charles Dixon, superintendent of information services for Aetna, the company has reaped publicity from its sponsorship. Although executives of the company have actively worked with the Hartford Symphony and recently retired company board chairman Henry S. Beers was vice president of the Symphony Society, this had little or nothing to do with the company's sponsorship.   (24)

527

How Corning Blended Self-Help, Public Service

Why does a major corporation sponsor a cultural event? How does it combine public service with self-interest? The experience of the Corning Glass Works of Corning, N. Y. in sponsoring last fall's telecast of the opening of Lincoln Center gives insight into the present increase in business activities in the arts.

Corning manufactures 35,000 different glass products, mainly for industrial and technical use, but also for the consumer market. It spends a considerable amount on national advertising and retains Batten, Barton, Durstine and Osborn as its advertising agency.

Last summer B.B.D.O. proposed that Corning sponsor a "CBS Special" on the Lincoln Center premiere. It gave as its reasons:

1. The program would strengthen the company's identity. Customers now using one Corning product might think of Corning's name in connection with other products as well.

2. Dignified advertising could inform the industrial audience that Corning was capable of solving special production problems for them by making glass goods for specific purposes.

3. Since many of Corning's products are relatively new, and it is likely to be introducing additional items in the future, wide exposure of its name to the public would make new product introduction easier.

4. The program would build employee morale and enthusiasm.

These objectives could, however, have been accomplished through sponsorship of many different kinds of programs. Why the Lincoln Center opening? What quality could a cultural program impart to Corning's advertising that other types of programs could not? The answer: a connotation of "excellence." According to *Printer's Ink* magazine, an advertising trade journal, Corning "wanted to define 'excellence' and then transfer that definition to the screen."

Once Corning had decided to go ahead, B.B.D.O. developed a series of dignified and informative commercials—a total of 12 minutes in all.

To maximize their effect, Corning widely publicized the forthcoming telecast in advance, both by ads placed in local papers, and by mailing pieces to customers, employees and stockholders.

What were the results of the program?

1. According to Nielsen ratings and standard broadcast industry audience projections, a total of 28,000,000 Americans viewed the dazzling premiere.

2. The company received 552 letters, almost all of them praising it for its sponsorship, over half of them specifically approving the commercials. More important from Corning's point of view, many of the letters asked about its products.

3. Widespread comment in the nation's press mentioned Corning and some papers also took the trouble to praise its commercials.

4. Corning salesmen reported "an almost immediate" reaction to the program among their customers and potential customers.

5. Employees of Corning, according to a company spokesman, "found it exciting to be in the big league, and to be able to say, 'We sponsored the opening night at Lincoln Center.'" The company noted a new interest in "excellence," a perceptible pick-up in production, and a drop off in absenteeism and minor injuries.

6. There has been a notable rise in attendance at the company's "Glass Center"—a museum in Corning, N. Y.

Said *Printer's Ink,* quoting a B.B.D.O. official: "They got the right response from the right people."

Such results indicate that other companies can also, through imaginative cooperation with the arts, blend their own interests with programs of definite public service. (12)

Why Not Try a Free Billboard?

An arts message may sometimes be placed on a huge billboard at a shopping center or beside a highway completely free of charge, if the regional branch office of the General Outdoor Advertising Company is asked at the right time.

Since the company was organized in 1925, it has been General Outdoor policy to donate billboard space for all kinds of public service campaigns, provided space is open. The decision on whether to donate, and to whom, is made at each of 36 company branches in the U. S. and Canada. This spring, for example, the Washington, D. C. branch office donated five billboards, including the art work, to aid the National Symphony in its fund drive. In the summer of 1960 the company promoted museum attendance on a national scale with poster reproductions of old masters. (5)

AM Survey
The Arts Get a Free Ride On Public Transit Systems

Free advertising space on public transportation vehicles is available to cultural institutions and groups in 38 of 57 cities responding to a survey by *Arts Management.* Space for displaying posters in busses, subways and streetcars can be obtained at a fraction of its regular cost in 18 reporting cities. Only one transit advertising company in a single city flatly refused to offer special treatment to cultural institutions.

Members of the National Association of Transit Advertising, Inc., representing about three-fourths of the total transit advertising volume in the U. S., indicated a marked willingness to cooperate with arts groups. Many cautioned, however, that free space for poster cards is available only under certain conditions.

The first is that there be vacant space. In the words of one leading company, "Our ability to accommodate institutions . . . depends on space availabilities. Our principal business is to sell the advertising space at the full rate to regular advertisers."

Nearly all those offering special consideration to cultural groups also specify that they must be non-profit in character. Some add that they must not charge admission to the public. Several state that applicants must be "non-controversial". One company will not take ads announcing dates for an event, inasmuch as it cannot guarantee to find vacant space at the appropriate time.

In general, however, there is no restriction on the content of advertising, within the bounds of simple good taste. Nor is there a limit, except in a few cities, on the number of times a group may approach the advertising company for space.

Companies that do not offer free space, but that do offer reduced rates, generally charge between 20 per cent and 50 per cent of the standard price. Some charge a flat labor fee of 20 cents or 25 cents per card placed.

In all but one case, the institution is responsible for the preparation of its own posters. Costs for these vary widely, depending upon the materials used, the number of colors printed, and the number of cards required.

Requests for free or cut-rate advertising space should, in general, be addressed to the head of a transit advertising company in your community. Many of these companies are linked through ownership or association into regional or national networks. These make it possible for national cultural organizations, as distinct from local institutions, to place a message in busses, streetcars and subways in dozens of cities at one time—at little or no cost. (1)

PART FOUR: BUSINESS AND THE ARTS

Chapter VIII – Corporate Support

Chapter VIII – Corporate Support

THE RATIONALE AND THE ORGANIZED FORCES

Sorensen Sees New Corporate Obligations

By

Theodore C. Sorensen

I congratulate those firms with the vision to recognize—and the initiative to act upon—the unmistakable fact that corporate support of art or culture, or corporate wars on poverty or prejudice, are indeed in their enlightened self-interest. Their actions are not only profitable—they are commendable. But are they enough? Is self-interest, no matter how enlightened, ever enough? Is a corporation to support the arts, or to engage in other public-spirited activities, only when it can find an economic benefit? Are there no broader motivations, no higher obligations?

I believe there are. I believe that gradually, almost imperceptibly to many of those closest to the scene, the modern corporation has evolved into a social as well as an economic institution. Without losing sight of its need to make a profit, it has concerns and ideals and responsibilities which go far beyond the profit motive. It is no more expected to confine itself to economic issues than the modern clergyman is expected to speak only of religion, or the modern educator only of education. It has become, in effect, a full-fledged citizen, not only of the community in which it is located, but of the country and world we all inhabit. And

535

what would become of that country and world if all of its citizens acted only out of self-interest? What if every citizen supported art or public charities or took part in public affairs only in the expectation of an economic gain?

When I was a student of law, the old casebooks on corporation law laid the same stress on economic self-interest as the literature pertaining to this conference. The old common law rule required the showing of a direct corporate economic benefit before the corporation's funds could be used for any outside purpose.

Today, as a lawyer, I am willing to predict that the courts of our time, if necessary, would uphold corporation expenditures for the public good even without a showing of even indirect economic benefit to the corporation.

The trend of the law merely reflects the trend of history. Two world wars, a depression, a civil rights revolution, the effects of industrialization and automation, and a host of other changes have impressed upon our corporations their obligations of citizenship. The decline of kings and clergy as patrons of the arts, and the reduced proportion of great personal fortunes as the result of tax structures, have combined to increase the role and responsibility of the corporation. Business enterprises, like all other citizens, recognize now more clearly than ever that they can survive and succeed only in an atmosphere of liberty, progress and prosperity—and that that atmosphere must be nation-wide, not merely local.

No doubt, in this age of specialization, many business leaders will plead that they have no interest in problems outside their business. That we cannot afford. We are all citizens first and businessmen or lawyers or doctors or whatever second. The corporation's influence upon our country, its power for good and for progress, imposes upon it obligations of citizenship and leadership which it has no choice, but to accept—in support of good art, yes, and in support of the good society as well.   (49)

— ◆ —

Gingrich Cites Stanton Talk on Business and Arts

By

Arnold Gingrich

Speaking before a joint meeting of the Arts Council of Columbus, Ohio, and the Columbus Area Chamber of Commerce, Dr. Frank Stanton of CBS observed that business is learning that "it is not an island unto itself and that it both nourishes and is nourished by all those other activities that give any society character, richness, variety and meaning."

No more eloquent answer than Dr. Stanton's has been given to the isolationism of those die-hard Business Firsters, whose heads are still stuck ostrich-like beneath the barren sands of such bleak dicta as Cal Coolidge's "the business of America is business" and Engine Charlie Wilson's "What's good for General Motors is good for the country." In the Columbus speech, Dr. Stanton forecast a new degree of empathy between commerce, industry and the arts, "fostered by a new breed of American ... a breed in league with the arts"—one who "rejects an environment that says that the only concern of business is the 30-day balance sheet."

Those in the field of financing and managing of the arts, who must still contend with specimens of the old breed, can find not only consolation, but also ammunition in some of Dr. Stanton's remarks.

Here are some of the cogent reasons he cited to explain why alert business managements are now expressing greater interest in the arts: to attract a larger share to business of the country's graduating college students than the mere twelve per cent of them who now make it their first choice; to provide added incentive in recruiting able employees for plant communities; to earn and keep the respect of the nation's public and private sectors; to better the understanding of the human values of business; and to elevate the level of business communications.

Citing the great wave of corporate support of education in the eight years from 1956 to 1964, when it rose by 127 per cent, Dr. Stanton foresaw a similar wave in the offing of corporate support of the arts: "Education, generally, has a much more easily observed relationship with all other institutions than the arts do, but I don't believe that it has an any more valid one. And I am not sure that the arts are not ultimately the meeting ground where liberal education and progressive business come together. The purpose of liberal education is, basically, to enable us to make distinctions. The essence of successful business practice is to operate on distinctions. The arts carry distinctions to their logical, and very often their illogical, extremes. And so the first place to worry about American life losing its vital qualities of individualism is in the arts. If this happens, no liberal education will save our kind of society, and no business enterprise will long prosper in what is left of it."

In Dr. Stanton's view, "Art is not a remote thing, responsibility for which can be bucked over to some far center of funds or authority. It is the thing that preserves for all life—including business life and perhaps, in a complex industrial society, especially business life—the human scale."

These are brave words, and heartening—for they underline the fact that Dr. Stanton himself exemplifies the new breed of businessman, the rise of whose influence he foresees. (55)

◄●►

American Corporations Overseas Create New Image Through Arts

By

Robert E. Kingsley

We live in an era which is moving towards what McLuhan calls the "Global Village," when the proliferation of mass media offers unprecedented opportunities and perils. But, paradoxically, the communications gap between nations, between cultures, grows. Words have become weapons or, at best, too often are used to frustrate understanding and to magnify differences. Fortunately, we are coming to see that the arts and their creators can play a mediating role by forging links of mutual respect and appreciation.

It is not surprising that the modern business corporation abroad, which can survive and prosper best in an atmosphere of international good will, has come to be an enthusiastic patron of the arts. The example of my own company is cited only because it is familiar to me. Esso affiliates throughout the world have been leaders in sponsoring the plastic arts, literature, music and other art forms.

Our motivation has been clearcut: to establish, through the arts, a community of interest with the host nation, to become a part of its cultural life as well as contributing to its economic well-being. We bring to these countries our capital, technology and management skills; in return, we hope to enrich *ourselves* by supporting the artists and intellectuals whose contributions to the future are as significant as our own.

Quite honestly, the overseas U. S. corporation is at times victimized by unreasoning nationalism which rejects everything foreign. The other side of the coin is the widespread belief, especially in underdeveloped areas, that the U. S. expatriate or businessman has little interest and less respect for the national culture. Yet both industry and the arts are needed if a nation is to develop to the full its material and cultural life.

I realize that in many ways Esso and other progressive U. S. corporations have been subversive in undermining the stereotype of callous and exploitive business. Our support of the arts has been one element in shattering the false image of U. S. business abroad. But it has brought us, more than any other effort has, closer to the creative people who are fashioning the new world in which we all want to live.   (62)

Public Relations Counsel Helps Spur Corporate Support of Arts

By

William Ruder

The public relations counselor is becoming increasingly effective as a management member of the American corporation. This gives him added leverage in the role he plays of helping to shape the relationship between the corporation and the arts. Furthermore, the "corporate conscience" has become more and more an area of public relations responsibility. Finally, the corporation has faced the inescapable fact that it must participate in the arena of public issues. It must take a stand. It must be involved in the social turmoil around us. This set of involvements is also part of the responsibility of the public relations counselor.

Some of us in the public relations field have discovered that the arts can become an important instrument through which corporate commitment to good citizenship can be expressed. We have also discovered that the arts speak in a universal language—and this can be most helpful in an environment in which the noise level is as high as it is in America.

We have found that through the arts we can express both our good citizenship and also develop a technique for communications that can reach individuals and groups as perhaps no other technique can. If the arts speak a universal language and have an ability to reach and touch as does nothing else—and if the corporation can build a communications program that includes art of real quality and integrity within it, then there is a unique set of forces at work.

These discoveries have been made only lately by some of us, though of course, the objective facts have been there waiting to be discovered for many years. But perhaps, these are the times that will tend to encourage a little venturesomeness and a little discovery.

The public relations field, as ''keepers of the conscience,'' as corporate communicators, and as participants in the development of corporate policy where it becomes part of public policy, can help to encourage a relationship between the arts and the business enterprise which can become one of the few clear channels through which society's and the corporation's interest can mutually be solved.   (63)

Group Formed to Spur Corporate Aid to Arts

A national advisory organization of corporate executives, created to spur increased business support to the arts, has just been organized and expects to be fully operational by January 1968. Called the Business Committee for the Arts, the group traces its origins back to a proposal made by David Rockefeller, president of the Chase Manhattan Bank, in an address to the annual meeting of the National Industrial Conference Board in September 1966. Mr. Rockefeller, at the time, proposed the establishment of a national council on business and the arts, to be composed of businessmen knowledgeable in the arts, cultural leaders and representative artists, whose purpose would be to broaden the base of corporate support to cultural organizations.

The positive response to his suggestion prompted Mr. Rockefeller to meet with other top corporate leaders and plan the development of the new organization. As now constituted, the committee will include 75 to 80 members, all top corporate officers, at the level of executive vice president and higher. The committee, to be located at 1270 Avenue of the Americas, New York City, will be chaired by C. Douglas Dillon, former Secretary of the Treasury and now president of the United States and Foreign Securities Corporation.

From within the overall membership, a board of directors and an executive committee of some six to ten members will be drawn. The new group will serve in an advisory capacity and while it will suggest ways in which corporations can assist the arts, it will not be a grant-giving organization itself. The committee hopes to support its activities through funds provided by a consortium of foundations.

Although cultural leaders and artists will not be included on the committee, as was originally proposed by Mr. Rockefeller, G. A. McLellan, who was recently hired as the committee's president, told *AM* that his organization will work closely with national arts organizations in the development of its program. Mr. McLellan, former administrative director of Plans for Progress and most recently director of public affairs at Olin Mathieson, outlined five working objectives of the committee: to research information on support of the arts for the business community; to counsel corporations interested in aiding the arts; to develop a nationwide public information program to inform corporations of new opportunities for support of the arts and to apprise art groups of corporate activity in the arts; to assist cultural organizations in presentations to corporations and encourage participation by businessmen in arts groups; and to represent business in cooperative endeavors with arts organizations and governmental arts agencies.

Most members of the committee will be drawn from large corporations, but several smaller firms will be represented as well. Both a geographic and industrial balance will be maintained. The group plans to hold its first meeting in January 1968. (57)

Chambers of Commerce Supporting the Arts

Chambers of Commerce are taking an increasingly active role in supporting arts activities in their communities, according to the results of a recently completed *Arts Management* survey. A detailed questionnaire drew responses from chambers in 181 cities in 44 states throughout the country. Responding chambers represent more than 125,000 business members.

Strikingly evident from survey results is the fact that chambers are establishing closer ties with their local arts groups. Seventy chambers, 40 per cent of those responding to the question, indicated that they have created special committees on the arts, with 33 of them organized within the past three years. Five other chambers include the arts in civic affairs or recreation committees. An *AM* chamber survey five years ago revealed that only 27.9 per cent of responding chambers had such committees. In the first three months of 1967 alone, eight chambers created new cultural committees and others are now being organized.

As another indication of increasing chamber interest in the arts, a surprisingly high 18.7 per cent of the chambers reported that they have published special brochures or pamphlets devoted to the arts of their communities. These ranged from mimeographed publications prepared at virtually no cost by two chambers in Indiana, to handsome brochures costing thousands of dollars.

In Winston-Salem, N. C., a chamber-published arts brochure cost $5,000; a report on the arts in Dallas cost the chamber $7,500; and a 1963 Atlanta, Ga. chamber brochure cost $12,000. The Houston, Texas chamber published brochures on the arts in 1963 and 1965, and the Minneapolis, Minn. chamber has twice published cultural brochures as a supplement to other chamber publications. Some chambers, such as those in Springdale, Ark. and Orlando, Fla., have published brochures for special arts events.

Some arts groups are receiving direct financial assistance from chambers in their communities. Nearly 20 per cent of responding chambers answered yes to the question: "Does your chamber make financial contributions to any local cultural organization or institution?" In Dayton, Ohio, the chamber contributes $6,000 to local arts organizations and produces 18 summer concerts in cooperation with the city and the local musicians' union at a total cost of $25,000. The Beloit, Wisc. chamber contributes $2,500 to a local art gallery; chambers in Hollywood, Fla. and Hartford, Conn. each contribute $1,500 to concert series; and the Asheville, N. C. chamber contributes $1,125 to the Thomas Wolfe Theatre.

Music and arts festivals receive financial support from chambers in North Little Rock, Ark., Harlan, Ky., Savannah, Ga., Kirkwood, Mo., Asheville, N. C., and Pawtucket, R. I. The Winter Park, Fla. chamber contributes $500 to the local symphony and the Amarillo, Texas chamber donates $500 to its fine arts council.

In Cherokee, Iowa, the chamber, in addition to contributing $100 to the arts council, spent more than $500, plus hundreds of hours of contributed time, to help promote a bond issue for a new community center. The Alhambra, Calif. chamber purchases the prize for an art competition. In Flagstaff, Ariz. the chamber helps finance the printing of brochures by various arts groups.

Over 80 per cent of responding chambers provide nonfinancial services to local arts groups. Although the most common form of assistance is the promotion and publicity of cultural events, chamber help is wide-ranging and varied. Chambers in Fort Dodge, Iowa, Louisville, Ky., and Oklahoma City, Okla., for example, offer counsel in fund raising campaigns. The Beckley, W. Va. chamber raises money for the West Virginia Historical Drama Association, and the Cincinnati, Ohio chamber "highlighted the need for business support of the Playhouse in the Park."

In a number of communities, chambers furnish meeting facilities for arts groups and provide secretarial and administrative services. The McKeesport, Pa. chamber provides quarters for its symphony orchestra, and the Hollywood, Fla. chamber does bookkeeping for its symphony. In Denver, Colo., the chamber helped establish the western offices of the National Folk Festival and in Orlando, Fla., the chamber is helping to organize a community arts council. Other chambers maintain arts calendars, help organize festivals, and present arts awards.

The Houston, Texas chamber, for example, conceived, organized and sponsored the city's first comprehensive arts festival, held in October, 1966. Two years of advance effort preceded the month-long program.

In Ypsilanti, Mich., the chamber is trying to save the Greek Theatre, which presented its first season last summer, but has been forced to cancel the 1967 season because of financial difficulties. The chamber has agreed to take over business management of the theater at the request of the theater's board of directors. In an attempt to insure a 1968 season, chamber members have been contacting foundations and soliciting funds.

How important are the arts in attracting tourists to a city? Only 6.8 per cent of responding chambers view the arts as a prime factor; 29.0 per cent see it as very important; 46.6 per cent see it as moderately important; and 17.6 per cent find the arts an insignificant tourist attraction.

The arts, however, play a more prominent role in attracting new industry to communities. Although only 3.4 per cent of the chambers see the arts as a prime factor, nearly 46 per cent consider the arts a very important factor and 39.8 per cent indicate that cultural activities are moderately important. The other 10.8 per cent view the arts as an insignificant factor.

One hundred and twenty five chambers estimated the percentage of their member companies making direct financial contributions to arts groups. The responses were: fewer than 10 per cent—thirty one chambers; 10 to 25 per cent—forty four; 25 to 50—twenty six; 50 to 75—fifteen; and over 75 per cent—nine chambers.   (55)

———— ◆ ————

Chamber of Commerce Spurs Arts in City

An important chamber of commerce program in Oklahoma City has provided a strong stimulus to the growth and maintenance of arts organizations there. Almost all the city's leading cultural institutions, including its symphony orchestra, its arts center, its theater and its museum, were established with the help of the chamber and have received its continuing support.

The chamber has mobilized the leadership and resources of the community to heighten local interest in the arts. "This goal has been consistently set forth throughout the years in the chamber's policies and projects, alongside the goals for industrial and commercial development," Lola Hall, secretary of the chamber's Committee on Education and the Arts, told *AM*.

As part of its policy, the chamber has frequently played an important role in leading fund raising drives to meet the financial needs of the city's cultural institutions. In 1962, the chamber helped to organize a special Danny Kaye Benefit Concert and Symphony Maintenance Fund Campaign, on behalf of the Oklahoma City Symphony, an orchestra it helped to found in 1938. More than $153,000 was raised in a single night to help the orchestra pay its accumulated debts and to place it on a sound financial footing. In addition, the chamber was instrumental in instituting the regularly scheduled network broadcasts of the orchestra which have been heard throughout the country for 20 years.

Another local group which has been aided by the chamber is the Mummers Theatre. In 1963, the Ford Foundation offered the theater a matching grant of $700,000 for a home and equipment. The chamber led an intensive, two-week

547

campaign in which the grant was more than matched by $750,000 raised from civic leaders.

The chamber also led a drive which resulted in the location in Oklahoma City of the National Cowboy Hall of Fame and Western Heritage Center, built by the 17 Western States. Oklahoma's share of $1,000,000 toward the center was raised through a drive spearheaded by the chamber.

To accelerate future cultural growth in the community, the chamber helped to establish the Oklahoma City Industrial and Cultural Facilities Trust last year. Funds from the trust were instrumental in financing the completion of the Cowboy Hall of Fame and in helping it to acquire a $1,000,000 collection of Charles M. Russell art.

Oklahoma City University, a large contributor to the city's cultural life, has benefited greatly from chamber support and leadership. Stanley Draper, managing director of the chamber, is chairman of the school's Campus Development Committee, with which the chamber worked to develop the university's plan to expand its facilities. Currently, a $600,000 addition to the university's music school is being undertaken. This addition will include space for speech, drama and ballet activities.

Other groups which the chamber supports are the Oklahoma City Junior Symphony, the Civic Music Association, (Mr. Draper is a member of the board of both) the Chamber Music Series and the Oklahoma City Civic Ballet. The chamber was instrumental in establishing the Oklahoma Art Center in 1935 and has given the institution its continued support from the beginning.   (47)

Businesswomen Aid Arts

Businesswomen are a new group to lend assistance to the arts. In Anaheim, California, 230 members of the Women's Division of the Anaheim Chamber of Commerce, have developed a widespread cultural program. This year, for example, the group co-sponsored and coordinated Anaheim Cultural Arts Month and the Carousel of Anaheim, a two-day community-wide arts festival. Through its cultural arts committee, the group has developed art exhibitions, sponsored an annual lecture and concert series, and assisted the local arts council. It is now planning to publish a brochure, *The Cultural Arts of Anaheim,* to be based on its survey of arts activity in the community.   (63)

A Chamber of Commerce Has Ten Year Arts Plan

The main program focus of a Southern chamber of commerce during the next decade will be on the arts. The Greensboro, North Carolina chamber, which celebrated its 90th anniversary last year, is planning for its centennial with a multi-faceted cultural program which will be climaxed by the presentation of a new symphonic drama in 1977.

As the first step in its ten year arts program, the chamber recently underwrote the engagement of Thomas Cousins for a two-year period as Greensboro's composer-in-residence. Cousins is the former conductor of the Greensboro Symphony Orchestra and former faculty member at the University of North Carolina in Greensboro. The chamber has also commissioned a work of sculpture, which, when

549

completed next month, will be placed in the downtown business area.

Among its other programs, the chamber is planning a study of the community's historic sites for restoration, a survey of Greensboro's cultural resources, and a closer liaison with the Greensboro Arts Council.

Members of another Southern chamber of commerce, in Jackson, Mississippi, provided unique assistance to the American Symphony Orchestra League. When the chamber's members learned that the League had been trying for two years to find funds to purchase a station wagon for the use of its headquarters staff, they raised the funds and presented the money to the Jackson Symphony League for transmittal to the ASOL. An official presentation of the automobile was made at a board meeting of the ASOL's Women's Council in Chicago last month. (59)

Key Business Group Features Arts in Program

Quietly, and without fanfare, an international organization with more than 2,300 top business leaders as members, has developed a significant program of education and idea exchange which includes the arts as one of its key aspects. The Young Presidents' Organization, which limits its membership to men and women who became the chief operating officers or presidents of their companies before their 40th birthday, (there are qualifying requirements also as to company size and business volume) emphasizes self-development for its members in all areas of personal and public responsibility. Although primary emphasis is on business subjects, the arts are regularly included as topics in na-

550

tional and regional meetings, and they have been the feature subject for national symposia as well.

This fall, for example, Y.P.O. will sponsor its fourth annual symposium on the arts at Lincoln Center. Open to all members, the program includes lectures on cultural topics by arts leaders and members' attendance at performances. The four areas of discussion are theater, ballet, opera and music.

In the spring of 1967, Y.P.O. sponsored a five-day West Coast Cultural Seminar in Los Angeles, which included visits to leading museums in the area, tours of U.C.L.A.'s fine and performing arts facilities, and a full-day at the Los Angeles Music Center for tours, meetings and attendance at a concert. Special class sessions, with faculty drawn from Los Angeles area cultural groups, rounded out the program for corporation presidents.

The annual University for Presidents, a week-long international gathering of Y.P.O. members, has included the arts as one of its four permanent divisions since 1967. The educationally-oriented program features approximately 100 different courses for attendees. At this year's University, held in Puerto Rico in April, R. Philip Hanes, Jr., vice-chairman of Associated Councils of the Arts, and a Y.P.O. member, served as arts dean, and Ralph Burgard, executive director of A.C.A., was his assistant. Members of the arts faculty were Maria Tallchief, Philip Johnson, Stan Vanderbeek, Jonathan Williams and Jules Irving, who discussed such subjects as the new theater and its significance to the community, new poetry, and architectural decay.

In addition to the programs Y.P.O. presents on a national and international level, it offers many additional meetings and seminars at the area level (the organization is divided into 11 major areas throughout the world) and at the chapter level. Each of the 35 chapters in the United States and in

30 foreign countries develops its own monthly program, independent of the international organization, and frequently
the arts are featured.

Although Y.P.O. as an organization does not underwrite
outside cultural activities or programs, its commitment to
betterment, and its treatment of the arts as an essential aspect of everyday life, is precedent-setting.   (61)

————————————◄●►————————————

Organized Labor Backs Pilot Arts Program

Greater support of the arts by organized labor is in the
offing. As a first step in this direction, the AFL-CIO's Department of Community Services, headed by national director, Leo Perlis, in cooperation with S.P.A.C.E., a group of
unions representing scientific, professional and cultural employees, is sponsoring a one-year demonstration project in
the arts which is being launched in four cities this year—
New York, Minneapolis, Louisville and Buffalo. If successful, the program will be expanded to include other cities
throughout the country. According to Mr. Perlis, "This is
the first time in the history of the labor movement that the
involvement of labor in the arts is being organized in a dis-
ciplined fashion."

The current program traces its beginnings back to the
annual meetings of the AFL-CIO in San Francisco two
years ago, when a resolution calling for greater labor participation in the arts was adopted in principle. The resolution
was then referred to the organization's executive council
which appointed a special subcommittee to study labor's
relationship to the arts. The subcommittee, after surveying
the activities of labor unions in the arts, recommended the
current program. Recently, Harlowe F. Dean, who will work

out of Washington, D. C., was named overall administrator for the program.

The cities picked for the demonstration program were selected from a list of 12 original possibilities on the basis of interested central labor leadership, an active community services program, good local cultural resources, and geographical location. In each of the cities, the labor leadership will take inventory of cultural facilities in the community, survey the current status of local labor participation in the arts, organize two-day seminars bringing together arts and labor leaders, and then develop a list of practical projects. Among the projects which Mr. Perlis told *AM* would be undertaken were: labor support in financing cultural programs; its sponsorship of special arts programs in schools and in poverty areas; the free use of union halls for performances; the organization of labor tours to museums; greater labor involvement on cultural boards; and arranging for arts leaders to speak regularly at local union meetings.

In Minneapolis, for example, Frank Sugrue, a representative of the national Department of Community Services, spent three days speaking to local arts leaders and union members recently to win their support for the program there. Plans for a seminar involving the arts and labor have been developed and business agents representing all member groups of the Central Labor Council have been meeting with officials of the Minneapolis Institute of Art in the hopes of developing a joint program.

Although funding of each demonstration project will be the responsibility of organized labor in the participating cities, the AFL-CIO, in its original resolution, appropriated $10,000 for the project. The national organization is now attempting to find additional funds for the project from various sources, including the Endowment for the Arts.

553

The program is a modest one, but as Mr. Perlis pointed out, "This is not a one-shot idea. We want to do a thorough program on a continuing basis." He admitted to *AM*, however, that the project is not on the high priority list of the AFL-CIO. (59)

Business & Arts Equal Partners in New Council

A Pioneer corporate aid to the arts program organized by the New York Board of Trade six years ago, has been restructured to include *equal* arts and business representation within its committee membership. The New Arts & Business Cooperative Council, which replaces the Board's Business and the Arts Advisory Council, plans to promote corporate support for all arts programs regardless of size, and serve as a business-arts voice on vital issues concerning the arts in the city.

As its first public action, the new committee presented a program for businessmen at Lincoln Center's Forum theater honoring neighboring arts activities and featuring brief performances by four community cultural groups. At the program, the committee announced that through it, Standard Oil of New Jersey had made a $52,500 grant to New York's borough arts councils to encourage cultural programs at the community level, and to enable the councils to continue their administrative services. (71)

Company Hires Culture Head, Nation's First

In a precedent-setting move, a leading American corporation, Dayton Hudson of Minneapolis, has filled a new slot in the business hierarchy—corporate director of cultural affairs. The position, believed to be the nation's first corporate job with full-time executive responsibility in the arts, will be manned as of January 2, 1973 by Orrel Thompson, former director of the Art Institute of Akron, Ohio. Elsewhere, other key developments are focusing increased national attention on the business role in the arts.

One of the nation's largest retailers with operations in 26 states and annual sales exceeding $1-billion, Dayton Hudson has long been involved in supporting cultural programs in cities where its department stores are located. One of the few companies to utilize its full five per cent tax deductible allowance for contributions, it has twice won the Esquire/BCA Business in the Arts Award.

The decision to create the new post was reached several months ago by board chairman Bruce Dayton and trustees of the Dayton Hudson Foundation who recognized the company's growing role in cultural affairs. "We decided that our principal thrust will be in the arts," said Robert W. MacGregor, vice president and executive director of the Dayton Hudson Foundation. "Instead of giving to everyone, a concentration of effort in the arts, under the professional direction of Mr. Thompson, will help us to use our funds more effectively and bring maximum benefits to the groups and artists we help."

In his new position Thompson will be responsible for coordinating the existing corporate arts program, after evaluating present priorities and developing sound criteria for arts support. He will establish also a program of continuing education and communications in the arts for company employees and develop, with the help of cultural groups and community leaders, new projects in a wide range of areas. He indicated to *AM,* however, that the overall Dayton Hudson arts program will take time to develop. "We can't establish a program in a vacuum," he said. "Before we can develop a serious program we will have to get out and explore where the needs are."

In a discussion with *Arts Management,* Thompson pinpointed some of the areas that he hopes to explore in the coming months including the development of far-reaching arts programs for shopping centers, free consultative help to cultural groups, discount ticket distribution to employees, lecture and dialogue programs in theater and music for community groups, and development of working statewide arts-business coalitions.

"We're looking to develop an exemplary arts program," he added, "which can demonstrate to other corporations what can be done. It's our goal to establish the kind of program that can help the cities in which we're located become major cultural centers."

Elsewhere, a government agency has become interested in the arts-business relationship. The United States Information Agency is now involved in the planning stages of an exhibit on business and the arts which, when completed sometime in the spring of 1973, will be offered to the 120 USIA agencies throughout the world for their possible use. Included in the exhibit will be articles and books, films, and visual materials.

Organizationally, there are continued developments of interest. The Business Committee for the Arts sponsored pilot business-arts meetings this fall in Wisconsin, Southern California and Oklahoma and full state-wide conferences in Indiana and Louisiana. Eight or nine additional meetings are expected to be held by mid-1973.

In New York City, the Arts & Business Cooperative Council of the New York Board of Trade, established seven years ago as the first organization of its kind, will take on a new structure and an important new role soon. The Council, an equal representation group of business and arts leaders, has just been incorporated as a not-for-profit organization and under its new name, the Arts & Business Council of New York City, Inc., will operate as an entity separate from the Board of Trade. This status will allow the Council to become a tax exempt body with a new action role—obtaining contributions from business to make grants to arts programs and cultural group in New York City.

Corporate involvement in the arts is attracting editorial attention as well. The *Harvard Business Review* is planning several future articles on the subject and this January, *The American Way,* the in-flight magazine of American Airlines which is read by hundreds of thousands of businessmen, features an illustrated cover story on the subject by *AM* editor Alvin H. Reiss. (78)

———◄●►———

CORPORATE DONATIONS, PROGRAM SPONSORSHIP AND COMMERCIAL INVOLVEMENT

Bank Becomes Partner in State Arts Project

State arts councils have found a new partner to assist them in the support of local and state-wide cultural programs—private corporations. In Maryland, the state council and the Maryland National Bank are co-sponsoring performances by Baltimore's Center Stage in communities throughout the state. The Council, which hopes that the example set by the bank may influence other corporations to support activities, claims that "it is the first time that a business organization and a state arts council have collaborated on a major arts project." The bank's total financial commitment to the project is $8,000.

In the pilot phase of the program, the Center Stage presented performances of *Pictures in the Hallway* in Salisbury and Hagerstown in November. Based on a favorable response to these performances, the Council now hopes to expand the program so that performances will blanket the entire state after the first of the year. Other productions to be presented including *Waiting for Godot, Under Milk Wood* and *The Marriage Proposal.*

As a follow-up, the Council is now planning the development of an advisory panel on business support. This small group of top corporate executives will work with the Council to help it uncover new sources of corporate support.

· In a separate project, the Council is now involved in discussions with a major national business concern regarding its support of a state-wide student art competition. "The development of meaningful business support for the arts," Mr. Marchand told *AM,* "is a major concern of the Council."

Meanwhile, in Wellsville, New York, a top local corporation, concerned with the paucity of professional arts attractions available to its employees and to community residents, approached the New York State Council on the Arts for help in developing a continuing cultural program. The query from the Air Preheater Company prompted the Council to send two staff members to Wellsville to meet with local leaders and officials of the corporation.

As a result of the meetings and the advice of Council officials, the new Wellsville Performing Arts Council was established, a performing arts series of four evening concerts and four free children's matinees was scheduled, and plans were developed to use the town library for traveling art exhibitions circulated throughout the state by the Council. Moreover, the Air Preheater Company agreed to underwrite all concert series costs not defrayed by ticket sales. The Council has continued to assist the new venture by providing technical assistance services to the neophyte community organization in such areas as organizational development, membership campaign, box office procedures, promotion and publicity, and ticket sales.

The community reacted enthusiastically to the new program and its three leading service organizations agreed to help sell series tickets and assist in promotion. The local newspaper responded with a long editorial calling for local support of the program and with continuing news stories. The editorial said, in part, "This is the first opportunity in some time for large scale participation in a series of cultural performances of a high order brought here for the primary benefit of area residents. The projected series is a highly commendable response by the Air Preheater Company, together with a number of civic-minded citizens and organizations, to the growing hunger in this region for improved cultural opportunity ... It is now up to the residents of this area to ensure the success of the project through strong support.''

Elsewhere, the Missouri State Council on the Arts, faced with the prospect of producing its first annual report, but lacking publication funds in its budget, turned to local corporations for assistance. As a result, seven Missouri firms underwrote the total cost of publishing the recently issued Missouri State Council on the Arts 1965-66 Annual Report, which summarizes the Council's accomplishments during its first two years of operation. The report is a handsomely designed and illustrated 40-page brochure with a two-color front and back cover featuring a reproduction of a work by St. Louis artist and sculptor, Ernest Trova.

In addition to providing financial support, one of the corporations, Hallmark Cards, Inc., of Kansas City, also contributed design, layout and production services for the report. Other firms who shared the publication costs were: the Kansas City Life Insurance Company; First National Bank of Joplin; Commerce Trust Company of Kansas City; Westab, Inc., a subsidiary of Meade Corporation, in St. Joseph; First National Bank of Kansas City; and Kansas City Southern Railway Lines.   (58)

Banks and Other Business Groups Aid the Arts

A leading New York bank was so impressed with the results of the first arts project it sponsored that it immediately undertook sponsorship of a second program. Subsequently it voted to allot 10 to 15 per cent of its 1967 advertising budget to the support of cultural programs.

Although several board members of the Trade Bank and Trust Company were personally interested and involved in the arts, the bank itself, had never considered sponsoring a cultural program. However, after several bank executives attended a conference on business in the arts at Lincoln Center last spring, at the urging of its sponsor, the Arts Advisory Council of the New York Board of Trade, their interest was stirred and they asked the Council if there were any projects which needed corporate support. The result, achieved after resistance by some bank board members was overcome, was the sponsorship of an exhibition of Herbert Migdoll dance photographs at Lincoln Center's Philharmonic Hall last fall. The exhibit was subsequently shown at the Museum and Library of Performing Arts, again under the bank's sponsorship, and at the bank's main office and two of its branches.

The exhibit drew a favorable response from the public and the press. As a result, the bank experienced little resistance in selling its board on sponsorship of a second program, "The Arts in Your Life," a series of six evening programs designed to introduce young people to the performing and visual arts. The programs, which are being held monthly through May 1967, at New York's Fashion Institute of Technology, feature demonstrations, performances and discussions by such groups as the New York City Ballet, the APA-Phoenix Theatre, and the New York City Opera. The final event in the series will feature a "happening" created by Michael Kirby.

Last month, following the successful first performance in the new series, the bank board voted to donate a percentage of this year's advertising budget to the support of arts programs. "Although we had to be sold initially on support of the arts," said bank vice-president Lawrence A. Meyers, "we're convinced now. In fact, our recently completed stockholders' report contained a page commenting on our sponsorship of cultural programs."

Other banks have also been active in supporting cultural events recently. In North Carolina, six banks are sponsoring performances of *Shakespeare Scene by Scene* in state public schools for the second consecutive year. In Baltimore, Maryland, the Equitable Bank and Trust Company sponsored seven free performances of Moliere's *The Miser* by the Center Stage at an estimated cost of $20,000.

In other instances of corporate involvement in the arts, Circle F Industries announced its sponsorship of an art exhibition, "Focus on Light," to be held at the New Jersey State Museum in Trenton beginning this May, and the Boston Herald-Traveler Corporation, which owns three newspapers and a radio and television station, announced that it was underwriting the complete costs of the first American Festival of Music '67, a four-day event to be held this April in Boston. For the past two years, the Herald-Traveler Corporation has sponsored a local repertory drama program.

Meanwhile, in Winston-Salem, North Carolina, the local Chamber of Commerce published 5,000 copies of a handsomely designed brochure titled, *The Arts in Winston-Salem: A Working Partner.* Especially significant is the fact that nowhere in the color brochure does the Chamber mention its role in the production of the publication.   (54)

--- ◆ ---

Survey Shows Increased Corporate Aid to Arts

Corporate support to the arts is increasing—it has quintupled in the past decade—but much more is needed if the problems of the arts are to be alleviated. This is one of the conclusions reached in the nation's first comprehensive survey of business support of the arts, undertaken by the National Industrial Conference Board on behalf of the Business Committee for the Arts. The completed survey is based on the results of a detailed seven-page questionnaire sent to corporations of varying sizes last summer, with 500 of the questionnaires selected at random for inclusion in the study.

Nearly 70 per cent of the respondents, 345 of 500 corporations, said they contributed to the arts. Based on BCA/NICB projections and interpolations with other studies, the report estimates that corporate contributions of funds and gifts in kind to the arts in 1968 totalled $45-million. This amount was nearly equalled, according to the report, by the additional $40-million corporations gave to the arts in 1968 through business expenses—items carried on the corporate books as advertising or promotional expenses, rather than contributions.

What kind of corporation is most likely to support the arts? A profile drawn from the survey shows it to be a relatively small, nonmanufacturing, publicly-held company, with fewer than 1,000 employees, which is primarily concerned with local markets. The most favored areas of corporate arts support are symphony orchestras, museums and cultural and civic centers in that order. Least popular are donations to experimental art forms and composers.

The survey explores many other aspects of corporate support in detail, including the rationale for giving and for non-giving. A complete analysis is contained in the newly-published B.C.A. book, *Business and the Arts '70.*

(67)

Canadian Firm Starts Million Dollar Arts Fund

In an unusual action which suggests a new model for corporations interested in aiding the arts, a Canadian cigarette manufacturer has established a performing arts council and committed $1-million to its support over the next five years. The du Maurier Council for the Performing Arts, with Canadian Senator Donald Cameron as chairman and four leaders of the arts and education communities as directors, will operate independent of its benefactor, du Maurier Cigarettes, in providing grants to existing Canadian performing arts groups. Emphasis will be on broadening the general public for the arts.

Over the years, du Maurier has been an active contributor to a variety of performing arts activities. The new program will enable it to maintain its involvement and support—its coordinator of arts activities will serve as liaison to the council—while removing from it the burden and responsibility of selecting grant recipients. Moreover, the cigarette company has agreed to provide marketing and public relations help to groups sponsored by the council. Organized in December, the council will meet twice a year to select grant recipients. As one of its initial actions it announced grants to six leading Canadian symphony orchestras in support of their special "pops" concert series. (74)

Marketing Firm Finds Corporations to Fund Arts

A commercial marketing firm, whose involvement in the arts is recent, helped to win corporate support for a costly national cultural program—and won itself an arts client in the process. The program was the first annual American College Theatre Festival, which brought together ten college theater companies for two weeks of performances in Washington, D.C.'s historic Ford's Theatre and newly-built Theatre on the Mall this spring. The performing troupes were selected from 176 colleges in a nation-wide competition which began last fall. The commercial firm was the National Student Marketing Corporation, which develops programs to help clients sell their products and services to high school and college customers.

Initially, the Festival producers, the American Educational Theatre Association and the American National Theatre and Academy, won corporate support on their own, when American Airlines responded to their proposal to become one of the Festival's three official sponsors, along with the Smithsonian Institution and the Friends of the John F. Kennedy Center. When it became evident, however, that the ambitious undertaking would require additional funds, an American Airlines public relations executive suggested that, because of the Festival's college orientation, the producers ask NSMC to help. The marketing firm had recently established a creative arts division under Mitchell Nestor, a former off-Broadway producer and director.

It was Nestor's job to put together a marketing package which he could sell to a corporate client—one which would win dollars for the Festival without exploiting it and at the same time, win good program identification for the corporate underwriter. He found the package in a souvenir journal and the company in the Chrysler Corporation.

In Chrysler's behalf, National Student Marketing prepared Festival journals and posters and distributed

565

500,000 of each of them to college campuses throughout the country, sent out releases on college productions entered regionally in the competition and gave away tape recorders to college theater departments. Chrysler, for the considerable amount of money it invested in the Festival, won the youth identification it sought. It received recognition as underwriters of the journal, had six pages of ads and editorial copy within the publication and was identified on all the posters.

Nestor and NSMC were to play one more vital role in the Festival. One of the sponsors, the Smithsonian Institution, was looking for a corporation to underwrite the $50,000 cost of the Theatre on the Mall, which was to be used for a variety of summer arts programs as well as for Festival productions. NSMC found an "angel"—Pepsi-Cola. (65)

Business Approach

Approaches to business for support should be made in a business-like manner. With this in mind, the Arts Council of Winston-Salem, North Carolina, asked business to support its annual fund raising drive in a letter accompanied by four pages of exhibits to show where contributed money would go. One point underscored by the arts council was that "many persons who make up your company's corporate family and their wives serve as directors or perform numerous of the tasks for member groups." The thought was backed up with statistics. (38)

A Dollar a Month

Many businesses now have "Buck of the Month" clubs where employees grant management the right to deduct $1.00 each month from their paychecks as donations to worthwhile causes. In plans of this type, employees are given an opportunity to select the organizations they wish to aid. Arts groups should seek out the businesses in their areas which have such plans, and then present their case for support to these companies and to their employees so as to be included in the plans. (33)

Annual Corporate Donations

Make sure that companies who have contributed to your fund drive in the past are gently reminded when contribution time comes around again. *AM* learned of one recent instance where a secretary, typing a corporation's annual contribution list, forgot to inspect one sheet of paper. The result? An arts group and several other nonprofit organizations failed to receive their annual contributions. (56)

Business Helps Neighborhood Arts

Neighborhood cultural groups in New York City have found a staunch advocate in a top corporation, Standard Oil of New Jersey. The company, which contributed more than $50,000 to the city's borough arts councils last year to encourage community-based cultural activity, has since stepped up its involvement. This summer it sponsored the Fiesta at Fordham, a two-week program of free performances by the Alliance of Latin Arts and underwrote the cost of an outside wall mural at the Henry Street Settlement Theatre by the Cityarts Workshop.

Early this fall the company premiered a new film documentary on neighborhood arts activity. *Hometown,* a 33-minute color film underwritten by Standard Oil and produced by the Arts and Business Council of the New York Board of Trade, depicts the activities of six performing arts groups in New York's five boroughs. *Hometown* will be shown overseas by the United States Information Agency and is available without charge from the distributors, A. A. Schechter Associates, 551 Fifth Avenue, New York, N.Y. 10017, for showings in America. A separate 28-minute version is available for television.

Standard Oil has agreed also, to underwrite all administrative costs of a massive new cultural auction, "The Possible Dream," for the benefit of New York City's community arts groups. The program, patterned after auctions held in St. Louis and elsewhere will culminate in a series of fall 1973 fund-raising events including community auctions and a gala dinner auction. Incorporated as an activity of the New York Board of Trade's Educational Foundation, the "Dream" will be administered as a united fund by a professional staff with proceeds to be disseminated by the borough arts councils to neighborhood arts activities. (76)

Brochure for Business

If your organization solicits funds from business and industry, a special brochure concisely setting forth your purposes can be an effective tool for reaching this audience. The Carnegie Institute of Technology, in Pittsburgh, for example, publishes a two-color, six-page brochure which, on the cover bears the message that "Carnegie Tech Gratefully Acknowledges . . . the support of Business and Industry." Inside, the brochure goes on to point out the many and varied services that the university provides for these sources and then lists companies as well as associations and organizations which contribute to its support.   (33)

––––––––––– ◄●► –––––––––––

Arts Score Low in Corporate Giving Plan

The arts fared poorly in an unusual corporate philanthropic program which could influence the giving pattern of American business. This summer, the *Reader's Digest* gave its staff members more than $500,000 to donate to non-profit organizations of their choice. The arts received less than $8,000 of the total contributed.

Of significance to cultural organizations is the fact that other corporations have expressed interest in the plan, according to DeWitt Wallace, owner and editor of the magazine. If the plan wins wide acceptance, it will have the effect of spreading money among many local groups in the communities served by the company. It will also make the individual worker a more important figure than he is now in the overall philanthropic picture.

The *Digest* authorized a total of $515,350 for distribution to various charities by 750 of its employees. The amount varied from a top of $6,000 for each of 15 executives to $200 for clerical workers. Each employee selected six organizations and divided the money among them as he preferred.

Of the money distributed, cultural organizations received less than two per cent, or a total of $7,925. Performing arts organizations, lumped in a category titled music, arts and theaters, received $3,550. Museums received $950, and historical and restoration societies received $3,425. Educational institutions and health organizations were the major beneficiaries, with each category receiving well in excess of $100,000. Religious organizations followed closely.

When asked by *Arts Management* why contributions to cultural groups were so low, Mr. Wallace, who conceived of the plan, replied, "Evidently, the arts didn't present their case well."

The *Digest* plan may appeal to other corporations for several reasons. First, it removes the burden of selecting gift beneficiaries from the corporation. Second, gifts donated in this manner, generally go to groups which serve the corporation's employees.   (43)

------◄●►------

Business Finds New Ways to Aid the Arts

There is an increasing trend by arts groups to develop programs based on continuing relationships with business, where the long-range potential supercedes the immediate gain.

In Stratford, Connecticut, for example, the American Shakespeare Festival Theatre recently developed an Industrial Council, with membership drawn from top Connecticut corporations of a thousand or more employees.

Members, including such firms as Charles Pfizer and Company, Avco, and the Electric Boat Division of General Dynamics, each have appointed a top executive to serve on the Council, which meets quarterly with Festival executives. The purpose of the Council, according to the Festival, is to link the "two most successful aspects of the State of Connecticut—its industrial growth and its cultural growth— to form a mutually beneficial relationship."

There are two key aspects to the program. First, the Festival makes it clear that membership in the Council is not a request for a financial donation. Second, the Festival provides a series of special benefits to each corporate member. These benefits include: making blocks of tickets available at preview performances during the Festival's student season; saluting individual member corporations at special performances; allotting a limited number of free dress rehearsal admissions to companies who place standing orders for house seats; arranging backstage tours for representatives of Council organizations and providing members with in-plant lectures and demonstrations by cast members; spotlighting Council members in local and national publicity and listing them in the Festival program; and providing members and their employees with monthly bulletins on the Council and its activities.

Another Connecticut arts group, the Long Wharf Theatre in New Haven, tied its first anniversary to the 100th anniversary of a local corporation, the Winchester Company. In a ceremony, which was locally publicized, Winchester presented several antique rifles from its collection as a gift to Long Wharf for use in future productions. This initial project triggered several others. The theater was invited to present a revue at Winchester's centennial dinner attended by executives of the corporation and stars of the Hollywood movie, *Stagecoach*. Also, Winchester is now

571

planning a Company Night for its employees at a Long Wharf performance to be followed by a gala champagne reception.

Meanwhile, in New York City, the City Center of Music and Drama, Inc., was the recipient of an unusual service provided free by the Interpublic Group of Companies, Inc. Twenty younger employees of the corporation, which is composed of several leading advertising and marketing companies, conducted a detailed market analysis of the City Center operation. Upon completion of the study, the employees presented a report, more than 60 pages in length, to the Center containing their recommendations on how the Center could achieve a broader and more stable base of financial support.

The employees, representing different companies in the Interpublic Group, participated in the two-month-long project as part of a special corporate training program designed to help promising employees improve their skills. The project participants made the choice of the cultural group as a vehicle for analysis, although commercial corporations are normally studied in the program. They received counselling from top executives in the corporation during the course of study and presented their findings to an Interpublic review board before presenting them to the City Center.

Recommendations included suggestions on improving the Center's direct mail and public relations programs and a plan to increase membership in the Friends of City Center. In addition, the study group analyzed various advertising outlets in the Metropolitan New York area and recommended specific media to use, and a proposed advertising schedule and budget for each. Three new radio commercials and three print advertisements accompanied the report.

According to Mrs. Nancy LaSalle, director of the City Center's Education Department, "the report was interesting as a confirmation of many things we already knew. However, several of the points contained in it may prove of use to us."

A long range program developed by a New York restaurant, the Cattleman, may prove beneficial to various arts groups. Early this summer, the restaurant invited the public, at a cost of $9.00 per person, to attend a week-long series of champagne suppers saluting the cast of a Broadway show, *Half a Sixpence*. The restaurant advertised the program in newspapers and on the radio, distributed invitations at theaters, and publicized it in its own newspaper and in table tents. The Cattleman assumed all costs and turned profits over to the Actors' Fund. Beginning this fall, the restaurant plans to resume the program on a regular basis for the benefit of the Actors' Fund and other arts groups, by saluting new shows and other cultural attractions regularly. To attract more people, however, it intends to substitute drinks and refreshments for supper and lower the admission price. (51)

Orchestras Gain Support from Unusual Sources

To mark the anniversary of its first year in a new building, the Northern States Power Company of Minneapolis, Minnesota, engaged the Minneapolis Symphony Orchestra to present a free public concert in the plaza adjoining the building, last September. The result was extra paid employment for the orchestra, its exposure before a new audience, and favorable publicity for the utility company.

The idea for the project was conceived by R. D. Furber, vice president of Northern States Power, and a board member of the Minnesota Orchestral Association, the parent body of the symphony. Planning for the concert began last May when the company contracted for the services of the orchestra at a fee of $2,500. A September date was agreed upon by both parties as the earliest possible time for the concert. Details of the musical program were left to the orchestra's music director, Stanislaw Skrowaczewski, who selected such works as Dvorak's *Symphony No. 4*, Glinka's Overture to *Russlan and Ludmilla*, and Respighi's symphonic poem, *The Pines of Rome*.

To mount the program, the corporation had to build a platform for the orchestra on top of a pool at one end of the plaza. The possibility of traffic noise was eliminated when nearby construction work closed streets to vehicles on both sides of the plaza, which is located in a busy section of downtown Minneapolis. The plaza's marble wall behind the musicians served as an orchestra shell.

Full-scale promotion began a week prior to the event, with the corporation running announcements over local television stations and placing full-page advertisements in Minneapolis newspapers. The concert, held on a Sunday, on a first-come, first-served basis, drew an enthusiastic overflow crowd of more than 3,000, including many families

574

and a surprisingly large number of children. The audience sat in chairs, stood, climbed a parking ramp across the street, and even sat on sawhorses, stacks of lumber, and mounds of earth at a nearby construction site.

According to E. J. Felton, of the power company's information department, the concert enhanced the symphony's prestige as a community organization and made it the beneficiary of a tremendous amount of newspaper publicity both prior to and following the event. The company, in turn, viewed the concert as a highly successful public relations activity which drew attention to its long-standing support of the symphony.

"We would like to arrange another symphony concert under our sponsorship next summer," Mr. Felton told *AM*. "We believe that our concert has prompted some thinking by other firms toward possible sponsorship of symphony concerts in the future."

Meanwhile, in St. Louis, a second symphony orchestra received support from an unusual source. In an effort to help the St. Louis Symphony recover losses suffered when the orchestra cut its 1965-1966 season by four weeks (due to a strike by orchestra members for higher pay) the St. Louis Cardinals, a professional football team, made the musical group the beneficiary of proceeds from an exhibition game, held prior to the start of the 1966 football season.

The benefit game, played last August between the Cardinals and the Baltimore Colts, raised $58,000 for the orchestra. This enabled the orchestra to lengthen its 1966-1967 season by one week and place the remainder of the proceeds into a fund for orchestra players' salaries. The football team handled the bulk of the promotion and publicity for the game, although the orchestra hired a publicity specialist for two months prior to the game to help increase attendance.

A third orchestra, Hofstra University's professional Pro Art Symphony in Hempstead, Long Island, was the recipient of an entire building. When the Donald E. Axinn Company, a local real estate firm, decided to move to new offices, it donated its former building, valued at $25,000, to Hofstra University. The one-story 34' by 44' wood frame structure, was moved eight miles to its new site on the Hofstra campus, where it will now serve as offices for the orchestra and the university's Institute of the Arts.   (54)

Standard Oil of N. J. Is Pragmatic Arts Patron; Aiding Projects Brings It Prestige and Goodwill

The increased use to which business has been putting the arts in public relations work is dramatically illustrated by the experience of the Standard Oil Company of New Jersey. The parent company and its affiliates, both in the United States and abroad, have been pace-setters in cultural patronage. Most notable recent example is the TV series "An Age of Kings," which brought Shakespeare's histories as acted by the Old Vic company into American homes.

Carl Maas, art director of Jersey Standard, told *Arts Management* the company is completely pragmatic about its activities in the arts. Its purpose is to build goodwill and prestige for the firm, and to promote its products in a highly competitive field. Proof that it has been effective is seen in the flood of commendatory letters that have come to Maas and his colleagues within the Jersey Standard complex.

Local arts groups seeking patronage should approach the company through its local affiliate, Maas told *AM*. He emphasized that applicants should be prepared to state what they think the company can gain from sponsoring a particular program. Jersey Standard policy is to look for the unusual, to the end that a cultural program will attract favorable attention and thus win commendation for the sponsor. Company public relations in the arts is oriented toward thought leaders, *AM* was told.

Maas said he receives many suggestions and requests for aid, a large number of which are for projects either too small or unsuited to the company's purpose. Every project is examined, however, and where appropriate is referred to the affiliate most likely to find a way to work it into its own program.

Jersey Standard's use of the arts as a means of visual communication goes back to 1942, when the company began to commission American painters to document the role of the oil industry in the war effort. By 1946 the company owned a sufficient number to warrant a traveling exhibition, which toured for five years and was shown in 125 university and museum galleries throughout the U. S. and Canada.

In 1944 the company started two other visual projects—the establishment of a photographic library and the production of its first motion picture. The photographs have since appeared in periodicals and books of many kinds, and some have appeared in museum exhibitions.

The first motion picture, produced by the late Robert Flaherty, was "Louisiana Story," an artistic, highly honored documentary about a boy of the bayous and the friends he found among the men who came to drill an oil well. The film's musical score, "Louisiana Story Suite," was composed by Virgil Thomson. It was played by the Philadelphia

Orchestra during a European tour and is available as a re-
recording.

Imperial Oil Limited, Jersey's Canadian affiliate, has
sponsored such films as "The Legend of the Raven" and
"The Seasons," which were distributed jointly with the National Film Board of Canada and by educational departments of Canadian provinces.

Imperial has also commissioned paintings and drawings
by some of the country's finest artists for use in its magazine, *Imperial Oil Review,* and has decorated the lobby of
its home office building in Toronto with two large murals
by R. York Wilson, one of Canada's leading painters.

Another Imperial Oil project in the arts is its purchase
of a collection of drawings by Charles S. Jefferys. The
company photographed and catalogued Jefferys' work and
distributed reproductions to schools.

In France the Jersey affiliate, Esso Standard S.A.F., has
employed outstanding sculptors to design figureheads for
the company's tankers. In Italy, the local company has held
art competitions and used works of avant garde artists to
illustrate the company magazine, *Esso Rivista.* The English
company has made a notable color film, "Our Native
Shores," of which the government Information Office has
made versions in several other languages.   (13)

Airline Sponsorship Helps Concert Program Grow

A concert program for young artists, limited in scope and regional in nature during the first three years of its existence, has grown to national prominence since receiving the support and sponsorship of a leading corporation, American Airlines.

American Youth Performs, an organization which arranges paid engagements for promising apprentice singers and instrumentalists to appear with youth symphonies and choirs, served a limited East Coast area from its founding in 1961 until 1965. Many of the concerts were booked into small towns and outlying areas of large cities. Artists' fees were paid for by schools and local education boards presenting the concerts, and the remaining costs were loaned to AYP by interested individuals.

In the spring of 1965, Charles Abdoo, the founder of AYP, approached American Airlines for support, after first studying the company and its basic philosophy. He discovered that the company was interested in local affairs, especially those involving the youth of a community. Also, it had sponsored good music programs on radio for a number of years. He suggested that the airline sponsorship of AYP be tested in several local markets first, as part of the company's community relations program.

The airline supported concerts in five cities initially, and it broadened its support considerably the following year, sponsoring concerts in 62 cities throughout the country. This support, including artists' fees, all travel expenses, and where necessary, auditorium rental fees and the printing of tickets and programs, enabled local schools to present the concerts without cost. Airline support averaged about $1500 per market, covering three to six concerts in

579

participating cities. As a highlight of its 1966 sponsorship, the airline underwrote the cost of a Carnegie Hall concert, featuring artists brought to New York from 50 cities, and subsidized the production and national distribution of a complimentary record album taped at the concert.

This year, under the sponsorship of American Airlines, AYP is presenting concerts in 60 to 65 cities. A second Carnegie Hall concert will be offered on April 20th, with young artists from 99 cities performing as orchestra members and as choristers. A record album of the concert again will be released and distributed without charge to school music supervisors throughout the country. In addition, airline sponsorship has enabled AYP to add performing educators to the program—orchestral and choral conductors and music clinicians—at the high school, university and conservatory level. These educators travel to various cities, where they work with youth orchestras.

Based on his own experience, Mr. Abdoo offers this advice to arts groups seeking corporate support: "When you get a good idea, shape it into a workable and tangible program before presenting it to a potential sponsor. When you do present it, make sure that your program is complete and that it works for the sponsor and not just for your organization. Also, try to develop programs which can be presented on a small test basis at first, and then expanded, if they work. Always give credit to the sponsoring corporation, even if they don't ask for it. And finally, be persistent."   (55)

Business Tapped for First Time Responds to Theater Fund Drive

Faced with a fund crisis, a suburban arts group enlisted the support of local business for the first time and found a willing angel in the wings. In Huntington, N. Y., the Performing Arts Foundation of Long Island, which has operated a successful year-round professional theater for six years, needed $50,000 to cover the conversion of a warehouse to its playhouse 22 months earlier. With creditor pressure mounting and the board unable to raise the funds, it was obvious that immediate and drastic action was necessary. Finally, early last December the board announced an emergency fund drive. Unless $50,000 could be raised by January 29th, the theater would close.

With no time for preparation, no experience in conducting a major drive and only seven weeks in which to reach its goal, the organization had a nearly impossible task before it. However, the drive received a financial and promotional boost when the Huntington Town Board passed a resolution awarding PAF $12,500. A leading local businessman, Robert Mitchell, former president of the chamber of commerce and head of his own Cadillac agency, helped spark support by personally buying time on radio station WGSM to appeal for funds. Mitchell, currently president of the Huntington Arts Council, was heard twice a day for a week. The station matched his contribution with free spots.

"Mitchell's appeal had a very positive effect on local business," executive director Clint Marantz told *AM*. The Huntington Chamber of Commerce passed a resolution pledging its support. The Village Merchants Association set aside January 20th as Save PAF Day and asked member firms to contribute five to ten per cent of their receipts to PAF that day and to place donation boxes in their stores.

Although the organized support of business had never before been solicited, the response was immediate. A leading area utility, Long Island Lighting, helped launch the drive with a $2,000 donation. Over 300 area merchants helped promote PAF Day and raised more than $500 from donation boxes in their stores. Some $3,000 was raised from Merchants Association members who contributed a percentage of their January 20th receipts to the Foundation. A non-member, MacDonald's, gave PAF over $1600 —50 per cent of the day's gross receipts from its two stands in Huntington. Some PAF business creditors noted the drive's success and responded. They either forgave indebtedness or accepted performance tickets and playbill advertising as payment.

By deadline date the board announced that the goal had been topped by $3,000. "Not only did we tap business," added Marantz, "but we developed a continuing ally. It's been decided already that the third Saturday of every January will be an annual event for local merchants— PAF Day."   (79)

------◆◆------

Business Sponsor

Perhaps you don't have "a friend at Chase Manhattan," but if a company in your area has a quality art collection, as a growing number of corporations do, you might borrow an idea from Chase and benefit your group. Recently, the bank presented the first public exhibition of its outstanding art collection as a benefit for the Dance Theatre of Harlem. The exhibition, held at Finch College in New York, featured a sparkling cocktail party opening with guests paying $25 each to view the collection and see a brief, informal performance by the dance company in the college auditorium. Net result? Good will for the bank and money in the bank, nearly $10,000, for the dance company.   (73)

Divide and Conquer

If arts groups can't find a single corporation willing to sponsor an entire project, they might be able to entice several companies into sharing the project, especially if it is one which can be easily divided like the pages of a publication. The January-March 1970 issue of the four-page newsletter, *Museum Matters,* published by the Orange County Community of Museums and Galleries in Goshen, New York, had three different corporate sponsors, one for page two, another for page three and a third sponsor for page four. Each was identified by name, address and telephone number and credited at the bottom of its sponsored page.   (67)

A Sporting Deal

If you have a professional athletic team in your area, you might find them a willing source of support or promotional aid. Past issues of *AM* have featured such examples of athletic largesse as a football team making its local symphony the beneficiary of proceeds from an exhibition game, (See *AM:* No. 54). Recently, a professional basketball team, the Utah Stars, gave $2500 to a dance company, Ballet West, as a way of thanking Utah citizens for the recognition and support accorded to the Stars. Said the team, "It is our pleasure to give this recognition to another Utah-based professional company that has received international acclaim for the excellence of their performance—Ballet West." (79)

Broadcasters Group Backs Canada Drama Festival

The Dominion Drama Festival in Canada, devoted to the stimulation of theatre art through national competitions, for three years has had the active backing of the Canadian Association of Broadcasters, an organization of 167 radio and 55 television stations. C.A.B. support, financial as well as promotional, has helped make the annual festival an event of importance.

An average of 95 theatre groups participate in regional and sub-regional drama competitions. This year eight organizations participated in the finals, held in Kitchener, Ont. The play-off festival is held in a different city each year. Regional festivals are judged by qualified drama professionals. The national competition is judged by a prominent theatre personality from outside the country. The top judge this year was Pierre Lefevre, head of the drama school of Centre del'Ouest, one of France's leading national theatres.

Financing has always been a problem for the Dominion Drama Festival. Each region is responsible for its own budget, and participating drama groups pay entry fees to the national body, but coordinating and running the festival program requires an annual budget of $69,000. This money goes not only to stage the national festival, but to operate a small office in Ottawa, with a staff consisting of a national director—Richard MacDonald, an assistant, and two clerical employees. The funds are raised from private contributions and a subsidy from the Canada Council, a government agency. From 1952 to 1960 the festival also had the support of Calvert Distillers, Ltd., which made an annual grant of $15,000. When this support was discontinued in 1960, however, the festival faced severe problems. It was at this point that the Canadian Association of Broadcasters stepped in.

585

The C.A.B., interested in encouraging Canadian talent and in building a better public relations image for itself, now donates $21,000 annually. This provides $1,000 in prize money for each of the regional winners, and an additional $1,000 for the winning drama group in the final festival.

The C.A.B., however, goes beyond its financial contribution. It actively promotes theatre in all parts of the country, and does much to promote ticket sales for both the regional and national festivals. For the regional meets, the television and radio stations broadcast spots, flashes, news items, interviews and feature stories on the presentations. For the final festival, the stations in the host city produce material for broadcast in the home cities of the participating groups and air their own shows about the festival. In addition, the Canadian Broadcasting Corp., the government-owned broadcast network, usually carries a live program about the presentation of the awards.

Awards go not only for the best production, but for the best plays (one in English, one in French), for the best director, outstanding actors and actresses, etc. There are cash prizes and a $3,000 scholarship awarded by the Province of Quebec for the most promising artist whose mother tongue is French.

The festival program has not only stimulated new interest in theatre, but promoted interest in bi-culturalism. In six regions French-speaking and English-speaking drama companies compete against one another. The festival appears to have demonstrated that the two-language factor is not a barrier.   (19)

Art Programs for Corporations Win New Members and Audience

Cultural institutions seeking to increase interest and support from the business community are wise to develop special programs for this group. A successful activity of this nature, was sponsored by the Minneapolis Institute of Arts.

An evening was set aside at the Institute for a "Treasure Party" exclusively for the employees of Corporate Members of the Minneapolis Society of Fine Arts, the governing and supporting organization of the Institute. Admission was free and the 105 business members—contributors of $100 or more to the Society's annual Guaranty Fund Drive—were sent handsome invitations and companies were asked to post these on their bulletin boards.

700 persons attended the three hour reception. Guided tours were held; behind-the-scenes visits were made to the museum workshop where works of art are cleaned and restored; a short film was shown; informal discussions took place with the museum's staff; and refreshments were served.

According to one official, "Many individual memberships were sold as a result of that night. We also know that events such as this one, which bring people into the Institute for the first time, increase our attendance from that night on, as the same people bring their friends." (8)

Breakfast With Business

Speeches by executives of cultural institutions, at meetings of leading organizations, are a good method of promoting the institution's activities. One important platform, frequently overlooked, is the business meeting or convention. Some companies, such as Prentice-Hall, Inc., in New York, have regular executive breakfasts at which experts in various fields address the company leaders.   (19)

Business as Sponsor

If your organization is planning to issue a regular publication, you should consider asking local businesses to sponsor it on a rotating basis. Thus, no one business will be asked to assume a continuing financial burden and the example established by one company may act as a spur to other companies. In Rockland County, New York, *South of the Mountain,* the quarterly publication of the Tappan Zee Historical Society, has been sponsored by a variety of local business organizations since its inception in 1957.   (23)

Bank Promotion Attracts Funds for Culture

By varying a tried promotional tactic, the free gift to new depositors, a New York City bank made a key contribution to a cultural fund-raising campaign and helped itself at the same time. Importantly, the technique used by the East New York Savings Bank to benefit the New York Public Library could be adapted by any company offering premiums to help cultural organizations in its community.

When East New York was planning the opening of a new branch on Manhattan's West 42nd Street earlier this year, it looked at its immediate neighborhood to see the local amenities with which it might identify. Foremost among them was the main branch of the city's library system, located across the street. The library was then about to launch a major fund-raising drive to match a $500,000 grant from the National Endowment for the Humanities by June 30th.

With the dual objective of helping the library's fund drive and promoting its own branch opening, the bank launched two consecutive 30-day promotional campaigns beginning on May 15th, the first in all nine Metropolitan area branches and the second at the 42nd Street branch alone. The traditional free gift offer used by banks to attract new customers was varied to permit new account openers to exercise an unusual option—they could accept a gift or they could donate its price to the library. If they opted for the donation, the bank agreed to match the gift.

The promotion was backed by the usual heavy advertising barrage which accompanies branch openings. In East New York's case this meant two ads every week in each of New York's dailies, double pages in tabloids and full-pages in the *New York Times,* plus a full schedule of weekly news-paper ads and radio announcements. A typical full-page *Times* ad showed bank chairman John P. McGrath stand-ing behind a table laden with gifts. The caption read, "East New York Savings Bank has a gift for you, but we'd rather you didn't take it . . . Instead—let us contribute the price of your gift to the New York Public Library. And we'll send an equal amount." Accompanying text described the library's financial needs and outlined the alternate gift plan. Library contributors were also given certificates of acknowledgment and a permanent identification label in a library book.

Although the amount raised through the bank was not a major part of the overall total raised by the library, it far surpassed expectations. During the initial campaign and the first two weeks of the second campaign, both coming prior to the matching grant deadline, 20 per cent of all new depositors waived the free gift and contributed to the library. Moreover, the bank received a number of library donations from non-depositors and its action helped to spur business contributions, some rather sizable. Perhaps most important to the library, however, was the tremendous ex-posure it received as a result of the bank promotion. "We received more than triple our advance expectation in con-tributions," the library's chief of public information, Ed-ward White, told *AM,* "and an immeasurable amount of exposure and good will." Three days prior to the matching grant deadline the library announced that it had topped its goal by nearly $200,000.

The bank was equally pleased with the results. Its vice-president for marketing, Edward J. Pfeiffer, said, "Forty second Street was the most successful branch opening we've ever had. We exceeded our maximum projection of the number of new accounts and the amount deposited by a good degree." The bank also received tremendous institutional recognition and its offices were flooded with hundreds of congratulatory letters.

"We feel it was a great benefit all around," added Pfeiffer. "We were able to perform a public service and still meet our marketing objectives. Any business offering any kind of substantial premium could make this kind of option available to its customers." (76)

———————◄●►———————

International Ties

Arts groups planning a program with an international flavor may get support for the event from a local business which has international ties. For example, an American company which had its origins in Switzerland recently contributed $300 to help sponsor an exhibition of Swiss Posters on loan from the Traveling Exhibition Service of the Smithsonian Institution. The exhibition was presented at a cultural institution in the company's home community. (45)

Corporate Gifts

The Whitney Museum in New York City has developed a successful corporate gift plan which might be adapted by other visual arts groups. Corporations contribute $3,000 to the museum to enable it to purchase any painting it wishes. Once the painting is selected by the museum, it then lends that work, or up to three others, to the corporation for one year. At the end of the year, the painting is returned to the museum to be added to its permanent collection. (58)

Floral Tribute

A fund raising technique used successfully by the Ballet Guild of Cleveland, Ohio, may be of interest to smaller arts groups. Each year, the Guild provides volunteers to man the display of a local florist at an annual flower show. The florist, in turn, contributes the "wages" earned by the volunteers to the Guild. (60)

Bank Floor is Unique Setting for Performance by Orchestra

The main floor of a leading bank will become an auditorium for the Buffalo Philharmonic Orchestra when it presents a concert there on December 12th. The Buffalo Savings Bank has donated space on its banking floor for the event and will pay the orchestra for the performance.

In addition, the bank will advertise the event without charge to the orchestra, and serve coffee and doughnuts to the 1,400 persons who are expected to attend the concert, which will take place between two and four P.M. on a Saturday. Seats for the performance are free and will be offered on a first come, first served basis.

Seymour L. Rosen, the orchestra's manager, told *AM* that his organization suggested the program to the bank last April and received approval for it in June. The bank will spend about $4,000 on the concert with the major portion earmarked for the orchestra's players.

The orchestra won support for the project by pointing out to the bank that it would be providing a service to the community generally and to its customers specifically. It was also maintained that community goodwill generated by the event would benefit the bank.

To gain bank approval, the orchestra's board members established personal contacts with board members of the bank. Although the bank had previously cooperated with the orchestra on limited projects such as sending out mailings on behalf of the orchestra, closer ties resulted from working on the event. The bank is now considering sponsoring other arts events.

Mr. Rosen feels that promotion of the performance will help generate interest in the orchestra since many persons who may attend the concert normally do not go to regular orchestral presentations. To appeal to a wide audience, a program of semi-classical and Christmas music is planned.

Advertisements of the presentation were scheduled to appear a week before the concert in the *Buffalo Courier-Express,* and the *Buffalo Evening News,* major city newspapers with a combined total circulation of more than 590,000. In addition, posters announcing the event will be displayed in the bank lobby, and spot radio and television announcements will be used. The bank also sent direct mail to its customers telling them of the concert.

Mr. Rosen said that the bank is ideally situated for the performance since it is in the heart of the downtown shopping district. (33)

Cultural Events Play Key Role In Employee Relations Program

Local businesses are becoming increasingly receptive to the sponsorship of cultural events on their premises as part of their employee relations program.

In Philadelphia, for example, the Professional Training Orchestra of the New School of Music recently presented a Saturday afternoon concert in the lunchroom of the Smith Kline & French Laboratories for employees of the company and their families.

Members of the all-student orchestra were paid for the performance which was sponsored jointly by the company and the Martha Baird Rockefeller Fund for Music, Inc. This was the first in a series of industrial concerts to be presented by the orchestra this season. A performance at the Philco Corporation plant in Philadelphia, will be held on February 21st.

Two years ago, the New School initiated its industrial program with its orchestra performing in a concert sponsored by the Krylon Paint Company of Norristown, Pennsylvania. The open-air concert, held at the local high school stadium, with employees of the company and their families in attendance, was given as part of Norristown's tercentenary celebration.

According to Max Aronoff, director of the school, "The purpose of these industrial concerts is to create a greater demand for live music and to develop a larger listening audience in the Philadelphia area." In addition, he said, "Such a project will also provide a 'learn and earn' program for orchestral students."

Meanwhile, in Hartford, Connecticut, the Travelers Insurance Company is offering its employees, free of charge, a series of lectures intended to spur interest in fine music and attendance at concerts, including those of the Hartford Symphony.

Lectures conducted by Mary Lane, a violinist with the Hartford Symphony, cover such specific topics as the role of the conductor, the role of solo instruments, the arrangement of instruments, the functions of a large symphony choir, and a discussion of the musical styles of the last three centuries which make up the symphonic repertoire.

Featured in the lecture series is a discussion of the major works which the Hartford Symphony will perform this season. (35)

Cable Television May Mean Income to Arts

Performing arts groups looking for new sources of income, might cast their eyes at the growing cable television industry. Although local cable systems throughout the country have incorporated cultural presentations in their programming from time to time, the arts involvement has been low-keyed and cultural benefits have been promotional rather than financial. Some arts groups, for example, have taken advantage of an FCC regulation which requires cable systems to provide one free noncommercial channel for public access. The start of a new kind of relationship may have been signalled, however, when Teleprompter Manhattan Cable TV presented the New York City Opera's "Le Coq D'Or" live and in color direct from the stage of Lincoln Center's New York State Theater on November 9th. The production, with Beverly Sills and Norman Treigle, was viewed by an estimated 12,800 of the 80,000 Teleprompter and Sterling Manhattan Cable subscribers in New York City.

The project was conceived by John Goberman of the New York City Opera, who approached Teleprompter with the idea. The cable company was extremely interested and after an agreement was reached, the opera company worked out the complicated special arrangements with unions and performers. "We were interested in doing live productions for our audience," Teleprompter's general manager Joseph C. Groth, told *AM*. "We did a number of audience studies and opera, ballet and theater always came out high."

Both the opera company and the cable system were delighted with the arrangement. Teleprompter promoted and advertised the event heavily in advance and was able to use it as a lure to sell its service to new subscribers. The New York City Opera received a fee from the cable system for the performance and everyone on the company payroll was paid once again for participation. Moreover, the production presented no special technical problems and neither theater audiences nor cast was inconvenienced. The arrangement worked so well, in fact, that the opera company and Teleprompter are now planning similar live broadcasts this spring. Moreover, according to an enthusiastic Mr. Groth, Teleprompter has entered into preliminary discussions on live cable telecasts with such groups as the New York Philharmonic, the Joffrey Ballet and the Repertory Theater of Lincoln Center. "I can envision the day," he said, "when there will be a domestic communications satellite system in cable television which will draw heavily on the arts." (73)

———————◄●►———————

Culture Center Also Retailer to Help Finance Arts Program

A New England arts group has found a unique way to help finance its non-profit operation. It has become a commercial retailer. Since this April, the National Center of Afro-American Artists, Inc., in Dorchester, Mass., which conducts an intensive training and performance program in dance, drama, music and art for black artists, has been partner as well as operator of the Capezio Dance Shop in Boston.

The Boston store, a long-established and successful operation, is one of six Capezio Dance shops throughout the country which are run as partnerships between the parent

597

company, Cap-Sal-Ballet Makers of New York, and local entrepreneurs. When Herbert Tieman the Boston operator died this February, Cap-Sal president Ben Sommers, who is also the president of the Capezio Foundation and a board member of several national dance organizations, began searching for a new local partner. Elma Lewis, nationally known arts educator and a good friend of the former owner was recommended. Instead of proposing herself as a partner, however, Miss Lewis suggested that the Afro-American Center, which she founded and directed along with the Elma Lewis School of Fine Arts, take over half ownership and manage the operation. "Whatever profits we make," she told Sommers, "can go back into the operation of the center and the school."

The idea of artists and dancers running a store which sold dance supplies, shoes and leotards had tremendous appeal to Sommers, as did the fact that both Miss Lewis and her operation were well-known and respected in the Boston area. Moreover, they would have a tremendous incentive to do well because the arts center would benefit. As Sommers told *AM,* "This was a tremendous opportunity for the Center, and we made it easy for them to acquire the partnership."

While it is highly unlikely that store profits will ever negate the need for Center fund raising, the new arrangement does provide it with an excellent source of added income which hopefully, will continue to grow over the years. Already, Miss Lewis told *AM,* the store is making plans to expand into such new sales areas as jewelry, books, and makeup.

In the first few months under the in-store managership of dancer Delores Brown, the store, according to Miss Lewis, "is doing marvelously. We're doing about twice as great a volume as the previous management and we're very excited about it." (71)

—————◄●►—————

Arts in Commercials

An arts group has found huge new audiences and an extra payday through television. For the past few months, a television commercial sponsored by the Foundation for Full Service Banks featuring the Detroit Symphony, has enjoyed frequent prime time network exposure. The commercial, one of a series designed to show how local banks serve their communities, was made in one afternoon this fall, with orchestra players receiving a fee for their participation. The sixty second vignette focuses visually on the orchestra, while telling viewers how the National Bank of Detroit sponsors morning coffee concerts by the orchestra to bring shoppers downtown and makes loans to its players for the purchase of rare instruments. (74)

—————◄●►—————

Port Authority Sponsors Orchestra Tour

A commercial reason for supporting the arts was acknowledged by the Delaware River Port Authority, which sponsored a month-long, seven-nation European tour by the Philadelphia Orchestra this spring. According to reports, the Authority underwrote the tour cost of $150,000 to promote European shipping to Philadelphia and other Delaware River ports. In each of 12 cities where the orchestra performed, Authority executives and Philadelphia Mayor James H. J. Tate greeted European shippers at pre-concert receptions. Prospective customers were given concert tickets, a booklet on Authority ports, and a new album recorded by the Orchestra for the trip, which featured the Philadelphia waterfront on its jacket.   (68)

—————◄•►—————

Gambling on the Arts

In California, horse racing at Santa Anita has enriched the offers of performing arts groups in Los Angeles. According to California Horse Racing Law, Chapter 4, Division 8, each racing association other than state, county or district fairs, must designate from three to five days as charity days, with net proceeds on these days contributed to non-profit organizations approved by the state racing board. In 1967 and 1968, the state distributed over $2.5-million from races to various charities. Santa Anita alone this year, distributed $470,000. Among its recipients was the Performing Arts Council of Los Angeles which received $20,000 for distribution to its members.   (66)

—————◄•►—————

FREE SERVICES AND PROMOTIONAL HELP

Corporate Planners Help Arts Identify Needs

Top corporate planning executives have joined lawyers, accountants and other business professionals who, within the past year, have developed programs of voluntary aid to the arts. Currently, as the precursor to a possible national effort, corporate planners in New York City are helping three arts groups with their long range planning.

The concept of a public service project which would transfer the planning methodology used in business to non-business areas on a voluntary basis, was conceived late last year by members of the New York chapter of the North American Society, for corporate planning. The Society with 10 chapters in the United States and Canada, has nearly 1,000 members overall.

When the idea took shape, R. J. Allio, director of corporate planning for Babcock & Wilcox, and president of the New York chapter, began to seek out non-business groups which had a need for planning and had a leader who recognized the need and was willing to work with volunteer consultants. Personally interested in the arts, Allio discussed the project with Nancy Hanks and asked the Business Committee for the Arts to suggest several groups. Of the seven projects later undertaken by the chapter, three were for arts groups—Hospital Audiences, Inc., the Municipal Art Society, and the U.S. Institute for Theatre Technology.

According to Allio, the job of the corporate planners (20 volunteer chapter members have worked on the seven projects) has been to provide primary skills in planning methodology in order to: focus on what were an organization's goals; to determine with the organization the strategies needed to reach these goals; and ascertain if the group had the skills to reach them. "We don't do the planning," Allio told *AM*. "Groups must do their own planning. We give them the format and provide advice and guidance. They try to fill in the empty spaces."

Participating New York arts groups have been unanimous in their praise for the expert volunteer help they've received over the past few months. In conversations with *AM* their directors have talked about the practical scenarios and plans prepared by the consultants which have helped their groups formulate new strategies and develop long range organizational plans. Said Michael Jon Spencer of Hospital Audiences, "The corporate planners have helped us to clarify priorities and think through solutions."

In addition to voluntary consultant activity, the New York chapter plans to issue a planning manual for nonbusiness groups within several months and hopes to conduct a seminar in the fall. Moreover, the program begun in New York may be expanded elsewhere. "We've got enough resources to do more," said Allio. "Other chapters have shown an interest and we hope to have their participation in the project." Arts groups interested in the program may reach Mr. Allio at Babcock & Wilcox, 161 E. 42nd St., New York, N. Y. 10017.

Meanwhile, across the country, a rehearsal room became a "war room" complete with charts and graphs earlier this season, as top local businessmen helped the Seattle Opera to determine its priorities. One evening a week for three months, the executives worked voluntarily with opera staff on a detailed management study which included the analyses of more than 50 different opera projects in production, administration and education, to determine their community reach, potential for success, and cost in relationship to possible return.   (71)

———————◄●►———————

Executive Help for Fund Drive Offered to Groups by Industry

Need trained and talented executives to help with your fund campaign on a free, but full-time basis? Health and welfare organizations for many years have been asking and getting precisely this kind of assistance from business organizations. The New York chapter of the Arthritis and Rheumatism Foundation, for example, has used personnel from such companies as the Metropolitan Life Insurance Company, the New York Telephone Company, I.B.M., and Sperry Rand in recent fund drives for a month or more of full-time work. Executives-on-loan have been used to meet with prospective donors, to handle clerical work, or to perform tasks demanding special skills like accounting.

Some concerns like the New York Life Insurance Company, have a regular plan for making retired employees available to non-profit organizations. These workers are paid full salary by the company. Other companies send young employees whose brightness and energy compensate for a lack of experience. According to one official, corporations rarely send out secretarial help.

The best approach to a corporation for the loan of executive help is a personal visit by a top official of a cultural organization. If nobody within your organization knows an executive of the firm, and if the company is a large one, outline your proposal in writing and send it either to the personnel director or the vice president for public relations of the company. Requests to smaller companies should be addressed to the president.

Be specific about your needs. Tell the company how many employees you require; what skills are most needed; what the duties of assigned workers will be; and the approximate length of time for which workers are needed. Larger corporations generally lend workers for a one month to six week period; smaller companies may send employees for several days. If a company requests that a specific worker be used only for certain kinds of duties, it is important that this request be honored. (16)

Borrowing Businessmen

Business executives can be key cogs in a fund raising campaign, especially if they are able to devote full time to it as 100 of them did in Boston. The executives spent eight weeks working on the 1965 Massachusetts Bay United Fund Campaign, with their salaries paid by their employers. Participating corporations indicated that this action helped them because executives received good training and experience, developed contacts, and generated good will for their companies. (50)

Dollars from Pop

Soft drinks may bring in hard cash. The Sacramento Symphony Orchestra, through a cooperative venture with the 7-Up Bottling Company of Sacramento, realizes about $100 at each of 16 concerts through the sale of soft drinks and coffee. While the Symphony Association pays the company for the actual cost of soda supplied to them, about four cents a drink, the bottling company provides free coffee, equipment, manpower, cups, and ice. The soft drinks are sold for 25 cents each and the coffee for 15 cents a cup. The project was initiated at the suggestion of the bottling company, to help raise money for the orchestra.

(65)

———◄●►———

Lawyers Form New Organization to Aid and Counsel the Arts

Legal aid for the arts is a reality. After a year of organization and planning, a New York-based group known as Volunteer Lawyers for the Arts has acquired offices, (space provided by Associated Councils of the Arts within its suite at 1564 Broadway, New York City) found seed money for a three year program, formulated a set of operational guidelines, and served its first "clients." Although one of V.L.A.'s principal activities is to provide free legal counsel to non-profit cultural groups which can't otherwise afford it, the organization also plans to issue publications of interest to the arts and undertake investigations of arts-related legal problems.

According to V.L.A. president and founder Paul H. Epstein, a New York lawyer, the organization has developed a pilot program, which, if proved successful, can be adapted by lawyers in other states. Already, lawyers in Boston and Washington have indicated interest in starting similar projects. (68)

Donated Services

Is your arts group looking to receive expert free counsel and service from lawyers, accountants, architects, personnel executives or other specialists? You might point out to them that they may be able to deduct a donated service as an advertising expense. According to the IRS, the expenses incurred by executives engaged in civic activities are a deductible business expense if these activities are of a type normally engaged in by their firm, and if they are undertaken primarily as a means of indirect advertising—a way of keeping their name before the public. (66)

Free Transportation

Importing something for an exhibition or show? If it's of considerable value or importance, a transportation company may carry the cargo free of charge in return for the publicity value. The Home Lines Steamship Agency of Canada provided round trip shipping from Europe to Canada for the important Héritage de France Art Exhibition. The same principle can be applied to local hauling as well. (4)

606

Conference Room?

Need a free meeting place for a regional get-together, a seminar or other group session? Many businesses—newspapers, particularly—offer cultural groups free use of their well-appointed conference rooms, if arrangements are made well in advance. (4)

Need Staff Members?

A major company in your community may be helpful in easing your personnel woes. Some companies will provide personnel services for you. They will work up job definitions; tell you prevailing wage scales; even conduct interviewing for you. Western Electric in Winston-Salem, North Carolina provides services like these for the Winston-Salem Arts Council. (15)

Advertising Industry Helps to Promote the Arts

Madison Avenue is helping to promote the arts in America. With growing frequency, advertisers are spotlighting their local cultural institutions in prominent national ads, in order to demonstrate the quality of life in their city or area. Also, a leading industry-wide association, the Advertising Council, is about to take its first organized step in behalf of the arts. While it is a small one, it could become the precursor for a mammoth promotional campaign which would solicit arts support throughout the country.

The Advertising Council conducts major national public service advertising campaigns on behalf of carefully selected causes, worth millions of dollars to the beneficiaries in the form of donated advertising services and contributed media space and time. Current campaigns include "Help Prevent Crime" for the U.S. Department of Justice, "Traffic Safety" for the National Safety Council and "United Community Campaigns" for United Community Funds and Councils of America.

Initially, the arts will be included in the Council's Public Service Advertising Bulletin, a publication listing Council-approved public service subjects which media and advertisers might wish to support by contributing free time and space. The Council will evaluate the overall response to the arts listing for some six months following its inclusion in the Bulletin, and could then decide, if the response has been favorable, to make the arts the subject of a full-scale, major campaign. In such an event, the Council would supervise an overall program which could be worth several millions of dollars in free ads to the arts in magazines, newspapers, television, radio, outdoor billboards, company publications and other media.

The current project had its genesis about a year ago, when national arts leaders representing the group known as "the President's Council," joined with the Business Committee for the Arts in suggesting the arts as a public service theme to the Advertising Council. The Business Committee has since followed up and has agreed to act as the sponsoring agency, responsible for preparing materials on the arts and providing them to media which request them.

Elsewhere, full-page color advertisements promoting arts groups are being used to help "sell" specific markets. In a *Business Week* ad, the Southern Company termed its four state area America's action frontier in the arts, and called attention to the region's 15 symphony orchestras, six opera companies, 18 community art museums, 17 civic ballet groups, 60 theater organizations and more than 100 art associations. In *Advertising Age,* the *Miami Herald and News* pointed to the Miami Philharmonic as proof of the importance of its market. "Remember when South Florida 'culture' meant some bathing cuties warbling en chorale?" asked the ad. "Forget it! Nowadays we thrill the air with Philharmonic excellence . . . You only see activity like this in a mature community. The kind of community that makes a rich market." In large black and white ads, which appeared in the *New York Times* and other publications, the Massachusetts Department of Commerce and Development pictured Leonard Bernstein and a caption stating, "Leonard Bernstein would be in the Boston Symphony audience if he had become a mathematician."

Perhaps the most unusual print media ad on a cultural theme appeared last fall in *Business Week.* The full-color, two page ad placed by Bankers Trust Company, showed views of Olana, the 19th century estate of Frederic Church, last of the Hudson River School of painters. It described how Banker's Trust, as executor of the estate, went against banking convention and saved Olana from destruction by allowing a preservation group time to raise money to buy the estate and preserve it as a museum.   (67)

Movie Theaters

If your group lacks facilities appropriate for fund raising events you can often find the space you need in local
movie theaters. For example, in West Springfield, Massachusetts, Cinema I & II invites community groups to use
their auditoriums for fund raising events during non-oper-
ating hours. The service is provided to non-profit organizations without charge.   (35)

—◆◆—

Corporations Lend Aid To Leading Art Museums

Although many corporations have provided services to
arts groups on a one-time basis, there are relatively few examples of corporations which have provided continued assistance over a period of years. One exception is the Baltimore Federal Savings and Loan Association.

Five years ago, in January 1963, the bank agreed to provide three large display cases in its West Room for exhibitions of works from the Walters Art Gallery. The idea originated because of the Gallery's acute shortage of display
space and its desire to reach a portion of the public who
might not otherwise come to the Gallery. At the time the
program began, the Gallery was launching a public drive
to raise funds for a building expansion.

Although the program began as an experiment, it has continued regularly since its initiation, with the bank sponsoring six exhibitions annually, each lasting two months. This
January and February, for example, the art of the lock-
smith was featured in an exhibition titled "Under Lock and
Key." "Japanese Lacquers" is now on display, to be followed by an exhibition of clocks titled "Timepieces."

The bank, which is a regular member of the Gallery, pays for transportation of the art, the insurance and publicity costs of the exhibition, and the printing of exhibition brochures. Located in the heart of the Baltimore business district, the exhibitions have been viewed by thousands of visitors since their inception.

Another museum which is benefiting from corporate support is New York City's Museum of Modern Art. For some time, the Museum has offered corporate members its Art Advisory Service, a consulting program in which the museum, on a fee basis, selects works of art for companies interested in either purchasing them or borrowing them to display in corporate headquarters. Now, for the first time, a corporate member, the posh Four Seasons restaurant, has used the consulting service to assemble a collection for public display. The exhibition, titled "Five Works in Light and Movement," features works on loan from leading private galleries. Mr. Charles Hesse, who is in charge of corporate relations for the Museum, told *AM*, "We hope that the idea of corporations using our service for public exhibitions may start a new trend, and may even encourage some firms to become corporate members."

In Canada, meanwhile, the Montreal Museum of Fine Arts has leased nine paintings by young artists to Benson & Hedges, Ltd. The large abstract and pop paintings now hang high above machines in the cigarette factory, where the 250 workers on the floor can view them daily. In addition to a rental fee, the company pays all insurance costs. (60)

———◄●►———

611

Artist Finds Company and Wins Studio, Materials, Commissions

A young Ohio artist interested in metal working but lacking the means to open a suitable studio, systematically solicited area industries until he found one interested in giving him free space without any strings attached. While Thomas W. Taylor envisioned a studio which always would be open to employees, he didn't wish to trade his artistic services for free space.

Although they had never met, Harvey Gittler, manager of manufacturing for the Tappan Air Conditioning plant in Elyria, Ohio, responded to the unusual suggestion. In March 1972, several weeks after the initial proposal was made, Taylor moved into his new studio tucked away in a maintenance department area used mainly for storage. The studio is large enough for his needs and includes such materials as an arc welder, portable crane and hoist, work bench and storage cabinet. In addition, virtually every tool in the maintenance department, from drill presses to abrasive saws, and tools in the plant's other departments have been made available to Taylor. "The paint line will send through anything that fits," said Taylor, "as long as I don't mind green and yellow, the color of the air conditioners and furnaces they manufacture." He also can take any material he wishes from the Tappan scrap yard without charge.

Officially identified as the company's artist in residence, Taylor has found the relationship beneficial both from an economic and production viewpoint. During the past year he's produced a variety of new works including a winged form made from old boiler shells and a rotating piece made from damaged air conditioner and furnace parts. He's also been working on modular building units based on pentagons and prism shapes.

Although, as Taylor puts it, "The present involvement does not solve all the problems of survival," he's found a customer for his work in Tappan. His decorative wall sculpture now hangs in the company's training room and a large steel form of his has been rented by Tappan for display in its front yard. Recently, the marketing department bought a large piece of his to highlight their exhibit at a trade show. The company also hired him as a color consultant to brighten areas within the plant and Harvey Gittler personally commissioned a steel structure and several abstract steel forms.

"Having Tom here has been an exciting experience for our employees," said Gittler. "Many regularly visit his studio and they now see artistic form in their everyday surroundings." (79)

———◄●►———

Alert Arts Groups Get Help From
Local Department Stores

Department stores represent an important source of potential help to cultural organizations, far beyond giving financial aid in fund drives. Because retailing is highly competitive, stores are constantly searching for new ways to make friends and build prestige in the communities they serve.

An energetic and alert arts manager can suggest many avenues of service to department store executives that can benefit his arts group and the store at the same time. For this reason he should learn as much as possible about local stores, their record of community service and who in their executive hierarchy makes decisions in such matters.

A community cultural group should make every effort to obtain the active service of a top executive of a leading store on its board. Not only can he guide the organization in work with store people who direct public relations, advertising and sales promotion, but he can also provide insight into the business community as a whole.

Among the ways department stores can help the arts: provide free window displays saluting an organization or a special event; feature organizations in pictorial institutional ads; provide volunteer workers; sponsor concerts and exhibitions; provide ticket sales booths; lend rooms for meetings; raise funds; and permit arts groups to use their mailing lists.

Among the many cultural activities of stores that have come to the attention of *Arts Management*: Abraham & Straus in Brooklyn, N. Y., has started a series of theatre seminars for high school students in cooperation with the American National Theatre and Academy that attracted 300 students to its first program; Burdine's in Miami, Fla.,

614

will sponsor an International Art Show in cooperation with the University of Miami; R. H. Macy in New York City recently helped finance a youth concert for 2,000 students presented by the West Side Symphony.

The National Retail Merchants Association has given a great impetus to retail store cooperation with the arts by joining *Reader's Digest* in sponsoring an annual awards competition for outstanding community service. The winning entries present fine examples of aid given cultural groups by stores.

In Inglewood, Calif., the Boston Stores devoted a special sales day to raising funds for local organizations. A store in South Carolina led a campaign to build a regional museum, and a South Dakota store helped build a community auditorium. Ackemann Brothers, Inc. in Elgin, Ill., helped lead a fund raising drive for a community band shell to be used by local music groups and the civic theatre.

The grand opening of Walker-Scott Company in San Diego, Calif., was used as a fund raising occasion to assist the local symphony orchestra. The New Orleans Symphony received a tremendous publicity boost from the Krauss-Company, which spelled out messages to the community in behalf of the orchestra in lighted letters six feet high above its marquee.

One of the most unusual services offered by a store is that provided by Loveman, Joseph and Loeb in Birmingham, Ala. The store added a children's drama consultant as a full-time member of its public relations staff. Employed by the store since 1957, this specialist tours schools throughout Alabama, Mississippi and Georgia, conducting workshops in creative drama for teachers and providing free consultative service in formal drama for children.   (9)

Department Store Offers Free Ads to Arts

Department stores can be important sources of free advertising for the arts. In Brooklyn, New York, for example, Abraham & Straus, a leading department store, places about 25 advertisements in six major metropolitan newspapers each year promoting cultural events. The advertisements, offered without charge to the arts institutions whose events are featured, generally include non-commercial messages about the department store.

Such organizations as the Delacorte Mobile Theater, the Brooklyn Ballet Guild and the Brooklyn Academy of Music are among the institutions that have benefited from the store's advertising program. In addition to paying for the cost of the advertisements, A & S also prepares the art work for them.

While advertisements vary in size, they usually are two to three columns wide and 150 lines long. At times, they fill an entire page. A full page advertisement in the *New York Times,* one of the newspapers most frequently displaying the advertisements, costs the store more than $5,000.

Furthermore, the store has sponsored performances by several of the organizations featured in the advertisements. This summer it presented the Delacorte Mobile Theater's production of Shakespeare's *A Midsummer Night's Dream,* which was held in Brooklyn's Prospect Park.

William Toby, vice president in charge of advertising, public relations and sales promotion for the store, told *AM* that his company pays for the advertisements to "identify itself with programs that arouse community interest." He said that letters received from the public indicate a warm response to these efforts.

No rigid formula exists for approaching the store for free advertisements, and each request is weighed individually.

However, organizations must have an official civic affiliation and must be non-profit.

In many cases, the store's efforts to promote arts groups have reached far beyond free advertisements and the sponsorship of events. It recently donated a booth on one of its floors to promote the membership drive of the Brooklyn Academy of Music. (32)

———— ◄•► ————

Good Neighbor Store Lends Meeting Room, Windows, Aid

One of the most important services that department stores can provide for the arts is free use of their space. In the Philadelphia area, Lit Brothers, a department store with six outlets, carries on a broad program of assistance to non-profit organizations in which it lends them not only space but also the use of personnel and other facilities.

Lit's has assigned a large room in each of its six branches as its Good Neighbor Room, for the use of cultural and other non-profit groups. The Good Neighbor Room may be reserved free of charge during store hours on a regular weekly or monthly schedule, depending on availability. The rooms range in size from a seating capacity of 50 to 500. They are equipped with a public address system, a movie screen, a grand piano and an electric organ.

Each Lit Brothers branch reserves one large window for community groups on a rotating two-week basis. Those using the window send their props to the display department of the store, which then takes care of dressing the window in a professional manner.

Lit Brothers employs a full-time Good Neighbor Director at each branch store to work directly with community organizations. She sees to the use of the rooms, the provision of window displays and the placing of weekly advertisements in the newspapers honoring individuals within those organizations that perform outstanding service to the community.

Among her other duties, the Good Neighbor Director cooperates with art centers in her locality and plans a comprehensive program of art exhibits and receptions which are held frequently in her store.   (14)

Department Store Gives Technical Aid to Arts

Cultural groups in New Jersey seeking advice on such promotional problems as publicizing productions, selling tickets, printing programs, placing ads, and selecting media, frequently find the answers to their problems in their local department store. Bamberger's, a chain of department stores in Newark and seven other New Jersey cities, offers technical assistance to arts groups as part of a comprehensive program in the cultural field.

Bamberger's active and unique program in the arts began in 1959 when it arranged for the Ballet Russe de Monte Carlo to appear at the Mosque Theatre in Newark. With the store backing the visit with an all-out promotional campaign, the performance was a sell-out, and Bamberger's became convinced that the community wanted good cultural attractions on a regular basis. The store arranged for yearly return visits by the ballet company and immediately launched a campaign to bring other top arts programs to New Jersey.

Since then, Bamberger's has arranged for many performing arts groups to visit Newark and other areas of the state where it has stores. This month, for example, it helped to bring the National Ballet Company from Washington, D.C., to Newark and to Trenton for two performances in each city. A Van Cliburn concert arranged by the store will take place in Newark soon. Although Bamberger's does not actually act as impresario for any of the visiting attractions, it does initiate many of the preliminary performance arrangements and its also pays for promotional expenses. In addition, it sells tickets, publicizes the events, advertises the performances and prints most of the programs free of charge.

The store, which assumed all responsibility for promotion and institutional advertising on behalf of the now defunct Garden State Concerts, now lends its full support to the New Jersey Symphony. The store, in fact, played one of the major roles in the planning and administration of the orchestra's annual Symphony Ball, and Arthur Manchee, Bamberger's chairman of the board, served as chairman for the affair. The store also wrote and printed the program for the ball, printed tickets and sold tables.

According to Martin Stuart, public relations director of Bamberger's, the store's informal program of technical aid to the arts helps two or three different cultural groups each week. Stuart and his three assistants, one in the Paramus store, one in the Cherry Hill store, and a third who travels among the other stores, see leaders of cultural organizations in their offices and advise them on promotion, advertising and other technical matters.

In the visual arts, Bamberger's presents a *Living With Art Show* each January. This exhibition, designed to uncover new artists, is open to any New Jersey resident. Although the store retains several of the paintings for its permanent collection, most of the works are available for purchase.

619

The retail chain has also been instrumental in developing a monthly calendar of cultural events with the assistance of the Greater Newark Development Council. It takes a regular ad in the calendar to help support its production and mails calendars free of charge to all who request copies. "We have a stake in our customers and the community," Stuart told *AM*, "and we believe that through our program in the arts we are offering a real service to the community." (27)

Retailers Aid Arts

Local cultural groups can pick up added financial support by lending a hand to local retailers. In North Carolina one successful gift shop owner gives a different arts group each year the money he would otherwise spend on 3,500 customer Christmas cards. In addition, he donates 10 per cent of the profits from all Christmas cards sold at his store and 10 per cent of the sales on a designated day to the cultural organization. The recipient group simply announces this policy to its members when mailing them their season tickets and thus encourages their patronage of the shop. (10)

Store Promotions

Many department stores now plan special promotions for a week or longer built around specific themes. Alert art organizations can suggest tieing in with the planned events. Often, the stores will help to promote the organizations affiliated with the events in advertising and publicity, and will sometimes give them window space.   (38)

————————◄•►————————

Store Windows Feature Work
Of Local Arts Organizations

Cultural organizations in and around Washington, D.C. received a generous promotional boost in July and early August from Woodward & Lothrop, the largest department store in the area. For a full month the store turned over two show windows in its main store, and 17 windows in four of its suburban stores, to exhibit the work of local arts groups and cultural institutions.

A luncheon at the store, attended by local cultural leaders, preceded the display program.

The Woodward & Lothrop display department asked each organization to help plan its own window and to furnish props and costumes wherever needed. Thus, Arena Stage provided costumes and props from its recently concluded production of *The Threepenny Opera.* Several art galleries offered either original pieces of sculpture and paintings or good reproductions.

Most spectacular display of all was a ballet scene from Tschaikovsky's *Swan Lake,* with mobile figures in brilliant costumes moving to ballet music that could be heard by side-

621

walk viewers. In displays where figures in contemporary dress were needed, the store supplied mannequins and clothed them attractively, without labels or prices. Nowhere did the store permit a commercial note to intrude on the cultural displays.

Each of the cultural groups involved in the store's promotion benefited by receiving free publicity in a new and colorful form. The event was reported in the newspapers, and stimulated a city-wide, word-of-mouth discussion. People interested in the work of particular arts groups visited the stores to view the windows, and many stayed to do some shopping.

The midsummer salute to Washington cultural groups fits into a pattern of month-long summer salutes developed by the store over the past several years. The cultural project was eight weeks in the planning and execution. Woodward & Lothrop's summer display is the second longest of the year, only the pre-Christmas windows staying in place longer.

Principal benefit for the store, a Woodward & Lothrop spokesman told *Arts Management,* is that the cultural windows attract traffic. Not only are Washington area people drawn to the displays, but tourists are attracted as well. In addition, the store benefits from the goodwill generated by rendering a public service in the community where it does business. (19)

Shopping Center Fare: Groceries and Culture

Shopping centers, an accepted part of suburban life, are beginning to play an important role in promoting cultural activities in the community.

A good example is the Monmouth Shopping Center, Etontown, New Jersey, which serves all of Monmouth County and the northern part of Ocean County.

One of the largest of its kind in the state, the center receives $100,000 per year from the Merchants Association (a group comprising the management of its 42 stores) to promote a community relations program.

Since the center opened in 1960, this fund has been used, among other things, to sponsor plays, concerts, puppet shows, films, lectures and art shows. These events are held on the shopping center's sidewalks or in the 400-seat Civic Auditorium.

Although the auditorium was built for use by the Center, commercial groups can rent it for $25 to $100 per day, depending upon the space used. Non-profit organizations are billed slightly less. The center charges no admission to any program it sponsors and makes no profit from renting the hall. The money received is used to pay for maintainance and personnel of the auditorium.

This year, on July 13, the center will hold its fourth annual outdoor art show, and over 600 professional and amateur artists from all over New Jersey are expected to participate. No fee is charged to enter the show. A panel of competent artists and art critics serves as judges.

To promote events and to keep the community informed, the center publishes its own newspaper, issues monthly bulletins to the stores' 900 employees so that sales personnel can inform shoppers of what the center is doing, distributes posters and advertises on highway billboards. The 800-member children's club, formed by the center, also receives a monthly calendar of events.

The center's stores, including Bamberger's, Montgomery Ward and Lerner's, donate window space, lend merchandise and contribute prizes for the various art shows.

Cultural groups seeking to enlist the aid of a shopping center should approach the manager of its largest store. If he himself cannot help, he will direct you to the proper person to whom you may present your plan for staging a performance or establishing an arts program within the shopping center.   (17)

------------◄•►------------

Arts Group Profits from Shopping Center Shows

Smaller performing arts organizations can win new audiences, achieve widespread publicity and realize financial gain by presenting productions in local shopping centers. Because shopping centers are highly competitive operations, their managers are constantly seeking promotional activities, such as performances, which will attract large numbers of customers. In Baltimore, Maryland, for example, the Baltimore City Ballet Company has given seven performances during the past year at a large shopping center before an aggregate audience of more than 10,000 people, many of them first time attendees at a ballet. According to Max Yerman, president of the ballet company, "These are the few projects from which we actually make a profit."

The ballet company got the idea of performing in shopping centers in the spring of 1963 and it sent letters to managers of the larger centers in Baltimore, inviting them to attend the ballet's second annual dance festival as guests of the company. As a result, a very large and profitable center, the Mondawmin Shopping Center, asked the Baltimore City Ballet to present four fifteen minute performances as an Easter promotion at a fee of $500. An audience of about 3500 people attended the performances and the management of the center was so pleased that it invited the ballet company to return for two Saturday performances at a fee of $600. Attendance exceeded 5000.

This spring the company again presented an Easter performance and it has also been invited back to the Mondawmin Center for a two performance, back-to-school promotion in the fall. According to Mr. Yerman, the shopping center and the ballet company now have a mutually happy relationship and from all indications the dance group will continue to work with the shopping center.

It has been especially significant to the ballet that Mondawmin promoted each of the performances to its mailing list of about 80,000 people, thus giving the Baltimore City Ballet excellent and widespread exposure.   (28)

Arts Program Draws Crowds to Shopping Center

Visitors to the Walt Whitman Shopping Center in Huntington Station, Long Island, enjoyed a free performance of ballet and orchestral music on a Sunday afternoon in the Fall. The unusual performance, presented by the Ballet Repertory Company and the Orchestra da Camera, was supported by the New York State Council on the Arts under its Professional Touring Performing Arts Program and sponsored by the Walt Whitman Shopping Center Merchants Association.

To highlight its week-long Mexican Festival, the association asked the Council to support a top cultural program. Once the program was approved, the association spent about $5,000 to get its covered malls prepared for the free presentation. Costs included heating the performance area, renting chairs for the audience, assembling a stage, providing dressing rooms and sound equipment and staffing the site for the event. The performance was presented on a Sunday when the 80-unit center, with more than a million square feet of space, is normally closed.

A capacity crowd of 2,000 attended the performance and 5,000 additional people were turned away. Omar Lerman, the Council's special consultant on the performing arts, termed the performance, "one of the most successful in the Council's history."

Alvin M. Goldberg, executive director of the merchants group, noted that the performance has spurred a continuing program of cultural events at the center, including organ recitals by Evan Wood on November 1st and Mark Bauer on November 8th. Each of the performances drew audiences of about 1,500 people.

Mr. Goldberg told *AM,* "The objective of the association is to make the shopping center a community center for culture as well as a good place to shop. We are attempting to duplicate in a small way what the Council is doing." He added that, "exposing the shopping center to an audience of arts lovers will ultimately pay off in good will."

To promote the event, the shopping center paid for advertisements in major Long Island newspapers.   (33)

Hotel Chain Creates Circulating Exhibit

A hotel chain, with 33 locations throughout the East and Midwest, is launching its own series of traveling art exhibitions. The Pick Hotels, located in 29 cities in 19 states, eventually hopes to mount an exhibition at each location.

The idea for exhibitions originated at Washington's Pick Motor Inn, where sales manager Dan Botkiss, a former art student, set aside an area in his mezzanine for a permanent display. The first exhibit featured the paintings of the Italian-born artist, Pietro Lazzari. The public received the idea so favorably that the chain's main office in Chicago decided to send exhibitions to each of its other hotels, with the chain paying for the cost of transporting both the paintings and the artist, whose works were on exhibition, to the next location.

Botkiss frankly admits that the exhibitions are designed as "art on the run" for guests who are too busy to visit art galleries outside the hotel. (22)

New Hotel Warms House with Gala for Arts Givers

A Washington cultural group raised more than $11,000 with relative ease, and a swank, new capital hotel made hundreds of friends in a unique cooperative venture.

The teamwork formula, carried out by the Washington Ballet Guild and the Georgetown Inn, can be adapted for benefit parties wherever the management of a new hotel or restaurant, properly situated and equipped, is willing to spend money for an opening splash to attract attention.

The Georgetown Inn, a small, beautifully-decorated hotel aiming at a clientele of discriminating taste, took the initiative. Long before construction was finished, Julius Epstein, Georgetown Inn operator, sought a cultural organization for which the hotel could stage an opening-week benefit, on the theory that its best friends locally would be people interested in the arts.

Mr. Epstein offered space, a cocktail reception and a lavish dinner with three wines, completely free of charge, at a cost to the hotel of more than $3,000. The National Symphony Orchestra was approached at first, but rejected the proposition because of space limits in the hotel dining rooms. The ballet, a smaller group, then accepted. It promoted the benefit tickets as both an aid to the guild and as admission to a special preview of a unique hotel-restaurant, amid a gala crowd of VIPs.

The benefit dinner drew 220 friends of the ballet guild and their guests, who paid $50 apiece to attend the evening affair. An added fillip was the presence of the Duke and Duchess of Windsor. Socially and financially, the Washington Ballet Guild found the joint enterprise a great success. George L. Williams, guild leader responsible for the benefit, wrote to the hotel management:

"I don't believe there could ever be another benefit so well done because the hotel management was so lavish in their contribution to the ballet. We all, trustees and patrons of the ballet, are very grateful and appreciative of what you did."

Mr. Epstein, who heads a firm that manages hotels in several cities, told *Arts Management.* "I am delighted with the results. The ballet benefit allowed us to show the Georgetown Inn to the flower of Washington philanthropy. These are the best people in the city, both from my viewpoint and that of the ballet guild." (5)

Hotel Help

Hotels can help to promote your arts program. Recently, Chait's, an art-oriented hotel in Accord, New York, mailed post cards to its former guests announcing the American premiere of a play at New York City's Renata Theatre. Headed "Dear Friends," the notices were signed by the hotel owners. Included on the cards were performance dates, ticket prices and a form for purchasing tickets which could be mailed directly to the theater. (47)

Resorts Provide Growing Market For Cultural Programs

Resort hotels are becoming more involved with the arts, and cultural groups near these resorts might well consider working with them. These hotels can help promote an arts program, gain publicity for an organization, and, in some instances, be a source of added income.

Art galleries have been established in some resorts; others have presented music and arts festivals; and many hostelries have added recognized art instructors to their payrolls.

A good example is Tamiment in the Poconos, Pennsylvania. For the past three years, this resort has aided the Poconos Arts Center by donating to it all proceeds from a chamber music festival the hotel sponsors. Concerts, held four days a week, are free to the hotel's guests, but visitors must purchase tickets for $2.00 each from the Arts Center. The Arts Center, in turn, promotes the performances. Last year, this organization realized several hundred dollars from the festival.

Tamiment is probably the only resort in the country to build a special hall just to house its annual chamber music festival. However, the hotel encourages the arts in other ways, too. It holds frequent art shows and schedules weekly lectures ranging from psychology to art appreciation. One evening a week concert recitals are held in the Tamiment Playhouse. Plays, jazz groups and ballet companies also are booked into the hotel.

Art groups interested in cooperating with local resorts should write or see the public relations director or program coordinator of the hotel.   (17)

------------◄●►------------

Arts Get Free Publicity From Travel Companies

Arts organizations may be able to obtain important promotional help from businesses in the transportation field if they plan in advance, if they are not easily discouraged, and if they develop imaginative programs geared to the individual needs of each business approached.

In Lake George, New York, for example, Fred Patrick, executive producer of the Opera Festival there, received continuous free advertising space from a bus company and an airline during his entire season last summer.

Beginning in December, 1962, Mr. Patrick approached nearly 150 companies involved with transportation, including airlines, railroads, gas and oil companies, and hotels, suggesting a joint promotional campaign built around Lake George's importance as a tourist center. In each instance, Mr. Patrick geared his approach to the particular promotional needs of the company. About 25 businesses responded and two, the Schenectady Bus Lines, Inc. and Mohawk Airlines, worked out definite programs with the festival.

The bus line established a special reduced rate service on Friday and Saturday nights for the 50-mile trip from Schenectady to the opera, and featured the opera festival in many free advertisements. The festival, in turn, promoted the concept of bus trips to the door of the opera performance.

The airline company, which flies to within nine miles of Lage George, put 11-inch stickers on the back of every seat in its planes. They read, "Lake George is an opera festival. Go there on Mohawk Airlines." It promoted the festival with the same slogan on billboards throughout New York City. The opera festival gave space in its program to the airline.

Hotels, motels and restaurants in the vicinity of Lake George also cooperated with the festival in the planning of a press trip. Mr. Patrick invited 15 writers from leading publications in New York City to attend the festival, and the local facilities provided free lodging and meals to the writers in the hope that their establishments and the area would receive favorable coverage from the reporters. As a result of this kind of cooperation, the festival's only expense was in providing round-trip automobile transportation for the writers from New York to the festival at a total cost of about $200. The Opera Festival at Lake George received widespread national publicity.

According to Mr. Patrick, the key to receiving promotional aid from transportation facilities lies in discovering how a cooperative program might benefit the business approached. Often, he claims, the key may be an obvious one.

(23)

Auto Dealer Gives Art Free Ride to Exhibits

A New York automobile agency is offering artists free studio-to-gallery transportation of their one-man exhibitions. According to Curt Gruber, general sales manager of Fifth Avenue Motors, a Volkswagen dealership which has exhibited art in its showrooms, his company launched the program in the hopes of finding prospective station wagon customers among artists. First announced in December, the promotion has already benefited 14 artists who have had one man shows transported to the exhibition gallery.

The offer appears as a monthly pull-out coupon advertisement in a publication, the *New York Arts Calendar*. Its only conditions are that the artist must accompany his works in the Volkswagen bus, dates be made at least ten days in advance, the transportation be limited to one delivery from studio to gallery in Manhattan. Although artists have called and requested the movement of furniture and other items, the offer is limited to the art scheduled to appear in one-man shows. Normal automotive insurance, provided by the automotive dealer, covers the vehicle and its contents.

The company, which now has several artists seriously interested in purchasing station wagons, is continuing the offer indefinitely and may even extend it to include group shows in the future. Also, according to Gruber, there is an excellent possibility that the program may become national. He has suggested adoption of the program in an article submitted to the special trade publication of Volkswagen dealers throughout the country. (25)

Newspaper, Railroad and Stratford Festival Bring Toronto to Shakespeare in Package Trip

By

Harry J. Allen, Jr.

The Stratford Shakespearean Festival at Stratford, Ontario, Canada, has a theatre-by-rail plan that guarantees it almost 10,000 patrons a season, about $10,000 worth of free advertising lineage, and thousands of news lines in a metropolitan newspaper. In cooperation with the Toronto *Telegram* and the Canadian National Railways, the Festival draws as many as 600 adult patrons a week for the two-hour trip from Toronto, a city of more than a million, 88 miles away by rail.

The 1962 season offers 14 Tuesday evening trains, including one afternoon special in behalf of the Actors' Fund. For an entire evening's package, the patron pays $11.25 and gets a $5 theatre ticket, or $9.75 with a $3.50 seat. He gets round-trip rail transportation, a festival ticket, dinner, bus transportation in Stratford and a beverage during or after the performance. In each case, the festival receives the full price for its ticket.

Victor Polley, festival general manager, says the joint promotion with the newspaper and railroad has helped to build the festival in Toronto, the large city closest to Stratford, and has encouraged many from Toronto to attend the theatre using other means of transportation. Polley says:

"There are still people who prefer to buy a package form of travel, in which they are given painless attendance at the theatre. We are fortunate in having a major newspaper like the *Telegram* to carry this promotion. It couldn't have been more ideal for us."

As many as six members of the newspaper's promotion staff are aboard each train to distribute booklets giving the layout of Stratford, a resume of the plays, and information about sights along the route. Attendants answer questions and pass out free roses, cigarettes, and wash 'n dry towels. In Stratford the patrons are carried by bus to a church where they are served dinner by one of the five church women's auxiliaries, and they are taken to the theatre. After the performance, the bus moves them back to the train for the trip home.

Announcement of the summer plans are made in March. The newspaper runs a three-column ad once and sometimes twice a week promoting the trains, and also provides considerable news lineage. The $10,000 value of this free advertising is equal to what Stratford spends for its entire United States advertising program.

The *Telegram* underwrites any losses incurred by the railroad. While some weeks show losses, compensating profits at other times keep the paper from losing money on the operation. The newspaper pays for its own ads, window cards and the staff it puts on the trains, as well as for the dinner.

Tickets are sold at the C.N.R. Toronto office, with Stratford allocating up to 500 tickets for each performance. If Stratford runs short of tickets, some of the Toronto ones are called back, with the box office keeping in close contact with the C.N.R. When the plan started eight years ago, 3,200 patrons made the trip; in 1959 and 1960, package patronage was close to 10,500 each year.

The *Telegram* also sponsors a student train in the first two weeks of September. This is nearly sold out, with more than 7,500 scheduled to "take the classroom to the theatre" in this way. There will be 12 trains running to matinee performances and two evening trains in the student program.

The *Telegram's* promotion has been emulated by two U. S. newspapers. The Buffalo, N. Y., *Catholic Union and Echo* charters a train and promotes through its columns some 1,500 tickets sold to Catholic high schools. The Detroit *News,* in addition, runs two trains a season to Stratford charging its readers $12.75 for the package. Both newspapers provide generous news coverage for the events.

The festival sends announcements to groups that have attended before, advising them to book early, and aids in arranging accommodations in Stratford.   (6)

Supermarkets Aid Arts at Checkout Counter

By gaining the cooperation of local merchants and their suppliers, cultural groups can create new avenues of advertising that effectively reach nearby audiences at a small cost. The Mummers Theater in Oklahoma City, Oklahoma, for example, arranged with the National Cash Register Company to let it imprint an advertisement reading, "Discover the Mummers, Subscribe Now," on the backs of cash register tapes the company sells to supermarkets for use as customer receipts.

The theater group then secured commitments in writing from three chain stores with 66 branches in the Oklahoma City area to use 35 cases of the imprinted tape rolls during the summer season. Safeway distributed the tapes to 20 stores, Humpty Dumpty to 19 stores and Seven-Eleven to 27 stores. Printing costs for the tapes were $70 for the logo and $6.64 for each caseload of tape, or a total of $232.40 for the entire promotion.

To guarantee the success of the promotion, chain stores needed to be assured by the tape supplier that they could purchase the comparatively small quantity of imprinted tapes used in the advertising campaign at the same price per case they paid for large quantities of clear tape. Speaking of the role played by the supplier in this aspect of the campaign as well as in the entire promotion, David Lunney of the theater group told *AM*, "the extra help of the local N.C.R. supplier is invaluable. He can really get things off the ground—if he wants to."

Greater effectiveness was given to the advertising drive by offering increased reductions during the campaign to season subscribers. Before the campaign started discounts of 15 per cent were offered on the purchase of tickets for the eight play season which runs from September, 1964 through June, 1965. However, during the month-long advertising drive, reductions were raised to 25 per cent. After the drive ended they reverted to the original 15 per cent discount, which will be available until the completion of the first play in the season's repertoire.

As a result of these and other promotional efforts, including the display of the Mummer logo on 15 billboards throughout the city, the theater company has excellent prospects of reaching record subscription totals. By midsummer the group had already obtained more than 3,500 season subscriptions. Included in the total were 1,100 new subscribers. This figure surpasses the 3,175 total subscriptions sold during all of last year. (30)

Record Shop Prospers By Giving the Arts a Hand

The record shop known as a center for good music can play a vital role in a city's cultural life well beyond that of selling fine recordings.

An example is the Discount Record Shop in Washington, D. C., which has recently expanded both its function and its title to the Discount Record, Book and Print Shop. Basic to the merchandising outlook of Robert Bialek, president of the firm, is that lovers of good music, books and graphic art in one city are very often the same people.

While records remain the anchor of the shop's business, broadening its cultural appeal has both stimulated patronage and sales and enabled it to render greater community service. The results have been mutually profitable, since the store's name is repeatedly connected with cultural activity. The shop:

—helps publicize performances by local cultural groups by displaying their posters;

—acts as a ticket sales point for benefit concerts;

—gives generously to fund drives by established groups like the National Symphony Orchestra and the Arena Stage;

—assists in sponsoring new organizations, like the local opera society;

—promotes the recordings of local artists to help them gain recognition; and

—publicizes visiting artists by interviews on the shop's weekly radio program carried by a good music station, WGMS.

Now rounding out its eleventh year in business, the Discount Record Shop has in the past four seasons stepped out on its own as impresario. It has booked into Washington comedians like Jack Paar and Tom Lehrer, and popular vocal groups like "The Limelighters" and "The Weavers." This season the shop has booked the Philadelphia Orchestra for a series of five Tuesday evening concerts conducted by Ormandy, Klemperer and Stokowski. It has also presented Peter Cook's "Establishment", a full length topical revue from London. In its role as impresario the shop works closely with the city's principal concert manager to avoid conflicts in bookings.

"We have a sense of civic responsibility in our business," Bialek told *Arts Management,* "so we try to fill a cultural need not met by others. From our experience with what sells in this shop we can tell what will go well in performance here.

"It would be very smart business for any good music store to become a center for ticket sales and arts publicity. People who come in for tickets often walk out having bought both tickets and records. But only if the store has the proper volume and the management know-how, should it try acting as impresario. Arts management of this kind is risky business."

Bialek estimates the number of customers entering his doors every week as "thousands." His mailing list, which is constantly renewed and is covered at least four times yearly with promotional material, he numbers "in the tens of thousands."

In its combined function as a retail cultural outlet and an interdisciplinary cross-roads for the community, Bialek believes his shop is unique. The idea of a retail store working closely with arts groups, however, may well be applicable in a good many communities.　(11)

Win Diners

Local restaurants can help to promote cultural groups. Many restaurants may be willing to have a printed message about an arts organization appear on the back of their customer checks, if the organization pays the small printing cost. When such a check is presented face down, the message of the cultural organization greets customers.   (29)

Illuminating the Arts

Looking for a unique way to advertise cultural activities in your community? Perhaps a local retail operation might lend you its facilities. In Huntsville, Alabama, for example, a laundry allowed the Arts Council of Huntsville to announce cultural events on its illuminated revolving sign. In 8 months, the Council displayed 46 announcements on the sign.   (51)

Fill 'em Up With Publicity

Local gas stations may be a good source of free publicity for events your organization is sponsoring. Supply them with fliers and announcements which they can pass out to motorists along with change and trading stamps. During the summer it's wise to emphasize events with particular appeal to tourists passing through your community.   (16)

639

Milkman Brings Publicity

Free advertising may be available from your local dairy. For example, one arts group arranged for two dairies in its community to print messages on the side of their milk containers promoting the cultural organization's season subscription program. These messages included information on ticket prices and the organization's telephone number. Although the promotion was made without cost to the group, it had to supply all the art work for the announcement. (30)

Business Promotions Help Win New Audiences

New audiences for the arts can be created through the establishment of imaginative joint promotions with local businesses. For example, Martin Tahse, a theatrical producer, has successfully promoted his touring productions to audiences who do not normally attend theater by tying in promotions with chain store supermarkets and travel agents. As a result, there has been a steady upswing in attendance at his two latest road productions, *After the Fall* and *A Funny Thing Happened on the Way to the Forum*.

Advertising was aimed specifically at young non-theatregoers by including brief descriptions of play content in the copy. Mr. Tahse also arranged to have advertising placed on grocery bags used in supermarkets prior to the arrival of the shows. Coupons on the bags encouraged shoppers to send in for tickets or to inquire about theater parties. In addition, free tickets were raffled off at the supermarkets.

Another promotion instituted by Mr. Tahse was a tie-in with the National Tea Company, which mentioned *A Funny*

Thing on radio and television spot commercials, in window posters, in newspaper advertisements and in about one-and-a half million promotional booklets mailed to Chicago-area families. In exchange, Mr. Tahse gave the 250 supermarket stores owned by the company a total of 5,000 tickets to be awarded to shoppers.

Travel agents provided Mr. Tahse with another novel outlet for promoting his shows in communities within 75-miles of performance sites. Mr. Tahse helped put together a "package" for the agents to offer their clients. The package consisted of transportation arranged by the agent, an orchestra ticket provided at the normal price and an original cast recording and a souvenir book, both sold to agents at cost.

The agents sold the package at a profit, but below the price the items would normally cost the theatergoer. In that way, both agent and patron benefited while Mr. Tahse attracted a new audience to his shows. (34)

———◄●►———

Phone Bill Can Ring a Bell

An increasing number of public service messages are appearing in leaflets distributed by telephone companies with their monthly bills. The February leaflet of the Chesapeake & Potomac Telephone Co., for example, carried notices and appeals for the Boy Scouts, Girl Scouts, an educational TV station, the Y.M.C.A., Heart Month and Brotherhood Week. Arts groups can find out how to get this kind of mass publicity by calling the public relations office of the local phone company. (2)

———◄●►———

Apartment Houses

Local realtors and builders can be a good publicity outlet
for the arts. In New York City the John Adams apartment
house calls attention to the cultural life in its neighborhood
by listing in its rental ads the nearby cultural events. Another new apartment house, the St. Germain, has invited
groups to furnish programs and posters for display in the
lobby. (10)

———————◄●►———————

Real Estate Office

The window of a real estate office in a residential neighborhood can be a regular showcase for arts group publicity.
Many real estate dealers look for new ways to attract attention to their offices through their windows, which too frequently display the same, tired old snapshots of houses for
sale. An arts display publicizing an upcoming event can
be designed in cooperation with the dealer to promote the
idea that living in his sales area is culturally rewarding.
(15)

———————◄●►———————

PART FIVE: THE ARTS AND THE COMMUNITY:

Private, Governmental, and Educational

Chapter IX – Government and Private

Chapter X – Education and the Arts

Chapter IX – Government and Private

THE CITY

Cities to Play More Important Role in Arts

By

Alvin Toffler

I think we can sketch some of the new relationships between art and the city that seem likely to take shape in the next decade and a half. In this exercise in conjecture, I am speaking of cities with populations of about 500,000 or over, of which we will have a good many more by 1980.

1) Any such city without *professional* theatre, or music, or dance, without a first-rate art gallery, or bookshops, museums and a culture-oriented radio or television station, will be regarded as an embarrassing relic of the past . . . States and, perhaps, the federal government will rush to provide technical assistance to these culturally underdeveloped areas.

2) By 1980, virtually all such cities will have something that passes for a culture center . . . New facilities will have been built in part with public funds . . .

3) Every such city will have an arts council . . .

4) By 1980, most cultural centers and arts councils will be regarded by many artists as being already hopelessly ossified . . . New arts groups will spring up outside, and in opposition to, the centers and councils . . . Each city will have a "culture establishment," and around its edges, the start of an anti-establishment movement.

645

5) One reason for this breakaway will be the explosion of new artistic media and forms made possible by the technological revolution . . . plastics, computors, video tape . . . Experimenters with these will be represented in the main cultural institutions, but will rebel and demand more time, money and attention . . . These artists will continue to face a difficult struggle because most philanthropy will be channeled through the "arts establishment."

6) Newspapers, radio and television will devote more attention to the arts . . . Critics will be more specialized . . . local critics will be more respected and powerful.

7) Local universities will become much bigger; the dollar volume of educational activity will climb. All schools will be enormously more important in the economic and political life of the city.

8) The dollar volume of cultural activity will also increase sharply . . . Arts groups will be linked more closely with the ascendant power of the education system. Taken together, educational and cultural activity will constitute a very significant factor in the city economy. This economic significance will be reflected in sharply increased political influence . . .

9) Every city will have a culture lobby that will parallel and often work together with a local education lobby. Arts lobbies will pressure city councils for various subventions and concessions . . . City officials will be increasingly receptive to them, because by 1980 arts lobbies will enjoy the active support of business, labor and other politically potent groups in the community.

10) Virtually every city government will have some agency devoted primarily to the coordination and encour-

agement of artistic activity or to maintaining liaison with private groups performing these functions . . . This agency will channel funds from counterpart state and federal agencies into the arts institutions of the city, most likely in support of riskless culture, the safe and the traditional. It will also compile detailed data about local arts activity and review all contemplated municipal decisions from the point of view of their potential impact on the arts . . . Cities can also be expected to levy a variety of imaginative taxes and charges to raise money for the arts.

As culture becomes legitimate grist for the local political mill, it is predictable that many groups outside the culture industry will make their weight felt in decisions concerning the arts.

If these predictions have any validity, it is clear that public agencies will play a far more important role in the development of the arts . . . Cities, by becoming more important as patrons, will further reduce the already declining significance of the individual donor—the only real source of support for venturesome arts projects.

This imbalance in the patronage structure can be offset somewhat by the city offering tax incentives to individual donors and by offering aid directly to artists, including— and especially—those not affiliated with any institutions. Loft studios could be designed into public housing projects and offered to painters at minimal rents. Similarly, cities could offer special low rent apartments to composers and performers.

Another way for cities to help creative artists is to give them some institutional connection as, perhaps, . . . artists-in-residence attached to libraries or to school systems at teachers' salaries . . . Cost would be minimal.

647

Concern for the quality of life will deepen in the next 15 years, mainly because powerful economic and social forces, acting on our value systems, are going to compel it to happen. People will care about their cities and will demand a higher level of cultural activity than ever before.

None of this means that utopia will have arrived. Each change has consequences not immediately visible and not necessarily good for the arts or the city or society.　(41)

'Culture Vote' Can Prod Cities to Assist Arts

The role of municipalities in culture is becoming increasingly important. Although the kind of assistance city governments give to the arts varies widely from community to community and their overall contribution is still relatively small, the potential of municipal support cannot be dismissed.

In Los Angeles, for example, the city supports programs in both the visual and performing arts. This includes sponsorship of band, choral and chamber music concerts, ballet recitals, and support for the Hollywood Bowl, the Los Angeles Philharmonic and several community orchestras. In addition, a Municipal Art Commission incorporated into the city charter since 1911, budgeted nearly $300,000 out of a total 1963-1964 city budget of $271,025,417 for cultural purposes. The Commission operates an all-city art festival in Barnsdall Park, is responsible for the design of all public buildings and for the acquisition and location of the city's art works.

What role can arts leaders play to encourage municipal support of the arts? Eddy S. Feldman, a member of the Los Angeles Board of Municipal Art Commissioners, suggests the following four point program:

1. Citizens should find out what cultural facilities the city provides and use them.

2. Citizens should concern themselves with the work of municipal agencies concerned with the arts. They should attend meetings, make suggestions and wherever possible participate in the work of the agency.

3. Citizens should demand from their city the cultural programs which they cannot provide for themselves. Even if budgetary problems exist, claims Mr. Feldman, the creation of imaginative programs can have the effect of mobilizing both legislative and popular support for them. In addition, every part of the city, not just a few fortunate sections, should be exposed to high level cultural programs.

4. Citizens should impress their needs through demands on city officials and upon those who are running or plan to run for municipal office. According to Mr. Feldman there is such a thing as a "culture vote" and this was demonstrated in the 1963 mayoralty campaign in San Francisco when the arts became a campaign issue. "Culture voters," says Mr. Feldman, "will lend prestige to office holders and seekers, will work hard for their election, and provide them with financial support. The culture voters have only to be encouraged."

Mr. Feldman points out that it is the city administration's responsibility to lead the way in creating and expanding cultural programs. "It is not elected simply to follow tested and unimaginative pathways," he says. "The administration may not always be aware of the desires of the populace to be involved, yet all that may be needed is simply the inspired call to action." (26)

———————◄●►———————

Community Interest Sparked by Lectures
on City Redevelopment

A free series of lectures, sponsored by a museum with the active support of local arts and business leaders, has helped to spark community-wide interest in the revitalization of downtown Portland, Maine, and has increased local awareness of the importance of good architecture and the arts to the city's future well-being. These positive reactions are especially significant at a time when local arts groups are urging the construction of a performing arts center in downtown Portland.

The program resulted from a request by the Portland Museum of Art for assistance in developing an important lecture series. A local committee, including representatives of the Greater Portland Arts Council, selected the theme "Rebuilding Portland" as one which would have the greatest community significance. Planning began in February, 1965, a year prior to the presentation of the series of five lectures. The program was strategically timed to precede the issuance of a report by Victor Gruen Associates on downtown Portland redevelopment.

During the entire planning period, the support and cooperation of community leaders helped the committee stay within its budget of less than $1500. A public relations firm volunteered its assistance, five local commercial banks underwrote the hiring of Frye Hall where the programs were presented, news media offered their full cooperation, and most of the speakers, who were well-known city planners and architects, waived lecture fees. Also, local television station WGAN made a film and video tape of the lectures.

With community interest high and with excellent pre-publicity, the lectures, held on Wednesday evenings in Feb-

650

ruary and March, attracted full houses of about 500 people each. Most attendees were men. The series consisted of lectures on the mid-century city, mid-century urban design, Portland today, Portland tomorrow—downtown, and Portland tomorrow—regional metropolis. Large dinners preceded the first and fourth lectures and informal parties at the museum followed the other three lectures. The museum also featured an exhibition related to the series.

According to Mrs. Sidney W. Thaxter, co-chairman of the lecture series and president of the arts council, "The series was very successful in opening the minds of the people to the many facets of redesigning a city today. The lectures really awakened several important business leaders to a new perspective." She told *AM* that since the series ended, one building has been bought and repaired and a colorful restaurant has been installed in it.

An equally important result, especially with the arts council attempting to engender interest in a new downtown arts center, has been the positive reaction of civic officials. "City councilmen," Mrs. Thaxter told *AM*, "have said they now realize the importance of downtown activity at night in the center city, a point emphasized by the lectures." The arts council is now awaiting the recommendations for downtown to be released in the forthcoming Gruen report, before any action on the arts center can take place.

As a subsidiary benefit of the series, the arts council gained 200 new members following the completion of the series, representing a 50 per cent membership increase.

(52)

Convention Bureau

St. Louis, through its Touring and Convention Bureau, gave $50,000 to the St. Louis Symphony for a special program designed to promote the city as a convention and tourist site. Some of the money will be used by the orchestra for two out-of-town concerts, in New York's Carnegie Hall on March 8th and at Washington's Kennedy Center on March 13th. Between 500 and 1,000 New York and Washington business leaders will be invited to each of these concerts and to receptions following them, which will promote the attractions of St. Louis. The rest of the money will provide St. Louis convention-goers with tickets to the orchestra's local concerts. (14)

Printing Help

Need flyers and press releases printed? Perhaps a municipal agency can help you. In San Francisco, the Art Commission has established a community printing service which all local cultural groups can use to promote their upcoming events. Charges are minimal and when organizations can't afford to pay, the service is free. (71)

Generous City Budget Supports Park, Recreation Arts Program

The arts are playing an increasingly important role in the planning of park and recreation agencies. An especially ambitious and comprehensive program is that run by the Bureau of Parks and Public Recreation in Portland, Oregon, which organizes and sponsors performing arts groups, offers training in the visual and performing arts, provides facilities to cultural organizations and presents a yearly sixteen-day arts festival in a municipal park.

Cultural programming by the Bureau is a full-scale, year-round operation involving considerable expense. Salaries of the specialists directing it come from the city budget. Park funds cover maintenance of physical facilities used by arts groups, some construction and general operating expenses. And for most productions under its sponsorship the Bureau does not charge admission.

Under the leadership of the Director of Recreation, Miss Dorothea M. Lensch, a staff of fourteen cultural specialists, nine full-time and five part-time, work on the Portland arts program. Activity is based at the neighborhood level in community centers and schools, where instruction is given. More advanced activities are carried on by city-wide groups in each of the artistic disciplines.

During the past five years, according to Miss Lensch, the municipal budget for cultural activities has increased markedly each year; so has participation in the programs.

The Bureau sponsors two dance groups: the Dance Repertory Group and Dance Apprentices. Both are open by audition and by invitation of the Bureau's director of the dance. A Ballet Center supplements the ballet classes offered in every neighborhood. It sponsors three workshop

653

companies which perform in public and on television, and give demonstrations throughout the city.

Opera in Portland is presented under the auspices of the Bureau, which sponsors three productions each year in city schools, in public halls and in the outdoor theatre of a city park. Produced by the Theatre Arts Opera Association, a volunteer company with a paid musical director, the performances are of professional quality, according to Miss Lensch. Winners of the Metropolitan and San Francisco Opera auditions have had preliminary training with the company.

The music program includes sponsorship of the Community String Orchestra, a group which gives regular concerts through the year and presents a summer series at Mt. Tabor Park. Distinguished professional musicians frequently appear with the orchestra as soloists. In the schools a comprehensive educational program is built around the Community Music Center, a children's conservatory.

The visual arts program is based in the Portland Junior Museum and the Craft House, sponsored by the Bureau. In theatre, the Bureau provides training for adults and children in each neighborhood. A more advanced Theatre Workshop provides talented youngsters with individual instruction in music, dance and voice. The Workshop presents a monthly television show and regularly performs before civic groups.

Highlight of the Bureau's cultural work each year is its coordinating the programs of several arts groups into the sixteen-day Washington Park Summer Festival, held in August. With its fourteenth season ahead, the Festival has become an attraction for visitors throughout the state of Oregon. Admission is free to all concerts and performances, except for a small program fee charged at the opera.

Another summer program sponsored by the Bureau, the Volcano Theatre, is unique in that programs are held in an outdoor theatre where stage and lights have been built into an extinct crater.

"There are no short cuts in our work," Miss Lensch told *Arts Management.* "It requires hours of dedicated service by volunteers and the department staff, often salted with disappointment and heartbreak. But the results are there."

(14)

Mayor's Proclamation

Do you have an important event coming up? A proclamation from the mayor of your city, properly publicized, may be helpful in focusing attention on it. When suggesting a proclamation to a civic official, however, be sure to emphasize the community-wide significance of the event. (48)

Arts Council City Tour Wins Friends and Funds

Arts groups in communities which attract large numbers of tourists might consider establishing guided tours of their city, to bring in extra revenue and to publicize their own organization. The Dallas Symphony has sponsored "Face of Dallas" tours for some time; last year the Coordinating Council for the Arts in Hartford, Connecticut, initiated tours on the theme: "This is Hartford."

When arts council leaders in Hartford several years ago conceived the idea of organized tours patterned after the Dallas operation, they first investigated the possible interest that visitors would have in such tours and the probable number of visitors to the city. One knowledgeable local resident then volunteered to check landmarks and points of interest, draw up suggested itineraries and determine the approximate time for each tour.

At this point, the council recognized that the job was too big and important for volunteer help. It hired a local housewife who had been active in volunteer work and who was interested in the city of Hartford and its history to serve as tour leader.

Last May, five regular tours for groups of fifteen or more were established. They ranged from a $3.50 per person, two and one-half hour "Heart of Hartford" tour for the visitor with limited time, to a deluxe tour by Cadillac limousine, with prices dependent upon length of time taken. The other three tours, costing $4.50 per person, are all three and one-half hours long.

Rather than operating on a regular schedule, tours are arranged by appointment, when there are a sufficient number of visitors interested in taking one. Mrs. Andrew Shepard, the guide, is able to adapt to this flexible schedule. She is paid $1.00 for each person taking the tour.

For a two and one-half hour tour of 20 people at $3.50 per person, the bus company gets $1.00 a person, admissions account for $.50, Mrs. Shepard receives $1.00 and the arts council receives $1.00. As the number of visitors goes up, the bus price per person goes down and the council receives the additional revenue.

Conventions are the mainstay of an effective tour program, according to Mrs. Shepard, since they bring large groups who are interested in seeing the highlights of the community quickly and in an organized way. Although the program has been developing slowly, and profits to the arts council are small, the tour sponsors hope that convention guests scheduled to visit Hartford this spring will help to boost attendance. A brochure describing the tour is helping to promote the program.

While few organizations may get rich on this kind of activity, its public relations benefits to the sponsoring organization and to the city can be compensation enough.   (14)

Artists in Residence Belong to Whole City

A unique artist-in-residence project, established last year for an entire community rather than for a single institution, is part of a comprehensive city-wide program for the arts and education in Flint, Michigan, a city of 200,000 residents.

A spur to the development of major cultural activities in Flint has been the Committee of Sponsors for the Flint College and Cultural Development, Inc., a non-profit organization founded in 1954. Since then, in community fund raising drives, the Committee has raised more than $30,000,000 from 12,000 donors for educational and cultural facilities. Already, nearly $8,000,000 has been turned over to the Flint Board of Education for the construction and maintenance of such educational and cultural buildings as the DeWaters Arts Center, the home of the Flint Institute of Arts, which was completed several years ago.

In addition, several Committee projects initially conceived in 1954, are now nearing realization. A theatre-auditorium seating 2,100 and a Museum of Transportation will be completed by 1965. The Museum will be the first unit of a complex which will eventually have additional wings for a museum of history, a museum of natural history, a children's museum and a science museum.

The artist-in-residence program originated when a group of prominent Flint residents, impressed with a concert by young pianist, Coleman Blumfield, suggested that he be brought to the community. Last year, Blumfield became Flint's first artist-in-residence in a program administered by the Flint Board of Education and underwritten by the W. S. Ballenger Trust and the Charles Stewart Mott Foundation.

The purpose of the program is two-fold. First, it is designed to stimulate the cultural life of the community and its music students by providing access to a top musical talent at no charge. Second, it gives recognition to an outstanding young artist.

During his recently concluded first season—he has been reengaged for this year—Blumfield taught master classes to promising students, performed with community groups, and gave concerts.   (22)

Community Artists-in-Residence
Stimulate Amateur Performers

A month-long experimental artist-in-residence program sponsored by the Fort Wayne, Indiana, Fine Arts Foundation, an arts council, proved so successful that it will become an annual program. It will alternate yearly between the performing and the graphic arts.

In cooperation with the Fort Wayne Ballet, the city's non-professional dance company, the Foundation engaged the First Chamber Dance Quartet as artists-in-residence beginning in May. The Quartet's dancers are former members of the New York City Ballet.

During its stay in the community, the Quartet presented three performances, including two premieres at the Fort Wayne Fine Arts Festival, and also performed with the

Fort Wayne Ballet. Its members taught advanced classes at the Ballet's school, created a ballet for the local company and gave lecture-demonstrations in the city's public schools.

In addition, the Quartet spent four days with ballet teachers and advanced students from other cities in Indiana and from neighboring states. They led a workshop on costuming and conducted master classes.

George M. Schaefer, executive director of the Foundation, told *AM*, "The Quartet gave our ballet students a new lease on life and completely won over school audiences.

"Furthermore," added Mr. Schaefer, "our experiment proved that the presence of professionals in no way lessens the pleasure of the amateur performer. On the contrary, it heightens his pleasure and stimulates him to improve his own abilities."

To enable the arts council to establish an annual artist-in-residence grant, the local Community Concert organization is booking a non-subscription performance by the Metropolitan Opera National Company. Proceeds will go to the Foundation.

Not only arts and education groups, however, are employing artists-in-residence. In an unusual development, the Norwegian lines M/S Viking Princess, has named an artist-in-residence for its forthcoming 106-day round-the-world cruise. John Day, an American painter, has been given studio facilities aboard the ship to prepare for his one-man show to be held in New York next March. During the trip, he will discuss painting daily with passengers.   (41)

Symphony Orchestra Tries Cooperative Approach

America's first cooperative symphony orchestra, the Boston Philharmonia, is actively working on plans for a fall season, after having completed its first series of three favorably-received concerts this April. Immediately ahead for the orchestra is a week of concerts this summer in five Boston neighborhoods, under the sponsorship of the city's "Summerthing" festival.

The 40-member orchestra, drawn from independent Boston-area musicians, was organized to supplement rather than compete with other Boston and New England musical groups, by reaching a wider new audience. Although successful cooperative orchestras exist in Europe, they are profit-making organizations in which players own shares of stock. The Philharmonia is incorporated as a non-profit, non-stock corporation.

However, the Philharmonia terms itself "100 per cent artistically cooperative," since the musicians are permanent corporate members of the Philharmonia Society, hold three permanent memberships on its board of trustees, have exclusive decision-making power on the selection of orchestra personnel, have an equal vote with the trustees on the engagement of conductors and orchestra management, and must be consulted on policy matters concerning the musical product. A Music Advisory Committee of three orchestra players, recently established to develop guidelines for programming, is chaired by Harvard composer Leon Kirchner.

Present plans call for the orchestra to continue its guest conductor policy through next season. Musicians who were paid on a per-concert basis this season, will be paid on a seasonal basis during 1968-1969, with the base above the local scale. Although funding eventually will come from a plurality of sources, the immediate fund drive is being aimed at large local corporations. (61)

———————◄●►———————

Citizens' Arts Panels Plan Ahead for Tulsa

A series of panel reports on the arts of Tulsa, Oklahoma, may help shape that city's cultural future. The reports, recently submitted to the board of the Arts Council of Tulsa, contained the findings and recommendations of five of the six panels appointed by the organization a year ago to investigate the city's cultural activities. The Council is expected to rely on the panel proposals in its planning.

For the first time in the city's history, the panels brought together local cultural leaders to develop a short term as well as a long range program for the arts. Each panel, consisting of 20-to-30 persons, met independently from four-to-five times during the year. Reports were submitted on theater; dance; the literary arts; galleries and the visual arts; and city planning, landscaping, architecture and interior design. A report by the panel on music will be issued shortly.

While each panel had specific suggestions, several overall recommendations, to which all the panels subscribed, were made. Most dramatic of these was the suggestion that a multi-purpose performing arts center be built in Tulsa.

All panels saw the need for better coordination by the arts council in the planning of cultural events and in the dissemination of information.

Agreeing that audience building was a crying need of the arts in Tulsa, the panels came forth with a series of recommendations calling for greater promotional activity. Interestingly, they called for more publicity for good imported

661

cultural events which tend to receive less editorial space than strictly local arts activities.

Each panel found many existing problems in its specific area of investigation, and recommendations were terse and practical. Quality performances and professionalism were frequently cited needs, and in general, there was a call for increased contemporary programming — more modern dance, experimental theater and modern art exhibitions.

(43)

------◄•►------

Council Sends Display on Tour To Help Promote Its Programs

A low-cost and easily transportable traveling display has provided an arts council with an efficient and successful method of promoting its programs and services to the community.

The idea of assembling the display was conceived in the fall of 1964 by the Arts Council of Columbus, Ohio, during the planning of its annual Winter Showcase of the Arts, a 10-day festival highlighting community cultural events. Originally, the display was planned as a promotional vehicle to be exhibited at specific events during the Showcase period and arouse audience interest in other Showcase attractions. However, the exhibit proved so popular that it has since gone into year-round use, circulating from facility to facility.

The display consists of posters, programs, and photographs from each of the arts council's member organizations, representing such organizational characteristics as artists, physical facilities, and program content. These are blown up and dry-mounted on various-sized colored, flexible, poster boards and then placed on an aluminum framework consisting of four triangular, curved, free-standing units, three-feet wide by six-feet high. There is flexibility in the use of the exhibit since the components can be assembled into one unit or set up separately in close proximity to each other.

One of the key features of the display is the low cost in assembling it and in reconstructing it. In 1965, when it was first built, it cost $175.00. This year when it was rebuilt for the Winter Showcase, it cost only $121.00, because the aluminum framework remained usable and several exhibits did not have to be replaced.

Because of the effectiveness of the display in reaching a wide range of people, including many who are not normally part of the arts audience, the council plans to continue using it indefinitely. Most recently, for example, it was shown at a library and then was transported to a neighborhood community center.

For other arts groups who may consider using a similar display, Mrs. Frank W. Bentley, public relations chairman of the council, offers this advice. ''Make sure that the display is easy to transport. Ours can be dismantled and then reassembled and transported easily in a station wagon. The exhibit should also be stable enough to transport. Our units fold so they can fit into each other easily.'' (51)

Local Arts Council Fights City Hall and Wins

The united voice of the arts has scored an impressive victory over the forces of City Hall in Greensboro, North Carolina. Unlike most cultural tilts with officialdom, however, this battle involved neither money nor censorship. It centered about municipal parking regulations.

When in mid-September, the Greensboro Traffic Department, concerned with the heavy traffic flow, issued an edict prohibiting parking at any time on Elm Street, where the United Arts Council of Greensboro, Inc., is located, community arts leaders were visibly upset. For with street parking banned, attendance at Council arts classes, lectures and board meetings would have diminished considerably. Determined to take a stand, the Council asked all its officials and the presidents of its 31 member and associate organizations to appear at a meeting of the City Council the following week. Prior to the meeting, arts leaders hired a local photographer to take photographs of the street in question every hour on the hour from nine a.m. to three p.m., to demonstrate that traffic was not as heavy as city engineers claimed it to be. A mathematical presentation, indicating the average space between moving vehicles, was also prepared.

Following an impressive presentation, the City Council ordered a new traffic count of the street. This indicated that about 3,000 less vehicles used the street daily than the original traffic estimate indicated. The result? Parking on Elm Street was restored, except for rush hour periods.

Elsewhere, parking difficulties and transportation problems have spurred another cultural institution to take action. The Brooklyn Academy of Music, in Brooklyn, New York, which presents major programs in every area of the

664

arts, is located just across the river from Manhattan, the hub of cultural activity in New York City. The distance is not great, but to some members of the arts audience, Brooklyn is unfamiliar territory and parking presents a problem. So, early in October, the Academy launched a special bus service leaving from central locations on the East and West sides of Manhattan, with return trips scheduled fifteen minutes after performances end. The round-trip fare is $1.25 per person. The service was initiated when the Living Theatre appeared at the Academy and has continued during the special season of dance, featuring many of America's leading companies.

According to Academy director Harvey Lichtenstein, the bus service, which has been operating at about 75 per cent capacity, has proved its value. "Although we're not quite breaking even on it yet," he said, "we think we're attracting some first-time Academy-goers." (63)

————◄•►————

Joint Presentation

A cooperative program presented by several arts groups can attract great attention and thus increase audience potential. In Baltimore, Maryland, for example, audiences were drawn to each of three institutions which joined in presenting a recent exhibition, *Two Thousand Years of Calligraphy*. The show was divided into three chronological parts, and the Walters Art Gallery, the Baltimore Museum of Art, and the Peabody Institute Library, each presented a separate part simultaneously. (41)

————◄•►————

665

Schools Join With Town to Present Arts Series

A college, a high school, and a group of public spirited citizens have formed an alliance in Cazenovia, New York, to bring a cultural program to the community of about 3,000 residents. The first Cazenovia Community Series, launched this October, is proving so successful that it is now envisioned as an annual event.

In the past, Cazenovia College, a two year liberal arts institution for women, conducted its own lecture series. However, because of limited seating facilities, townspeople were unable to attend the programs. Last year a group of citizens, determined to bring cultural events to the community at large, formed a special sub-committee of the Citizens Advisory Committee for Town and Village Planning and with support from the State Council on the Arts, presented a January, 1963, performance by the Metropolitan Opera Studio in Cazenovia.

The townspeople responded so enthusiastically, that support was rallied for a regular community-wide program. The college offered to make its own series, supplemented by additional programs, available to everyone. The high school offered the use of its auditorium, which, with 650 seats, had double the capacity of the college facility. Thus, the Cultural Affairs Committee for the Cazenovia Community Series, with four members each from college, high school and town, was formed.

For its first season, a series of six presentations, including a ballet performance, four lectures, and the State Council-sponsored touring performance of the Irish Players in *Playboy of the Western World,* was arranged. Working as a team, the committee divided its work so that its high school and college members were in charge of staging and production and the community members in charge of tickets, sales promotion and general arrangements. Students have helped with lighting and props, and the college service club provided free ushers.

Attendance thus far has been close to capacity. Nearly 200 season tickets at $6.50 each were sold to townspeople and all 363 college students received season tickets as part of their school payments. High school students pay half price for all performances. As a special bonus, the committee offered a free State Council-sponsored performance of *The Worlds of Shakespeare* to subscribers.

As a guide to its future programming, the committee has been conducting an evaluation session following each performance. Both in advance of performance and following them, special educational programs relating to them have been conducted for students. The college's drama instructor, for example, led a special student symposium on Irish drama prior to the appearance of the Irish Players, and high school and college students held classroom discussions following the appearance of British lecturer, Fergus Montgomery, M.P.

According to Mrs. Dorothy W. Riester, chairman of the committee, the blending of students and adults in the Cazenovia series is proving very successful. "Students enjoy going to the lectures and performances with an adult audience," she told *AM*. "I think the series will become an important event in the Cazenovia area." (22)

Cooperation Among Arts Groups Reaps Benefits

Cooperation between a theater and a ballet company in Philadelphia has expanded the promotional reach of each group and has resulted in dollar savings on pooled services. The Theatre of the Living Arts and the Pennsylvania Ballet Company exchange program advertisements, feature each other in lobby displays, pool recreational personnel, insert each other's brochures in programs, and jointly purchase printing supplies. In addition, the groups share a press agent with a third organization, the Philadelphia All-Star Forum, which presents touring attractions at the local Academy of Music. Acting on behalf of the three groups, the press agent was able to convince the Philadelphia Tourist and Convention Bureau to send out a national press release promoting the performing arts in Philadelphia, the first time the Bureau had ever done this.

Recently, the theater and ballet company joined with the All-Star Forum in sponsoring the publication of an eight-page newspaper supplement, designed to promote all three groups and sell tickets to their programs. Titled "Crescendo," the supplement was published as part of the *Jewish Exponent,* (circulation 70,000) with an overrun distributed with the *Jewish Times,* (circulation 28,000). An additional 100,000 copies were mailed to the list of Philadelphia Cultural Communications, a non-profit organization which maintains a computerized mailing service for 13 local non-profit organizations. The $6,800 cost of the cooperative effort was divided among the groups.

The initial returns were good, although it is too early to determine the overall effectiveness of the promotion. Moreover, there were some surprising side benefits. John Bos, producing director of Theatre of the Living Arts told *AM,*

"We stirred up a lot of local interest. We also received at least 100 letters from people who read 'Crescendo,' and assuming it to be a permanent publication, requested subscriptions."

As a result of this reaction, and other positive benefits resulting from the cooperative effort, the three supplement sponsors invited representatives of the Philadelphia Orchestra and the Temple University Music Festival to join them at an upcoming meeting designed to explore pragmatic ways they could work together in such areas as ticket sales, promotion, and winning greater support from city agencies. Also on the agenda was a plan to make "Crescendo" a regular publication of Philadelphia performing arts organizations.

In another city, Youngstown, Ohio, a symphony orchestra and ballet company joined together in a "marriage" which has brought great benefits to both groups. Nearly two years ago, the Youngstown Symphony Society invited the then four-year-old Youngstown Ballet Guild to join its organization as an affiliate. After board approval by both organizations in March 1967, the merger was completed. Although the Guild still maintains its own board and operates autonomously in programming performances of its dance company, the affiliation has helped to solve many problems encountered by a young regional ballet company.

The Symphony Society, for example, now includes the budget within its own, coordinates all publicity, and assumes responsibility for such business details as insurance. Several times a year, the ballet company and orchestra perform together, with the Society handling ticket sales and other arrangements.

In a cooperative effort of a different nature, musicians in New York City have recently organized America's second co-op orchestra, the Symphony of New York. Under the direction of conductor Joseph Eger, the musicians have elected their own board of directors which has complete control over all artistic matters. A separate board of trustees composed primarily of top businessmen, is concerned with fund raising. The orchestra received excellent reviews following its first concert at New York's Carnegie Hall last December, a mixed media program which included dance sequences, narration by staging director, Burgess Meredith, and lighting by the Joshua Light Show. It is now planning two late-February programs—a Lincoln Center concert and the first performance ever given by a symphony orchestra at Harlem's Apollo Theater.   (64)

Tourist Attraction

Passing motorists can be motivated to visit cultural institutions through a system of directional signs posted along major thoroughfares in an organization's area. In Winston-Salem, North Carolina, the Gallery of Fine Arts and Old Salem have cooperated with a number of other institutions in posting a "view-way," a series of signs that directs tourists to the major attractions of the community.   (32)

THE COUNTY

Federation of 11 Museums Serves Entire County

Within recent months, increased attention has been focused on the efforts of museums to better reach and serve their communities. The Smithsonian Institution in Washington, D. C., for example, recently opened a branch museum in a deprived neighborhood under a $250,000 program financed by the Carnegie Corporation of New York, and the Whitney Museum in New York City will soon open a branch under the same program; New York City's Metropolitan Museum has been awarded a $100,000 grant from the New York State Council on the Arts to develop a pilot program for high school students; the Metropolitan and the Brooklyn Museum have announced a co-operative program including joint exhibitions, pooling of personnel and loans of important works; Boston's Museum of Fine Arts loaned nearly a million dollars worth of art to local banks for exhibition purposes; and finally, the Regional Plan Association, in its report on New York City museum-going, which predicted a doubling of Sunday attendance by the year 2000, suggested the establishment of major museums in suburban areas.

Museums in less populated areas, sharing a similar concern for service to their communities, might benefit from the experience of the Orange County Community of Museums and Galleries, a confederation of 11 visual arts institutions in Orange County, New York, who have banded together in an unusual county-wide cooperative program. Although organized in 1961 for the prime purpose of attracting a regional museum conference to the area, the Community has since expanded its activities into a variety of areas includ-

671

ing publications, broadcasting, research, and administrative services to members. It has helped to promote the visual arts in the county, increase attendance at local museums, and stimulate professionalism among member institutions. Moreover, the association, which started as a voluntary operation, now employs a full-time paid director and an associate director and has embarked upon an ambitious 11-project program.

From the period of its origin in November 1961, until 1965, when the Community operated strictly on a voluntary basis, it published 11 issues of *VIEWS,* a magazine devoted to the history and culture of Orange County, doubled the number of officially appointed local historians in the county, prepared copy for brochures and travel guides, and hosted the Northeast Museums Conference in October 1963.

Paid professional help was available for the first time in the summer of 1965, when the New York State Council on the Arts awarded a 10-week research associate internship to Malcolm Booth, one of the founders of the organization and the editor of *VIEWS.* During this period, Booth, who is now director of the organization, prepared a slide program, "The Story of Orange County," compiled a bibliography of local history and helped to develop future projects for the federation. Following Booth's internship, the organization returned to a volunteer basis for one year, during which time it developed a personnel aid program for member groups and sponsored a joint workshop for museum directors and social studies teachers.

In September 1966, New York's State Council approved the Community's request for a three year grant to cover the salary of a full-time director to operate a pilot program in cooperative museum activities. Under this program, directed by Mr. Booth, several notable achievements have already been realized, including publication of a quarterly newsletter, *Museum Matters,* airing of a weekly radio series, establishment of a clearing house for county cultural events, publication of a county museum directory, sponsorship of local cultural and historic programs, and development and maintenance of a master file of organizational program chairmen for possible speaking engagements.

Other current projects include the sponsorship of round-table meetings, a consultation service to members, conference attendance and reports, abstracting articles from journals, and assistance with financial matters, including the preparation of grant proposals to foundations and government agencies. A major Title III proposal involving the establishment of a regional museum service center has been submitted recently.

Commenting on the significance of the OCCM&G, Mr. Booth told *AM,* "The museum profession has long needed a project of this type. It brings us up to the point that the library profession reached 20 years ago. New York State's pioneering steps in regional library systems is now being followed up with an experiment that, I believe, will lead to regional museum systems across the country. It's long overdue." (57)

Look to County Recreation Department for Help

The role that a county government can play in sponsoring and promoting arts activities should be taken into consideration when planning your next cultural program.

Westchester County, one of the wealthiest communities in New York State, through its Department of Parks, Recreation and Conservation, actively participates in and gives financial support to many arts programs presented in the community.

Last month the county, in cooperation with the Westchester Federation of Women's Clubs, sponsored the first annual arts festival in Westchester. It allocated $3,500 to its music division to help defray costs of printing and mailing promotional material, royalties, costumes and production costs. The 4,200-seat County Center, owned by the county, was donated free to the festival for an entire week. The Center's staff, ushers, ticket takers and sellers, as well as its publicity and promotion departments, were all made available for the festival. Tickets, sold at $1.00 each, permitted the festival-goer to attend every event scheduled for the week. About 5,000 attended the arts festival.

Throughout the year, the Department of Parks sponsors or co-sponsors much of the cultural activity in Westchester. To promote the Youth Symphony, the Department sent notices and press releases; paid the conductor's fee when the performance was free, and paid the conductor an honorarium if the concert was for a fund-raising group. Rooms at the County Center were sound-proofed so that the orchestra could rehearse in them each week.

Besides the Youth Symphony, the county backed the Junior Orchestra (which feeds into the Youth Symphony), the Westchester County Concert Band, which schedules 60 concerts during the winter, and the Westchester Pops Band, active during the summer. At a cost of $8,000 to the county, 26 union men were hired to play with the Pops Band last year. In addition, a brass quintet and woodwind ensemble were sent by the Department to local recreation departments.

The Department of Parks also conducts a summer music school at the County Center, open to all Westchester children between the ages of 8 to 18. The program, costing about

$18,000 to administer, offers group instruction on every instrument plus composition. About $16,000 is realized from this, since each child entered in the course pays $30 to attend classes five weekday mornings for a six-week period. This money goes into the County treasury fund to help defray expenses.

The County, presently considering formation of a fine arts council, supplements work of local groups by sending them demonstrators and technical specialists in their fields. This year drama specialists will be dispatched to work with local theatres. Groups wishing to start a theatre may obtain help from the Park Department on how to organize and publicize their work. A directory is published listing every drama group in the county, giving its production schedule and indicating whether or not the group is willing to lend its equipment to others.

In the fall the Department conducts a choral reading clinic to which every music publisher is invited to send his latest choral literature. The Recreation Department invites 200 choral directors, pays for the demonstrating director and accompanist and furnishes space for the clinic.

This summer the Department will also sponsor a free weekly course in orchestral conducting, open to professional musicians, teachers and qualified students. (17)

Politics and Art

In December, 1971, the Erie County Legislature voted to withhold a $25,250 grant from the Studio Arena Theatre's school unless the theater guaranteed not to sponsor "morally objectionable presentations." At issue was the theater's earlier sponsorship of several performances of *Hair* by a touring company. Studio Arena's board stood up to the challenge and issued a public statement supporting the management and artistic direction of the theater. It asserted that "great art is free art" and asked the Legislature to reconsider its action and "grant us funds without contingencies." Buffalo newspapers in their editorial coverage of the situation were strongly critical of the Legislature's stand.

The following months, when the Legislature's Education and Cultural Affairs Committee reviewed the grant situation, it received a statement from theater trustees declaring that the school "never sponsored or produced 'morally objectionable presentations' and has no intentions of doing so in the future." This statement apparently provided a way out of the situation. The committee recommended approval of the grant without strings attached and several days later the Legislature concurred.

In New York City, a leading arts institution unwittingly became involved in a political tale involving a movie, the mayor and money. The film, *The Hot Rock*, which raised more than $300,000 as a controversial benefit showing for the Lindsay for President campaign, had been shot at the Brooklyn Museum. (20th Century Fox reportedly paid the museum an $8,000 fee plus overtime for personnel.) According to reports, the political benefit killed the possibilities of a planned museum benefit in Brooklyn, which would have netted about $40,000. (74)

Arts Groups Rely on County Recreation Agency

When performing arts groups in a Washington, D.C. suburb need help they turn to their county recreation agency, and invariably, they receive it. Unlike park and recreation departments whose concern is limited to the avocational aspects of culture, the Recreation Division of the Arlington County, Virginia, Department of Environmental Affairs is seriously involved in day to day arts activity. The division, in fact, through its full-time performing arts section, acts almost as an arts council does in providing local art groups with varied services and in some instances, funding.

The recreation division's involvement with local cultural groups dates back to the 50's when a children's theater and ballet group both grew out of classes it was conducting. Several years later the division helped organize a new opera program and agreed also to pay part of the salary of the Arlington Symphony's music director. In 1967, the division decided to go "all the way" in the arts. The performing arts section was reorganized to include six full-time arts professionals and non-profit Arlington County arts groups were invited to affiliate with the section and draw upon it for services and salaries.

The performing arts section, whose staff includes a technical director, costume coordinator, production and program supervisors and a part-time publicity coordinator, operates on an annual budget of $104,000; 80 per cent for salaries and 20 per cent for programs. Part of this is used to pay the full or partial salaries of the directors of affiliated arts groups. Throughout the year the section conducts workshops, discussion programs, classes and helps present about 25 to 30 public performances of its affiliated groups. Administrative and technical services include training volunteer workers in the technical aspects of theater, working with boards and artistic directors and developing community support and outside funding.

In addition to its regular day to day activity, the performing arts section is involved in short and long-range special projects. Last spring, for example, it helped develop and find outside funds for a pilot program in dance which resulted in the Arlington Dance Theater becoming a professional company. Currently the group is engaged in a special 30-week county residency.   (72)

Culture Thrives in a Former "Arts Poor" County

A poor rural area considered something of a "cultural wasteland" just three years ago, has since developed an ongoing program that has brought the arts into the daily life of the community. In Marlboro County, South Carolina, an area of 27,000 residents with the third lowest per capita income in the state, and a county seat, Bennettsville, located 100 miles from the nearest city with available arts activity, three years of effort have resulted in such achievements as: the organization of several permanent cultural groups; the introduction of arts programs into the schools; a regular calendar of performances, workshops and exhibitions including the first local concerts ever given by a full symphony orchestra and a ballet company; remodeling of the school auditorium; initiation of a regular newspaper column and radio program on the arts; creation of a county arts commission; and the continued involvement and support of individuals, local government and business.

678

The spark that lit the local fire was an experimental $5,000 grant by the South Carolina Arts Council to pay the salary of a community arts coordinator, who, it was hoped, could spur cultural activity in the county. At the time, in November 1969, the only county groups were some music clubs, dance bands and church choirs, and there was no organized force to promote the arts, hold workshops, and sponsor performances. Within three months local leaders with the help of the coordinator, Mrs. W. H. McIntyre, Jr., the mother of eight, had organized the Marlboro Area Arts Council in Bennettsville and in April, the new council, as part of the state tricentennial week, sponsored an arts festival, presented a full symphony orchestra concert, helped coordinate a three-performance historical pageant created by local citizens, and supervised a participatory collage by townspeople installed in the Bennettsville town square.

In subsequent months the new council helped organize two new arts groups, Marlboro Players Theater and Marlboro Arts and Crafts Guild, sponsored additional performances and developed a range of projects designed to involve the entire area in the cultural program. As a result of a clean-up of the four-acre city-owned gardens with the help of the Jaycees and Boy Scouts, the City Council voted to hire a leading landscape architect to further improve the gardens. Summer classes in the arts were introduced and the Marlboro Players initiated weekly workshops for teenagers. The local Merchants Association cooperated on a sidewalk art exhibit and the Recreation Department worked with the council on a parks and recreation study. Involvement with the school system resulted in county education authorities using emergency assistance act funds to start a program of arts instruction in the schools and

679

council initiation of a program to remodel the 1902 school auditorium for performances won the active support and participation of local industry, schools, and organizations.

A major test for the embryonic organization came in 1971 when it initiated a membership and funding campaign to supplement funds granted by the state council on a decreasing three-year basis (a total of $8,660). The resulting drive brought in 650 members—the largest enrollment of any organization of any type in the county. In addition, both new organizations founded by the council, the Players and the Arts and Crafts Guild, conducted their own separate membership drives successfully.

According to coordinator Lucy McIntyre, the effects of three years of "analyzing, planning, pursuing, hoping and backing up" are really beginning to show. "Marlboro County had little of this before and I think it improved our area. People are asking to help", she told *AM*, "and are casting aside personal prejudices to work side by side." Small signs indicate the progress. The movie theater owner, for example, scheduled good children's films all summer as a result of discussions with the council. The county now sends arts council resumes to industries considering the area for the location of new plants.

Currently, the council is engaged in its largest undertaking—sponsorship of a concert by the Atlanta Symphony Orchestra on January 12th in Bennettsville, a program that will cost $2,000. An all-out campaign was launched in late November with the appointment of "ticket ambassadors", development of in-school programs on the symphony orchestra, a poster contest and a ticket sale program offered by service and civic clubs in the area. On the first ticket sale day, one-fourth of all tickets were sold. The council is optimistic that the performance will be sold out well in advance.

Even with its record of success thus far, the council isn't sitting still. Future plans include a broader art and music program in the schools, greater professionalism in arts undertakings, a yearly cultural festival, regular Saturday workshop programs in the crafts, and presenting several high calibre concert groups as well as opera, ballet or symphony programs every season.   (78)

THE STATE

State Uses Orchestra to Attract New Industry

Although it is not uncommon for corporations to promote local cultural groups as part of their employee recruitment programs, it is not often that arts organizations become active partners in a program established to lure new industry to a state. Yet, the State of Utah has acknowledged the fact that it is helping to underwrite out-of-state tours by the Utah Symphony as a means of influencing leading corporations to relocate in the state. According to James N. Kimball, deputy director of the State's Coordinating Council, Department of Development Services, "I feel confident in saying that the Symphony tours have played a significant part in the attraction of many new industries to our state."

This June, Utah will underwrite about one-third of the cost of the orchestra's first concert tour to four Pacific Coast cities—Los Angeles, San Francisco, Portland and Seattle. A press release from the Symphony board, which announced the new concert program, credited Utah Governor Calvin L. Rampton with originating the idea for the tour and quoted him as saying, "In today's intense competition for industry, music and cultural events, such as those provided by the Symphony orchestra, are important factors that help sell this area. The June tour will again focus the attention of thousands of people on Utah."

The State's Coordinating Council for Development Services will help to coordinate concert arrangements in each of the four cities in cooperation with the orchestra and with local committees composed of former residents of Utah. Committees will direct the local sale of tickets and will help

682

in arranging buffet receptions immediately prior to each concert for invited corporate executives and other guests. The "sell Utah" theme will be inherent in each reception, right down to the food served—all of which will be Utah produced under the supervision of a state consumer marketing specialist.

Milton L. Weilenmann, managing director of Utah's Coordinating Council, views the upcoming tour as an important means of reaching industrial leaders. "It has been our experience," he said, "that through the cultural exposure provided by the Symphony on such tours, we have been able to meet successfully the national leaders of business and industry and thereby better tell the story of our state's phenomenal economic development. Tangible results of the Utah Symphony's assistance in the industrial growth of Utah were the contacts made in New York City prior to the Orchestra's concert at Carnegie Hall last fall."

Queried as to the "tangible results," Mr. Kimball mentioned the decision of General Instruments to locate an electronics facility in Salt Lake City. "It was during the September 1966 Utah Symphony concert at Carnegie Hall," he told *AM,* "that we made our initial contact with General Instruments. They attended a reception held by the State of Utah at the Waldorf-Astoria prior to the concert and expressed an interest in relocating one of their research plants in our state. The decision was consummated in subsequent meetings." (58)

How to Build a Regional Base for Your Institution

Cultural institutions interested in extending their services and their sphere of interest to nearby communities can profit from the experience of the Virginia Museum of Fine Arts in Richmond. This institution, which was founded in 1936 as the nation's first state-supported art museum, has, for the past four years, conducted a unique program which links it with cultural groups in 18 other communities in the State.

Well before inauguration of the confederacy plan, the Museum had pioneered in bringing art to scores of communities throughout the state. It invented the "artmobile," a traveling art gallery on wheels which toured the state, and it also arranged a series of boxed art exhibits which were shipped regularly to schools, colleges, libraries, and clubs. Seeking a means of developing a closer relationship with citizens in communities outside Richmond, the Museum, in 1960, sent a representative to visit arts leaders in other areas of the state.

As a result of this trip, 14 local chapters of the Museum were organized, including many in communities where little or no art activity had existed earlier. In addition, four cultural organizations with already existing programs and buildings were brought into the confederation as affiliates. Although the number of chapters and affiliates has remained the same—one chapter dropped out and another was added —they have grown in size and their programs have increased.

Each of the groups in the confederation functions as an autonomous unit under local volunteer leadership and has its own program of exhibitions, speakers and films. Although the Museum encourages the various organizations to work as independently as possible, it does urge their use of Museum services, and it gives constant programming and administrative aid to them. In return for its many services, including full membership privileges at the Richmond museum for each individual member of a confederate group, the Museum receives $3.25 from the membership fee of each chapter or affiliate member. Thus, the confederation program is financed entirely through membership fees.

Among the services offered by the Museum to all members of confederate groups are a monthly Museum bulletin with news of chapters and affiliates; a subscription to *Arts in Virginia* magazine; free Museum admission; preview and lecture invitations; guest privileges at the Museum; ticket and sales reductions; counsel on arts programs; and admission to theatre, dance and music programs held at the Museum.

In each affiliate organization's own community the Museum provides two Artmobile visits a season, each featuring an installed exhibition of original art objects; noted guest speakers; art teaching kits; a loan-own art service; and bus safaris to the Museum in Richmond. In addition, the Museum circulates some 80 traveling exhibitions.

According to William Gaines, head of the programs division at the Virginia Museum of Fine Arts, the public reaction to the confederation program has been more than favorable and membership in the local organizations continues to grow. "Other cultural organizations," said Gaines, "if interested in extensions of their services either through programs originating from the headquarters or by the organization of satellite organizations, would profit much from a study of our program." (28)

———— ◄●► ————

Paintings In Artmobile Tour Throughout State

An "Artmobile," which is actually a traveling wing of the Arkansas Arts Center of Little Rock, is rolling through the Arkansas countryside bringing an exhibit of original paintings to the people in the manner of a library bookmobile.

The Arkansas Artmobile cost $65,000. It is the gift of Winthrop and David Rockefeller and of the Barton Foundation of Arkansas. Gasoline to keep the Artmobile on the road is donated by the Lion Oil Refining Company, founded by the late Colonel T. H. Barton of the Barton Foundation.

Dedicated on December 13, 1962 with an address by Winthrop Rockefeller, the unusual vehicle has set out on a two-year tour of the state. Stops are scheduled for one, three or five days in a given town. It carries seventeen paintings from the Netherlands.

Air-conditioned and heated for visitors' comfort and for protection of the paintings, the Artmobile maintains constant temperature and humidity. The precious canvases are mounted on specially constructed walls, screwed into place with heavy steel rods holding their backs firm.

The unusual appearance of the Artmobile acts itself as promotion, as its shining steel sides are lettered with its name and the cargo it carries. Blue and green pennants fly from two poles attached to the roofed rear platform, which when opened extends the length of the Artmobile to 67 feet.

(13)

New Custom-Designed Mobile Gallery Now in Use

A new museum on wheels, believed to be the first such vehicle specifically designed for this purpose, and intended as a prototype for mobile units being developed by organizations throughout the country, has recently been completed and is now touring Illinois. In comparison to other traveling museums now in use, which are usually standard trailers converted to their new function, the new unit, called the Art Resources Traveler, has been completely custom designed and includes many unique features.

The mobile museum, which consists of a tractor and an exhibit trailer 40 feet long by 10 feet wide, was designed by Frank Carioti for the Illinois Department of Public Instruction with funds provided by the Educational Facilities Laboratories, a non-profit organization established by the Ford Foundation to help American schools and colleges with their physical problems. The Department which owns and operates the unit, has received additional project support through the Title V program of the Elementary and Secondary Education Act.

Completed in August 1967, the Traveler is equipped with sculpture and paintings loaned by leading museums and private collectors. Manned by a driver and lecturer, it began touring the state on September 12th.

Among the features of the new unit are: seamless display walls designed to make it easier to mount and dismount exhibits; climate and humidity controls said to be superior to those in most museums; built-in projection and sound systems to accommodate films, slides, tapes or any type of audiovisual material; an incandescent lighting system programmed into pre-recorded lecture systems; an air suspension system to provide maximum protection to the collection

687

when in transit; special safety controls; distinct exterior design with smooth panel construction to assure no visual identification with other mobile units; and a built-in wall stage which serves as a lecture platform.

The unit is heavier than standard commercial trailers and it is said to be far more durable. Also, it is self-supporting, with parts and equipment replaceable and repairable at the most remote location, and with all electric and hydraulic systems operable by hand.

Prior to the Traveler's arrival in a community, posters and press releases are sent to schools and other local agencies. Teachers receive filmstrips and instruction manuals which relate to the 35-to-40-minute programmed lectures presented to students in the trailer. Programmed lectures are planned also for adult groups and for teacher training classes. The unit accommodates 20 people for lectures and about 30 for regular viewing of the collection. Although the prototype cost $100,000 to build, it is estimated that additional units could be constructed at a cost of between $70,-000 to $80,000.

Meanwhile, in Rochester, New York, another unusual new mobile unit is providing local schoolchildren with a rare cultural experience—the opportunity to see movies, filmstrips and slides of places of interest, while they are *traveling* to these facilities. The theater on wheels, which looks like an ordinary yellow school bus on the outside, has a sloping theater floor, seats for 40 children, a screen, projectors, tape recorders, special control panel, and six loudspeakers in the bus and five outside it. Built with funds provided under Title I of the Elementary and Secondary Education Act, the bus cost $43,910. Local officials claim that it is the only bus in the country which can show visual materials while in motion.

During its first four months in operation, which began in September, some 4,000 Rochester children will have taken trips on the bus to museums, art galleries, industrial sites and college campuses. Along the way, lecturers will prepare them for their visits with audiovisual materials and special commentary. Tape recordings of gallery talks and lectures will be made at stopover points and played back later in the bus.   (57)

State Arts Report

Last spring, the New York State Commission on Cultural Resources, which was organized following the record $18-million legislative appropriation to the arts in 1970, issued a detailed report titled *State Financial Assistance to Cultural Resources*. The Commission, in addition to voicing its approval of the state arts council program and recommending an increase in council staff and regional offices, issued a series of other suggestions and recommendations, 15 overall. Among them was the recommendation that the state's emergency aid to the arts program be continued on a permanent basis and that the $18-million appropriation, which it deemed inadequate, be increased to $30-million.

Now, several months later, another specially created state arts study group, The Advisory Commission on Financing the Arts in Illinois, has issued its report. Unlike the New York report, however, the Illinois study, does not recommend an immediate and drastic increase in state aid to the arts. It suggests instead, what Commission chairman Joel F. Henning terms, "bread and butter recommendations—most of which can be implemented *now*, at the current level of State appropriation." In a statement

689

accompanying the report, Henning says, "The Commission recognizes the very desperate need for substantially increased arts appropriations. . . . Realistically, however, we know that additional funds will not be available from the State until the crushing weight of the welfare burden is lifted. We therefore recommend that the appropriation for the Illinois Arts Council increase over a five year period from its current level which amounts to $.05 per Illinois citizen to $1.00 per citizen, or from $600,000 to $11-million."

Among the 27 additional recommendations were several key proposals relating to the operation and program of the state arts council. The basic thrust of these was that the council change its program orientation and concentrate its efforts on providing facilitative services and technical aid to arts groups and artists instead of making grants or producing its own arts activities. Included in the recommendations was a proposal to reorganize the state council to meet the suggested new objectives.

Another provocative recommendation related to the state's major established arts institutions. The Commission asked these groups to reconstitute their boards of trustees and committees to "give more than token representation to men and women who can help attract new sources of support as well as to youth and labor, and increased attention to ethnic and cultural diversity." . . .

(72)

———————◄●►———————

Communications Link

A pilot project in New York is providing the state arts council with an important communications link to scores of small cultural groups throughout the state. At the same time, it is providing the small groups with a day to day informational resource and an ear receptive to their needs and problems.

The project, which is being undertaken for the state council by the Performing Arts Association of New York through a council grant, underwrites the part-time services of six young arts administrators from different areas of the state. As the association's regional representatives, they are charged with learning everything they can about their areas and about the arts groups within them. Since the program began last May, the representatives have become known to scores of arts groups and they have helped them by pinpointing available local resources and by explaining the state council program and how its various services can best be utilized. They have also acted as catalysts, consultants, and as information gatherers on arts programming. In one community a representative encouraged the library to provide meeting space to arts groups; in another, the representative helped expand the reach of an arts council by bringing cultural groups in nearby cities into its program.

The representatives maintain weekly phone communications with a program coordinator. In addition, they send the coordinator monthly written reports on their activities.

(73)

———————◆●▶———————

NATIONAL AND INTERNATIONAL

Arts and Humanities Foundation Established

Federal subsidy to the arts is here. After Congress rejected financial aid to the arts for more than a decade, it passed a bill establishing the National Foundation on the Arts and Humanities last month.

The bill authorizes, but does not guarantee, up to $10,-000,000 a year, for three years, for the arts and an equivalent sum for the humanities. In addition, up to $500,000 a year, for three years, will be available to the Commissioner of Education to strengthen instruction in the arts and the humanities. Although funds have been authorized, they have not been appropriated. A request for funds is expected to be submitted to Congress soon.

In signing the bill on September 29th, President Johnson pinpointed as Foundation priorities: the creation of a national repertory theater; support of a national opera and national ballet company; creation of a national film institute; commissioning of new musical works by American composers; support of symphony orchestras; and grants to bring artists-in-residence to schools and universities.

The legislation, which its Senate manager, Clairborne Pell of Rhode Island, termed "the most meaningful of its kind we have ever considered," establishes two fund-granting agencies under the new Foundation, a National Endowment for the Arts and a National Endowment for the Humanities. The chairman of each arm has complete authority to make grants in his area.

A newly established Federal Council on the Arts and Humanities will "advise and consult" with the two Endowments and will "promote coordination" between them.

The National Council on the Arts, established last year by Congress, will review applications for financial assistance made under the act and will make recommendations on them to the Arts Endowment chairman. Neither the national nor the federal council, however, will have veto power over grant-giving decisions made by the chairmen of the two Endowments.

Under provisions of the Arts Endowment, grants-in-aid will be available to non-profit, tax-exempt arts organizations, state agencies, and "in appropriate cases," to individuals. Although the legislation primarily is aimed at support for professional arts activities, funds are also available for amateur "workshop" activities.

Most often, grants to groups will be on a matching basis, and will not exceed 50 per cent of the total cost of a project or production. In some instances, however, groups may obtain more than 50 per cent if they can show they were unsuccessful in attempts to raise funds equal to the amount they requested of the Arts Endowment.

Projects eligible for Arts Endowment support, as outlined in the bill, include: artistically significant productions emphasizing professional excellence and "American" creativity; professional productions which would be unavailable to many citizens without such support; projects that help artists to achieve standards of professional excellence; workshops encouraging public appreciation of the arts; and other relevant projects including surveys, research, and planning in the arts.

The Humanities Endowment will award grants, loans and fellowships to institutions and individuals for training and workshops in the humanities and support research, study and the publication of scholarly works.

Of the approximately $20,000,000 a year authorized to be appropriated equally between the arts and the humanities,

$5,000,000 may be available immediately to each. In addition, the Endowments, which are eligible to receive donations of money and other properties, may receive funds matching the gifts received—up to $5,000,000 a year for the humanities and $2,250,000 for the arts.

An important beneficiary of the Arts Endowment will be state arts councils; $2,750,000 a year can be allocated to their programs with each state council eligible to receive up to 50 per cent of the total cost of an approved project. In addition, those states without councils may receive up to $25,000 for the purpose of conducting a study which will lead to the establishment of a council.

According to the law, the chairman of each Endowment will have, in effect, complete control over his operation. In addition to grant making powers, he will have the authority to accept gifts, order payment withheld if recipients of grants fail to comply with provisions of the law, appoint employees and consultants, establish an office and "make other necessary expenditures."

The chairman of the Arts Endowment, who will have a four year term of office, will be "the individual appointed as Chairman of the National Council on the Arts." Roger L. Stevens is the Council chairman.

The law authorizes specific funds only until June 30, 1968. After that date, Congress will have to authorize additional funds.

Of special importance to arts leaders who fear government control is Section 4 (c) of the legislation. This prohibits government supervision or control over the policy or administration of any non-Federal agency, institution, organization, or school. (42)

Government Groups Question Arts Program

Several events last month raised anew the question of whether government support of the arts might mean government interference in program content. In California, the Los Angeles County Board of Supervisors demanded that several of the tableaus of artist Edward Kienholz, in his exhibition at the Los Angeles County Museum of Art, be altered on the grounds that they were pornographic in nature. The Board threatened to withdraw public support from the museum, or order closing of the exhibition, if the suggested alterations were not made. The exhibition opened as scheduled with one alteration made—the door of one of the works, *Back Seat Dodge* remained closed. However, the museum refused to remove a reclining figure from the work *Roxy*.

In a unique response to the situation, the California Arts Commission, a state agency, issued a public statement deploring the County Board's action. It read, "In view of the recent effort to censor work of Edward Kienholz in Los Angeles, the California Arts Commission wishes to reaffirm its policy with respect to the freedom of artistic expression. The Commission declares and strongly condemns any efforts on the part of any political or legislative bodies to control or censor the free expression and exhibition of artistic works. It contends that the decisions and appraisals regarding performance and exhibitions be left to the discretion of the boards and professional staff of artistic institutions, organizations and museums, and to the discernment of the public."

Meanwhile, in Washington, D. C., some Congressmen questioned the content of the program of the National Endowment on the Arts. They contended that, among other

695

things, the Endowment was not telling them in advance how funds were to be disbursed. In a report to the House of Representatives on the Endowment's budget requests, the House Appropriations Committee suggested that "Extreme care must be exercised that those responsible for the administration of the program do not unduly influence through the award of grants the type of style of art which is to be cultivated in this country." The report also recommended that "in the early phases of this program more emphasis be placed on the award of grants to established foundations, organizations and institutions rather than to numerous individuals in the field." (49)

––––––––––◄•►––––––––––

Roger Stevens Reviews Endowment Program

(The National Endowment for the Arts initiated its program under the direction of Chairman Roger L. Stevens. In this exclusive 1967 interview with AM editor A. H. Reiss, Mr. Stevens discussed the Endowment's past program and examined its future prospects.)

Q: Mr. Stevens, are you satisfied with the progress made by the Arts Endowment?
A: Yes, considering the small amount of money we were given. In our first two years we've granted $6½-million for programs and $2-million to state arts councils. For fiscal year 1968 our budget will be $4½-million for programs and $2-million for states.

Q: Do you anticipate problems with budget appropriations in the future?
A: I think that Congressional support for the Endowment is growing. One of our handicaps has been that the big def-

696

icit in the entire government program affects us, and for this reason, it is difficult to secure the full authorization.

Q: How big a budget would you need to do the job you would like to do?

A: About $150-million a year. This is not an unrealistic figure, when it is considered that the Science Foundation receives $500-million a year. By fiscal year 1969, we will ask for $25-million and the following year we will ask for $50-million. It is reasonable to think that we can get these amounts authorized, but whether they will be appropriated is another question.

Q: What are your future program plans?

A: Up till now, the one area of the arts that has received insufficient attention is music, and we would like to undertake some important programs in this discipline. We are organizing a completely separate music panel to examine what can be done. Ideally, we would need $25-million for music alone. The Ford Foundation has helped to stem the tide, but there are still many needs.

Q: How have art leaders responded to the Endowment program thus far?

A: On the whole, the response has been excellent. Specifically, our visual arts program has been highly praised, and the establishment of the so-called laboratory theater groups has been very well received. We are now planning to establish another such group in the Watts area of Los Angeles.

Q: The development of state arts councils has been slow until now. Do you think it was correct to authorize study funds before state councils had proven themselves?

A: The appropriation of funds for state council studies was included in the legislation creating the Endowment, and

697

it is something that we have to honor. By July 1st, we will review all of the state council reports, and we will tell the councils if we think they are making mistakes in their planning. We do not plan to dominate the councils or impose our thinking on them, but we would like to exercise our right of review and be as helpful as we can, in an advisory capacity.

Q: What about the Endowment's relationship to private organizations, such as foundations? Can this be strengthened?
A: We have research and staff facilities in the arts far surpassing anything the foundations have. We encourage foundations, and corporations also, to come to us and we will be very happy to work with them in the development of programs. Not enough do so now. In order to develop better coordination between our office and large foundations active in the arts, we've held several meetings with them recently.

Q: The Endowment has been slow in developing programs in the area of arts administration. Why is this so?
A: The only two times I have been turned down by the National Council on the Arts has been when I suggested arts administration programs. For some reason the Council is not attuned to the needs in this area. I still have hopes that the situation will change and that arts administration programs can be developed in the near future.

Q: What are the remaining unsolved problems facing the arts?
A: I think that the most pressing problem is education, and everything relates to this. For example, let me illustrate four separate areas of concern. First, teachers in primary and secondary schools generally do not have a good back-

698

ground in the arts. Second, most colleges do not look favorably on high school arts credits. Third, except for those who specialize in the arts, the average college graduate isn't sufficiently exposed to the arts. Last, we are not sufficiently educating the audience we're trying to develop. The public must realize that preparation is needed to fully appreciate the arts. We hope to work closely with the U.S. Office of Education in a coordinated approach to these problems. (56)

———— ◄●► ————

Nancy Hanks Discusses Endowment Program

(Shortly after Miss Nancy Hanks assumed the chairmanship of the National Endowment for the Arts, Arts Management editor A. H. Reiss interviewed her for this publication. Now, three years later, Mr. Reiss again interviews Miss Hanks to discuss the Endowment's progress since 1969 and its future prospects.)

Q: How would you evaluate the progress of the Endowment in the past three years? What do you think were the most important accomplishments during this period?

A: We feel there was much progress made toward greater public awareness of the needs of the arts, and the great potential they have for improving the quality of life. This change in attitude may have been the most important accomplishment of this period. In addition, Congress and the President continued to give strong bipartisan support to the arts both in public statements and with greatly increased funding for the National Arts Endowment.

Q: In regard to programs, what do you consider to be the major developments?

A: A number of important new programs were estab-

699

lished. The Museum Program which began in 1971 with $1,000,000, last year accounted for more than $4,000,000 of our budget. The Expansion Arts Program, designed to encourage community based, professionally directed activities, began in fiscal 1971 and in one year went from $307,600 to $1,137,088. We hope that funding for this area will continue to increase. During the same period, we undertook a new program in public media and we are now beginning to see some very excellent results from it. We were also pleased with the growth of the Artists-in-Schools program and the tenfold development of the Jazz Program.

Q: The Endowment will be up for re-authorization in the next few months. What would be the ideal kind of action that could be taken in Congress regarding authorization and funding?

A: We hope that we will be re-authorized for three years, and that Congress will continue to give us the kind of firm support which it has in the past. Since fiscal 1971 our budget has been increased nearly fivefold. Our experience of the past three years has confirmed our belief in the basic validity of the legislation as originally drawn by Congress, and therefore, we would hope it would remain substantially the same.

Q: A figure of $200,000,000 in federal funds for the arts by 1976 has been suggested. Do you consider this to be a realistic goal?

A: The "art of budget" at the Endowment is designed to be responsive to the demands of people and the arts. We are hardly through our planning for Fiscal Years '74 and '75, and planning for fiscal '76 is in a very preliminary stage.

Q: What do you feel are the greatest challenges facing you and the Endowment now?

A: The challenge to maintain the flexibility to be responsive to the greatly changing demands of the public and the resultant needs of the arts. I am speaking both in terms of policies and procedures.

Q: What is the possibility of arts workers throughout the country having a greater voice in the Endowment's future policy planning?

A: We are constantly looking for new ways to involve people and welcome ideas and suggestions from anyone. The staff is always glad to talk with people when they are in Washington and when they are out on field visits. Much of our work is accomplished with state arts councils at the state level and we plan to continue our strong emphasis on input from this source with meetings and conferences held in regional areas. We also rely on our advisory panel members who are listed by name and area in our annual reports. They are all distinguished practitioners in their respective fields and we find their insights and advice to be based on very practical experience.

Q: What are the prospects for increased state funding of the arts?

A: There have been significant break-throughs in funding for the arts in several states in recent years which appears to be a trend. Funds for the councils and commissions in the states themselves have gone from $2,664,640 in fiscal 1966 to approximately $23,600,000 in the current fiscal year, a figure that will probably be increased in coming months. In addition, there are a number of special projects funded from the Arts Endowment through the states, particularly the Artist-in-Schools program and the Coordinated Residency Touring Program.

Q: Are there any new plans for increased attention to the funding of programs to train arts administrators at

701

every level?

A: Yes, we would hope there would be more recognition from the field of the important need for this training which we feel is a very critical area. We are very pleased with the pilot training programs we have established and hope to see them expanded.

Q: What do you consider to be the remaining major unsolved problems facing the arts?

A: It is not "the problems facing the arts" that I am worried about; there will always be problems and they will always be solved. What concerns me most is the continuing lack of understanding of the potential of the arts for all of our society.

Q: What can arts groups and individuals do in the coming months to help the Endowment best state its case to Congress?

A: Write on! (79)

New Government Agency To Promote Improvement of Education in the Arts

The goal of the recently established Cultural Affairs Branch in the federal Office of Education is to develop programs and activities designed to promote extension and improvement of education in the arts at all levels.

Kathryn Bloom, branch director, summed up her new agency's relation to arts organizations this way for *Arts Management*: "I see this as a friendly adviser kind of relationship between government and the arts. We do not intend to represent a benevolent Uncle Sam intent on control."

Because the Cultural Affairs Branch is part of the Office

of Education, under the Department of Health, Education and Welfare, Miss Bloom said that there must be some kind of educational relevance in its activities. But this does not mean that the work of her branch will be restricted to schools, or to school-age pupils.

Attention will be given to arts education programs for adults as well as for young people, whether they are offered by community art, music, theatre or dance groups, or by museums, cultural centers or arts councils.

Since her appointment to direct the branch last July, Miss Bloom has been building her staff. Dr. Harold Arberg assists her as music education specialist. When the table of organization is filled, they will be joined by educational specialists in museum, graphic art and performing arts work, plus research and clerical staff members. The branch budget comes from the overall appropriation for the Office of Education.

A principal activity of the branch, Miss Bloom said, will be to collect "comprehensive and definitive information regarding the state of the arts in American life and education. It is planned that a fact-finding program will be developed in order that information may be gathered in a continuing and orderly fashion, and that this will be interpreted and disseminated widely.

"Needless to say, this will not take the place of research regarding the arts which is carried on by professional associations and individuals, but should provide a general and comprehensive background for such surveys and studies."

In addition, the branch will emphasize research in arts education, and has funds authorized by Congress to support special projects in this area. A seminar on music education was held at Yale University last summer, with federal support, and the Office of Education is publishing the seminar proceedings.

703

A third area of branch activity is in publications to meet specific needs in arts education. For example, the Office is publishing "Curriculum Guides for Music," an annotated bibliography of guides in use by states and the larger cities and counties. Branch experts also write articles for professional publications. There is no regular branch periodical in sight yet, however.

The fourth area of Cultural Affairs Branch work lies in consultative services and the exchange of information. Staff members are available to render technical assistance through interviews, correspondence and attendance at conferences. It has already been represented at recent meetings on music education in Japan, and on art education in Montreal.

Close cooperation and working relationships with professional organizations is considered a basic part of her unit's work, Miss Bloom told *AM*.

The director is particularly well fitted for her unique and pioneering position in federal government. A graduate of the University of Minnesota, Miss Bloom has been progressively an art teacher in public schools, art museum lecturer, supervisor of art education at the Toledo Museum of Art, and from 1957 to 1963, consultant on the arts for the Association of Junior Leagues of America.　　　　(23)

Top Education Leader Discusses Title III

(In this 1968 interview with AM *editor A. H. Reiss, Miss Kathryn Bloom, director of the Arts and Humanities Program of the U.S. Office of Education, discussed the Elementary and Secondary Education Act and its past and future relevance to the arts.)*

Q: The Elementary and Secondary Education Act of 1965 has recently been extended by Congress for two years. Can you please explain what this extension means in terms of funding and program?
A: Because Congress feels that great progress has been made thus far, it is continuing its support of the program with a recommendation for an increase in funds. For Title III alone, $525-million has been authorized for the two years beginning in fiscal year 1969, although the money has not been appropriated as yet. During the past three years, there has been a significant increase in Title III appropriations: $75-million in 1966; $162-million in 1967; and $187-million in 1968. Also, beginning in 1969, Title III administration will be phased out of the Office of Education directly to state education agencies. In 1969, state agencies, which have been greatly strengthened by their participation in the program, will administer 75 per cent of the funds, and in 1970, 100 per cent.

Q: Under the various titles of the Act, how much money has been expended on the arts since 1965?
A: The figures are not available for all titles of the Act as yet. However, we do know that in 1966, $15-million of Title III funds went to support arts programs.

Q: The express purpose of Title III was to develop innovative programs. Has this objective been fully realized in projects involving the arts?
A: A high percentage of the programs have been innovative in terms of community need. Schools have learned what arts resources exist in their communities and they now know how to use those resources. Broadly speaking, several kinds of innovations in education, like team teaching and flexible scheduling of arts courses, have been major advances in im-

705

proving arts instruction in the schools.

Q: What are the reasons that some of the programs have been less than innovative and meaningful?
A: A major initial difficulty was the breakdown of communications between arts and education leaders. They both found it difficult to understand each other's problems. Also, on the arts side, many organizations erroneously thought of Title III grants as operating funds. Some of the resulting projects were for children, but they were not really educational; other projects were rushed into development before the participants were ready for them.

Q: What can be done to improve communications between education and the arts?
A: Professional associations in both areas can be extremely helpful in explaining needs to their constituents through programs, seminars and printed materials. Understanding, however, really begins at the local level and here a catalytic agent, like an arts council, chamber of commerce, or the mayor's office, can play a key role.

Q: What is the future of ongoing Title III projects involving the arts?
A: Even though Federal support for education has increased substantially, the Federal Government is very definitely a junior partner in providing funds for schools. The majority of financial support comes from state and local funds. Title III projects are supported on a three-year basis. Hopefully, these projects will demonstrate their value as an ongoing part of the curriculum of the schools which initiated them.

Q: Has the overall program in the arts worked out as well as your office hoped it would?

A: Overall, very much so. The kind of exposure available through the program has been very valuable. Many schools have learned how to work with arts organizations, and with poets, musicians, and artists, who, before the program was initiated, were seldom looked on as resources for educating children.

Q: Some people in the arts feel that participation in Title I and Title III programs can subvert their true artistic purpose. How do you feel about this?

A: Participation doesn't have to subvert true artistic purposes. It is up to the artistic director of a group to determine how much time he wants to devote to adult audiences and how much to children. If he feels he shouldn't participate in these programs, then by all means he shouldn't. Arts leaders must remember, however, that while participation in a program is not intended to meet an arts program deficit, it can open the door to possible future funds and new audiences.

Q: What can we look for in the future of this program and in the future relationship between education and the arts?
A: A positive climate has already been established. With proper understanding, the interdependence and interrelationship between the arts and education will continue to grow. Our office (Arts and Humanities Program, U.S. Office of Education, Washington, D.C. 20202), would welcome hearing from any arts leaders who have suggestions on strengthening the ties between these two significant areas.

(59)

Arts Council in Britain Tries New Approach

By

Marjorie Deane

An April 1, Nigel Abercrombie, 54 year old ex-university professor, ex-civil servant, took over as chief executive of the Arts Council of Great Britain. This change in leadership occurred as the Council experiments with new budgetary and organizational arrangements in an effort to increase financial support of the arts at the local level.

Under a new scheme, the Council can budget for three years instead of one: the money, from the government treasury, will amount to £2,730,000—approximately $7,644,-000—in his first 12 months in office, rising annually by 10 per cent in the next two years. There is scant hope of increasing these sums. Abercrombie's main task is to get more money for the arts out of local funds.

Not that he, or his council, has any control over local funds. Unlike the decentralized network of arts councils in the United States, there is only one Arts Council in Britain. Evolving from the wartime C.E.M.A. (Council for the Encouragement of Music and the Arts), which started as a voluntary effort financed by the Pilgrim Trust, Britain's Arts Council is the official instrument for distributing Government subsidies to artistic organizations throughout the length and breadth of the country.

It does not handle, however, all government assistance to the arts. Some organizations get direct grants. London's National Gallery, the Tate and the Victoria and Albert Museum are among national museums financed entirely by the Treasury and subject to the same sort of control as government departments. Certain independent bodies, such as the

708

Royal Music Colleges, also receive grants, but this represents only part of their income. The power of the Arts Council is that it has entire control of the way it spends its annual grant from Parliament, apart from the slice earmarked for Covent Garden Opera House. This leaves the council over $5,000,000 for distribution, out of the $28,000,-000 of taxpayers' money which goes to the arts as a whole, including the upkeep of historic buildings.

Far more bodies ask for Arts Council money than get it. In choosing, the Arts Council insists that recipients must be non-profit organizations. It also likes them to be capable of developing exemplary standards. The council gives money to metropolitan activities like the Saddler Wells Opera Company and will pay $364,000 a year to the new National Theatre to be built on the South Bank of the Thames. It aids great provincial orchestras like the Halle and Liverpool Philharmonic and endless activities up and down the country—art centers, music clubs, festivals such as the annual Edinburgh event, repertory companies, touring ballet companies and poetry societies. It also sends out a flow of art exhibitions, great and small—there were 346 separate showings last year.

The Council does not insist on local support for the theatres and orchestras it helps. But it would like to do so and sometimes does strike a pound-for-pound deal. Its latest report highlights startling evidence that, of the total income of the beneficiaries of the Arts Council, box office receipts cover rather less than two-thirds, the Arts Council provides 30 per cent and local authorities under five per cent. "The time is bound to come," warns the retiring secretary-general, "when the Arts Council will disclaim this unreasonable burden of responsibility."

Some local authorities, like the London County Council,

are quite generous, others niggardly. Altogether, the amount collected for the arts in Britain from ratepayers (local taxpayers who pay on the rateable value of their property) has been about one-sixtieth of what legally could be levied.

The Arts Council has long preached the advantage of tackling the arts regionally in a balanced way, but its organization until now has been centralized. Institutions received aid directly from it, and there was no provision for arts organizations in the same community to work together as they do through arts councils in the U.S. Now associations in three regions have been organized to bring together several municipalities and such other regional interests as universities, television, amateur societies, voluntary bodies and adult education.

All this is excitingly new in Britain. These new associations can apply to the Arts Council for help. Still unresolved is an acceptable formula for sharing the costs of the arts between the central and local funds. But it is hoped that through such regional or local organizations it will be possible to increase the flow of local or regional funds into the arts.

Only through personal contacts can the civic pride of local dignitaries in the arts be stimulated. Some critics have suggested that Abercrombie's Whitehall experience may not equip him for getting around Britain to stir up local interest. It is to be hoped they are proved wrong.   (15)

Government Subsidy Overseas Has Pros and Cons

Salzburg, Austria, site of the world-famous summer music festival, is also the home of a combined theatre-opera repertory company whose economic structure holds lessons for Americans interested in the controversy over federal aid to the arts.

The Salzburg Landestheater is one of six regional theater and/or opera companies that form the core of Austrian cultural life outside Vienna. It stages professional high-quality opera and theatre seven nights a week, for a full ten-month season. Performances are given in an attractive 820-seat hall provided free by the city. The company consists of 130 actors and singers, 70 orchestra members, and 60 technical and administrative personnel. It is headed by Dr. Helmuth Matisek, who at 32, is a veteran manager-director. Two of his top staff members are only 26. One, who among other things is responsible for public relations, is Dr. Werner Schneyder, a poet and playwright whose work the company performs.

The theatre operates on an annual budget of about $600,-000, of which only about $200,000 comes in from the box office. The remaining $400,000 is provided in equal thirds by the city of Salzburg, the province of Salzburg, and the federal Ministry of Education in Vienna.

Largest single item of expense for the theatre, of course, is the payroll. All artists work under one-year contracts that guarantee them nearly six months' advance notice, if the management decides not to renew their engagement. Minimum pay, guaranteed by a federal law, is about $1,120 a year. However, average payments run considerably higher. Thus the average actor receives $1,680. Singers average $2,000. Orchestra players, higher on the scale, are likely to receive $2,300. These salaries compare roughly with those of white collar workers or teachers in Salzburg, meaning they are niggardly.

These scales are so low, in fact, that the Salzburg Landestheater is frequently raided for talent by its counterpart companies in better-paying cities, and especially by state-supported opera theatres in Germany.

Like all Austrian workers, artists receive free medical care. In addition, 30 of the theatre's employees, chosen on the basis of need rather than merit, are given furnished apartments by the city. These rent at rates 50 per cent lower than comparable housing elsewhere.

Clearly, the $400,000 in direct government subsidy does not make possible a lavish life for the artist. What it does do is make possible an extraordinary low schedule of ticket prices. Thus the most expensive seat in the house sells for about $1.80. The cheapest seats can be had for as little as 40 cents (theater) or 48 cents (opera), about what it might cost for a night at the local movie. Even lower prices are available to season ticket buyers.

These price levels are fixed for the theatre by the *theateranschuss*—a committee of members of the Salzburg city council and the provincial legislature. These politicians, aware that any price increase is unpopular with their constituents, keep the scales low, even though the Landestheater management would like to increase its revenues by boosting the ceiling a bit.

Politics enters into the operation in other ways, too. Thus the basic budget for any year is determined jointly by representatives of city and province. The national government then announces how much it can add. In the annual scramble for federal funds, the six landestheaters tend to lobby together for bigger budgets, complaining that the Ministry of Education gives too large a share of its available funds to the Bundestheaterverwaltung—another agency that finances the famed Staatsoper in Vienna and three other performing arts organizations.

But it is the *theateranschuss* that actually doles out the subsidy money to the theatre, and also chooses its director or intendant. In theory, once he is chosen he has absolute control over both the artistic and business aspects of the operation, and he cannot be fired. Nor can his funds be withdrawn. The only power of the *theateranschuss* to influence his actions is its power not to renew his contract.

How does this work in practice? "Financial men," says Dr. Schneyder, "always think they are artistic experts. All over the world. They want the theatre to balance its books, and to be always popular. But the amount of political influence on, for example, the programming, is directly related to the personality and ability of the intendant. If he is good, and he has popular support, the politicians are silent. If the public is unhappy with his work, the politicians may grumble. But the truth is, this is not a major problem for us at all. I cannot remember our ever having to change our programming because of pressure from the government."

In short, at least at this institution, the artistic management finds it no more difficult to live with its public subsidizers than management of an institution in the U.S. might find getting along with private patrons. Conflicts exist, no doubt, but there is nothing automatic about the notion that government funds bring with it political control of program content or quality.

On the other hand, there is also abundant evidence here that public subsidy is no panacea. Complaints about finances seem as prevalent here as they do at home.   (16)

Chapter X – Education and the Arts

THE COLLEGE CULTURAL MARKET

Impresarios on Campus Report Salaries, Programs, Audience

The percentage of full-time, paid college concert managers increased from 12 to 25 per cent over the past six years. During the same period, there was a discernible trend towards greater professionalization among part-time managers, who constitute a majority of those in the field. In 1965 no salary was budgeted for 75 per cent of the impresarios, while today, only 32 per cent program without either compensation or released time.

These and other conclusions relating to college arts programming and programmers were reported in the Association of College and University Concert Managers' recently released *Profile Survey IV*. Survey results based on the 1970-71 season, were drawn from a sample of 42 per cent of ACUCM's 339 member institutions.

The annual profile, which covered managers' salaries for the first time, showed a monthly average salary of $1142 and a median salary range between $1000 and $1200. However, 23 per cent of the managers reporting, had salaries above $1400 a month and six per cent were paid between $2000 and $3500 monthly.

In an analysis of concert manager salaries the report concluded, "If one wants to make the maximum amount of money in the concert management field, he should be male, have a PhD, be over 60, be located in a public college that has between 10,000 and 20,000 students and be a part time manager. The difference between male and female monthly salaries [male, $1193 and female, $850] may not be as significant because males have higher academic degrees than females."

In terms of budget, 64 per cent of college concert fees were spent on five program types—rock, symphony, theater, popular and instrumental recitals. The average fee for all program types was $3169, up 12 per cent from $2189 a year earlier. About 46 per cent of the programs cost less than $3500 and 54 per cent cost more. The trend towards the use of larger facilities for all types of events continued, perhaps in response to increased fees. Happily, however, at 70 percent of the institutions, programs were subsidized.

Average attendance for all events was 1335 and average gross attendance was 59 per cent of capacity, down five per cent from the previous year. Students were a significant part of the audience, representing 59 per cent of the gross attendance, an annual increase of 11 per cent. Moreover, at 70 per cent of the institutions they helped make booking decisions through student committees.

The most popular "classical" event among all audiences in terms of average gross attendance was theater, followed by ballet, instrumental recitals and symphony. Least popular was vocal recitals, whose existence on campus the report termed "marginal." Among students, ballet easily led the way—student attendance soared from 44 to 78 per cent in a year—followed by contemporary dance, theater and chamber music.   (72)

————◄•►————

715

Colleges Surveyed on Their Cultural Programs

Midwestern colleges and universities generally present more cultural programs than institutions of comparable size elsewhere, have larger staffs to administer the programs, and provide greater program support than institutions in other areas. These were among the conclusions reached in a survey of members of the Association of College and University Concert Managers, based on the 1966-1967 season, which was conducted by California Institute of Technology last summer. Of the 213 respondents, 57 per cent were representatives of public institutions, 37 per cent represented independent private colleges and universities and the remainder were from parochial or other institutions. Median, rather than average, figures were used to avoid distortion.

The annual number of cultural events presented by colleges and universities has increased in the past few years and will continue to grow according to the survey. The median number of events in 1966-67 was 44, an increase of 15 over the 1964-1965 season. By 1968-1969, it is anticipated that the median will rise to 50. The most frequent types of attractions, expressed in the median number of programs presented during the 1966-1967 season were: non-travel films, 12; curricular music concerts, 10; public lectures, 8; professional classical music, of which 30 per cent were solo recital performances, six; and "pop" artists, three. The median for professional drama was two, and for professional dance, only one. Respondents cited "great" artist and "pop" artist concerts and professional drama productions as the most successful events, and solo recitals, chamber music and dance concerts as the least successful.

Where are college cultural programs presented? Sixty per cent of the institutions included in the survey have at least one major performance hall seating over 1,000, and 80 per cent have one or more smaller performance halls. An additional 42 per cent of the A.C.U.C.M. institutions use field houses for cultural programs and 14 per cent use Greek theaters.

Half of the respondents listed equipment deficiencies which prevent them from programming certain kinds of events. Among the deficiencies noted by this group (nearly all listed deficiencies in at least three of the following categories), were: stage rigging, 73 per cent; lights, 62 per cent; stage area, 56 per cent; dressing rooms, 52 per cent; stage furniture, 48 per cent; sound, 42 per cent; projection equipment, 38 per cent; and others, 28 per cent.

Subsidy, in some form, is essential to college cultural programming, with only nine per cent of the responding institutions supporting fee charge events solely through ticket sales. The box office, in fact, returns only a median 41 per cent of the total operating budget, and 51 per cent of the respondents use student and tuition fees to cover deficits and 31 per cent use allocations from general operating funds for this purpose. Nevertheless, ticket prices for the general public remain fairly low, ranging from a median $2.00 to $4.00 for professional music, drama, dance and "pop" programs. For faculty and students, the median ticket range is $1.50 to $4.00 for these programs.   (59)

College Audiences Surveyed

Traditional performing arts forms are finding it increasingly difficult to attract college student audiences. According to a survey of professional arts programs on campus, recently completed by the Association of College and University Concert Managers, the best student-attended programs are, in order of average attendance, rock, popular, jazz, folk music, and contemporary dance. Programs with the lowest average student attendance, are vocal recitals, chamber music, instrumental recitals, symphony, opera and choral. However, when the analysis was broadened to include the total campus audience, non-students as well as students, the figures showed that except for rock (72 per cent), ballet and symphony have the highest average gross attendance, with 71 per cent of capacity. Figures were based on responses from 170 college concert managers who spent an aggregate $5,262,586 on the 1,867 events they presented in 1969-1970.

How do college concert managers feel about the future? Last month some 300 delegates attended A.C.U.C.M.'s annual conference in New York City. According to the organization's executive secretary, Mrs. Fannie Taylor, "The managers were looking to the future. The note was one of optimism, flexibility, and a willingness to find and try new forms of artistic expression."   (69)

Culture on Campus is Big Business at UCLA

The rise of cultural activity on college campuses has created a new kind of faculty member, the educator-impresario. This increasingly important member of the arts management profession not only must cope with such familiar problems as ticket pricing, publicity, seating, scheduling, booking and budgeting, but must also deal with three special problems.

First, he is responsible, as a rule, for a program that combines both amateur and professional activity. Second, the program usually includes several artistic disciplines. Third, this program must, in some way, be integrated with the activities of the faculty.

One school that has successfully integrated a vast program through the instrument of a central coordinating agency—a kind of arts council on campus—is the University of California at Los Angeles. U.C.L.A. runs one of the most ambitious campus cultural programs in the country. Its attractions last year drew an aggregate audience of 284,155 and ran up box office sales of about $500,000. More impressive even is the scope of the program. The 1961-1962 season included 151 performances of professional theatre; 89 performances of academic theatre; 59 concerts; 40 film showings; 110 public lectures; and scores of other events like art exhibitions and dance recitals. This level of activity compares favorably with that in many a good-sized city.

A single agency, the Committee on Fine Arts Productions (C.F.A.P.) is responsible for planning and coordinating this tremendous program. Set up in May, 1954, C.F.A.P. is "a kind of holding company for the receiving and disbursing of funds needed to present student and professional offerings."

719

C.F.A.P. consists of eight sections. A Concert Section is responsible for presenting professional events in the fields of music and dance. These are supplemented by student productions put on by the Music Section and the Dance Section. Thus, in these fields, amateur and professional activity are divided. Similarly, there is a Film Section that presents documentaries and other special movies, and a Film Production Section which completes three to six student movie productions each year. In the field of art, however, a single section is responsible for both amateur and professional shows, and a Children's Programs Section stages both student and professional programs in a variety of disciplines. An eighth section for Theatre Arts, is responsible for student dramatic productions.

These regular sections are supplemented by Theatre Group, a wholly professional quasi-independent drama company headed by M.G.M. producer John Houseman and tied organizationally to C.F.A.P. (Frances Inglis, C.F.A.P.'s executive officer, sits on the Theatre Group board.)

Started four years ago, Theatre Group was given $15,000 by the university regents and told to sink or swim. Since then it has received no additional funds from the university, and has been so successful in paying its own way, it is now planning to build its own theatre. The regents have given it a piece of land and authorized it to raise construction funds through public solicitation. Theatre Group thus does not draw on C.F.A.P. for funds, although it receives certain services from C.F.A.P.

In contrast, each spring, the Sections present budgets to C.F.A.P. to cover their proposed programs. Student productions are only partially subsidized by university funds, so that even these usually require money from C.F.A.P. After careful screening C.F.A.P. makes an allocation to each section. At the end of the fiscal year each section must return to C.F.A.P. all its earned income.

Sections are expected to balance their books and turn over any profits made. Failure to repay the full amount of the allocation (which is, in effect, a loan) results in a more critical screening of the section's next budget request. C.F.A.P. provides, therefore, a reserve financial pool for cultural units on campus. Over the years, profits by some sections have balanced losses by others, so that the pool has not only maintained its level, but increased slightly.

When C.F.A.P. has a good year, the "profits" are plowed back into higher quality productions, the purchase of higher-fee artists' services, etc.

C.F.A.P., itself, receives little financial support from the university. It is granted $25,000 a year to help cover administrative expenses that actually run to twice that amount. Its staff of 13 includes the executive officer; a public relations representative; three administrative assistants (one for theatre, one for concert and films, one for ticket sales); a secretary for public lectures; a programmer for films; and six clerical aides. Its job—tying together the many-faceted arts activities on the campus—demands a high level of arts management. That the job is done well is reflected in the success of the U.C.L.A. program.   (8)

Local Citizens Spur Interest In University's Arts Program

A college performing arts series, sponsored by a group of private citizens, draws record crowds, is over-subscribed regularly, and is a "profitable" non-profit enterprise. In Raleigh, N. C., The Friends of the College, Inc., have sponsored an annual "top name" concert series for the past eight years in the 12,000 seat William Neal Reynolds Coliseum on the campus of North Carolina State University. More than 18,000 individuals subscribe to the seven concert series, at $7.00 per subscription. Although each attraction is presented two or three times, there is a long waiting list for subscriptions.

The college provides the services of an executive director and secretary for the arts program, but the Friends play a leading role in promoting and supporting the program, suggesting attractions, and approving all bookings made by the director. In spite of the fact that the operation runs on a balanced budget and frequently shows a surplus (this year's surplus may be used to improve the facility) the president of the Friends, Charles York, told *AM*, "We've never turned down an available attraction because of a high fee. If we feel that program is worthwhile, we book it regardless of its cost."

There are no reserved seats for any of the performances and the Coliseum generally begins to fill up at least 30 minutes before curtain time. In several instances, subscribers have been turned away fifteen minutes before curtain time because of a full house, and had to return for the second or third performance by an artist. The subscription audience is supplemented by North Carolina State University students, who receive two free tickets for each concert in the series. More than 9,000 students are currently enrolled at the University.

In addition to subscription sales, income for the program is derived from contributions from many sponsors and patrons, including leading local corporations and a variety of small businesses.

The program has become so successful that it draws subscribers from as far as a hundred miles away, and it is estimated that about 50 per cent of all audiences are non-residents of Raleigh. Attractions featured in the 1966-1967 season are: The American Ballet Theatre; violinist Erica Morini; opera stars Anna Moffo and Richard Tucker; Jose Greco and Company; a Pops Concert with Arthur Fiedler; Van Cliburn; and the Concertgebouw Orchestra of Amsterdam. (54)

Town-Gown Shares Stage

A college and a community "make beautiful music together" in Ames, Iowa, where a unique cooperative effort has resulted in a successful annual concert series. For the past five years, the Music Council of Iowa State University and the Ames Concert Association have jointly presented the Town and Gown Concert Series, a program open to both college students and townspeople.

The University Music Council suggested the partnership when the Association, which previously had its own series, was about to disband following a poor season. As now constituted, the series of four programs is presented at the Ames High School Auditorium on a reserved seat basis. The Association guarantees to sell half the house and the college uses the other half for students.

723

According to Mrs. William McCormack, president of the Concert Association, "This arrangement gives townspeople a talent budget of twice the amount they are paying in. On the other hand, the Music Council share is purchasing for the students a value that is twice the actual cost." Additional savings are effected through independent direct buying of talent by the University's concert office. Talent is selected by a committee composed of three townspeople and three University people.

Although the details of organization and presentation are handled by the University, the Concert Association has its own kick-off ticket drive each spring, as other civic concert groups do, to sell its half of the house. This year's series, budgeted at $7,500, will present the Chamber Symphony of Philadelphia, pianist Abbey Simon, the Oberlin Choir, and the Guarneri String Quartet. (62)

College and Orchestra In Summer Partnership

A symphony orchestra and a university are cooperating in a unique summer project which extends the orchestra's season and provides the university with an important program of education and entertainment. Called Summer Music at Minnesota, the project, initiated last year, features the participation of Minneapolis Symphony Orchestra players in a series of workshops, lecture-demonstrations and concerts during their five-week summer residency at the University of Minnesota.

The program had its beginnings three years ago, when symphony representatives and the University's music department organized a two-day symposium to discuss how the orchestra might be best utilized during the summer. A plan for a broad arts program at the University evolved from these meetings, encompassing opera and dance in addition to symphonic music. It was decided, however, to concentrate on symphonic music during the first few summers and expand the program to other areas later.

This year's program, budgeted at $150,000, features five Friday night "family twilight" concerts by the orchestra. In addition, orchestra members will participate as demonstration units in two credit courses offered by the University: Music 60, a nine-session introduction to orchestral repertoire, and the contemporary music workshop, a five-day program co-directed by Stanislaw Skrowaczewski, the orchestra's conductor, and Elliott Carter, the composer.

Two special programs for high school students and teachers will utilize the talents of orchestra members. A high school musicians' project will bring 141 gifted young students to the Minneapolis campus for four weeks, and a high school music teachers' workshop will draw 40 teachers to an intensive five-week session.

Other facets of the program include elementary and secondary music education workshops and an opera workshop.

(56)

University Becomes Arts Patron and Buys Tickets for Students

A foundation grant has enabled a university to become a patron of the arts, and has opened an important new audience-building avenue for cultural organizations in the New York City area. Under the program, which was instituted last month, the Brooklyn Center of New York's Long Island University has received $25,000 from the Youth Educational Council, a foundation. The funds will permit about 500

725

L.I.U. students a year, for five years, to attend theater, dance and musical performances in New York City, as part of their regular academic course. The university will endeavor to raise additional funds to extend the program beyond its original five years.

Such a program, if adopted by foundations elsewhere, could greatly aid arts groups by guaranteeing fully subsidized student attendance at performances. To attract student audiences, many arts groups now offer them substantial discounts on ticket purchases. Under this program, the university receives only slight discounts for buying tickets in bulk.

Students participating in the program are drawn from all grades and divisions of the school, including business administration and the natural sciences. They attend three-to-five performances during the year, with special seminars at the university following each performance. A student-faculty committee administers the program and selects the events.

Dr. William M. Birenbaum, vice president and provost of L.I.U's Brooklyn Center, said that the program is enabling the school to use the city's theaters and concert halls as "curricular workshops." Students are attending performances this season at the city's Lincoln Center for the Performing Arts, and at the Brooklyn Academy of Music. Plans call for broadening the program next fall to include performances of off-Broadway theater groups and of other small but significant arts organizations.

This pioneering program is the Educational Council's first in the arts. During its two year existence, it has supported programs for under-privileged children. Mrs. Marty N. Lipschutz, chairman and organizer of the foundation, expressed hope that other organizations would follow its lead in this area. She told *AM,* ''The Council was moved to make the grant because many courses of study, like engineering, have missed the cultural aspects of life.''   (45)

Ticket Sales Pay The Full Costs Of An Unusual College Theatre

A summer theatre owned and operated by a women's college provides training for its students in every phase of the theatre arts while supporting itself solely through ticket sales.

Stephens College of Columbia, Missouri has run the Okoboji Summer Theater outside its home state in Spirit Lake, Iowa, at a profit for five summers. Its efforts have proved an artistic, educational and commercial success that may hold lessons for colleges and arts groups elsewhere.

Stephens in 1958 started as operator of the theatre under a profit-sharing arrangement with the local group which owned it and was given ownership of the theatre this year.

The college has taken a completely professional approach to the management of its theatre. A two-year college for women, at which a limited number of students are candidates for the three-year Bachelor of Fine Arts degree, Stephens is noted for its curriculum in the arts. It combines operation of the theatre with an undergraduate summer session in theatre arts.

The staff for this program includes six male faculty members. During the academic year they are also members of Stephens' resident professional acting company, which presents eight productions at the campus playhouse. They are assisted by faculty responsible for business management, set and stage design, and props. There is also a coun-

727

selor for the residence hall, an additional instructor for the summer courses and a public relations specialist. The professionals direct each production and play the male roles, with female parts played by students.

During the eight-week summer season a new play is presented weekly, each production running for six nights. Matinees are devoted to children's plays. The theatre holds 354 seats. Tickets, at $2.00, bring in the entire operational revenue of the theatre.

Candidates for the new Bachelor of Fine Arts degree in theatre arts spend two summers at the Okoboji Theatre. They can earn up to eight semester hours of college credit each summer from courses in acting, production, theatre history and theatre management. Lecture courses are supplemented by actual work on each of the productions. The class in theatre management, for example, meets four hours a week for nine weeks and covers theatre organization and accounting, publicity, public relations, advertising, house management, stage management and box office.

During the summer students take part in all theatre operations, including acting, scenery building, lighting, costuming, and ticket selling. (10)

Students Take Over Management, Win New College Arts Audience

With the rise of professional cultural impresarios on campuses throughout the country, at least one college is providing a contrast to this trend. At East Carolina College in Greenville, N. C., students have taken over the management of the campus arts program from the faculty and scored a great success.

728

Working with a yearly budget of almost $25,000, a student entertainment committee selects guest artists for two concert series of five programs each. Students also book the artists, sell tickets and publicize the program. As evidence of the seriousness with which student leadership is taken, the college paid expenses for two student managers to attend a recent conference of the Association of College and University Concert Managers.

Until 1961, the arts program at East Carolina was managed by a faculty committee, with a student entertainment committee providing a rubber stamp for their decisions. Then Tom Mallison, an undergraduate who is now president of the Student Government Association, was appointed head of the entertainment committee. He resolved that students should run the entire arts program aided by faculty advisors.

The student constitution was changed so as to establish a rotating student committee of eight members and four faculty advisors with authority to conduct the program. A strong student government, which administers an overall yearly budget of $130,000, provides the framework in which the entertainment committee functions.

When students took over the program in 1961, attendance had been sparse and interest was low. In two years student attendance has zoomed upward, and season ticket sales to the community have increased by 800 per cent. The students courted their crowds first by engaging artists with immediate name value, but now they are gradually introducing new names into the program.

In its first year the committee operated with a $24,600 budget, a $7,000 increase over the budget used by the faculty committee the preceding year. Money comes from a portion of the $15 student activity fee paid by students each quarter, and students are entitled to receive tickets to all concerts in the fine arts and pops series, space permitting.

At first, student activity tickets were punched at the door. But since turn-away crowds became the rule, students must present their activity cards at the box office from three to ten days before a performance in order to obtain tickets. All tickets not picked up three days before the concert are sold to townspeople at $2 each for the fine arts series and $3 a seat for the pops series. In addition, the student committee is authorized to sell up to 500 fine arts season tickets to townspeople at $7 per subscription. All money realized from outside sales ($2,000 last year) goes back into a general student fund.

Arrangements for the following year's concert season begin in the spring when at least half the artists are signed, subject to faculty approval. An approximate budget is approved by a student-faculty budget committee in May, and the rest of the programs are filled in the summer and early fall.

This year the fine arts series includes William Warfield, Alexander Brailowsky, the Jose Limon Dancers, Judith Anderson and the North Carolina Symphony. The pops program includes such names as the Limelighters, Dave Brubeck, the Four Preps and the Smothers Brothers. The budget is split 50-50 between the fine arts and pops programs.

Student fine arts attendance is thus far averaging 75 per cent of capacity, up from 50 per cent last year. Pops concerts are about 99 per cent filled. Both figures are a great increase over the days of faculty management. The overall budget includes $1,500 a year for operating expenses. Paid help is limited to students manning the box office and working as ushers at 75¢ an hour. All other services are contributed free by students and faculty advisors.

Mallison says increased publicity has been important in boosting attendance. Releases go regularly to some 75 newspapers in Eastern North Carolina.

In addition to administering the arts program, the students are participating in a drive to raise $20,000 for an acoustical shell. Under a special arrangement, the students were promised a penny for each empty pack of Liggett & Myers cigarettes returned to the company. Thus far, nearly 250,000 empty packs have been collected, netting $2,500 towards the shell.

"A program such as we run," Mallison told *Arts Management,* "can work at other schools provided there is a strong student government and administration support."

(13)

Universities Must Adjust to the Role of Artists on Campus

In recent years, there has been a growth in the number of artists teaching at colleges and universities. According to Robert Iglehart, chairman of the University of Michigan Department of Art, however, the artist is still a somewhat odd fish on the campus.

"His curious implements, nude models, and puzzling products raise doubts in the minds of our colleagues in history and classical studies," says Iglehart. "As a matter of fact, it could be argued that the artist is more uneasy on campus than the campus is to have him. He has long been in exile. He tends to think of himself as in revolt. Suddenly he is an associate professor with a regular income and a vote in the faculty senate. He fears domestication and suspects that neglect and oppression are necessary to his career."

Iglehart claims we have developed a sort of folklore image of the artist which would have surprised the decorators of Solomon's temple or Leonardo da Vinci. "Isn't it somewhere nearer the truth," he claims, "to say we expect the artist to be rather thin, dressed with some eccentricity, probably moody and unreliable in practical affairs and unreasonably hostile to ideas held as a matter of course by the rest of us. Even when we meet an artist who turns out to be fat, conventionally attired, happy, reliable, and not unprosperous, we view him as the exception which proves the rule, and hold fast to our familiar image."

Iglehart concludes that there are problems of adjustment on the part of both the universities and the art faculties. "Nevertheless," he says, "both stand to gain from the association. The artist on campus integrates the arts into the accepted disciplines. And the university provides the physical and human resources the artist needs to solve the problems of art." (25)

New Auditorium at University Spurs Interest in the Arts

What happens when a campus gets a new concert hall or theatre? The answer: an increase in cultural activity and arts consciousness. That, at least, has been the experience of Butler University in Indianapolis, which opened a new $3,500,000 auditorium in October, 1963.

The 2,200-seat hall became the home of the Indianapolis Symphony Orchestra. It also booked a heavy schedule of imported cultural attractions—far more than the community or the campus was accustomed to getting. In all, during its first year of operation, Clowes Memorial Hall is presenting 67 offerings. This represents an $88,000 outlay for artists' fees alone.

The availability of the big, new, auditorium with its 300-seat supplementary recital hall, has made it possible for many attractions to visit the city for the first time. Public response has been enthusiastic. During a single one-month period subscribers bought 1,642 out of a total of 1,899 tickets for a 10-attraction series. This represented an income of $71,689. Box office sales of single tickets boosted the total gross.

This season the hall is presenting, in addition to the Indianapolis Symphony concerts, touring professional performances of *Brecht on Brecht, A Man for All Seasons, Camelot,* and other Broadway and off-Broadway plays and musicals. The National Repertory Theatre will perform in February. Community Concerts and university drama productions will help round out the program.

The size of the hall makes it economically feasible for touring productions to appear there. Thus it has been pointed out by *Variety* that, at a suggested top price of $7.50, *Camelot* would be able to gross more than $98,000 for eight performances. For a straight play giving only two performances, with a $4.50 top, the potential gross would be $15,500.

Elsewhere, too, colleges are increasingly active culturally. Miles College in Birmingham, a Negro institution, made news recently by sponsoring a recital by coloratura Mattiwilde Dobbs in Birmingham's Municipal Auditorium. The event was desegregated. It drew an audience of approximately 3,000.

In the Midwest, the University of Wisconsin student union presented a month-long Far Eastern Festival aimed at the many student groups, faculty members and departments with a special interest in the culture of the Orient. The program included recitals by Shanta Rao, the Indian dancer, Kimio Eto, a koto player, and Suzushi Hanayagi,

733

a classical Japanese dancer. There were art exhibits, films, and discussion of contemporary Far Eastern literature.

These events reflect the national trend for increasing sponsorship of cultural activities by colleges and universities. (23)

New Groups Lend Support to Cultural Programs

Arts and artists are winning support from new sectors, as some recent developments indicate. Performing arts departments at Cornell University in Ithaca, New York, for example, are being aided by school alumni who have just created the Cornell Council for the Performing Arts. The new council, whose members include many arts notables, initiated its activities with a cocktail party this October, at which faculty members of the University's departments of theater arts and music discussed current and future programs. The new council plans to promote and encourage the construction and maintenance of first class performing arts facilities at Cornell, interest alumni in the arts to donate their papers and records to the institution, and encourage these alumni to lecture at the institution. The group is now planning the first alumni performing arts weekend at Cornell.

Elsewhere, performing artists are being helped through a program now reaching its fruitional stage after three years of development. Linking performers, universities and, hopefully, corporations as sponsors, the Affiliate Artists program offers young professional artists employment at universities at an annual salary of $6,500. Unlike artists-in-residence programs, however, performers spend only about 56 days a year on campus, spread over four to six visits, and are free during the remaining time to perform professionally elsewhere. On campus, artists' duties are flexible and are not tied to specific classroom assignments — they perform, participate in student seminars, and sometimes lecture.

Matching artists and universities is the job of Affiliate Artists, Inc., the non-profit organization which conceived the program and administers it. Artists interested in participating (there are now 300 on file) submit background information to the organization at 155 West 68th Street, New York, N. Y. 10023. Resumes are screened by an advisory committee, which then reaches its final decisions following attendance at auditions or performances. Schools expressing interest in the program are visited by an organizational representative who evaluates the school and the department to be involved. Two or three artists are then recommended to the school. The selected artist visits the school with an official of Affiliate Artists to work out the year's program. Colleges and universities pay 20 per cent of the total fee for each artist and outside sponsors pay the balance.

From one artist in 1966, the program has grown to 15 in 1967 and to 26 this year. Major support, thus far, has come from foundations, the National Endowment for the Arts, and church organizations, but a key to future growth is business sponsorship, as Plato S. Karayanis, the organization's director of artist activities indicated to *AM*. "We are much encouraged by the progress we have made in securing corporate underwriting," he said, "and we hope to have most of our appointments for 1969-70 underwritten fully by corporate sponsors." (63)

ELEMENTARY AND SECONDARY SCHOOLS

Drive to Broaden Arts in Education Gains

The movement to broaden the arts role in public education has accelerated considerably as a result of positive developments on several fronts. They include:

• Several pilot arts in education programs have completed or are about to complete their initial funding phases successfully and their prospects for renewed funding from local sources are excellent. Moreover, they can now provide education systems with models to be studied and emulated.

• A broad and multi-faceted national arts in education program, Project Arts/Worth, has completed its initial organization and is now entering a new action-oriented phase.

• The North American Society of State and Provincial Arts Agencies has joined the campaign by issuing a strong eight point resolution calling for an expansion of the arts in education.

• Imaginative new programs linking the arts with school systems are being developed.

• A growing number of school administrators, including some who were skeptical initially, have witnessed arts programs as part of the curriculum and have become convinced of their value.

• A philosophical rationale for infusing the arts into the educational system is winning acceptance by many thought leaders.

The program with perhaps the greatest immediacy to cultural institutions is Project Arts/Worth, conceived and initiated by the National Council of the Arts in Education to "establish more firmly the role of the arts in general education." Funded through June 1973 by a three year planning grant of $200,000 from the National Endowment for the Humanities, Arts/Worth during its first year has: researched needs and planned its overall approach; gathered information on existing arts in education programs; begun to develop a network of 25 regional representatives throughout the country; organized five special consultative committees; and established its identity in both the arts and education communities.

Now, the program is moving into a direct action phase with several tangible projects on the horizon. On February 25-26, for example, Arts/Worth will sponsor the first in a series of regional symposiums on the arts role in education developed with the aid of its regional representatives. These representatives, according to Arts/Worth director Allen Sapp, will be "our organization's eyes and ears around the country." Upcoming in March is a White Paper on the arts role in education, which also defines the aims and purposes of Arts/Worth and by summer the organization will begin publishing a national newsletter. Later this year, Arts/Worth will launch a national public relations campaign aimed at educators, legislators and school administrators and finalize plans for a centralized information resources center.

Sapp, on leave from his dual post as professor of music and director of cultural affairs at the State University of New York in Buffalo, told *AM,* "We're developing a case and taking it to the people who can help to redefine priorities and switch goals in the education system—to school administrators, rural teachers, and legislators. We're also helping people to learn to use the resources on hand, the millions of untapped dollars, to develop new and permanent cultural programs in our schools. We hope that people will

737

come to us and learn to use us." Write to Project Arts/ Worth at 60 East 42nd St., New York, N.Y., 10017.

Elsewhere, imaginative pilot arts programs in public schools funded by the Arts in Education Program of the JDR 3rd Fund have succeeded in making a positive impact on local education leaders. In University City, Mo., for example, the foundation funded a program which incorporated the arts into the general curriculum of all classes from kindergarten through grade 12. When the three year grant ended several months ago, the local board of education voted to assume financial support for a fourth and fifth year.

In Mineola, L.I., where a three year foundation-funded project dealing with widespread student exposure to artists and arts groups ends this year, serious local attention is being given to ways in which the program can be continued. At P.S. 51 in New York City, a foundation project to train teachers to teach the arts, is continuing after expiration of the grant period, through the initiative of the principal. As a result of the program's success, the JDR 3rd Fund has just awarded a grant to the Bank Street College of Education to develop a program aimed at training school administrators in the arts. Recently, other JDR 3rd Fund grants have been given to school districts in Oklahoma City, Okla. and Jefferson County, Colo., to enable them to draw on the experiences of the pilot projects.

In five schools elsewhere, another pilot project is completing the initial funded phase of its operations this June and here too, the prospects for program continuance and additional funding look good. Project Impact, a $1-million program funded by the U.S. Office of Education for two years, has involved an integration of the arts—dance, theater, film, music and visual art—into all aspects of the elementary and middle school program. Indications thus

738

far are that the project has changed the environment in participating schools, and that the arts have become a more normal part of the school day. Administrators in cities with Impact schools—Philadelphia; Troy, Ala.; Columbus, Ohio; Glendale, Calif.; and Eugene, Ore.—have agreed to underwrite efforts to work cooperatively and seek outside funding to keep the programs going. Locally, attempts are being made to find money from community resources and state education departments.

In Rhode Island, the Arts in Education Project funded by the Arts Endowment and Office of Education has achieved positive results in communities throughout the state. Now in the second year of a three year grant, the program uses local arts groups to provide cultural programs in schools and train teachers. A program initiated this fall by Lincoln Center, is enabling each of 12 performing artists to be in residence at a city high school twice a week for 30 weeks. These resource professionals work with 150 students regularly at each school to encourage their involvement in the arts. Classroom activities, which include student experimentation in dance, music, and writing, are supplemented by discussion and by student attendance at performances and rehearsals. (74)

Sponsored Trip to Exhibitions
Important Adjunct to Teaching

A state art society is helping its public school art teachers to improve the level of local instruction by exposing them to a variety of collections and styles not available to them in their own communities. Now in its second year, the Art Teacher Study Tour, sponsored by the North Carolina State Art Society, provides a week-long all-expense-paid trip for selected teachers to Washington, D. C. and New York City, where they visit museums, galleries, and artists' studios. Following the trip, each participant summarizes his experience in a written report to the Society and also addresses groups and classes in his own community.

Community sponsors submit teacher nominations annually to the State Art Society. Each year, four are selected for the tour and the $300 cost of the week-long program is shared equally between the Art Society and the local sponsor. However, other nominated teachers are free to participate in the program at their own expense. All tour arrangements are planned in advance by the supervisor of art of the North Carolina State Department of Public Instruction.

This year's tour, held in February, began when the group assembled in Raleigh to receive their tour materials, meet officers of the Art Society, and see the collection of the North Carolina Museum of Art. The following day the group went to Washington for visits to the National Gallery of Art and the Phillips Gallery. Four days were then spent in New York visiting ten art galleries, participating in an art education seminar at New York University, visiting artists in their studios, and seeing the collections of the Guggenheim, Cooper Union, Metropolitan, Whitney, Gallery of Modern Art, Contemporary Crafts and Modern Art museums.

Some of the participants were visiting New York City for the first time, and as one teacher commented, "Seeing and studying first hand, has put a deeper meaning into my teaching of art." (55)

School Program Brings Art Exhibits to Students

Nearly 4,000 schoolchildren in Bethlehem, New York, a suburb of Albany, are viewing original works of art daily as a series of loan exhibitions circulates throughout the entire Bethlehem school system. The unusual program, now in its second year, stems from a belief by school officials that constant exposure to fine art would be a meaningful experience for students in the six elementary schools, the junior high school and senior high school which comprise the school district.

The program had its beginnings in June, 1962, when Hamilton Bookhout, supervising principal of Bethlehem Central Schools, appointed an art appreciation committee composed of two art teachers and a librarian from the school system to devise a visual art program. During the summer, the committee, under the leadership of Mrs. Wilma F. Collins, librarian at Bethlehem Junior High School, borrowed 50 original contemporary paintings, all of them the work of artists in the area. The Albany Institute of History and Art, for example, lent 30 paintings, including 16 which were prizewinners in the *Artists of the Hudson Valley* competi-

741

tion. None of these works was painted before 1945; all the artists were alive and painting. The Albany Artists Group and individual local artists also made paintings available.

Paintings were arranged by general subject matter and divided into eight different exhibits with each of the schools in Bethlehem receiving a new exhibit every month on a rotating basis. They were displayed in libraries, classrooms and guidance offices, and art teachers used the paintings for instruction purposes. Interest in art was so high by the end of the school year that the school system purchased a painting and received two others from grateful parents.

This year, art was borrowed to create four separate exhibits, one each of oils, water-colors, prints and photographs. It was soon discovered, however, that additional art was needed to meet the demand. Early in December, the school system borrowed 16 paintings from the Albany Institute of History and Art, all of them works by artists of the Hudson River school. These have been divided into two additional exhibits of eight paintings apiece. Because the paintings have historic value, they are also being studied by history classes.

According to Mrs. Collins, chairman of the art appreciation committee, the positive reaction by youngsters has exceeded all expectations. When an exhibition was removed, for example, she found that many of the students complained of missing paintings which they had enjoyed seeing. Mrs. Collins also thinks that the exhibitions featuring the work of local artists have been particularly significant because, "if youngsters see that we esteem local artists, they will be inspired to create art themselves."

The Bethlehem art exhibitions, now considered a permanent feature of the school program, may be extended to include sculpture and mobiles in the future. Communities

seeking to set up similar programs are advised by Mrs.
Collins to ascertain first if there is a good source of original
art available locally.   (23)

New York Museums Collaborate on Combined Resources Program

An important cooperative program, designed to bring
museum resources into schools and communities not adequately served by museums, is beginning in New York
City. Through the new Museums Collaborative, eighteen
New York museums, including all its major ones, will work
together to develop new kinds of educational programs and
materials, exhibitions, teaching services and loans. The
Collaborative plans to explore also such joint projects as
a film on museum resources for schools and communities,
an educational TV program, and establishment of community museums.

The idea for the Collaborative developed from discussions held last spring between museum directors, and staff
members of two key government arts agencies—New York
City's Department of Cultural Affairs and the New York
State Council on the Arts. Following additional visits and
completion of a survey last October, a state council grant
to the New York City Cultural Council enabled the Collaborative to be established under the aegis of the Department of Cultural Affairs. The Collaborative staff,
headed by Emily Dennis of the city department, provides
research and development services and acts as liaison between communities, school districts, school boards and the
museums.

As one of its initial projects, the group will help develop a prototype exhibition and associated teaching programs for two city schools districts.   (69)

————— ◄•► —————

Theater Woos Young Audiences With Help of Student Leaders

Although many arts organizations recognize youth as an important part of their audience, few make a concerted effort to attract it to their door. One organization which has benefited greatly by aiming promotions at teen-age audiences is the Manitoba Theatre Centre, a professional repertory theater group in Winnipeg, Canada. It has increased its audience and gained significant publicity by initiating a series of programs specifically aimed at high school students.

Stuart Baker, director of the Theatre School—one arm of the Centre—told *AM,* "M.T.C.'s policy has always been to build up its young audiences." A survey made by the Centre last year showed that over 40 per cent of its audience was under 21 years old.

An unusual and successful project for youth initiated by the Theatre School last Fall was the creation of a Drama Youth Council—composed of students who promote theater in Winnipeg. The Council is student managed and financed.

As its initial project, the Council held a contest for the

best display of theater posters, costume designs, set designs, and programs drawn by high school students.

The contest, which ran for five weeks, was conceived by Mr. Baker, but was executed and publicized by the Council. Winners of the contest had their posters displayed at the downtown branch of the Winnipeg Public Library as part of "Young Canada Book Week."

The student-publicized event received wide-spread coverage on regional network television and in local newspapers. Information on the winners and their exhibits was distributed to all Winnipeg schools.

The Council, composed of 41 members, is also involved in other projects to promote theater to youth. It is working on the Theatre School's newsletter which is intended to better communications between high school drama clubs. It is also handling public relations and "front-of-house" work for M.T.C.'s fourth Inter-High School Drama Festival, which gives young persons working in school drama a public showcase.

Other Centre efforts aimed at youth include the presentation of plays that relate to the high school curriculum, reduced ticket rates for students, touring performances in the schools and programs with school drama clubs.   (36)

——————— ◄●► ———————

Advance Program Woos Students to the Theatre

The National Repertory Theatre, a touring drama company headed by Eva Le Gallienne, has developed a comprehensive program of work with schools in the communities where it performs.

The detailed approach to student audiences begins several months in advance of performance, with letters sent to

745

every college, university and high school within a 100-mile radius of a city where a performance is scheduled. Lists of relevant reading and suggestions for classroom assignments are enclosed. About six weeks prior to the performance by the N.R.T., the organization's advance representative visits schools and colleges interested in the program and arranges discount ticket sales for students; makes plans for displays and announcements about the performances; schedules interviews and tape discussions by cast members for use in classrooms and on radio and television; and assists teachers who wish to use the educational material developed by the N.R.T.

Two weeks later, a second advance representative arrives. He meets with schools who have not responded to correspondence from the N.R.T. and attempts to make special ticket and transportation arrangements for them. He also supervises the scheduling of special promotional events and addresses classes and assemblies on the productions to be performed.

At the time of the opening, a younger member of the company who has been appointed student representative supervises final arrangements for backstage visits by students and lectures by cast members in classrooms. Eight members of the cast are available for lectures, and everyone associated with the production and lighting personnel, remains backstage after each performance to discuss the work with interested students. (21)

Culture for Kids?

If you stage an exhibit or performance in a school, you can build interest and enthusiasm by providing teachers with a mimeographed sheet of proposed activities built around your show. The Tri-Cities Opera Workshop, Binghamton, N. Y., issues a one-page bulletin. Sample from the sheet that went out before a performance of *Boheme*: "History—what was happening in Paris or Italy or America in 1830, the time the opera was written? . . . Home Economics —Italian or French recipes . . . Language—Students from families of Italian descent could be very helpful here in building interest." Sheet then lists Italian words, phrases from opera libretto. Activity ideas help teachers as well as kids, and make for return engagements. (3)

For the Young

One way to interest more young people in the arts is to bring news to students through students, as the Warwick Arts Foundation did. *The Rhode Island Evening Bulletin* annually sponsors a Youth Awards Dinner commending those high school students whose contributions to the youth pages of the paper have been exceptional. By sponsoring an "arts award" within this competition, the Foundation provided the impetus for a wide range of student-written articles on the arts during the past year. As a result of the program's success, the Foundation and the paper now hope to establish annual workshops in arts reviewing for high school correspondents. (62)

Key Pilot Project Described

A detailed description of a stunning educational achievement, a pilot project which successfully integrated all the arts into the program of an entire school district, is the subject of a newly-released report. Published by the Arts and Education Program of the JDR 3rd Fund (50 Rockefeller Plaza, New York, N. Y. 10020) and available without charge, *All the Arts for Every Child* focuses on the University City, Mo. school district where, beginning in May 1968, the JDR 3rd Fund established and supported the first of three pilot programs designed to determine whether all the arts could be made integral to the education of every child from kindergarten through high school.

Written by project director, Stanley S. Madeja, the report describes key aspects of the projects beginning with the establishment of goals and continuing with staffing, development of instructional units and complementary resources, local artists and arts institutions and evaluating progress. Although the report does not indulge in wild horn-tooting, the project's success is clearly evident from reading the report and hopefully the document will serve as a model for school districts throughout the country. Another indication of the project's success is its acceptance by students, parents and school administrators. The University City school district has gradually absorbed it into its regular budget and when JDR 3rd Fund support ends this June, the school district will assume full financial responsibility for permanent incorporation of the new arts program into the curriculum . . . (79)

Comic Approach

A comic approach with a serious purpose, turning school children on to art, is being used effectively by the Michigan Council for the Arts. To help youngsters prepare for their visits to Artrain, a museum on tracks which travels the state, (in January Artrain will begin an eight month tour of the Rocky Mountain States) the Council distributes copies of "Artrain Comics" in advance to teachers and students. The booklet, featuring a comic strip about art and a story, "The Artrain Ghost," alerts students to ideas they will be exposed to on the train. The back page, "Make your own art," suggests activities which can be done in any classroom and the whole inside is a wall poster to take home and hang as a lasting reminder of the visit.   (78)

School Children Study For Orchestra Concert

A grammar school program in North Carolina offers some lessons in developing future audiences who will understand, appreciate and participate in the arts. It is also a good example of school support for an orchestral group.

Teachers of fifth and sixth grade students in North Carolina's Greensboro and Guilford Counties believed that their pupils get most benefit and enjoyment from something they understand. Weeks before a May 14 performance of the North Carolina Symphony orchestra the teachers began preparing their students for the concert.

Recordings of the concert's program were played to give the children a familiarity with the music. Sometimes the pupils simply listened — at other times they danced or painted their reactions to the music. They learned two songs

749

based on the music, and those who could play simple instruments learned a score written especially for these instruments.

They learned what instruments comprise a symphony orchestra and how these instruments are arranged on the stage for a concert. Films, pictures and live demonstrations were used to show what each instrument looked like and how it sounded.

Trips to the school library taught them something about the lives of the composers whose music they would hear. On the basis of research, they wrote reports about the composers, prepared bulletin boards showing events in their lives and painted or drew pictures of these events.

On the day of the concert more than 400 students played their recorders, harps and bells along with the orchestra, and the whole group joined in the songs.   (18)

Summer Program Can Help Keep Arts Group Busy

An arts group need not languish during summer, if imagination is applied to developing a summer program. In doing so, don't overlook the possibility of activity in the schools. In addition to working directly with school authorities, you may get valuable assistance from the local PTA. In the 1959-60 school year the National Congress of Parents and Teachers organized a Cultural Arts Committee. Some local PTA councils now also have such committees, and are seeking ways to help promote the arts.

In Muskegon, Michigan, for example, the local PTA sparked the creation of a community-wide Children's Cultural Activities Council that brought together a number of arts groups, the PTA, itself, and a local bank which provided financial support. This city-wide group has developed an imaginative and highly successful vacation program that can set a pattern for summertime activities elsewhere.

The pilot project, begun last year, brought together over 20 children for summer classes in creative art, dancing, drama, literature and music. Sessions, two hours a day, five days a week for four weeks were so enthusiastically attended that this year the program will offer daily three-hour sessions for a full six week period. Enrollment is expected to top 60. Last year teachers worked on a volunteer basis. This summer they will be paid.

Families were charged $10 tuition per child. Additional financial backing was secured through donor memberships, with minimum gifts set at $10.00. (4)

Schools, Children, Volunteers Back Professional Music Series

School children are leading adults to concerts of the Long Island Little Orchestra. This is the result of a unique concert series organized by a professional chamber orchestra in the suburbs of New York City, in cooperation with school officials and community committees of music sponsors.

The series of concerts, at an adult rather than juvenile level, has grown from three performances in its first year to twelve now. In one community, attendance tripled at the second annual concert.

The orchestra first enlists the superintendent of schools in each community, obtaining a guarantee of several hundred dollars and free use of an auditorium. The concert program is then explained to pupils in the fourth through twelfth grades through talks and detailed printed material supplied by the orchestra. The school prints programs and tickets, provides lighting crews, and ushers. With the help of a chapter of local sponsors, the orchestra puts up posters, sells tickets and publicizes the event.

Thanks to the classroom preparation, student interest is high, and family groups attend together. Conductor Clara Burling Roesch advises other orchestras considering similar suburban programs to organize in several towns so that a series can be arranged. Preliminary work with a volunteer committee in each town is essential. (4)

CHRONOLOGICAL REVIEW OF BOOKS AND REPORTS: 1969-1973

America's Museums: The Belmont Report, had its genesis in June, 1967, when President Johnson asked the Federal Council on the Arts and Humanities to "study thoroughly the status of American museums and report to me. What is their present condition? What are the unmet needs of America's museums? What is their relationship to other educational and cultural institutions?" A 16-member committee of the American Association of Museums completed the study in May 1968 and it was presented to President Johnson in November 1968 by Roger L. Stevens, chairman of the Federal Council. Now, the report has been introduced into the Senate and House of Representatives as the subject of upcoming hearings.

Relying on existing data, rather than new research findings, the report clearly indicates the growing demands for museum services, the key role that museums play in the educational system, and the desperate financial condition of most museums today. It pinpoints ten current priority needs and develops a cogent case for Federal support of museums, "somewhere between 35-million and $60-million for the first year." The report indicates that if authorized funds are appropriated and certain amendments to statutes made, the Government can help meet museum priority needs, from within existing machinery. (65)

Two books, although oriented to the arts in specific cities, have tremendous value for managers everywhere. *Persuade and Provide* by Michael Newton and Scott Hatley (Associated Councils of the Arts, $7.50) is the informative story of the development of the Arts and Educational Council of Greater St. Louis, as told by its directors. *The Arts*

In Boston by Bernard Taper, (Harvard University Press, $6.00) subtitled "An outsider's inside view of the cultural estate," is a slim yet provocative book which analyzes cultural development in the city and seeks answers to a number of key questions.

Bricks, Mortar and the Performing Arts (Twentieth Century Fund, $1.00) is a report of the nine-member Twentieth Century Fund Task Force on Performing Arts Centers. Among the panel's key recommendations, designed to help arts centers avoid financial disaster, were: remodelling be considered before constructing new centers and centers be made self-supporting by allocating some space to commercial ventures. The 99-page report includes a background paper on performing arts centers by Martin Mayer. Several newly published reports add immeasurable documentation to sparsely covered areas of interest. *The Arts Education, and the Urban Sub-Culture,* by Don D. Bushnell, is an insightful national survey of performing arts for inner city youngsters. The study (Grant #OEC-0-8-071104-1742) was undertaken for the Office of Education of the United States Department of Health, Education and Welfare, Washington, D. C. *Labor Relations in the Performing Arts* by Michael H. Moskow (Associated Councils of the Arts, $2.50) not only offers an excellent beginning look at a complex subject, but also pinpoints current and possible future problem areas. *The Theatre Today in England and Wales* by the British Arts Council Theatre Enquiry 1970, is a terse, on-target report on the arts scene in a foreign country. Especially interesting to American readers is the summary of priorities, the description of organizations and the statistical table on subsidy.   (68)

How does an art council disperse $18-million? A complete listing of the 596 cultural groups funded under the

New York State Council on the Arts 1970-71 program of direct aid to cultural groups, including amounts and descriptions of funded programs, has been published by Associated Councils of the Arts. Material in the report, which also includes some important overall findings, was provided by the state council. (70)

An important publication for administrators is the Arts Endowment's *Economic Aspects of the Performing Arts— A Portrait in Figures,* (U.S. Government Printing Office, $.30). The slim booklet, compiled by former Endowment staffer, Sureva Seligson, offers readers a picture of the 1969-70 income and expenditures figures for 187 professional non-profit performing arts groups with budgets exceeding $100,000 annually, and gives financial estimates for 1970-71. Among the highlights: the cost of staffing and operating the 187 groups was $144-million in 69-70 and is estimated at $160.5 million in 70-71, an 11 per cent increase. Earned income from subscription and box office sales and fees from services will increase 14 per cent from 69-70's $80-million to 70-71's $90.5-million, and income from contributions, grants and endowments is expected to increase seven per cent from $59-million to $63-million. Gross deficits, however, will probably rise eight per cent from $65-million to $70-million and net deficits will rise 21 per cent from $6-million in 69-70 to $7-million in 70-71. (71)

Bach, Beethoven and Bureaucracy: The Case of the Philadelphia Orchestra (The University of Alabama Press, $7.50) was written by Edward Arian, a Philadelphia Orchestra member for 20 years and currently professor of political science at Drexel University, where he is developing an arts administration program. The short, critical work analyzes the orchestra's operation since its beginning and takes it to task for a bureaucratic approach which the author contends has emphasized economy and efficiency at the expense of quality, artistic experimentation, the musicians and audience development. Janet Schlesinger's *Challenge to the Urban Orchestra—The Case of the Pittsburgh Symphony,* (soft-covered, spiral- bound, available from the University of Pittsburgh, $3.80) is less detailed and less critical than the Arian book, but like the latter it does strongly emphasize the need for change in the future operation of urban orchestras.

Fiction, infrequently used to explore the world of the arts in the past, has made up for this oversight and within recent months three new "culture novels" have been published. *Philharmonic,* (Coward-McCann, $6.95) written by Margalit Banai and another former orchestra player, Herbert Russcol, chronicles the activities of a symphony orchestra, at home and on tour, and the personal relationships of its players, conductor, management and board. A concert artist and the people she works and deals with, impresarios, conductors and personal managers, are subjects of George Selcamm's book, *57th Street,* (W. W. Norton, $6.95). A former Museum of Modern Art staff member, Robert A. Carter, takes the reader inside the day to day world of a large New York museum in *Manhattan Primitive* (Stein & Day, $6.95). The novel is up-to-date in the situations and conflicts it treats and several scenes will seem familiar to the discerning arts administrator.

The new *1971 Financial and Salary Survey* just published by the American Association of Museums in Washington, D.C. and available for $5.00, should be of interest to arts managers interested in fiscal operations. The report, based on questionnaire responses from more than 950 museums, discusses museum salaries according to discipline, geographic location and size of budget, and lists data on such financial aspects as sources of museum funding, budgets, and attendance. Some fascinating bits of information unfold along the way including: 44 per cent of American museums ran at a deficit in 1970 and 30 per cent charged admission fees. (72)

An essential work is the fourth edition of the *Foundation Directory*, (The Foundation Center, $15.00). The 642-page volume, which is being distributed by the Columbia University Press, lists 5,454 foundations with assets of $500,000 and over or which made grants of $25,000 in the year of record. Foundations are listed by state and each entry includes such data as names of key personnel and donors, assets, grants and purposes and activities. In addition, a useful index lists areas of interest, donors, trustees and administrators.

Lincoln Center for the Performing Arts, (Prentice-Hall, $14.95) is a big and handsomely illustrated book with 32 pages of full color and 100 black and white photos. Following an introductory section on development of the Center, there are sections on the constituent groups. Readers looking for a guided tour rather than a social document will enjoy browsing through the book.

Museums and the Environment: A Handbook for Education (American Association of Museums, $12.95) was designed by the Association for use by its member institutions and community groups. The handsomely illustrated book contains articles by experts on various aspects of ecology followed by suggestions on how museums and other groups can develop exhibits, projects and activities dealing with the environment. Illustrated examples of successful programs are given. (73)

Museums in Crisis, (George Braziller, Inc., $6.95) is a useful aid to understanding the complex role of museums in contemporary life and the mounting problems which threaten their survival. Edited by Brian O'Doherty with a foreword by Nancy Hanks, the book is comprised of a series of essays which originally appeared in the July-August 1971 special museum issue of *Art in America*.

(74)

Lincoln Center has taken a year-long, in-depth look at its 11-year old student program and other cultural programs for youngsters and reached some interesting conclusions. Titled, *The Hunting of the Squiggle: A Study of a Performing Arts Institution and Young People*, the report, prepared under the direction of Lincoln Center's education director, Mark Schubart, envisions a new kind of performing arts organization designed specifically for young people. Such an organization would present many programs outside the formal education system and traditional performing areas. The result would be a range of interdisciplinary programs in more informal spaces involving a wider number of participants—artists, educators, community agency leaders and youth.

Lincoln Center is now developing a three-year program to explore and implement the study's recommendations.

(75)

Culture & Company, a book which has aroused considerable interest prior to its release, will be published by Twayne ($8.95) on June 20th. Subtitled, "A critical study of an improbable alliance," the 309-page book by Alvin H. Reiss, editor of *Arts Management*, probes the relationship of the arts and business to a changing society and to each other. In the process, it delves deeply into such key areas as: arts power; new programming and cultural tokenism; commercial partnerships between business and the arts; and the influence of government, labor and minority groups.

Arnold Gingrich, *Esquire* publisher and co-sponsor of the annual Business in the Arts Awards, calls *Culture & Company* "the definitive account . . . the most detailed and comprehensive blueprint for the still struggling movement's future—this is the one book toward which so many others have been pointing." In his preface, Alvin Toffler, author of *Future Shock,* terms the book "a piece of social reportage that will be of considerable significance to the cultural historians of tomorrow." The book will be available in most stores but copies may be ordered directly from Twayne Publishers, 31 Union Square West, New York, N. Y. 10003.

The ultimate cultural center, set down in the heartland of America, Culture City, South Dakota, provides the setting for still another in a recent string of novels about the arts. *Bringing Down the House,* by Richard P. Brickner (Scribners, $6.95) is a satire, and at times a very funny one.

The *Visual Artist and the Law,* is the first of-its-kind, a terse, yet surprisingly comprehensive monograph, which guides the artist through such areas as copyright, publication, gallery and museum relations, sales and commissions, and tax problems. A joint effort of Associated Councils of the Arts (1564 Broadway, New York, N. Y. 10036), the New York City Bar Association and Volunteer Lawyers for the arts, it is available from ACA in paperbacks for $4.00 and in hardcover for $9.00. *The Business of Music* (Billboard Publications, $15.00), a completely revised and enlarged edition of a standard in its field, is a comprehensive guide to virtually every aspect of the music record-tape industry. The 575-page hardcover includes over 100 pages of sample forms and contracts.

Anyone interested in government's role in the arts, will be grateful to Francis V. O'Connor for the superb job he has done in assembling. *The New Deal Art Projects: An Anthology of Memoirs* (Smithsonian Institution Press, $12.50). The 332-page book with 63 illustrations, offers the candid, first-hand observations of ten individuals who participated as artists and administrators in such important government-sponsored arts projects of the 30's and early 40's as the WPA and Treasury Department programs.　　　　　　　　　　　　　　　　(75)

Management and the Arts: A Selected Bibliography, (UCLA Graduate School of Management, $3.00) should be a useful reference tool for administrators. The 51-page booklet succeeds a 1970 bibliography published by the school and contains many new listings among its 150 titles. Earlier, Associated Councils of the Arts published three important new directories. *State Arts Councils,* ($5.00) includes a detailed analysis of funding and programming for all the councils as well as information on membership and staffing. The *Directory of Community Arts Councils,* ($3.00) is a listing and survey of 254 councils throughout the country with data on their memberships, areas of activity and funding. An updated and expanded edition of an earlier ACA publication, *Directory of National Arts Organizations* ($3.00) includes data on 52 non-profit service groups.

An 83-page publication, which describes all the programs of the National Endowment for the Arts and procedures for funding, will be of primary interest to arts organizations. Titled *Our Programs,* the booklet, Stock Number 3600-0011, is available for $1.00 from the Superintendent of Documents, U.S. Government Printing Office, Washington, D.C., 20402. A guide to government activity in the arts, *Millions for the Arts: Federal and State Cultural Programs*, (Washington International Arts Letter, $10.50) is a reprint of a survey originally undertaken for the U.S. Senate by the Congressional Research Service. Described as a handbook for artists and art dealers, *Marketing Art*, (Gee Tee Bee, $12.75) deals specifically with the business aspects of the contemporary art market.

New hardcover books provide insights into several areas of the arts. Stuart W. Little's *Off-Broadway*, (Coward, McCann & Geoghegan, $7.95), is a comprehensive and absorbing study of a key movement and its leaders. In *At the Vanishing Point*, (Saturday Review Press, $8.95) critic Marcia B. Siegel looks at American dance activity from 1967-1971. *The History of Art for Young People*, (Harry N. Abrams, $15.00) is an abridgement and rewriting of H. W. Janson's earlier work *History of Art*, tailored to the needs of students. Included in the 414-page book are 74 full-color illustrations.   (76)

More and better trained arts administrators, a broadening of the base of public support for culture and the establishment of new arts priorities throughout the broadcast and printed media are among the key recommendations of the new Concert Environment Study. Prepared by the Association of College and University Concert Managers, the study investigated the cultural patterns of colleges and communities in 12 states. "In the broadest sense," states the report, "what this study has demonstrated is the need to integrate the arts with the total educational and social development of this country and to stimulate a national consciousness that recognizes the importance of doing so."
(76)

A comprehensive study of the nonprofit cultural industry in New York State, undertaken by the National Research

Center of the Arts, pinpoints the arts impact on the economy for perhaps the first time and should provide useful ammunition to arts administrators throughout the country. The 543 professional arts groups surveyed on their activities during 1970-71 had a total income of $168.6-million, employed 31,000 people and attracted an audience of over 70 million. However, operating costs were $177-million and 54 per cent of the groups surveyed showed net income gaps for the year. Copies of the 194-page study are available for $3.00 from the Performing Arts Association of New York, Saratoga Performing Arts Center, Saratoga, N. Y. 12866.

Museums: Their New Audiences, a report by a special committee of the American Association of Museums, assesses the present and potential public service role of the urban museum. Prepared under a grant from the U.S. Department of Housing and Urban Development, the report, which includes brief case studies of 16 urban museums, concludes with 16 recommendations designed to strengthen the museum relationship to the community. Included were such suggestions as community representation on museum boards and the establishment by AAM of a new urban information center. Reports are available free from the AAM 2233 Wisconsin Ave. N. W., Washington, D. C. 20007.

The Big Foundations, just issued by the Twentieth Century Fund ($10.95), is a critical study of 33 of America's largest foundations, those with assets of $100-million or more. Author Waldemar A. Nielsen concludes that as a group the large foundations are neither creative nor experimental in their programs, unwilling to take risks, and tend to give preference to familiar and "generally sound" applicants. Upcoming next month (McGraw-Hill, $7.95) is a more positive view of foundations, *Private Money and*

Public Service—The Role of Foundations in American Society. Author Merrimon Cuninggim recently resigned as president of the Danforth Foundation.

Negotiating and Contracting for Artists and Attractions is a slim but practical booklet (Association of College and University Concert Managers, $5.00) written for educational and nonprofit institutions. (77)

For a book about an arts administrator, albeit an uncommon one, Sir Rudolph Bing's *5000 Nights at the Opera* (Doubleday, $10.00) is creating quite a stir and deservedly so. The Bing memoir is lively, anecdotal, witty and quite revealing of the man and the arts institution he ran.

A four-volume treatise on the legal aspects of the performing arts—theater, film, dance, music, literature, cassettes and television—has been written by theatrical lawyer Joseph Taubman for an audience of arts producers, administrators and lawyers. *Performing Arts Management and Law,* (Law-Arts Publishers) probes such areas as contracts, copyrights, related marketing agencies, derivative rights and the law as it relates to the performer and organization. Two volumes of text at $50 are available now. The remaining volumes, forms for the television and motion picture fields, will be published later this year.

Arts in Common, the newsletter initiated as a quarterly publication for community arts councils last year, will be published on a ten times a year basis beginning this December. Each issue will cover a different topic of interest—the initial issue on gambling for the arts discusses lotteries, and horse and dog racing. Copies are available from Associated Councils of the Arts, 1564 Broadway, New York, N. Y. 10036.

The California Dance Directory, listing several hundred dance companies and sponsors in California has been published by the Association of American Dance Companies and the California Arts Commission as step one of a project which will soon include a pilot artist management service. Copies are available on request from AADC, 245 W. 52nd St., New York, N. Y. 10019. Another key reference work, *A Directory of American Poets,* (Poets and Writers, Inc., $4.00) is now available in a revised and enlarged edition with information about 1200 contemporary writers.

A booklet prepared by the Fort Wayne Fine Arts Foundation, an arts council, may be of interest to administrators elsewhere as a discussion document on the arts and the artist's role in the community. Free copies of *A Proposal to Establish a Community Arts School* are available from the Foundation at 324 Penn Ave., Fort Wayne, Ind. 46305. The second edition of *Grants and Aid to Individuals in the Arts* (Washington International Arts Letter, $10.95) lists 1500 sources, 200 more than the first edition. (78)

The beginning of the year is directory time in the arts and several important updates have recently been published. *Dance Magazine 73* (Danad Publications, New York, N. Y., $5.00) has been expanded greatly since last year. In addition to listing some 2,000 dance attractions the directory has doubled the number of categories and includes, for the first time, such listings as dance advisory panels of state arts councils, public educational television stations and arts councils and museums which sponsor dance. *Musical America's 1973 Directory of the Performing Arts* (Billboard Publications, Great Barrington, Mass., $6.00) is a 344-page compendium of orchestras, dance companies, theater programs, schools, festivals, music organizations of every kind here and abroad, plus a city-by-city survey of music activity.

The new 1973 edition of the *Official Museum Directory* (National Register Publishing Co., Skokie, Ill., $35.00) is a massive 855-page volume published by the American Association of Museums in cooperation with National Register. For each of the 5100 museums listed geographically by state and city in the United States and Canada, there is concise information on personnel, governing authority, collections, activities, hours, etc. Alphabetical, categorical and personnel indexes add to the directory's usefulness.

A first-time *Theatre Directory* listing information on 140 non-profit professional theaters has recently been published by the Theatre Communications Group, 15 East 41st St., New York, N. Y. 10017. It is available for 75 cents although it's free to non-profit theaters.

Administrators looking for fund raising and promotional ideas may find several new titles useful. *The Handbook of Special Events for Nonprofit Organizations* (Association Press, New York, N. Y., $12.95) is a how-to and how-it-was-done compilation of money-making and publicity ideas. Included are over 100 case histories contributed by local and national organizations and checklists for such events as bazaars, fairs and fashion shows. A slim booklet, *The Anatomy of an Art Auction* (Arnold Harvey Associates, Commack, N. Y., $2.98), presents a step-by-step program for organizing, promoting, conducting and following-up this kind of fund raising event.   (79)

——————————◄●►——————————

Checklist – Relevant Reading

A selective memo on relevant reading—including a few titles from places not on the beaten cultural path.

1969—1973

- *Can the Artist Be More 'Businesslike'?* Wall Street Journal, June 17, 1969, p. 22.

- *The Arts and Business,* Evergreen, July 1969, p. 63.

- *Livelier than Broadway,* (on regional theater), This Week, July 6, 1969, p. 10.

- *Honor to Those who Honor the Arts,* Esquire, July 1969, p. 6.

- *Orchestras Over Oil Wells,* New York Times, May 25, 1969, Section 2, p. 29.

- *The American Culture 'Complex',* Bravo, Volume VIII, No. 9, p. 4.

- *The Artist and the University,* Harpers, June 1969, p. 12.

- *Whatever Happened to the Kennedy Cultural Center?,* U.S. News and World Report, September 22, 1969, p. 17.

- *Some Sour Notes, But Not a Bad Town to Work in, Philharmonicsville (pop. 106),* New York Times Magazine, September 28, 1969, p. 26.

- *How to Make Politics From Art, and Vice Versa,* Harper's, August 1969, p. 21.

- *Businessmen Turning Toward the Art World,* New York Times, October 12, 1969, Section 3, p. 12.

- *Who Will Build the Financial Bridge?* Variety, January 7, 1970, p. 133.

- *Artists Use an Industrial Palette,* Business Week, November 8, 1969, p. 96.

- *Aiding Arts Keeps Nancy Hanks Busy,* New York Times, December 24, 1969, p. 12.

- *Manhattan Arrangement of Art and Money,* New York Magazine, December 8, 1969, p. 34.

- *Arts Seen in Demand-Cost Squeeze,* New York Times, January 16, 1970, p. 28.

- *Despite Budget Pinch, Federal Aid for Arts Wins Broad Support,* The Wall Street Journal, July 24, 1970, p. 1.

- *Black Arts for Black Youth,* Saturday Review, July 18, 1970, p. 43.

- *The Lively Ones: Black Theater on the Brink,* by Robert Hooks, Signature, June 1970, p. 16.

- *Bleak Picture: The Art Market Is Feeling the Financial Pinch, Too,* Barron's, July 6, 1970, p. 11.

- *The Artist As Teacher,* Saturday Review, December 19, 1970, p. 51.

- *Can the Transistor Save the Arts?,* Forbes Magazine, January 15, 1971, p. 18.

- *Across the Land, the Arts Are Lively,* The New York Times, December 31, 1970, p. 10.

- *Performing Arts, Financing the Future,* The Christian Science Monitor, (series of 5 articles) December 3, 4, 7, 9, and 10, 1970.

- *His Best Advice: Small City Arts Merger Unwise,* Variety, January 6, 1971, p. 148.

- *The Man Who's Made 'the most solid contribution to the arts of any President since F.D.R.,'* New York Times Magazine, February 14, 1971, p. 14.

- *Man on the Spot,* (John Hightower), Newsweek, January 25, 1971, p. 82.

- *Cultural Policy—a Modern Dilemma,* Unesco Courier, January 1971, p. 5.

- *Arena Stage: Full Speed Ahead,* Saturday Review, March 27, 1971, p. 63.

- *At Harvard Museums, Budgetary Blues,* Wall Street Journal, August 9, 1971, p. 8.

- *The Arts and Quality of Life,* Saturday Evening Post, Summer 1971, p. 72.

- *Business: The New Arts Patron,* by Alvin H. Reiss, Cue, August 21, 1971, p. 7.

- *The Kennedy Center: Culture Comes to Washington,* Show, August 1971, p. 32.

- *Museum in Action,* Newsweek, June 7, 1971, p. 69.

- *If An Artist Wants to Be Serious And Respected and Rich, Famous and Popular, He Is Suffering From Cultural Schizophrenia,* New York Times Magazine, September 26, 1971, p. 12.

- *Federal Aid to the Arts: Unnecessary and Unwise,* National Observer, October 9, 1971, p. 13.

- *Guthrie Troupe: The Cinderella Theater,* Associated Press national release, October 10, 1971.

- *Ethnic Nights Are a Box Office Hit,* Business Week, October 23, 1971, p. 94.

- *Troubled Museums—Many U. S. Exhibitors Reel Under Burden of Own Popularity,* Wall Street Journal, November 1, 1971, p. 1.

- *And Now the Arts Lobby,* Christian Science Monitor, November 17, 1971, p. 12.

- *The Hottest Show in Town is Joe Papp!* New York Magazine, November 29, 1971, p. 33.

- *New Music Man,* Life, November 12, 1971, p. 42.

- *Will Our Cultural Institutions Collapse?* Los Angeles Times syndicated article, October 26, 1971.

- *A Slowdown in Giving by Major Firms—the Reasons,* U.S. News and World Report, January 24, 1972, p. 37.

- *Animating Disney's Dream,* (on the California Institute of the Arts) Saturday Review, January 29, 1972, p. 33.

- *Hurok and Others More Than Just 10 Percenters,* New York Times, January 28, 1972, p. 18.

- *The Plasterer Plays Figaro,* The Lamp, Winter 1971, p. 16.

- *Washington Must Do More for the Arts,* Saturday Review, April 22, 1972, p. 18.

- *Classical Radio Stations Find Dollars are Harder to Come By Than Fans,* Wall Street Journal, April 5, 1972, p. 1.

- *The Battle in the Museums: Exhibition Vs. Education,* New York Magazine, February 21, 1972, p. 56.

- *Citizens' Lobby for Arts Gains Power,* New York Times, April 14, 1972, p. 21.

- *How Much is a Good Museum Worth?,* Wall Street Journal, August 25, 1972, p. 6.

- *Nixon as Top Arts Patron,* Variety, July 5, 1972, p. 1.

- *Public Money and a Public Mission for American Museums,* Saturday Review, August 12, 1972, p. 48.

- *The American Indian and the Performing Arts,* The American Way, July 1972, p. 24.

- *Humanities Endowment Thrives Amid Internal Strife,* New York Times, August 18, 1972, p. 32.

- *Nonprofit Show Biz Economics: Ask Corporation Gifts as Final Stopgap,* Variety, July 12, 1972, p. 20.

- *Since Grantsmanship Doesn't Work, Why not Roulette?* Saturday Review of the Society, November 1972, p. 65.

- *A Computer Aids in Picking Plays,* Business Week, September 16, 1972, p. 84.

- *Mr. Hoving's Lemonade Stand,* New York Times, October 15, 1972, Section 2, p. 1.

- *Standard Oil of N. J. Shells Out Substantial Coin to Assist Arts,* Variety, October 4, 1972, p. 57.

- *Teaching Schoolchildren that There is an Art to Seeing Beauty,* New York Times, October 20, 1972, p. 29.

- *A Change in the Weather,* New York Magazine, October 30, 1972, p. 71.

- *The Inside Story of the Mellon Art Collection,* The Atlantic Monthly, December 1972, p. 68.

- *The Art Squad,* Saturday Review of the Arts, December 1972, p. 33.

- *The Unlikely Alliance of Business and the Arts,* by Alvin H. Reiss, The American Way, January 1973, p. 12.

- *Philharmonic, Citing a $449,000 Crisis Deficit, Inserts Plea for Donations in Program Bills,* New York Times, November 14, 1972, p. 52.

- *Tax Money for Arts: What it is Buying,* U. S. News & World Report, February 5, 1973, p. 84.

- *The Growing Corporate Involvement in the Arts,* Art News, January 1973, p. 21.

- *The Metropolitan Museum—It's Worse Than You Think,* New York Magazine, January 15, 1973, p. 54.

- *Challenge of Arts Funding: Increase Foundation Support,* Fund-Raising Management, January-February 1973, p. 28.

- *The Boom in Art for Corporate Use,* New York Times, January 28, 1973, Sec. 3, p. 3.

BIOGRAPHICAL NOTES ON CONTRIBUTORS

HARRY J. ALLEN, JR.; Presently Secretary and General Manager, CHIC RADIO LIMITED; Heywood Broun Award Winner as reporter with "The Telegram," Toronto, when contributor to *Arts Management*.

W. J. BAUMOL; Professor of Economics at Princeton University, is co-author with W. G. Bowen of *Performing Arts: The Economic Dilemma*. The article which appears in this handbook is excerpted from a paper presented before the American Economics Association.

WELTON BECKETT; Deceased, President of Welton Beckett and Associates, Architects and Engineers, when contributor to *Arts Management*.

W. G. BOWEN; Professor of Economics at Princeton University, is co-author with W. J. Baumol of *Performing Arts: The Economic Dilemma*. The article which appears in this handbook is excerpted from a paper presented before the American Economics Association.

WILLIAM A. BRIGGS, A.I.A.; Head of William A. Briggs architectural planning consultants and the author of *Night and Day*.

DUNCAN F. CAMERON; Presently President of Janus Museum Consultants, Ltd. and National Director of the Canadian Conference of the Arts, formerly Director, Public Relations Research, Canadian Facts, Ltd. when contributor to *Arts Management*.

MARJORIE DEANE; Deputy Business Editor of the *London Economist*.

THOMAS FICHANDLER; Executive Director of Arena Stage Company, Washington, D. C.

KAY FLIEHR; Consultant in Community Relations; President of the American Community Theatre Association (ACTA).

BIOGRAPHICAL NOTES ON CONTRIBUTORS

CARILLO GANTNER; Formerly Drama Office, Australian Council for the Arts; now General Manager, The Melbourne Theatre Company, Russell Street Theatre, Melbourne, Australia.

ARNOLD GINGRICH; Publisher of *Esquire* and author of *Business and the Arts: an Answer to Tomorrow.*

SIDNEY GREEN; President of Sidney W. Green Associates, fund raising consultants.

RICHARD W. HYNSON; Home Life Insurance Company, New York.

MYRON I. KANDEL; Executive Vice-President, Institutional Investor Systems, Inc.

E. R. KESSLER; Presently retired, formerly Vice President of Pinkerton's National Detective Agency when contributor to *Arts Management.*

ROBERT E. KINGSLEY; Executive of the Standard Oil Company of New Jersey.

RALPH KOHLHOFF; Presently Acting Director of Fort Wayne Fine Arts Foundation, Inc., Fort Wayne, Indiana; formerly staff member in the University of Wisconsin's Office of Adult Education Research when contributor to *Arts Management.*

KYRAN M. McGRATH; Director, American Association of Museums.

THOMAS GALE MOORE; Professor of Economics at Michigan State University, formerly member of the economics faculty at Carnegie Institute of Technology when contributor to *Arts Management.* The author of "The Economics of the American Theater" (Duke University Press, 1968).

BRADLEY G. MORISON; President, Arts Development Associates Inc., of Minneapolis and New York, consultants in arts planning and management; co-author of "In Search of An Audience."

A. H. REISS; Editor of *Arts Management,* and "Culture and Company."

JOSEPH J. REIS; Presently Director, Division of Interpretation, Milwaukee Art Center, formerly staff member in the Office of Adult Education Research, University of Wisconsin when contributor to *Arts Management.*

WILLIAM RUDER; President of Ruder and Finn, Inc., a public relations firm.

GEORGE M. SCHAEFER; Presently General Manager of the St. Paul Opera, formerly Executive Director of the Fort Wayne Fine Arts Foundation, Inc. when contributor to *Arts Management.*

ELEANOR OSHRY SHATZKIN; Presently head of Shatzkin & Company Consultants, Inc., formerly Senior Consultant in the management department of J. K. Lasser & Company when contributor to *Arts Management.*

THEODORE C. SORENSON; New York attorney. The article which appears in this handbook is condensed from a speech delivered by Mr. Sorenson at a conference on Business in the Arts co-sponsored by the New York Board of Trade and *Esquire* Magazine.

GAIL STOCKHOLM; Music Critic of the "Cincinnati Enquirer."

ALVIN TOFFLER; Author of "The Culture Consumers," and "Future Shock."

RICHARD TRENBETH; Presently Director of Development for the Chicago Symphony Orchestra, and development and marketing mail consultant; formerly Development Director for the Art Institute of Chicago when contributor to *Arts Management.*

ARTHUR VIDICH; Professor of Sociology and Anthropology, Graduate Faculty of Political and Social Science of the New School for Social Research. The article which appears in this handbook is a portion of a larger study,

The Third American Revolution, Harper and Row, written by Dr. Vidich in collaboration with Dr. Joseph Bensman.

George C. White; President of Eugene O'Neil Memorial Theatre Foundation.

H. Lawrence Wilsey; Vice President of Booz, Allen & Hamilton, Inc.

Joseph L. Wyatt, Jr.; Los Angeles attorney specializing in tax, trust and probate law.

KEY TO ARTICLE PUBLICATION DATE

Issue Number   *Issue Date*

1 _____ February, 1962
2 _____ March, 1962
3 _____ April, 1962
4 _____ May, 1962
5 _____ June, 1962
6 _____ July, 1962
7 _____ August, 1962
8 _____ September, 1962
9 _____ October, 1962
10 _____ November, 1962
11 _____ December, 1962
12 _____ January, 1963
13 _____ February, 1963
14 _____ March, 1963
15 _____ April, 1963
16 _____ May, 1963
17 _____ June, 1963
18 _____ July, 1963
19 _____ August, 1963
20 _____ September, 1963
21 _____ October, 1963
22 _____ November, 1963
23 _____ December, 1963
24 _____ January, 1964
25 _____ February, 1964
26 _____ March, 1964
27 _____ April, 1964
28 _____ May-June, 1964
29 _____ July-August, 1964
30 _____ September, 1964
31 _____ October, 1964
32 _____ November, 1964
33 _____ December, 1964
34 _____ January, 1965
35 _____ February, 1965

KEY TO ARTICLE PUBLICATION DATE

Issue Number   *Issue Date*

Issue Number	Issue Date
36	March, 1965
37	April, 1965
38	May, 1965
39	June, 1965
40	July-August, 1965
41	September, 1965
42	October, 1965
43	November, 1965
44	December, 1965
45	January, 1966
46	February, 1966
47	March, 1966
48	April, 1966
49	May, 1966
50	June-July, 1966
51	August-September, 1966
52	October, 1966
53	November-December, 1966
54	January-February, 1967
55	March-April, 1967
56	Summer, 1967
57	September-October, 1967
58	November-December, 1967
59	January-February, 1968
60	March-April, 1968
61	Summer, 1968
62	September-October, 1968
63	November-December, 1968
64	January-February, 1969
65	Spring-Summer, 1969
66	September-October, 1969
67	Winter, 69-70

INDEX

Humorous approach to arts, 69, 164-
66, 188, 236-37, 329-30, 356-57, 447,
476-78, 524-26, 749
Humpty Dumpty Stores, 635
Hunter College, 200;
Concert Bureau, 526
Huntington Arts Council, 307, 581
Huntington Chamber of Commerce,
581
Huntsville, Ala., 393, 639
Huntsville Arts Council, 639
Husak, Mrs. Erna, 151, 455-6
Hutchinson, Kansas, 511
Hynson, Richard W., 262

IBM, 133, 603
Illinois Arts Council, 690
Illinois; Department of Public In-
struction, 687; Advisory Commis-
sion on Financing the Arts in
Illinois, 689
Independence Hall, 189-90
Indianapolis, Ind., 476
Indianapolis Symphony Orchestra, 63,
109, 177, 188, 338, 399, 437, 476,
732-3;
"Symphony A-Go-Go", 476
Indians, 153-54
Institute for Retired Professionals, 254
Institutional Investor, 13
Insurance, 55, 297-99, 527, 603
Internal Revenue Service, 17, 60, 247,
262-4, 606
Interpublic Group of Companies, Inc.,
572
Irving, Jules, 551
Iselin, John Jay, 14
Israel, 112
Ithaca, N.Y., Festival, 470, 495
Inglewood, Calif., 615
Irish Players, 666-7
Iowa State University, 723;
Music Council 723
Inglis, Frances, 720
Inglehart, Robert, 731-2

Jackson, Miss., 393
Jackson Symphony League, 550
Jazzmobile, 177
JDR 3rd Fund, 738, 748
Arts in Education Program, 738-9,
748
Jefferson County, Colo., 738
Jefferys, Charles S., 578
Jeffreys, David, 246
Jelleff's, 357
Jennings, Frank, 15
Jennings, Robert, 416, 419
Jersey Journal, 415
Jewish Chronic Disease Hospital, 461,
479-81
Jewish Exponent and *Jewish Times*,
668
Joffrey Ballet, 243, 353, 597
Johansen, John, 361
Johnson, Philip, 551
Jones Company, John Price, 39, 66-7
Jones, John Price, 53
Johnson, President Lyndon, 692
Joplin, Mo., First National Bank, 560
Jorda, 433
Jory, Jon, 169
Joshua Light Show, 670
Juneau, Alaska, 392
Junior Leagues, 100, 255-57, 317-18

Kaderlan, Norman, 279-81
Kalamazoo, Mich., 389
Kansas, J. K., 314
Kansas City, Missouri, Philharmonic
Rock Band, 85
Kansas City Life Insurance Company,
560
Kansas City Southern Railways Lines,
560
Karayanis, Plato S., 735
Katims, Milton, 196
Kaye, Danny, 547
Kennedy Center for the Performing
Arts, 184, 652;
Friends of, 565

Membership, 70-1, 114, 141, 223-38, 331-32, 344, 398, 520-22, 587, 617, 685
Memphis, Tenn., 392
Memphis Commercial Appeal, 416, 419
Meredith, Burgess, 670
Meredeth, Margaret May, 167
Metro Council, 120
Metropolitan Life Insurance Company, 603
Metropolitan Museum of Art, 102, 112, 491, 510, 671, 740; Cloisters, 510
Metropolitan Opera, 350; National Company, 659
Meyers, Lawrence A., 561
Miami, Florida, 374, 385
Miami Herald and News, 609
Miami Philharmonic, 609
Miami Valley Arts Council, 351
Michelangelo, 112
Michigan Council for the Arts, 749
Midland, Michigan, 369
Midland Arts Center (England), 279
Midland Community Theatre, Inc., (Texas), 236-7
Migdoll, Herbert, 561
Miles College, 733
Milk and Honey, 147
Millikin University, 392
Milwaukee, Wisc., 382, 459
Milwaukee Art Center, 391, 459
Milwaukee Repertory Theater, 260, 281
Mineola, L.I., 738
Miner, Paul, 521
Minneapolis, Minn., 133, 135, 389, 544, 552-3, 555, 574
Minneapolis Institute of Art, 553, 587
Minneapolis Society of Fine Arts, 587
Minneapolis Symphony, 136, 190, 227-8, 574-5, 724-5
Minorities, 153-58, 288-9
Mintz, Edward N., 461, 479
Mississippi Arts Festival, 255
Missouri State Council on the Arts, 560

MIT, 15
Mitchell Dance Company, 177
Mitchell, Howard, 192-3, 258, 358
Mitchell, Robert, 581
Moffo, Anna, 723
Mohawk Airlines, 630-1
Moliere, 562
Mondawmin Shopping Center, 625
Monmouth County Shopping Center, N.J., 623
Monroe, La., 391
Montgomery County Arts Center, 376
Montgomery, M. P., Fergus, 667
Montgomery Ward, 624
Monticello College, 195, 379
Montreal, Canada, 500
Montreal Museum of Fine Arts, 611
Moore, George, 283
Moore, Henry, 388
Moore, Thomas Gale, 23, 142
Mooreville, West Virginia, 116
Morgan, Dr. Glen, 317
Morini, Erica, 723
Morison, Bradley G., 126-29
Mosque Theatre, 618
Mott Foundation, Charles Stewart, 658
Mousesian, Nance, 159
M/S Viking Princess, 659
Mummers Theatre, 361-2, 501, 547, 635
Muscular Dystrophy Association (MDA), 81-3
Museum of the City of New York, 258
Museum of Modern Art, 69, 317, 510, 514, 611, 741; Arts Advisory Service, 611
Museums, 14-17, 20, 34, 90-1, 125, 137-41, 162-64, 181, 183, 186-87, 189-90, 223-24, 227-31, 238, 241-42, 258, 305, 327, 331-32, 354, 368-69, 381-85, 390-93, 446-47, 481, 484-86, 491, 507-08, 510, 514-15, 520-23, 583, 587, 592, 610-11, 665, 671-73, 676, 684-85, 695, 708, 740-44, 753, 756-58, 762, 765

Reiss, Alvin H., 34, 397-414, 557, 696-9, 699-702, 704-7

Remington-Rand, 309

Renata Theatre, 629

Repertory Theatre of Loretto-Hilton, 113, 180

Respighi, 574

Restaurants, 140, 190, 194-96, 308, 573, 582, 639

Reynolds Coliseum, 722

Rhode Island, 739

Rhode Island Evening Bulletin, The, 747

Rice University, 490

Richardson and Sons, James, 121

Richmond, Va., 391, 522-3

Rich's, 339

Riester, Mrs. Dorothy W., 667

Riggs, Annie, 368-9

Rio (Switzerland Co.), 481

Roanoke, Va., 374, 393

Roberson Memorial Center, 117, 222, 235, 250-1, 464, 513

Robertson, Jr., Mrs. William, 339

Rochester, N.Y., 109, 385, 387, 389, 470, 688-9

Rochester Civic Music Association, 109-11

Rochester Civic Orchestra, 109

Rochester Gas and Electric, 110

Rochester Philharmonic, 109, 166, 370

Rochester Tiny Tots Concerts, 109

Rochester Times Union, 416

Rockefeller Brothers Fund Report, 35, 197

Rockefeller, David, 542, 686

Rockefeller Foundation, 23, 50

Rockefeller Fund for Music, Martha Baird, 595

Rockefeller, Nelson, 442

Rockefeller, Winthrop, 686

Roffman, Fred, 201

Rollins College, 282

Romeo and Juliet, 430

Rosen, Seymour L., 593-4

Roslyn, N.Y., 111

Ross, Glynn, 150-1, 200, 430

Royal Ontario Museum, 137-8

Royal Shakespeare Theatre, 279

Royal Winnipeg Ballet, 119-20, 482

Ruder, Williams, 540-1

Ryerson Polytechnical Institute, 282

Rao, Shanta, 733

Roesch, Clara Burling, 752

S & H Green Stamps, 348

Sabrey, Sheila, 33

Sacramento, California, 99-101, 605

Sadler Wells Opera (Eng.), 709

Sacramento Symphony Orchestra, 99-100, 114-5, 605

Sacramento Union, 114-5

Safeway, 635

Saginaw, Mich., 391

Sahm-Chun-Li dance group, 195

St. Germain Apartments, 642

St. Joseph, Mo., 560

St. Louis, Mo., 113, 118, 185, 384, 575

St. Louis City Art Museum, 180

St. Louis Cardinals, 575

St. Louis Democrat, 184

St. Louis Museum and Zoo, 77

St. Louis Symphony, 113, 341, 575, 652

St. Louis Touring and Convention Bureau, 652

St. Paul, Minnesota, 172

St. Paul Pioneer Press, 345

St. Paul Opera, 345

St. Paul Science Museum, 172

St. Paul's Community Theatre (Brooklyn), 185

St. Petersburg, Florida, 382

Saint-Saens, 166

Salisbury, Md., 558

Salt Lake City, Utah, 172, 436, 517-9

Salzburg, Austria, 711-13;

Salzburg Landestheater, 711-12

San Antonio, Texas, 392

San Antonio Express and News, 420

San Antonio Fine Arts Commission, 256

San Diego, Calif., 118, 355, 430, 615